Lecture Notes in Computer Science 2677

Edited by G. Goos, J. Hartmanis, and J. van Leeuwen

T0223625

Rogério de Lemos
Cristina Gacek
Alexander Romanovsky (Eds.)

Architecting
Dependable Systems

 Springer

Series Editors

Gerhard Goos, Karlsruhe University, Germany
Juris Hartmanis, Cornell University, NY, USA
Jan van Leeuwen, Utrecht University, The Netherlands

Volume Editors

Rogério de Lemos
University of Kent, Computing Laboratory
Canterbury, Kent CT2 7NF, United Kingdom
E-mail: r.delemos@ukc.ac.uk

Cristina Gacek
Alexander Romanovsky
University of Newcastle upon Tyne, School of Computing Science
Newcastle upon Tyne NE1 7RU, United Kingdom
E-mail: {cristina.gacek, alexander.romanovsky}@ncl.ac.uk

Cataloging-in-Publication Data applied for

A catalog record for this book is available from the Library of Congress

Bibliographic information published by Die Deutsche Bibliothek
Die Deutsche Bibliothek lists this publication in the Deutsche Nationalbibliographie;
detailed bibliographic data is available in the Internet at <http://dnb.ddb.de>.

CR Subject Classification (1998): D.2, D.4

ISSN 0302-9743
ISBN 3-540-40727-8 Springer-Verlag Berlin Heidelberg New York

Springer-Verlag Berlin Heidelberg New York
a member of BertelsmannSpringer Science+Business Media GmbH

http://www.springer.de

© Springer-Verlag Berlin Heidelberg 2003

Typesetting: Camera-ready by author, data conversion by Christian Grosche, Hamburg.
Printed on acid-free paper   SPIN: 10927540   06/3142   5 4 3 2 1 0

Foreword

As software systems become more and more ubiquitous, the issues of dependability become more and more critical. And, as solutions to these issues must be planned in from the beginning of a system – grafting them on after the system has been built is very difficult – it is appropriate that these issues be addressed at the architectural level.

However, how they are to be addressed at this level is a critical question. Are the solutions to these dependability issues to be considered explicitly in the architecture, or are they to be considered implicitly by being buried in the design and implementation instead of the architecture? If they are to be considered explicitly, are they integral to the entire architecture or are they componentized within that architecture?

An example analogy for whether to make solutions explicit or implicit can be found in the issue of distribution. Do you want to make distribution an architecturally explicit issue or do you want the architecture to be independent of placement and topological issues. For example, in the quest for a generic architecture to cover a product line that ranged from centralized to a variety of distributed systems, it was decided to make the architecture distribution free (IWSAPF3, LNCS 1951, Springer-Verlag, 2000). The solution incorporated an ORB (Object Request Broker)-like architectural entity in the system and buried the details of placement and topology into that component, thereby removing distribution as an explicit architectural issue. Similarly we might treat dependability issues in the same way, burying them in components that worry about how to provide them rather than making them explicitly part of the architecture.

If we decide to make solutions explicit, then there is still the issue of whether they are integral across the entire architecture or whether they are componentized within that architecture. If integral, then one way to ensure that all the components in an architecture conform appropriately would be to define a dependability-property-specific architectural style (Perry/Wolf, SEN 17:4, Oct. 1992) that all components in the architecture must conform to. An example of this use of an architectural style for fault handling was defined and used in the above-mentioned product line architecture.

Far more interesting architecturally is an attempt to find solutions to dependability problems that are compositional, or additive, and that can be viewed as independent components (Brandozzi/Perry, WADS 2002). The logical distinction between components and connectors is very suggestive in this direction. Connectors can be much richer than just means of communications (their initial and basic use). Indeed, the entire Coordination conference series is built around the premise of separating coordination from computation – in effect using connectors among computations to provide their coordination. We can approach dependability problems in the same way or by pushing the envelope of connectors even further. Not only can connectors be coordinative, they can be mediative as well (Keynote, Coordination97). Indeed, mediation is often precisely what we want to do in the context of making our systems more dependable.

In this book we have a variety of approaches for considering the problems of dependability architecturally. Some push in these new and interesting directions, others continue in more traditional modes. It is my belief that we will make our most significant progress exploiting these new possibilities in looking for compositional means for achieving dependability.

July 2003

Dewayne E. Perry
Motorola Regents Chair in Software Engineering
The University of Texas at Austin

Preface

Architectural representations of systems have been shown to be effective in assisting the understanding of broader system concerns by abstracting away from details of the system. The dependability of systems is defined as the reliance that can justifiably be placed on the service the system delivers. Dependability has become an important aspect of computer systems since everyday life increasingly depends on software. Although there is a large body of research in dependability, architectural-level reasoning about dependability is only just emerging as an important theme in software engineering. This is due to the fact that dependability concerns are usually left until too late in the process of development. Additionally, the complexity of emerging applications and the trend of building trustworthy systems from existing untrustworthy components are demanding that dependability concerns be considered at the architectural level.

This book results from an effort to bring together the research communities of software architectures and dependability. It was inspired by the ICSE 2002 Workshop on Architecting Dependable Systems (WADS 2002), where many interesting papers were presented and lively discussions took place. The book addresses issues that are currently relevant towards improving the state of the art for architecting dependable systems. Its contents are a selection of peer-reviewed papers stemming from some original WADS 2002 papers and some invited ones. The book is structured in four parts: software architectures for dependability, fault tolerance in software architectures, evaluation of dependability at the architecture level, and industrial experiences.

Part 1 is on architectures for dependability. It consists of five papers proposing special architectural solutions enhancing system dependability. Dependability is a generic multi-faceted concept encompassing a number of attributes characterizing various properties of a computer system. The papers included in this part address different aspects of dependability. The first paper entitled "Intrusion-Tolerant Architectures: Concepts and Design" was written by Veríssimo, Neves, and Correia. The authors introduce the ideas of intrusion tolerance, describe the fundamental concepts behind it, tracing their connection to classical fault tolerance and security, discuss the main strategies and mechanisms for architecting intrusion tolerant systems, and report on recent advances in distributed intrusion tolerance system architectures. The second paper, "Improving Dependability of Component-Based Systems via Multi-versioning Connectors," by Medvidovic, Mikic-Rakic, and Mehta, presents an architectural solution intended for achieving higher dependability of software systems in which components can be upgraded. The approach makes use of the diversity between the old and the new versions of a component and leverages explicit software connectors, called multi-versioning connectors, to ensure dependable system composition and evolution, possibly during run time. The paper discusses implementation and evaluation results in the context of a family of architectural implementation platforms. In the next paper, "Increasing System Dependability through Architecture-Based Self-Repair," Garlan, Cheng, and Schmerl introduce mechanisms that allow a system to adapt at run time in order to accommodate varying resources, system errors, and changing requirements. In particular, the paper outlines a solution in which stylized architectural design models are maintained at run time as a vehicle for automatically monitoring system behavior, for detecting when that behavior falls outside of acceptable ranges, and for deciding on a high-level repair strategy. The next paper of part 1, "Dependability in the Web Services Architecture," was written by Tartanoglu, Issarny, Romanovsky, and Levy. This paper discusses approaches to building dependable systems based on the Web services architecture. More specifically, it surveys the basic fault tolerance mechanisms, considering both backward and forward error recovery mechanisms, and shows how they are adapted for dealing with the specific characteristics of the Web in the light of ongoing work in the area. The last paper of Part 1, "A Component Based Real-Time Scheduling Architecture" by Fohler, Lennvall, and Dobrin, proposes a component-based architecture for schedule reuse. Instead of using traditional approaches tying the temporal constraints, scheduler, and system architecture together, the authors put forward methods that allow for the reuse of existing schedules on various system architectures. In particular, they show how a schedule developed for a table-driven, dynamic or static priority paradigm can be reused in the other schemes. The proposed architecture disentangles actual scheduling from dispatching and other kernel routines and introduces a small common interface suitable for a variety of scheduling schemes viewed as components.

Part 2 of the book addresses issues of fault tolerance in software architectures. Its papers are based on the common underlying assumption that faults will always be present in software systems and consequently must be tolerated at run time. Unlike previous efforts, these papers address fault tolerance at the architectural level, rather than focusing only on the implementation. The first paper, "A Fault-Tolerant Software Architecture for Component-Based Systems" by Guerra, Rubira, and de Lemos, presents an approach for structuring fault-tolerant component-based systems based on the C2 architectural style. The aim is to leverage the dependability properties of component-based systems by providing a solution at the architectural level that is able to guide the structuring of unreliable components into a fault-tolerant architecture. The paper by Dias and Richardson, "The Role of Event Description in Architecting Dependable Systems," discusses the importance of event description as an integration element for architecting dependable systems and presents how the authors' current work in defining an interchangeable description language for events can support the development of complex systems. The final paper in Part 2, "Architectural Mismatch Tolerance" by de Lemos, Gacek, and Romanovsky, moves towards ensuring that components in complex software systems are interconnected in a way that allows architectural mismatches to be tolerated, the resulting architectural solution being a system based on existing components that are independent in their nature but are able to interact in well-understood ways. Towards fulfilling this goal, the authors apply general principles of fault tolerance in the context of dealing with architectural mismatches.

Dependability models allow us to compare different architectural solutions and run analysis for identifying both dependability bottlenecks and critical parameters to which the system is sensitive. The four papers of Part 3 of the book deal with dependability modeling and analysis at the architectural level of systems. The first paper "Quality Analysis of Dependable Systems: A Developer Oriented Approach" by Zarras, Kloukinas and Issarny presents an architecture-based approach for the quality analysis of dependable systems. Instead of the traditional approaches that employ methods and tools that have a strong formal basis, the authors advocate as a starting point the representation of a system using an architectural description language. Based on this representation, the qualitative and quantitative analysis can then be performed using, respectively, for example, model checking tools like SPIN, and a reliability analysis tools like SURE-ASSIST. In the second paper, entitled "Stochastic Dependability Analysis of System Architecture Based on UML Models," the authors Majzik, Pataricza, and Bondavalli describe an approach in which dependability modeling is performed on the architectural representation of a system, which is extended by the parameters needed for the dependability analysis. This approach avoids building a dependability model from scratch, thus guaranteeing by the process a consistency between the architectural and dependability models. The quantitative evaluation of the system availability and reliability is performed by transforming UML diagrams to Timed Petri Net models. In the third paper entitled "Specification-Level Integration of Simulation and Dependability Analysis," the authors Gokhale, Horgan and Trivedi outline an approach that seeks a three-way integration, namely, formal specification, simulation and testing, and performance and dependability analysis. The basis for this integration is provided by the measurements obtained during simulation and testing, which are then used to parameterize the quantitative model of the system. The approach is facilitated by the Telcordia Software Visualization and Analysis Tool Suite (TSVAT), developed at Telcordia Technologies for architectural specifications of systems, which uses the Specification and Description Language (SDL) and Stochastic Reward Nets (SRNs). In the final paper of Part 3, "Using Architectural Properties to Model and Measure Graceful Degradation," Shelton and Koopman present a scalable architectural solution for modeling and measuring the graceful degradation of systems. Considering that graceful degradation is a viable approach for improving system dependability, the authors have explicitly defined it as a system property, which can be represented at the architecture level, thus enabling an analysis of how well the system degrades in the presence of multiple component failures. The approach consists of a software data flow graph for determining dependency relationships among components, and a utility model that provides a framework for comparing the relative utility of system configurations. Dependency relationships among components enable efficient elimination of invalid configurations, thus reducing the complexity of determining the utility function for all possible system configurations.

Dependability is a crucial aspect of computer systems that obviously directly impacts organizations developing safety-critical systems, yet other organizations are also impacted, since having more dependable products facilitates maintaining, if not increasing, market share. Part 4 of this book provides some insights on dependability in current industrial settings. It consists of the paper "Dependability Experience in Philips" by van der Linden, where an overview of dependability issues encountered in 12 years within several business units of Philips is presented. The main focus is on architectural concepts and patterns that help to solve dependability issues in systems.

The topic of architecting dependable systems is very timely and work should continue in this area. The follow-on ICSE 2003 Workshop on Software Architectures for Dependable Systems (WADS 2003) is one of the means to foster related further work. As editors of this book, we are certain that its contents will prove to be invaluable for the area and are greatly thankful to the many people who contributed towards its success. These include the authors of the various contributions for the excellence in their work, the WADS 2002 participants for their active support and lively discussions, and Alfred Hofmann from Springer-Verlag for believing in the idea of this book and assisting us in getting it published. Last, but not least, we are also thankful to the reviewers who devoted their time and effort towards guaranteeing the high-quality level found in the various contributions. They are L. Andrade, M.S. Dias, D. Garlan, P.A. Guerra, V. Issarny, C. Kloukinas, P. Koopman, N. Levy, N. Medvidovic, N.F. Neves, D.E. Perry, P. Puschner, D. Richardson, B. Schmerl, C.M.F. Rubira, C. Shelton, F. van der Linden, and anonymous reviewers.

July 2003   Rogério de Lemos
                                                                        Cristina Gacek
                                                             Alexander Romanovsky

Table of Contents

Part 1. Architectures for Dependability

Part 2. Fault Tolerance in Software Architectures

Part 3. Dependability Analysis in Software Architectures

Part 4. Industrial Experience

Author Index

Architectures for Dependability

Intrusion-Tolerant Architectures:
Concepts and Design*

Paulo Esteves Veríssimo, Nuno Ferreira Neves, and Miguel Pupo Correia

Univ. of Lisboa, Faculty of Sciences
Bloco C5, Campo Grande, 1749-016 Lisboa - Portugal
{pjv,nuno,mpc}@di.fc.ul.pt
http://www.navigators.di.fc.ul.pt

Abstract. There is a significant body of research on distributed computing architectures, methodologies and algorithms, both in the fields of fault tolerance and security. Whilst they have taken separate paths until recently, the problems to be solved are of similar nature. In classical dependability, fault tolerance has been the workhorse of many solutions. Classical security-related work has on the other hand privileged, with few exceptions, intrusion prevention. Intrusion tolerance (IT) is a new approach that has slowly emerged during the past decade, and gained impressive momentum recently. Instead of trying to prevent every single intrusion, these are allowed, but tolerated: the system triggers mechanisms that prevent the intrusion from generating a system security failure. The paper describes the fundamental concepts behind IT, tracing their connection with classical fault tolerance and security. We discuss the main strategies and mechanisms for architecting IT systems, and report on recent advances on distributed IT system architectures.

1 Introduction

There is a significant body of research on distributed computing architectures, methodologies and algorithms, both in the fields of dependability and fault tolerance, and in security and information assurance. These are commonly used in a wide spectrum of situations: information infrastructures; commercial web-based sites; embedded systems. Their operation has always been a concern, namely presently, due to the use of COTS, compressed design cycles, openness. Whilst they have taken separate paths until recently, the problems to be solved are of similar nature: keeping systems working correctly, despite the occurrence of mishaps, which we could commonly call faults (accidental or malicious); ensure that, when systems do fail (again, on account of accidental or malicious faults), they do so in a non harmful/catastrophic way. In classical dependability, and mainly in distributed settings, fault tolerance has been the workhorse of the

---

* Navigators Home Page: http://www.navigators.di.fc.ul.pt. Work partially supported by the EC, through project IST-1999-11583 (MAFTIA), and FCT, through the Large-Scale Informatic Systems Laboratory (LaSIGE), and projects POSI/1999/CHS/33996 (DEFEATS) and POSI/CHS/39815/2001 (COPE).

R. de Lemos et al. (Eds.): Architecting Dependable Systems, LNCS 2677, pp. 3–36, 2003.

many solutions published over the years. Classical security-related work has on the other hand privileged, with few exceptions, intrusion prevention, or intrusion detection without systematic forms of processing the intrusion symptoms.

A new approach has slowly emerged during the past decade, and gained impressive momentum recently: intrusion tolerance (IT) [1]. That is, the notion of handling— react, counteract, recover, mask— a wide set of faults encompassing intentional and malicious faults (we may collectively call them intrusions), which may lead to failure of the system security properties if nothing is done to counter their effect on the system state. In short, instead of trying to prevent every single intrusion, these are allowed, but tolerated: the system has the means to trigger mechanisms that prevent the intrusion from generating a system failure.

It is known that distribution and fault tolerance go hand in hand: one distributes to achieve resilience to common mode faults, and/or one embeds fault tolerance in a distributed system to resist the higher fault probabilities coming from distribution. Contrary to some vanishing misconceptions, security and distribution also go hand in hand: one splits and separates information and processing geographically, making life harder to an attacker. This suggests that (distributed) malicious fault tolerance, a.k.a. (distributed) intrusion tolerance is an obvious approach to achieve secure processing. If this is so obvious, why has it not happened earlier?

In fact, the term "intrusion tolerance" has been used for the first time in [19], and a sequel of that work lead to a specific system developed in the DELTA-4 project [16]. In the following years, a number of isolated works, mainly on protocols, took place that can be put under the IT umbrella [10, 31, 22, 2, 24, 4, 21], but only recently did the area develop explosively, with two main projects on both sides of the Atlantic, the OASIS and the MAFTIA projects, doing structured work on concepts, mechanisms and architectures. One main reason is concerned with the fact that distributed systems present fundamental problems in the presence of malicious faults. On the other hand, classical fault tolerance follows a framework that is not completely fit to the universe of intentional and/or malicious faults. These issues will be discussed below.

The purpose of this paper is to make an attempt to systematise these new concepts and design principles. The paper describes the fundamental concepts behind intrusion tolerance (IT), tracing their connection with classical fault tolerance and security, and identifying the main delicate issues emerging in the evolution towards IT. We discuss the main strategies and mechanisms for architecting IT systems, and report on recent advances on distributed IT system architectures. For the sake of clarifying our position, we assume an 'architecture' to be materialised by a given composition of components. Components have given functional and non-functional properties, and an interface where these properties manifest themselves. Components are placed in a given topology of the architecture, and interact through algorithms (in a generic sense), such that global system properties emerge from these interactions.

---

[1] Example pointers to relevant IT research: MAFTIA: http://www.maftia.org. OASIS: http://www.tolerantsystems.org.

2   The Case for Intrusion Tolerance

Dependability has been defined as that property of a computer system such that reliance can justifiably be placed on the service it delivers. The service delivered by a system is its behaviour as it is perceptible by its user(s); a user is another system (human or physical) which interacts with the former [5].

Dependability is a body of research that hosts a set of paradigms, amongst which fault tolerance, and it grew under the mental framework of accidental faults, with few exceptions [19, 17], but we will show that the essential concepts can be applied to malicious faults in a coherent manner.

2.1   A Brief Look at Classical Fault Tolerance and Security

Malicious failures make the problem of reliability of a distributed system harder: failures can no longer be considered independent, as with accidental faults, since human attackers are likely to produce "common-mode" symptoms; components may perform collusion through distributed protocols; failures themselves become more severe, since the occurrence of inconsistent outputs, at wrong times, with forged identity or content, can no longer be considered of "low probability"; furthermore, they may occur at specially inconvenient instants or places of the system, driven by an intelligent adversary's mind.

The first question that comes to mind when addressing fault tolerance (FT) under a malicious perspective, is thus: *How do you model the mind of an attacker?*

Traditionally, security has evolved as a combination of: preventing certain attacks from occurring; removing vulnerabilities from initially fragile software; preventing attacks from leading to intrusions. For example, in order to preserve confidentiality, it would be unthinkable to let an intruder read any confidential data at all. Likewise, integrity would assume not letting an intruder modify data at all. That is, with few exceptions, security has long been based on the prevention paradigm. However, let us tentatively imagine the tolerance paradigm in security [1]:

- assuming (and accepting) that systems remain to a certain extent vulnerable;
- assuming (and accepting) that attacks on components/sub-systems can happen and some will be successful;
- ensuring that the overall system nevertheless remains secure and operational.

Then, another question can be put: *How do we let data be read or modified by an intruder, and still ensure confidentiality or integrity?*

2.2   Dependability as a Common Framework

Let us observe the well-known fault-error-failure sequence in Figure 1. Dependability aims at preventing the failure of the system. This failure has a remote cause, which is a fault (e.g. a bug in a program, a configuration error) which, if activated (e.g. the program execution passes through the faulty line of code), leads to an error in system state. If nothing is done, failure will manifest itself in system behaviour.

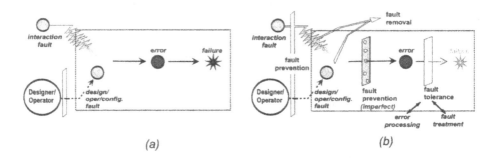

Fig. 1. Fault-> Error-> Failure sequence

In consequence, achieving dependability implies the use of combinations of: fault prevention, or how to prevent the occurrence or introduction of faults; fault removal, or how to reduce the presence (number, severity) of faults; fault forecasting, or how to estimate the presence, creation and consequences of faults; and last but not least, fault tolerance, or how to ensure continued correct service provision despite faults. Thus, achieving dependability vis-a-vis malicious faults (e.g. attacks and vulnerabilities) will mean the combined use of classical prevention and removal techniques with tolerance techniques.

This roadmap seems convincing, but in concrete terms, *how can tolerance be applied in the context of attacks, vulnerabilities, intrusions?*

2.3   Open Problems

Let us analyse a few open problems that arise when intrusion tolerance is analysed from a security or fault tolerance background.

To start with, what contributes to the risk of intrusion? Risk is a combined measure of the probability of there being intrusions, and of their severity, that is, of the impact of a failure caused by them. The former is influenced by two factors that act in combination: the level of threat to which a computing or communication system is exposed; and the degree of vulnerability it possesses. The correct measure of how potentially insecure a system can be (in other words, of how hard it will be to make it secure) depends: on the number and nature of the flaws of the system (vulnerabilities); on the potential for there existing attacks on the system (threats). Informally, the probability of an intrusion is given by the probability of there being an attack activating a vulnerability that is sensitive to it. The latter, the impact of failure, is measured by the cost of an intrusion in the system operation, which can be equated in several forms (economical, political, etc.).

Should we try and bring the risk to zero? And is that feasible at all? This is classical prevention/removal: of the number, power, and severity of the vulnerabilities and the attacks the system may be subjected to. The problem is that neither can be made arbitrarily low, for several reasons: it is too costly and/or too complex (e.g., too many lines of code, hardware constraints); certain attacks come from the kind of service being deployed (e.g., public anonymous servers on the Internet); certain vulnerabilities are attached to the design of the system proper (e.g., mechanisms leading to races in certain operating systems).

And even if we could bring the risk to zero, would it be worthwhile? It should be possible to talk about *acceptable risk*: a measure of the probability of failure we are prepared to accept, given the value of the service or data we are trying to protect. This will educate our reasoning when we architect intrusion tolerance, for it establishes criteria for prevention/removal of faults and for the effort that should be put in tolerating the residual faults in the system. Further guidance can be taken for our system assumptions if we think that the hacker or intruder also incurs in a *cost of intruding*. This cost can be measured in terms of time, power, money, or combinations thereof, and clearly contributes to equating 'acceptable risk', by establishing the relation between 'cost of intruding' and 'value of assets'.

How tamper-proof is 'tamper-proof'? Classically, 'tamper-proof' means that a component is shielded, i.e. it cannot be penetrated. Nevertheless, in order to handle the difficulty of finding out that some components were "imperfectly" tamper-proof, experts in the area introduced an alternative designation, 'tamper-resistant', to express that fact. However, the imprecision of the latter is uncomfortable, leading to what we call the "watch-maker syndrome":

- *"Is this watch water-proof?"*
- *"No, it's water-resistant."*
- *"Anyway, I assume that I can swim with it!"*
- *"Well yes, you can! But... I wouldn't trust that very much..."*

A definition is required that attaches a quantifiable notion of "imperfect" to tamper-proofness, without necessarily introducing another vague term.

How can something be trusted and not trustworthy? Classically, in security one aims at building trust between components, but the merits of the object of our trust are not always analysed. This leads to what we called the "unjustified reliance syndrome":

- *"I trust Alice!"*
- *"Well Bob, you shouldn't, she's not trustworthy."*

What is the problem? Bob built trust on Alice through some means that may be correct at a high level (for example, Alice produced some signed credentials). However, Bob is being alerted to a fact he forgot (e.g., that Alice is capable of forging the credentials). It is necessary to establish the difference between what is required of a component, and what the component can give.

How do we model the mind of a hacker? Since the hacker is the perpetrator of attacks on systems, a fault model would be a description of what he/she can do. Then, a classical attempt at doing it would lead to the "well-behaved hacker syndrome":

- *"Hello, I'll be your hacker today, and here is the list of what I promise not to do."*
- *"Thank you, here are a few additional attacks we would also like you not to attempt."*

In consequence, a malicious-fault modelling methodology is required that refines the kinds of faults that may occur, and one that does not make naive assumptions about how the hacker can act. The crucial questions put in this section will be addressed in the rest of the paper.

3   Intrusion Tolerance Concepts

What is Intrusion Tolerance? As said earlier, the tolerance paradigm in security: assumes that systems remain to a certain extent vulnerable; assumes that attacks on components or sub-systems can happen and some will be successful; ensures that the overall system nevertheless remains secure and operational, with a quantifiable probability. In other words:

- faults— malicious and other— occur;
- they generate errors, i.e. component-level security compromises;
- error processing mechanisms make sure that security failure is prevented.

Obviously, a complete approach combines tolerance with prevention, removal, forecasting, after all, the classic dependability fields of action!

3.1   AVI Composite Fault Model

The mechanisms of failure of a system or component, security-wise, have to do with a wealth of causes, which range from internal faults (e.g. vulnerabilities), to external, interaction faults (e.g., attacks), whose combination produces faults that can directly lead to component failure (e.g., intrusion). An intrusion has two underlying causes:

Vulnerability - fault in a computing or communication system that can be exploited with malicious intention

Attack - malicious intentional fault attempted at a computing or communication system, with the intent of exploiting a vulnerability in that system

Which then lead to:

Intrusion - a malicious operational fault resulting from a successful attack on a vulnerability

It is important to distinguish between the several kinds of faults susceptible of contributing to a security failure. Figure 2a represents the fundamental sequence of these three kinds of faults: attack → vulnerability → intrusion → failure. This well-defined relationship between attack/vulnerability/intrusion is what we call the *AVI composite fault model*. The AVI sequence can occur recursively in a coherent chain of events generated by the intruder(s), also called an intrusion campaign. For example, a given vulnerability may have been introduced in the course of an intrusion resulting from a previous successful attack.

Vulnerabilities are the primordial faults existing inside the components, essentially requirements, specification, design or configuration faults (e.g., coding faults allowing program stack overflow, files with root setuid in UNIX, naive passwords, unprotected TCP/IP ports). These are normally accidental, but may be due to intentional actions, as pointed out in the last paragraph. *Attacks* are interaction faults that maliciously attempt to activate one or more of those vulnerabilities (e.g., port scans, email viruses, malicious Java applets or ActiveX controls).

The event of a successful attack activating a vulnerability is called an *intrusion*. This further step towards failure is normally characterised by an erroneous state in the system which may take several forms (e.g., an unauthorised privileged account with telnet access, a system file with undue access permissions to the hacker). Intrusion tolerance means that these errors can for example be unveiled by intrusion detection, and they can be recovered or masked. However, if nothing is done to process the errors resulting from the intrusion, failure of some or several security properties will probably occur.

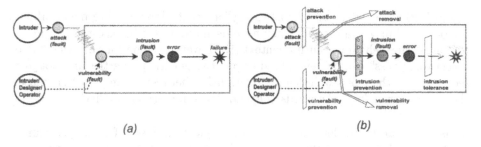

(a)   (b)

Fig. 2. (a) AVI composite fault model; (b) Preventing security failure

Why a composite model? The AVI model is a specialisation of the generic fault → error → failure sequence, which has several virtues. Firstly, it describes the mechanism of intrusion precisely: without matching attacks, a given vulnerability is harmless; without target vulnerabilities, an attacks is irrelevant. Secondly, it provides constructive guidance to build in dependability against malicious faults, through the combined introduction of several techniques. To begin with, we can prevent some attacks from occurring, reducing the level of threat, as shown in Figure 2b. *Attack prevention* can be performed, for example, by shadowing the password file in UNIX, making it unavailable to unauthorised readers, or filtering access to parts of the system (e.g., if a component is behind a firewall and cannot be accessed from the Internet, attack from there is prevented). We can also perform *attack removal*, which consists of taking measures to discontinue ongoing attacks. However, it is impossible to prevent all attacks, so reducing the level of threat should be combined with reducing the degree of vulnerability, through *vulnerability prevention*, for example by using best-practices in the design and configuration of systems, or through *vulnerability removal* (i.e., debugging, patching, disabling modules, etc.) for example it is not possible to prevent the attack(s) that activate(s) a given vulnerability. The whole of the above-mentioned techniques prefigures what we call *intrusion prevention*, i.e. the attempt to avoid the occurrence of intrusion faults.

Figure 2b suggests, as we discussed earlier, that it is impossible or infeasible to guarantee perfect prevention. The reasons are obvious: it may be not possible to handle all attacks, possibly because not all are known or new ones may appear; it may not be possible to remove or prevent the introduction of new vulnerabilities. For these intrusions still escaping the prevention process, forms of *intrusion tolerance* are required, as shown in the figure, in order to prevent system failure. As will be explained later, these can assume several forms: detection (e.g., of intruded account activity, of Trojan horse activity); recovery (e.g., interception and neutralisation of intruder activity); or masking (e.g., voting between several components, including a minority of intruded ones).

3.2   Trust and Trustworthiness

The adjectives "trusted" and "trustworthy" are central to many arguments about the dependability of a system. They have been often used inconsistently and up to now, exclusively in a security context [1]. However, the notions of "trust" and "trustworthiness" can be generalised to point to generic properties and not just security; and there is a well-defined relationship between them— in that sense, they relate strongly to the words "dependence" and "dependability".

Trust - the accepted dependence of a component, on a set of properties (functional and/or non-functional) of another component, subsystem or system

In consequence, a trusted component has a set of properties that are relied upon by another component (or components). If A trusts B, then A accepts that a violation in those properties of B might compromise the correct operation of A. Note that trust is not absolute: the degree of trust placed by A on B is expressed by the set of properties, functional and non-functional, which A trusts in B (for example, that a smart card: P1- Gives a correct signature for every input; P2- Has an MTTF of 10h (to a given level of threat...)).

Observe that those properties of B trusted by A might not correspond quantitatively or qualitatively to B's actual properties. However, in order for the relation implied by the definition of trust to be substantiated, trust should be placed *to the extent of* the component's trustworthiness. In other words, trust, the belief that B is dependable, should be placed in the measure of B's dependability.

Trustworthiness - the measure in which a component, subsystem or system, meets a set of properties (functional and/or non-functional)

The trustworthiness of a component is, not surprisingly, defined by how well it secures a set of functional and non-functional properties, deriving from its architecture, construction, and environment, and evaluated as appropriate. A smart card used to implement the example above should actually meet or exceed P1 and P2, in the envisaged operation conditions.

The definitions above have obvious (and desirable) consequences for the design of intrusion tolerant systems: trust is not absolute, it may have several degrees, quantitatively or qualitatively speaking; it is related not only with security-related properties but with any property (e.g., timeliness); trust and trustworthiness lead to complementary aspects of the design and verification process. In other words, when A trusts B, A assumes something about B. The trustworthiness of B measures the *coverage* of that assumption.

In fact, one can reason separately about trust and trustworthiness. One can define chains or layers of trust, make formal statements about them, and validate this process. In complement to this, one should ensure that the components involved in the above-mentioned process are endowed with the necessary trustworthiness. This alternative process is concerned with the design and verification of components, or of verification/certification of existing ones (e.g., COTS). The two terms establish a separation of concerns on the failure modes: of the higher level algorithms or assertions (e.g., authentication/authorization logics); and of the infrastructure running them (e.g., processes/servers/communications).

The intrusion-tolerance strategies should rely upon these notions. The assertion 'trust on a trusted component' inspires the following guidelines for the construction of modular fault tolerance in complex systems: components are trusted to the extent of their trustworthiness; there is separation of concerns between what to do with the trust placed on a component (e.g., building fault-tolerant algorithms), and how to achieve or show its trustworthiness (e.g., constructing the component). The practical use of these guidelines is exemplified in later sections.

3.3   Coverage and Separation of Concerns

Let us analyse how to build justified trust under the AVI model. Assume that component C has predicate P that holds with a coverage Pr, and this defines the component's trustworthiness, $\langle P, Pr \rangle$. Another component B should thus trust C to the extent of C possessing P with a probability Pr. So, there can be failures consistent with the limited trustworthiness of C (i.e., that $Pr < 1$): these are "normal", and who/whatever depends on C, like B, should be aware of that fact, and expect it (and maybe take provisions to tolerate the fact in a wider system perspective).

However, it can happen that B trusts C to a greater extent than it should: trust was placed on C to an extent greater than its trustworthiness, perhaps due to a wrong or neglecting perception of the latter. This is a mistake of who/whatever uses that component, which can lead to unexpected failures.

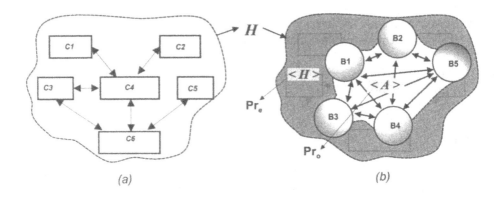

Fig. 3. Building trust

Finally, it can happen that the claim made about the trustworthiness of C is wrong (about predicate P, or its coverage Pr, or both). The component fails in worse, earlier, or more frequent modes than stated in the claim made about its resilience. In this case, even if B trusts C to the extent of $\langle P, Pr \rangle$ there can also be unexpected failures. However, this time, due to a mistake of whoever architected/built the component.

Ultimately, what does it mean for component B to trust component C? It means that B assumes something about C. Generalizing, assume a set $\mathcal{B}$ of participants $(B_1 - B_n)$, which run an algorithm offering a set of properties A, on a run-time support environment composed itself of a set $\mathcal{C}$ of components $(C_1 - C_n)$. This modular vision is very adequate for, but not confined to, distributed systems. Imagine the environment as depicted in Figure 3a: $\mathcal{C}$ is architected so as to offer a set of properties, call it H. This serves as the support environment on which $\mathcal{B}$ operates, as suggested by the shaded cushion in Figure 3b.

Observe that $\mathcal{B}$ trusts $\mathcal{C}$ to provide H: $\mathcal{B}$ depends on the environment's properties H to implement the algorithm securing properties A. Likewise, a user of $\mathcal{B}$ trusts the latter to provide A. Without further discourse, this chain of trust would be: if $\mathcal{C}$ is trusted to provide H, then $\mathcal{B}$ is trusted to provide A.

Now let us observe the trustworthiness side. H holds with a probability Pr_e, the environmental assumption coverage [30]:

$$Pr_e = Pr(H|f) , f \text{ - any fault}$$

Pr_e measures the trustworthiness of $\mathcal{C}$ (to secure properties H). Given H, A has a certain probability (can be 1 if the algorithm is deterministic and correct, can be less than one if it is probabilistic, and/or if it has design faults) of being fulfilled, the coverage Pr_o or operational assumption coverage:

$$Pr_o = Pr(A|H)$$

Pr_o measures the confidence on $\mathcal{B}$ securing properties A (given H as environment). Then, the trustworthiness of individual component $\mathcal{B}$ (to secure properties A given H) would be given by Pr_o.

As we propose, these equations should place limits on *the extent* of trust relations. $\mathcal{B}$ should trust $\mathcal{C}$ to the extent of providing H with confidence $Pr_e \leq 1$. However, since the user's trust on $\mathcal{B}$ is implied by $\mathcal{B}$'s trust on $\mathcal{C}$, then the user should trust $\mathcal{B}$ not in isolation, but conditioned to $\mathcal{C}$'s trustworthiness, that is, to the extent of providing A with confidence:

$Pr_a = Pr_o \times Pr_e = Pr(A|H) \times Pr(H|f) = Pr(A|f)$, f - any fault

The resulting chain could go on recursively. Pr_a is the probability that a user of the system composed of $\mathcal{B}$ and $\mathcal{C}$ enjoys properties A, in other words, it measures its trustworthiness.

4   IT Frameworks and Mechanisms

After introducing intrusion tolerance concepts, we begin this section by briefly analysing the main frameworks with which the architect can work in order to build intrusion tolerant systems: secure and fault-tolerant communication; software-based intrusion tolerance; hardware-based intrusion tolerance; auditing and intrusion detection. We will also look at several known security frameworks [33] under an IT perspective. Then we review error processing mechanisms in order to recover from intrusions.

4.1   Secure and Fault-Tolerant Communication

This is the framework concerning the body of protocols ensuring intrusion tolerant communication. Essentially, relevant to this framework are secure channels and secure envelopes, and classic fault tolerant communication.

Several techniques assist the design of fault-tolerant communication protocols. Their choice depends on the answer to the following question: *What are the classes of failures of communication network components?*

For the architect, this establishes the fundamental link between security and fault tolerance. In classical fault tolerant communication, it is frequent to see omissive fault models (crash, omissions, etc.). In IT the failure mode assumptions should be oriented by the AVI fault model, and by the way specific components' properties may restrict what should be the starting assumption: arbitrary failure (combination of omissive and assertive behaviour). In fact, this is the most adequate baseline model to represent malicious intelligence.

4.2   Software-Based Intrusion Tolerance

Software-based fault tolerance has primarily been aimed at tolerating hardware faults using software techniques. Another important facet is software fault tolerance, aimed at tolerating software design faults by design diversity. Finally, it has long been known that software-based fault tolerance by replication may also be extremely effective at handling transient and intermittent software faults [33].

Let us analyse what can be done under an IT perspective. In the case of design or configuration faults, simple replication would apparently provide little help: errors would systematically occur in all replicas. This is true from a vulnerability viewpoint: it is bound to exist in all replicas. However, the common-mode syndrome under the AVI model concerns intrusions, or attack-vulnerability pairs, rather than vulnerabilities alone.

This gives the architect some chances. Consider the problem of common-mode vulnerabilities, and of common-mode attacks, i.e. attacks that can be cloned and directed automatically and simultaneously to all (identical) replicas. Design diversity can be applied, for example, by using different operating systems, both to reduce the probability of common-mode vulnerabilities (the classic way), and to reduce the probability of common-mode attacks (by obliging the attacker to master attacks to more than one architecture) [9]. Both reduce the probability of common-mode intrusion, as desired.

However, even mere replication with homogeneous components can yield significant results. How? When components have a high enough trustworthiness that claims can be made about the hardness of achieving a successful attack-vulnerability match on one of them (e.g. "breaking" it). In this case, we could apply the classical principle of achieving a much higher reliability of a replica set than the individual replicas' reliability. For example, simple replication can be used to tolerate attacks, by making it difficult and lengthy for the attacker to launch simultaneous attacks to all replicas with success.

4.3   Hardware-Based Intrusion Tolerance

Software-based and hardware-based fault tolerance are not incompatible design frameworks [33]. In a modular and distributed systems context, hardware fault tolerance today should rather be seen as a means to construct *fail-controlled* components, in other words, components that are prevented from producing certain classes of failures. This contributes to establish improved levels of trustworthiness, and to use the corresponding improved trust to achieve more efficient fault-tolerant systems.

Distributed algorithms that tolerate arbitrary faults are expensive in both resources and time. For efficiency reasons, the use of hardware components with enforced controlled failure modes is often advisable, as a means for providing an infrastructure where protocols resilient to more benign failures can be used, without that implying a degradation in the resilience of the system to malicious faults.

4.4   Auditing and Intrusion Detection

Logging system actions and events is a good management procedure, and is routinely done in several operating systems. It allows a posteriori diagnosis of problems and their causes, by analysis of the logs. Audit trails are a crucial framework in security.

Intrusion Detection (ID) is a classical framework in security, which has encompassed all kinds of attempts to detect the presence or the likelihood of an intrusion. ID can be performed in real-time, or off-line. In consequence, an intrusion detection system (IDS) is a supervision system that follows and logs system activity, in order to detect and react (preferably in real-time) against any or all of: attacks (e.g. port scan detection), vulnerabilities (e.g. scanning), and intrusions (e.g. correlation engines).

An aspect deserving mention under an IT viewpoint is the dichotomy between error detection and fault diagnosis, normally concealed in current ID systems [1]. Why does it happen, and why is it important? It happens because IDS are primarily aimed at complementing prevention and triggering manual recovery. It is important because if automatic recovery (fault tolerance) of systems is desired, there is the need to clearly separate: what are errors as per the security policy specification; what are faults, as per the system fault model. Faults (e.g., attacks, vulnerabilities, intrusions) are to be diagnosed, in order that they can be treated (e.g. passivated, removed). Errors are to be detected, in order that they can be automatically processed in real-time (recovered, masked).

ID as error detection will be detailed later in the paper. It addresses detection of erroneous states in a system computation, deriving from malicious action e.g., modified files or messages, OS penetration by buffer overflow. ID as fault diagnosis seeks other purposes, and as such, both activities should not be mixed. Regardless of the error processing mechanism (recovery or masking), administration subsystems have a paramount action w.r.t. fault diagnosis. This facet of classical ID fits into fault treatment [1]. It can serve to give early warning that errors may occur (vulnerability diagnosis, attack forecasting), to assess the degree of success of the intruder in terms of corruption of components and subsystems (intrusion diagnosis), or to find out who/what performed an attack or introduced a vulnerability (attack diagnosis).

4.5   Processing the Errors Deriving from Intrusions

Next we review classes of mechanisms for processing errors deriving from intrusions. Essentially, we discuss the typical error processing mechanisms used in fault tolerance, under an IT perspective: error detection; error recovery; and error masking.

Error detection is concerned with detecting the error after an intrusion is activated. It aims at: confining it to avoid propagation; triggering error recovery mechanisms; triggering fault treatment mechanisms. Examples of typical errors are: forged or inconsistent (Byzantine) messages; modified files or memory variables; phoney OS accounts; sniffers, worms, viruses, in operation.

Error recovery is concerned with recovering from the error once it is detected. It aims at: providing correct service despite the error; recovering from effects of intrusions. Examples of backward recovery are: the system goes back to a previous state known as correct and resumes; the system having suffered DoS (denial of service) attack, re-executes the affected operation; the system having detected corrupted files, pauses, reinstalls them, goes back to last correct point. Forward recovery can also be used: the system proceeds forward to a state that ensures correct provision of service; the system detects intrusion, considers corrupted operations lost and increases level of security (threshold/quorums increase, key renewal); the system detects intrusion, moves to degraded but safer operational mode.

Error masking is a preferred mechanism when, as often happens, error detection is not reliable or can have large latency. Redundancy is used systematically in order to provide correct service without a noticeable glitch. As examples: systematic voting of operations; Byzantine agreement and interactive consistency; fragmentation-redundancy-scattering; sensor correlation (agreement on imprecise values).

4.6   Intrusion Detection Mechanisms

As to the methodology employed, classic ID systems belong to one (or a hybrid) of two classes: behaviour-based (or anomaly) detection systems; and knowledge-based (or misuse) detection systems.

Behaviour-based (anomaly) detection systems are characterized by needing no knowledge about specific attacks. They are provided with knowledge about the normal behaviour of the monitored system, acquired e.g., through extensive training of the system in correct operation. As advantages: they do not require a database of attack signatures that needs to be kept up-to-date. As drawbacks: there is a significant potential for false alarms, namely if usage is not very predictable with time; they provide no information (diagnosis) on type of intrusion, they just signal that something unusual happened.

Knowledge-based (misuse) systems rely on a database of previously known attack signatures. Whenever an activity matches a signature, an alarm is generated. As advantages: alarms contain diagnostic information about the cause. The main drawback comes from the potential for omitted or missed alarms, e.g. unknown attacks (incomplete database) or new attacks (on old or new vulnerabilities).

Put under an IT perspective, error detection mechanisms of either class can and should be combined. Combination of ID with automated recovery mechanisms is a research subject in fast progress[1, 14, 23, 11].

5   Intrusion Tolerance Strategies

Not surprisingly, intrusion tolerance strategies derive from a confluence of classical fault tolerance and security strategies [33]. Strategies are conditioned by several factors, such as: type of operation, classes of failures (i.e., power of intruder); cost of failure (i.e., limits to the accepted risk); performance; cost; available technology. Technically, besides a few fundamental tradeoffs that should always be made in any design, the grand strategic options for the design of an intrusion-tolerant system develop along a few main lines that we discuss in this section. We describe what we consider to be the main strategic lines that should be considered by the architect of IT systems, in a list that is not exhaustive. Once a strategy is defined, design should progress along the guidelines suggested by the several intrusion-tolerance frameworks just presented.

5.1   Fault Avoidance vs. Fault Tolerance

The first issue we consider is oriented to the system construction, whereas the remaining are related with its operational purpose. It concerns the balance between faults avoided (prevented or removed) and faults tolerated.

On the one hand, this is concerned with the 'zero-vulnerabilities' goal taken in many classical security designs. The Trusted Computing Base paradigm [36], when postulating the existence of a computing nucleus that is impervious to hackers, relies on that assumption. Over the years, it became evident that this was a strategy impossible to follow in generic system design: systems are too complex for the whole design and configuration to be mastered. On the other hand, this balance also concerns attack prevention. Reducing the level of threat improves on the system resilience, by reducing the risk of intrusion. However, for obvious reasons, this is also a very limited solution. As an example, the firewall paranoia of preventing attacks on intranets also leaves many necessary doors (for outside connectivity) closed in its way.

Nevertheless, one should avoid falling in the opposite extreme of the spectrum —assume the worst about system components and attack severity— unless the criticality of the operation justifies a 'minimal assumptions' attitude. This is because arbitrary failure protocols are normally costly in terms of performance and complexity.

The strategic option of using some trusted components— for example in critical parts of the system and its operation— may yield more performant protocols. If taken under a tolerance (rather than prevention) perspective, very high levels of dependability may be achieved. But the condition is that these components be made trustworthy (up to the trust placed on them, as we discussed earlier), that is, that their faulty behaviour is indeed limited to a subset of the possible faults. This is achieved by employing techniques in their construction that lead to the prevention and/or removal of the precluded faults, be them vulnerabilities, attacks, intrusions, or other faults (e.g. omission, timing, etc.).

The recursive (by level of abstraction) and modular (component-based) use of fault tolerance and fault prevention/removal when architecting a system is thus one of the fundamental strategic tradeoffs in solid but effective IT system design. This approach was taken in previous architectural works [29], but has an overwhelming importance in IT, given the nature of faults involved.

5.2   Confidential Operation

When the strategic goal is confidentiality, the system should preferably be architected around error masking, resorting to schemes that despite allowing partial unauthorised reads of pieces of data, do not reveal any useful information. Or schemes that by requiring a quorum above a given threshold to allow access to information, withstand levels of intrusion to the access control mechanism that remain below that threshold. Schemes relying on error detection/recovery are also possible. However, given the specificity of confidentiality (once read, read forever...), they will normally imply some form of forward, rather than backward recovery, such as rendering the unduly read data irrelevant in the future. They also require low detection latency, to mitigate the risk of error propagation and eventual system failure (in practical terms, the event of information disclosure).

5.3   Perfect Non-stop Operation

When no glitch is acceptable, the system must be architected around error masking, as in classical fault tolerance. Given a set of failure assumptions, enough space redundancy must be supplied to achieve the objective. On the other hand, adequate protocols implementing systematic error masking under the desired fault model must be used (e.g. Byzantine-resilient, TTP-based, etc.). However, note that non-stop availability against general denial-of-service attacks is still an ill-mastered goal in open systems.

5.4   Reconfigurable Operation

Non-stop operation is expensive and as such many services resort to cheaper redundancy management schemes, based on error recovery instead of error masking. These alternative approaches can be characterized by the existence of a visible glitch. The underlying strategy, which we call reconfigurable operation, is normally addressed at availability- or integrity-oriented services, such as transactional databases, web servers, etc.

The strategy is based on intrusion detection. The error symptom triggers a reconfiguration procedure that automatically replaces a failed component by a correct component, or an inadequate or incorrect configuration by an adequate or correct configuration, under the new circumstances (e.g. higher level of threat). For example, if a database replica is attacked and corrupted, it is replaced by a backup. During reconfiguration the service may be temporarily unavailable or suffer some performance degradation, whose duration depends on the recovery mechanisms. If the AVI sequence can be repeated (e.g., while the attack lasts), the service may resort to configurations that degrade QoS in trade for resilience, depending on the policy used (e.g., temporarily disabling a service that contains a vulnerability that cannot be removed, or switching to more resilient but slower protocols).

5.5   Recoverable Operation

Disruption avoidance is not always mandatory, and this may lead to cheaper and simpler systems. Furthermore, in most denial-of-service scenarios in open systems (Internet), it is generically not achievable.

Consider that a component crashes under an attack. An intrusion-tolerant design can still be obtained, if a set of preconditions hold for the component: (a) it takes a lower-bounded time T_c to fall; (b) it takes a upper-bounded time T_r to recover; (c) the duration of blackouts is short enough for the application's needs.

Unlike what happens with classic FT recoverable operation [33], where (c) only depends on (b), here the availability of the system is defined in a more elaborate way, proportionate to the level of threat, in terms of attack severity and duration. Firstly, for a given attack severity, (a) determines system reliability under attack. If an attack lasts less than T_c, the system does not even crash. Secondly, (a) and (b) determine the time for service restoration. For a given attack duration T_a, the system may either recover completely after T_r ($T_a < T_c + T_r$), or else cycle up-down, with a duty cycle of $T_c/(T_c + T_r)$ (longer attacks).

Moreover, the crash, which is provoked maliciously, must not give rise to incorrect computations. This may be achieved through several techniques, amongst which we name secure check-pointing and logging. Recoverable exactly-once operation can be achieved with intrusion-tolerant atomic transactions [33]. In distributed settings, these mechanisms may require secure agreement protocols.

This strategy concerns applications where at the cost of a noticeable temporary service outage, the least amount of redundancy is used. The strategy also serves long-running applications, such as data mining or scientific computations, where availability is not as demanding as in interactive applications, but integrity is of primary concern.

5.6   Fail-Safe

In certain situations, it is necessary to provide for an emergency action to be performed in case the system can no longer tolerate the faults occurring, i.e. it cannot withstand the current level of threat. This is done to prevent the system from evolving to a potentially incorrect situation, suffering or doing unexpected damage. In this case, it is preferable to shut the system down at once, what is called *fail-safe* behaviour. This strategy, often used in safety- and mission-critical systems, is also important in intrusion tolerance, for obvious reasons. It may complement other strategies described above.

6   Modelling Malicious Faults

A crucial aspect of any fault-tolerant architecture is the fault model upon which the system architecture is conceived, and component interactions are defined. The fault model conditions the correctness analysis, both in the value and time domains, and dictates crucial aspects of system configuration, such as the placement and choice of components, level of redundancy, types of algorithms, and so forth. A system fault model is built on assumptions about the way system components fail.

What are malicious faults? In the answer to this question lies the crux of the argument with regard to "adequate" intrusion fault models. The term 'malicious' is itself very suggestive, and means a special intent to cause damage. But how do we model the mind and power of the attacker? Indeed, many works have focused on the 'intent', whereas from an IT perspective, one should focus on the 'result'. That is, what should be extracted from the notion of 'maliciousness' is a technical definition of its objective: the *violation of several or all of the properties of a given service*, attempted in any possible manner within the power available to the intruder.

Classically, failure assumptions fall into essentially two kinds: controlled failure assumptions, and arbitrary failure assumptions.

Controlled failure assumptions specify qualitative and quantitative bounds on component failures. For example, the failure assumptions may specify that components only have timing failures, and that no more than f components fail during an interval of reference. Alternatively, they can admit value failures, but not allow components to spontaneously generate or forge messages, nor impersonate, collude with, or send conflicting information to other components. In the presence of accidental faults this approach is realistic, since it represents very well how common systems work, failing in a benign manner most of the time. However, it can hardly be directly extrapolated to malicious faults, under the above definition of maliciousness.

Arbitrary failure assumptions ideally specify no qualitative or quantitative bounds on component failures. In this context, an arbitrary failure means the capability of generating an interaction at any time, with whatever syntax and semantics (form and meaning), anywhere in the system. Arbitrary failure assumptions adapt perfectly to the notion of maliciousness, but they are costly to handle, in terms of performance and complexity, and thus are not compatible with the user requirements of the vast majority of today's on-line applications.

Note that the problem lies in how representative are our assumptions vis-a-vis what happens in reality. That is, a problem of *coverage* of our assumptions. So, how to proceed?

6.1   Arbitrary Failure Assumptions

Consider operations of very high value and/or criticality, such as: financial transactions; contract signing; provision of long term credentials; state secrets. The risk of failure due to violation of assumptions should not be incurred. This justifies considering arbitrary failure assumptions, and building the system around arbitrary-failure resilient building blocks (e.g. Byzantine agreement protocols), despite a possible performance penalty.

In consequence, no assumptions are made on the existence of trusted components such as security kernels or other fail-controlled components. Likewise, a time-free or asynchronous approach must be followed, i.e. no assumptions about timeliness, since timing assumptions are susceptible to be attacked. This limits the classes of applications that can be addressed under these assumptions: asynchronous models cannot solve timed problems.

In practice, many of the emerging applications we see today, particularly on the Internet, have interactivity or mission-criticality requirements. Timeliness is part of the required attributes, either because of user-dictated quality-of-service requirements (e.g., network transaction servers, multimedia rendering, synchronised groupware, stock exchange transaction servers), or because of safety constraints (e.g., air traffic control). So we should seek alternative fault model frameworks to address these requirements under malicious faults.

6.2 Hybrid Failure Assumptions Considered Useful

Hybrid assumptions combining several kinds of failure modes would be desirable. There is a body of research, starting with [25] on hybrid failure models that assume different failure type distributions for different nodes. For instance, some nodes are assumed to behave arbitrarily while others are assumed to fail only by crashing. The probabilistic foundation of such distributions might be hard to sustain in the presence of malicious intelligence, unless their behaviour is constrained in some manner. Consider a component or sub-system for which given controlled failure assumptions were made. How can we enforce trustworthiness of the component vis-a-vis the assumed behaviour, that is, coverage of such assumptions, given the unpredictability of attacks and the elusiveness of vulnerabilities?

A composite (AVI) fault model with hybrid failure assumptions is one where the presence and severity of vulnerabilities, attacks and intrusions varies from component to component. Some parts of the system would justifiably exhibit fail-controlled behaviour, whilst the remainder of the system would still be allowed an arbitrary behaviour. This might best be described as *architectural hybridisation*, in the line of works such as [28, 34, 13], where failure assumptions are in fact enforced by the architecture and the construction of the system components, and thus substantiated. That is (*see* Section 3) the component is made *trustworthy* enough to match the *trust* implied by the fail-controlled assumptions.

The task of the architect is made easier since the controlled failure modes of some components vis-a-vis malicious faults restrict the system faults the component can produce. In fact a form of fault prevention was performed at system level: some kinds of system faults are simply not produced. Intrusion-tolerance mechanisms can now be designed using a mixture of arbitrary-failure (fail-uncontrolled or non trusted) and fail-controlled (or trusted) components.

Hybrid failure assumptions can also be the key to secure timed operation. With regard to timeliness and timing failures, hybridisation yields forms of partial synchrony: (i) some subsystems exhibit controlled failure modes and can thus supply timed services in a secure way; (ii) the latter assist the system in fulfilling timeliness specifications; (iii) controlled failure of those specifications is admitted, but timing failure detection can be achieved with the help of trusted components [13].

7 Architecting Intrusion-Tolerant Systems

In this section, we discuss a few notions on architecting intrusion-tolerant systems.

7.1 (Almost) no Assumptions

The fail-uncontrolled or arbitrary failure approach to IT architecture is based on assuming as little as possible about the environment's behaviour (faults, synchronism), with the intent of maximizing coverage. It provides a conceptually simple framework for developing and reasoning about the correctness of an algorithm, satisfying safety under any conditions, and providing liveness under certain conditions, normally defined in a probabilistic way.

Randomised Byzantine agreement protocols are an example of typical protocols in this approach. They may not terminate with non-zero probability, but this probability can be made negligible. In fact, a protocol using cryptography always has a residual probability of failure, determined by the key lengths. Of course, for the system as a whole to provide useful service, it is necessary that at least some of the components are correct. This approach is essentially parametric: it will remain correct if a sufficient number of correct participants exist, for any hypothesised number of faulty participants f. Or in other words, with almost no assumptions one is able to achieve extremely resilient protocols.

This has some advantages for the design of secure distributed systems, which is one reason for pursuing such an approach. In fact, sometimes it is necessary and worthwhile to sacrifice performance or timeliness for resilience, for example for very critical operations (key distribution, contract signing, etc.)

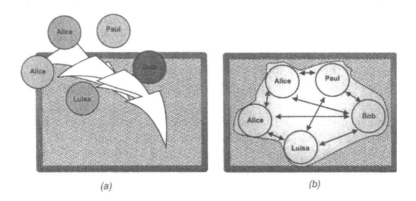

(a)   *(b)*

Fig. 4. Arbitrary failure approach

Figure 4 shows the principle in simple terms. The metaphore used from now on is: greyer for hostile, malicious, and whiter for benign, correct. Figure 4a shows the participants being immersed in a hostile and asynchronous environment. The individual hosts and the communication environment are not trusted. Participants may be malicious, and normally the only restriction assumed is in the number of ill-behaved participants. Figure 4b suggests that the protocol, coping with the environment's deficiencies, ensures that the participants collectively provide a correct service (whiter shade).

7.2 Non-justified Assumptions, or the Power of Faith

Alternatively, IT architecture may take the fail-controlled approach. Sometimes, it may simply be assumed that the environment is benign, without substantiating those assumptions. This is often done in accidental fault tolerance, when the environment is reasonably well-known, for example, from statistic measurements. Is it a reasonable approach for malicious faults?

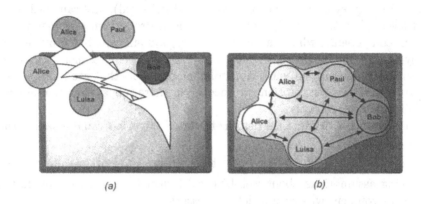

(a)   (b)

Fig. 5. Non-justified assumptions

Figure 5a shows the participants being immersed in an assumed moderately benign environment (essentially white, with a thin dark part, according to our metaphors). For example, it is usual to consider that the individual hosts (local environment) are trusted, and that the communication environment, though not trusted has a given limited attack model. Some user participants may be malicious.

The implementation is bound to work most of the times. However, it should not be surprising that a behaviour that is assumed out of statistic evidence (or worse, out of faith...) and not by enforcement, can be defrauded by an intruder attacking the run-time environment. Thus, it may turn out that the latter behaves in a manner worse than assumed (e.g., hosts were not that trustworthy, or the communication support was more severely attacked than the model assumed), as suggested in Figure 5b where, say upon an attack, the environment is shown actually more aggressive than initially thought in Figure 5a.

In consequence, making assumptions that are not substantiated in a strong manner may in many cases lead to the lack of trustworthiness (coverage) on the properties of a component or subsystem (suggested in our example by the dark shade partially hitting the participants and protocol). This may be problematic, because it concerns failures not assumed, that is, for which the protocol is not prepared, and which may be orchestrated by malicious intelligence. Their consequences may thus be unpredictable. We discuss a correct approach below.

7.3   Architectural Hybridisation

Architectural hybridisation is a solid guiding principle for architecting fail-controlled IT systems. One wishes to avoid the extreme of arbitrary assumptions, without incurring the risks of lack of coverage. Assuming something means trusting, as we saw earlier on, and so architectural hybridisation is an enabler of the approach of *using trusted components*, by making them *trustworthy* enough.

Essentially, the architect tries to make available black boxes with benign behaviour, of omissive or weak fail-silent class [33]. These can have different capabilities (e.g. synchronous or not; local or distributed), and can exist at different levels of abstraction. A good approach is to dress them as run-time environment components, which can be accessed by system calls but provide trustworthy results, in contrast with calls to an untrusted environment. Of course, fail-controlled designs can yield fault-tolerant protocols that are more efficient than truly arbitrary assumptions protocols, but more robust than non-enforced controlled failure protocols.

The tolerance attitude in the design of hybrid IT systems can be characterized by a few aspects:

- assuming as little as possible from the environment or other components;
- making assumptions about well-behaved (trusted) components or parts of the environment whenever strictly necessary;
- enforcing the assumptions on trusted components, by construction;
- unlike classical prevention-based approaches, trusted components do not intervene in all operations, they assist only crucial steps of the execution;
- protocols run thus in an non-trusted environment, single components can be corrupted, faults (intrusions) can occur;
- correct service is built on distributed fault tolerance mechanisms, e.g., agreement and replication amongst participants in several hosts.

7.4   Prevention, Tolerance, and a Bit of Salt

On achieving trustworthy components, the architect should bear in mind a recipe discussed earlier: the good balance between prevention and tolerance. Let us analyze the principles of operation of a trusted third party (TTP) protocol, as depicted in Figure 6a. Participants Alice, Paul and Bob, run an IT protocol amongst themselves, and trust Trent, the TTP component, to provide a few services that assist the protocol in being intrusion tolerant. What the figure does not show and is seldom asked is: is the TTP trustworthy?

In fact, the TTP is the perfect example of a trusted component that is sometimes (often?) trusted to an extent greater than its trustworthiness.

In Figure 6b we "open the lid" of the TTP and exemplify how a good combination of prevention and tolerance can render it trustworthy. To start with, we require certificate-based authentication, as a means to prevent certain failures from ocurring in the point-to-point interaction of participants with the TTP (e.g., impersonation, forging, etc.). Then, if we replicate the TTP, we make it

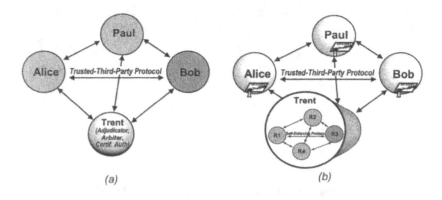

Fig. 6. (a) TTP protocol; (b) Enforcing TTP trustworthiness

resilient to crashes, and to a certain level of attacks on the TTP server replicas, if there is enough redundancy. Furthermore, the replicas should communicate through self-enforcing protocols of the Byzantine-resilient kind, if malicious faults can be attempted at subsets of server replicas.

The user need not be aware of the additional complexity and distribution of the TTP, a usual principle in fault tolerance. In fact, we should "close the lid" so that participants see essentially a single logical entity which they trust (as in Figure 6a). However, by having worked at component level (TTP), we achieve trustworthy behaviour of the component as seen at a higher level (system). Note that in fact, we have prevented some system faults from occurring. This duality prevention/tolerance can be applied recursively in more than one instance. Recently, there has been extensive research on making trustworthy TTPs, for example by recursively using intrusion tolerance mechanisms [1, 38].

7.5 Using Trusted Components

The relation of trust/trustworthiness can be applied in general when architecting IT systems, as we saw in the last section. However, particular instantiations of trusted components deserve mention here.

IT protocols can combine extremely high efficiency with high resilience if supported by *locally accessible* trusted components. For example, the notion of security kernel in IT would correspond to a fail-controlled local subsystem trusted to execute a few security-related functions correctly, albeit immersed in the remaining environment, subjected to malicious faults.

This can be generalised to any function, such as time-keeping, or failure detection. In that sense, a local trusted component would encapsulate, and supply in a trusted way, a set of functions, considered crucial for protocols and services having to execute in a hostile environment. The use of trusted hardware (e.g. smart cards, appliance boards) may serve to amplify the trustworthiness of these special components. In Figure 7a we see an example of an architecture featuring LTCs (local trusted components). Inter-component communication should

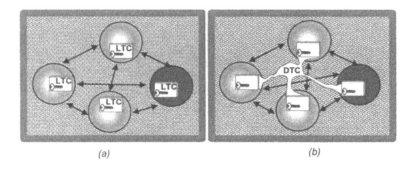

Fig. 7. Using trusted components: (a) Local; (b) Distributed

ensure that correct components enjoy the properties of the LTC despite malicious faults. On the other hand, the implementation of the LTC should ensure that malicious components, such as the one on the right of Figure 7a, do not undermine the operation of the LTC, making it work incorrectly.

Figure 7b shows a distributed trusted component (DTC). It amplifies the power of a LTC, since it assumes the existence of not only local trusted execution, but also a trusted channel among LTCs. This makes it possible to implement distributed trust for low-level operations (e.g., distribution of message authentication codes- MACS). It can be built for example with appliance boards with a private control channel, such as a second network attachment in a host.

A DTC can assist protocols in number of ways, which we discuss with more detail in later sections of the paper, but the fundamental rationale is the following:

- protocol participants have to exchange messages in a world full of threats, some of them may even be malicious and cheat (the normal network);
- there is a channel that correct participants trust, and which they can use to get in touch with each other, even if for rare and short moments;
- they can use this channel to synchronise, disseminate, and agree on, simple but crucial facts of the execution of a protocol, and this limits the potential for Byzantine actions from malicious participants.

8   Some Example Systems

The term "intrusion tolerance" appeared originally in a paper by Fraga and Powell [19]. Later their scheme –Fragmentation-Redundancy-Scattering– was used in the DELTA-4 project to develop an intrusion-tolerant distributed server composed by a set of insecure sites [16].

In the following years a number of isolated IT protocols and systems emerged. BFT [10] is an efficient state-machine replication algorithm [32]. It has been used to implement an intrusion-tolerant NFS server. Rampart provides tools for building IT distributed services: reliable multicast, atomic multicast and membership protocols [31]. SecureRing is a view-synchronous group communication system based on the Totem single-ring protocols [22]. Both Rampart and SecureRing can be used to build servers using the state-machine replication approach. Fleet [24] use Byzantine quorum systems [2] to build IT data stores, respectively for data abstractions like variables and locks, and for Java objects. The protocol suite CLIQUES supports group key agreement operations for dynamic groups of processes [4, 3]. More recently, two projects have focused on intrusion tolerance, OASIS and MAFTIA, developing several results that will be detailed ahead.

8.1   OASIS

Organically Assured and Survivable Information System (OASIS) [2] is a US DARPA program with the goal of providing "defence capabilities against sophisticated adversaries to allow sustained operation of mission critical functions in the face of known and future cyber attacks against information systems". The program has a strong focus in intrusion tolerance. Its objectives are:

- to construct intrusion-tolerant systems based on potentially vulnerable components;
- to characterize the cost-benefits of intrusion tolerance mechanisms;
- to develop assessment and validation methodologies to evaluate intrusion tolerance mechanisms.

OASIS is financing something like 30 projects. It is not possible to describe all of them so we survey a few that we find interesting and representative.

Intrusion Tolerance by Unpredictable Adaptation (ITUA) aims to develop a middleware to help design applications that tolerate certain classes of attacks [14]. The ITUA architecture is composed by security domains, that abstract the notion of boundaries that are difficult by an attacker to cross (e.g., a LAN protected by a firewall). An intrusion-tolerant application usually has to adapt when there are attacks. ITUA proposes unpredictable adaptation as a means to tolerate attacks that try to predict and take advantage of that adaptation. Adaptation in ITUA is handled by the QuO middleware and group communication is implemented as intrusion-tolerant layers in the Ensemble toolkit.

Intrusion Tolerant Architectures has the objective to develop a methodology based on architectural concepts for constructing intrusion-tolerant systems. The project developed an IT version of Enclaves, a middleware for supporting secure group applications in insecure networks, like the Internet [18]. IT-Enclaves has several leaders from which at most f out of $n \geq 3f+1$ are allowed to be compromised. The leaders provide all group-management services: user authentication, member join and leave, group-key generation, distribution, and refreshment. Each member of the group is in contact with $2f+1$ leaders.

COCA is an on-line certification-authority for local and wide-area networks [38]. COCA uses replicated servers for availability and intrusion-tolerance. The

---

[2] http://www.tolerantsystems.org/.

certificates that it produces are signed using a threshold cryptography algorithm. COCA assumes an adversary takes a certain time to corrupt a number of servers, therefore from time to time keys are changed (proactive security). Replication is based on a Byzantine quorum system.

8.2 MAFTIA

Malicious- and Accidental-Fault Tolerance for Internet Applications (MAFTIA)[3] is a recently finished EU IST project with the general objective of systematically investigating the 'tolerance paradigm' for constructing large-scale dependable distributed applications. The project had a comprehensive approach that includes both accidental and malicious faults. MAFTIA followed three main lines of action:

- definition of an architectural framework and a conceptual model;
- the design of mechanisms and protocols;
- formal validation and assessment.

The first line aimed to develop a coherent set of concepts for an architecture that could tolerate malicious faults [1]. Work has been done on the definition of a core set of intrusion tolerance concepts, clearly mapped into the classical dependability concepts. The AVI composite fault model presented above was defined in this context. Other relevant work included the definition of synchrony and topological models, the establishment of concepts for intrusion detection and the definition of a MAFTIA node architecture. This architecture includes components such as trusted and untrusted hardware, local and distributed trusted components, operating system and runtime environment, software, etc.

Most MAFTIA work was on the second line, the design of IT mechanisms and protocols. Part of that work was the definition of the *MAFTIA middleware*: architecture and protocols [7]. An asynchronous suite of protocols, including reliable, atomic and causal multicast was defined [8], providing Byzantine resilience by resorting to efficient solutions based on probabilistic execution. Work was also done on protocols based on a timed model, which relies on an innovative concept, the *wormholes*, enhanced subsystems which provide components with a means to obtain a few simple privileged functions and/or channels to other components, with "good" properties otherwise not guaranteed by the "normal" weak environment [35]. For example, the Trusted Timely Computing Base developed in MAFTIA (see next two sections) is based on a wormhole providing timely and secure functions on enviroments that are asynchronous and Byzantine-on-failure. Architectural hybridisation discussed earlier is used to implement the TTCB. In the context of MAFTIA middleware, an IT transaction service with support for multiparty transactions [37] was also designed.

Intrusion detection is assumed as a mechanism for intrusion tolerance but also as a service that has to be made intrusion-tolerant. MAFTIA developed a

---

[3] http://www.maftia.org/.

distributed IT intrusion detection system [15]. Problems like handling high rates of false alarms and combining several IDSs were also explored.

Trusted Third Parties (TTPs) such as certification authorities are important building blocks in today's Internet. MAFTIA designed a generic distributed certification authority that uses threshold cryptography and IT protocols in order to be intrusion-tolerant. Another TTP, the distributed optimistic fair exchange service, was also developed.

MAFTIA defined an *authorization service* based on fine grain protection, i.e., on protection at the level of the object method call [26]. The authorization service is a distributed TTP which can be used to grant or deny authorization for complex operations combining several method calls. The service relies on a local security kernel.

The third line of work was on formalizing the core concepts of MAFTIA and verifying and assessing the work on dependable middleware [27]. A novel rigorous model for the security of reactive systems was developed and protocols were modelled using CSP and FDR.

In the next sections, we describe some of our own work in more detail: the construction of a Trusted Timely Computing Base using the principle of architectural hybridisation, and a protocol using the TTCB wormhole.

Architectural Hybridisation in Practice. The Trusted Timely Computing Base (TTCB) is a real-time secure wormhole [13]. The TTCB is a simple component providing a limited set of services. Its architecture is presented in Figure 8. The objective is to support the execution of IT protocols and applications using the architectural hybridisation approach introduced before.

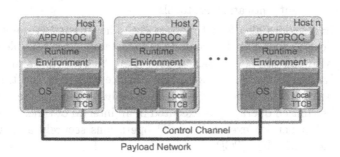

Fig. 8. System architecture with a TTCB

This experimental implementation of the TTCB was based on COTS components. The hosts are common Pentium PCs with a real-time kernel, RT-Linux or RTAI. The hosts are interconnected by two Fast-Ethernet LANs. One corresponds to the payload network in Figure 8, while the other is the TTCB control-channel. It is thus a configuration aimed at local environments, such as sites, campuses, etc. Wide-area configurations are also possible, as discussed in [35].

The design of a system has both functional and non-functional aspects. Next we describe the functionality of the TTCB –its services– and later we discuss the how the security and timeliness (real-time) are enforced in the COTS based TTCB.

The TTCB provides a limited set of services. From the point of view of programming they are a set of functions in a library that can be called by processes in the usual way. We use the word "process" to denominate whatever uses the TTCB services: a normal process, a thread, or another software component.

The TTCB provides three security-related services. The Local Authentication Service allows processes to communicate securely with the TTCB. The service authenticates the local TTCB before a process and establishes a shared symmetric key between both, using a simple authenticated key establishment protocol. This symmetric key is used to secure all their further communication. Every local TTCB has an asymmetric key pair, and we assume that the process manages to get a correct copy of the local TTCB public key. The Trusted Block Agreement Service is the main building block for IT protocols. This service delivers a value obtained from the agreement of values proposed by a set of processes. The service is not intended to replace agreement protocols in the payload system: it works with "small" blocks of data (currently 160 bits), and the TTCB has limited resources to execute it. The service provides a set of functions that can be used to calculate the result. For instance, it can select the value proposed by more processes. A parameter of the service is a timestamp that indicates the last instant when the service starts to be executed. This prevents malicious processes from delaying the service execution indefinitely. The last security-related service is the Random Number Generation Service that provides uniformly distributed random numbers. These numbers can be used as nonces or keys for cryptographic primitives such as authentication protocols.

The TTCB provides also four time services. The Trusted Absolute Timestamping Service provides globally meaningful timestamps. It is possible to obtain timestamps with this characteristic because local TTCBs clocks are synchronized. The Trusted Duration Measurement Service measures the time of the execution of an operation. The Trusted Timing Failure Detection Service checks if a local or distributed operation is executed in an interval of time. The Trusted Timely Execution Service executes special operations securely and within an interval of time inside the TTCB.

RT-Linux and RTAI are two similar real-time engineerings of Linux. Linux was modified so that a real-time executive takes control of the hardware, to enforce real-time behaviour of some real-time tasks. RT tasks were defined as special Linux loadable kernel modules so they run inside the kernel. The scheduler was changed to handle these tasks in a preemptive way and to be configurable to different scheduling disciplines. Linux runs as the lowest priority task and its interruption scheme was changed to be intercepted by RT-Linux/RTAI. The local part of a COTS-based TTCB is basically a (non-real-time) local kernel module, that handles the service calls, and a set of two or more RT tasks that execute all time constrained operations.

The local TTCB is protected by protecting the kernel. From the point of view of security, RT-Linux/RTAI are very similar to Linux. Their main vulnerability is the ability a superuser has to control any resource in the system. This vulnerability is usually reasonably easy to exploit, e.g., using race conditions. Linux capabilities are privileges or access control lists associated with processes that allow a fine grain control on how they use certain objects. However, currently the practical way of using this mechanism is quite basic. There is a system wide *capability bounding set* that bounds the capabilities that can be held by any system process. Removing a capability from that set disables the ability to use an object until the next reboot. Although basic, this mechanism is sufficient to protect the local TTCB. Removing the capability CAP_SYS_MODULE from the capability bounding set we prevent any process from inserting code in the kernel. Removing CAP_SYS_RAWIO we prevent any process from reading and modifying the kernel memory.

For the COTS-based TTCB we make the assumption that the control channel is not accessed physically. Therefore, security has to be guaranteed only in its access points. To be precise, we must prevent an intruder from reading or writing in the control channel access points. This is done by removing the control network device from the kernel so that it can only be accessed by code in the kernel, i.e., by the local TTCB.

The control channel in the COTS-based TTCB is a switched Fast-Ethernet LAN. The timeliness of that network packet is guaranteed preventing packet collisions which would cause unpredictable delays. This requires that: (1) only one host can be connected to each switch port (hubs cannot be used); and (2) the traffic load has to be controlled. The first requirement is obvious. The second is solved by an access control mechanism, that accepts or rejects the execution of a service taking into account the availability of resources (buffers and bandwidth).

A Wormhole-Aware Protocol. This section presents an IT protocol based on the TTCB wormhole [4]. This protocol illustrates the approach based on hybrid failure assumptions: most of the system is assumed to fail in an arbitrary way, while the wormhole is assumed to be secure, i.e, to fail only by crashing. The system is also assumed to be asynchronous, except for the TTCB which is synchronous.

The protocol is a *reliable multicast*, a classical problem in distributed systems. Each execution of a multicast has one sender process and several recipient processes. In the rest of the section, we will make the classical separation of *receiving* a message from the network and *delivering* a message – the result of the protocol execution.

A reliable multicast protocol enforces the following two properties [6]: (1) all correct processes deliver the same messages; (2) if a correct sender transmits a message then all correct processes deliver this message. These rules do not imply any guarantees of delivery in case of a malicious sender. However, one of two things will happen, either the correct processes never complete the protocol

---

[4] The protocol is a simplified version of the protocol presented in [12].

execution and no message is ever delivered, or if they terminate, then they will all deliver the same message. No assumptions are made about the behaviour of malicious (recipient) processes. They might decide to deliver the correct message, a distinct message or no message.

The protocol –BRM (Byzantine Reliable Multicast)– is executed by a set of distributed processes. The processes can fail arbitrarily, e.g., they can crash, delay or not transmit some messages, generate messages inconsistent with the protocol, or collude with other faulty processes with malicious intent. Their communication can also be arbitrarily attacked: messages can be corrupted, removed, introduced, and replayed.

Let us see the process failure modes in more detail. A process is *correct* basically if it follows the protocol until the protocol terminates. Therefore, a process is *failed* if it crashes or deviates from the protocol. There are some additional situations in which we also consider the process to be failed. A process has an identity before the TTCB which is associated to the shared key. If that pair *(id,key)* is captured by an attacker, the process can be impersonated before the TTCB, therefore it has to be considered failed.

Another situation in which we consider a process to be failed is when an attacker manages to disrupt its communication with the other processes. Protocols for asynchronous systems typically assume that messages are repeatedly retransmitted and eventually received (reliable channels). In practice, usually a service which is too delayed is useless. Therefore, BRM retransmits messages a limited number of times and then we assume "isolated" processes to be failed. In channels prone only to accidental faults it is usually considered that no more than Od messages are corrupted/lost in a reference interval of time. Od is the *omission degree* and tests can be made in concrete networks to determine Od with the desired probability. For malicious faults, if a process does not receive a message after $Od + 1$ retransmissions from the sender, with Od computed considering only accidental faults, then it is reasonable to assume that either the process crashed, or an attack is under way. In any case, we will consider the receiver process as failed. The reader, however, should notice that Od is just a parameter of the protocol. If Od is set to a very high value, then BRM will start to behave like the protocols that assume reliable channels.

Formally, a reliable multicast protocol has the properties below [20]. The predicate $sender(M)$ gives the message field with the sender, and $group(M)$ gives the "group" of processes involved, i.e., the sender and the recipients (note that we consider that the sender also delivers).

- *Validity:* If a correct process multicasts a message M, then some correct process in $group(M)$ eventually delivers M.
- *Agreement:* If a correct process delivers a message M, then all correct processes in $group(M)$ eventually deliver M.
- *Integrity:* For any message M, every correct process p delivers M at most once and only if p is in $group(M)$, and if $sender(M)$ is correct then M was previously multicast by $sender(M)$.

BRM-T Sender protocol

```
1   tstart = TTCB_getTimestamp() + T0;
2   M := (elist, tstart, data);
3   propose := TTCB_propose(elist, tstart, TTCB_TBA_RMULTICAST, H(M));
4   repeat Od+1 times do multicast M to elist except sender od
5   deliver M;
```

BRM-T Recipient protocol

```
6    read_blocking(M);
7    propose := TTCB_propose(M.elist, M.tstart, TTCB_TBA_RMULTICAST, ⊥);
8    do decide := TTCB_decide(propose.tag);
9        while (decide.error ≠ TTCB_TBA_ENDED);
10   while (H(M) ≠ decide.value) do read_blocking(M) od
11   repeat Od+1 times do multicast M to elist except sender od
12   deliver M;
```

Fig. 9. BRM protocol

An implementation of BRM can be found in Figure 9. The sender securely transmits a hash of the message $(H(M))$ to the recipients through the TTCB Agreement Service and then multicasts the message $Od + 1$ times. This hash code is used by the recipients to ensure the integrity and authenticity of the message. When they get a correct copy of the message they multicast it $Od + 1$ times. The pseudo-code is pretty much straightforward so we do not describe it with detail and refer the reader to [12].

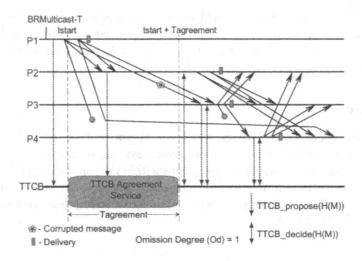

Fig. 10. Protocol execution

Figure 10 illustrates the behavior of the protocol. The horizontal lines represent the execution of processes through time. The thicker line represents the TTCB as a whole, even though, each process calls a separate local TTCB in its host (this representation is used for simplicity). The sender calls the TTCB agreement and then multicasts the message twice ($Od = 1$). These messages are received in the following way: P2 receives the two copies of the message, P3 receives the first copy corrupted and the second well, and P4 does not receive the first copy and the second is delayed. The example assumes that the first message sent to P3 is corrupted only in the *data* part, and for that reason it is still possible to determine this protocol instance. When a message arrives, the recipient calls the TTCB agreement to get the result with the reliable value of $H(M)$. Both processes P2 and P3 get this value almost immediately after the end of the agreement. They use the hash to select which of the messages they received is correct, and then they multicast the message to all the other recipients. P4 asks for the result of the agreement later, when it receives the first message from the protocol. Then, it multicasts the message.

9   Conclusion

We have presented an overview of the main concepts and design principles relevant to intrusion tolerant (IT) architectures. In our opinion, Intrusion Tolerance as a body of knowledge is, and will continue to be for a while, the main catalyst of the evolution of the area of dependability. The challenges put by looking at faults under the perspective of "malicious intelligence" have brought to the agenda hard issues such as uncertainty, adaptivity, incomplete knowledge, interference, and so forth. Under this thrust, researchers have sought replies, sometimes under new names or slight nuances of dependability, such as trustworthiness or survivability.

We believe that fault tolerance will witness an extraordinary evolution, which will have applicability in all fields and not only security-related ones. We will know that we got there when we will no longer talk about accidental faults, attacks or intrusions, but just (and again)... faults.

Acknowledgements

Many of the concepts and design principles presented here derive both from past experience with fault-tolerant and secure system architectures, and from more recent work and challenging discussions within the European IST MAFTIA project. We wish to warmly thank all members of the team, several of whom contributed to IT concepts presented here, and collectively have represented a fenomenal thinking tank.

References

1. Adelsbach, A., Alessandri, D., Cachin, C., Creese, S., Deswarte, Y., Kursawe, K., Laprie, J.C., Powell, D., Randell, B., Riordan, J., Ryan, P., Simmonds, W., Stroud, R., Veríssimo, P., Waidner, M., Wespi, A.: Conceptual Model and Architecture of MAFTIA. Project MAFTIA IST-1999-11583 deliverable D21. (2002) http://www.research.ec.org/maftia/deliverables/D21.pdf.
2. Alvisi, L., Malkhi, D., Pierce, E., Reiter, M.K., Wright, R.N.: Dynamic Byzantine quorum systems. In: Proceedings of the IEEE International Conference on Dependable Systems and Networks. (2000) 283–292
3. Amir, Y., Kim, Y., Nita-Rotaru, C., Schultz, J., Stanton, J., Tsudik, G.: Exploring robustness in group key agreement. In: Proceedings of the 21th IEEE International Conference on Distributed Computing Systems. (2001) 399–408
4. Ateniese, G., Steiner, M., Tsudik, G.: New multi-party authentication services and key agreement protocols. IEEE J. of Selected Areas on Communications 18 (2000)
5. Avizienis, A., Laprie, J.C., Randell, B.: Fundamental concepts of dependability. Technical Report 01145, LAAS-CNRS, Toulouse, France (2001)
6. Bracha, G., Toueg, S.: Asynchronous consensus and broadcast protocols. Journal of the ACM 32 (1985) 824–840
7. Cachin, C., Correia, M., McCutcheon, T., Neves, N., Pfitzmann, B., Randell, B., Schunter, M., Simmonds, W., Stroud, R., Veríssimo, P., Waidner, M., Welch, I.: Service and Protocol Architecture for the MAFTIA Middleware. Project MAFTIA IST-1999-11583 deliverable D23. (2001) http://www.research.ec.org/maftia/deliverables/D23final.pdf.
8. Cachin, C., Poritz, J.A.: Hydra: Secure replication on the internet. In: Proceedings of the International Conference on Dependable Systems and Networks. (2002)
9. Canetti, R., Gennaro, R., Herzberg, A., Naor, D.: Proactive security: Long-term protection against break-ins. RSA CryptoBytes 3 (1997) 1–8
10. Castro, M., Liskov, B.: Practical Byzantine fault tolerance. In: Proceedings of the Third Symposium on Operating Systems Design and Implementation. (1999)
11. Connelly, K., Chien, A.A.: Breaking the barriers: High performance security for high performance computing. In: Proc. New Security Paradigms Workshop. (2002)
12. Correia, M., Lung, L.C., Neves, N.F., Veríssimo, P.: Efficient Byzantine-resilient reliable multicast on a hybrid failure model. In: Proceedings of the 21st IEEE Symposium on Reliable Distributed Systems. (2002) 2–11
13. Correia, M., Veríssimo, P., Neves, N.F.: The design of a COTS real-time distributed security kernel. In: Proceedings of the Fourth European Dependable Computing Conference. (2002) 234–252
14. Cukier, M., Lyons, J., Pandey, P., Ramasamy, H.V., Sanders, W.H., Pal, P., Webber, F., Schantz, R., Loyall, J., Watro, R., Atighetchi, M., Gossett, J.: Intrusion tolerance approaches in ITUA (fast abstract). In: Supplement of the 2001 International Conference on Dependable Systems and Networks. (2001) 64–65
15. Debar, H., Wespi, A.: Aggregation and correlation of intrusion detection alerts. In: 4th Workshop on Recent Advances in Intrusion Detection. Volume 2212 of Lecture Notes in Computer Science. Springer-Verlag (2001) 85–103
16. Deswarte, Y., Blain, L., Fabre, J.C.: Intrusion tolerance in distributed computing systems. In: Proceedings of the 1991 IEEE Symposium on Research in Security and Privacy. (1991) 110–121
17. Dobson, J., Randell, B.: Building reliable secure computing systems out of unreliable insecure components. In: Proceedings of the International Symposium on Security and Privacy, IEEE (1986) 187–193
18. Dutertre, B., Crettaz, V., Stavridou, V.: Intrusion-tolerant Enclaves. In: Proceedings of the IEEE International Symposium on Security and Privacy. (2002)

19. Fraga, J.S., Powell, D.: A fault- and intrusion-tolerant file system. In: Proceedings of the 3rd International Conference on Computer Security. (1985) 203–218
20. Hadzilacos, V., Toueg, S.: A modular approach to fault-tolerant broadcasts and related problems. Technical Report TR94-1425, Cornell University, Department of Computer Science (1994)
21. Hiltunen, M., Schlichting, R., Ugarte, C.A.: Enhancing survivability of security services using redundancy. In: Proceedings of the IEEE International Conference on Dependable Systems and Networks. (2001) 173–182
22. Kihlstrom, K.P., Moser, L.E., Melliar-Smith, P.M.: The SecureRing group communication system. ACM Transactions on Information and System Security **4** (2001) 371–406
23. Knight, J., Heimbigner, D., Wolf, A., Carzaniga, A., Hill, J., Devanbu, P.: The Willow survivability architecture. In: Proceedings of the 4th Information Survivability Workshop. (2001)
24. Malkhi, D., Reiter, M.K., Tulone, D., Ziskind, E.: Persistent objects in the Fleet system. In: Proceedings of the 2nd DARPA Information Survivability Conference and Exposition (DISCEX II). (2001)
25. Meyer, F., Pradhan, D.: Consensus with dual failure modes. In: Proc. of the 17th IEEE International Symposium on Fault-Tolerant Computing. (1987) 214–222
26. Nicomette, V., Deswarte, Y.: An Authorization Scheme for Distributed Object Systems. In: IEEE Symposium on Research in Privacy and Security. (1996) 31–40
27. Pfitzmann, B., Waidner, M.: A model for asynchronous reactive systems and its application to secure message transmission. In: Proceedings of the IEEE Symposium on Research in Security and Privacy. (2001) 184–200
28. Powell, D., Seaton, D., Bonn, G., Veríssimo, P., Waeselynk, F.: The Delta-4 approach to dependability in open distributed computing systems. In: Proceedings of the 18th IEEE International Symposium on Fault-Tolerant Computing. (1988)
29. Powell, D., ed.: Delta-4: A Generic Architecture for Dependable Distributed Processing. Springer-Verlag (1991) Research Reports ESPRIT.
30. Powell, D.: Fault assumptions and assumption coverage. In: Proceedings of the 22nd IEEE International Symposium of Fault-Tolerant Computing. (1992)
31. Reiter, M.K.: The Rampart toolkit for building high-integrity services. In: Theory and Practice in Distributed Systems. Volume 938 of Lecture Notes in Computer Science. Springer-Verlag (1995) 99–110
32. Schneider, F.B.: The state machine approach: A tutorial. Technical Report TR86-800, Cornell University, Computer Science Department (1986)
33. Veríssimo, P., Rodrigues, L.: Distributed Systems for System Architects. Kluwer Academic Publishers (2001)
34. Veríssimo, P., Rodrigues, L., Casimiro, A.: Cesiumspray: A precise and accurate global clock service for large-scale systems. Journal of Real-Time Systems **12** (1997) 243–294
35. Veríssimo, P.: Uncertainty and predictability: Can they be reconciled? In: Future Directions in Distributed Computing. Springer-Verlag LNCS 2584 (2003) –
36. Veríssimo, P., Casimiro, A., Fetzer, C.: The Timely Computing Base: Timely actions in the presence of uncertain timeliness. In: Proceedings of the International Conference on Dependable Systems and Networks. (2000) 533–542
37. Xu, J., Randell, B., Romanovsky, A., Rubira, C., Stroud, R.J., Wu, Z.: Fault tolerance in concurrent object-oriented software through coordinated error recovery. In: Proceedings of the 25th IEEE International Symposium on Fault-Tolerant Computing. (1995) 499–508
38. Zhou, L., Schneider, F., van Renesse, R.: COCA: A secure distributed on-line certification authority. ACM Trans. on Computer Systems **20** (2002) 329–368

Improving Dependability of Component-Based Systems via Multi-versioning Connectors

Nenad Medvidovic, Marija Mikic-Rakic, and Nikunj Mehta

Computer Science Department
University of Southern California
Los Angeles, CA 90089-0781, USA
{neno,marija,mehta}@usc.edu

Abstract: The promise of architecture-based software development is that complex systems can be built and evolved reasonably quickly and reliably using coarse-grained components. However, practice has shown that many problems of traditional software development still persist in a component-based setting, and even that new problems are introduced. A class of such problems stems from the opportunity to perform system upgrade at the component level. The problems include errors in the functionality introduced by a new version of a component, decreased reliability of a new component version, inefficiency of components designed for reuse, component interaction mismatches, and so on. This paper presents an approach intended to alleviate the problems caused by component upgrades. Our approach focuses on software architectures both at system design and implementation levels. Specifically, our approach leverages explicit software connectors, called multi-versioning connectors (M-V-Cs), in ensuring dependable system composition and evolution, possibly during runtime. M-V-Cs unintrusively collect and analyze the execution statistics of one or more running components versions, and address three aspects of dependability: correctness, reliability, and efficiency. Our approach has been implemented and evaluated in the context of a family of architectural implementation platforms. We illustrate our approach with the help of an example application developed in coordination with a third-party organization.

Keywords: Software architecture, software component, software connector, dependability, architectural style, architectural middleware.

1 Introduction

Software architecture is an area of software engineering that focuses on notations, techniques, and tools for constructing software systems out of *components* (computational modules) and *connectors* (interaction modules) [31,35]. The promise of software architectures is that ever larger, more complex software systems can be built and evolved reasonably quickly and reliably by composing coarse-grained, possibly pre-fabricated software components and connectors. Indeed, component-based software development and software reuse have become topics of increasing interest to software researchers and practitioners. A number of component-based

R. de Lemos et al. (Eds.): Architecting Dependable Systems, LNCS 2677, pp. 37-60, 2003.
© Springer-Verlag Berlin Heidelberg 2003

technologies have emerged in the past decade, potentially enabling development of entire software systems from off-the-shelf (OTS) modules. At the same time, a number of well-documented problems may arise when attempting software reuse [6,7,15,21,24,33]:

- OTS components may be implemented in different programming languages;
- they may be poorly documented;
- they may not provide the exact functionality required;
- different OTS components may assume different types of interaction within the system (e.g., synchronous procedure calls vs. asynchronous event notifications);
- specialization and integration of OTS components may be unpredictably hard; and
- the costs associated with locating, understanding, and evaluating a component for reuse may be higher than engineering the component anew.

A specific instance of software reuse deals with *incorporating into a system a new version of an already existing component* [12]. Several of the reuse challenges outlined above may not be as pertinent in the context of component upgrades. Typically, vendors try to maintain the old component version's key properties (e.g., implementation language and interaction paradigm), while enhancing its functionality (by adding new features) and/or reliability (by fixing known bugs). However, component upgrades raise another set of questions, including whether the new version correctly preserves the functionality carried over from the old version, whether the new version introduces new errors, whether there is any performance discrepancy between the old and new versions, and so forth. Depending on the kinds of problems a new component version introduces and the remedies it provides for the old version's problems, this scenario can force an engineer to make some interesting choices:

- replace the old version of the component with the new version in the system;
- retain the old version (in case the new version introduces too many problems); and
- maintain both the old and new versions of a single component in the system.

Prior to making one of these choices, the engineer must somehow assess the new component in the context of the environment within which the old component is running. A simplistic solution to this task is to try to replicate the execution environment and test the new component within the replicated environment; the results of testing are then compared with those produced by the old component. However, this solution has several drawbacks. First, it may be difficult to faithfully replicate the execution environment, especially in heterogeneous, highly distributed systems. Second, multiple versions of a given system may be deployed in the field [16]; each such system version may employ different versions of (different) components, rendering the "off-line" testing approach impractical. Third, assuming that the new component version passes a "quality threshold" such that the engineer decides to add it to the deployed system (either as a replacement for the old version or in addition to the old version), the above strategy does not make any provisions for deploying such a component without disrupting the operation of the running system(s).

In this paper, we present an approach that addresses these three challenges. This work was inspired by Cook and Dage's technique for reliable upgrade of software at the level of individual procedures [12]. Our approach is predicated upon an explicit architectural focus, both at system modeling-time and run-time. To this end, we have leveraged an architecture description language (ADL) [16] and a family of architectural implementation platforms [23]. The specific objective of our work is to minimize the interdependencies of components, such that new component versions may be added to a (running) system more easily. In particular, we employ explicit software connectors as component intermediaries [2,27,31,35]. By "explicit software connectors" we mean implementation-level facilities [23] that directly correspond to the much more frequently used architectural model-level software connectors [35]. Specifically, we have developed special-purpose connectors, called *multi-versioning connectors (M-V-Cs)*, to ensure dependable system composition and evolution. M-V-Cs allow multiple versions of a component to execute "side-by-side" in the *deployed* system. M-V-Cs unintrusively collect and analyze the execution statistics of multiple component versions and perform comparisons of their performance (i.e., execution speed), reliability (i.e., number of failures), and correctness (i.e., ability to produce expected results). In response to the analysis results, M-V-Cs allow reverting the system and its constituent components to any previous state during their execution ("architectural undo"). Our implementation of M-V-Cs is evaluated in terms of the impact they have on the size and speed of an application. We illustrate our approach with the help of an example application developed in coordination with a third-party organization. While this paper will demonstrate that M-V-Cs can play an important role in improving the dependability of component-based systems, we also discuss a number of issues our current work has not addressed.

The remainder of the paper is organized as follows. Section 2 presents a brief overview of software architecture, software connectors, and middleware, which serve as the basis of this work. Section 3 briefly describes an example application used to illustrate the concepts throughout the paper. Section 4 details our approach, while Section 5 describes its current implementation. Section 6 presents evaluation of our approach and discusses several open issues. Finally we discuss related work in Section 7 and our conclusions in Section 7.

2 Background

2.1 Software Architectures

Our support for reliable component upgrades leverages explicit *software architectural* models. As software systems have grown more complex, their design and specification in terms of coarse-grain building blocks has become a necessity. The field of software architecture addresses this issue and provides high-level abstractions for representing the structure, behavior, and key properties of a software system. Software architectures involve (1) descriptions of the elements from which systems are built, (2) interactions among those elements, (3) patterns that guide their composition, and (4) constraints on these patterns [31]. In general, a particular system is defined in terms of a collection of *components*, their interconnections (*configuration*), and interactions among them (*connectors*).

Another key architectural concept is *architectural style*. An architectural style defines a *vocabulary* of component and connector types and a set of *constraints* on how instances of these types can be combined in a system or family of systems [35]. When designing a software system, selection of an appropriate architectural style becomes a key determinant of the system's success. Styles also influence architectural evolution by restricting the possible changes an architect is allowed to make. Examples of styles include pipe and filter, layered, blackboard, client-server [35], GenVoca [5], and C2 [37].

2.2   Software Connectors

Although components have been the predominant focus of researchers and practitioners, they address only one aspect of large-scale development. Another important aspect, particularly magnified by the emergence of the Internet and the growing need for distribution, is *interaction* among components. Component interaction is embodied in the notion of *software connectors*. Software components perform computations and store the information relevant to an application domain; software connectors, on the other hand, perform the transfer of control and data among components. In [35] connectors are defined as follows:

Connectors mediate interactions among components; that is, they establish the rules that govern component interaction and specify any auxiliary mechanisms required.

Connectors manifest themselves in a software system as shared variable accesses, table entries, buffers, instructions to a linker, procedure calls, networking protocols, pipes, SQL links between a database and an application, and so forth [35]. In large, and especially distributed systems, connectors become key determinants of system properties, such as performance, resource utilization, global rates of flow, scalability, reliability, security, evolvability, and so forth.

Software architecture-based approaches have come furthest in their treatment of connectors. They typically separate computation (components) from interaction (connectors) in a system. In principle, architectures do not assume component homogeneity, nor do they constrain the allowed connectors and connector implementation mechanisms. Several existing architecture-based technologies have provided support for modeling or implementing certain classes of connectors [2,34]. Most architectural approaches that have explicitly addressed connectors have either provided mechanisms for *modeling* arbitrarily complex connectors or *implementing* a small set of simple ones, but never both.

Our previous work on classifying software connectors has helped further our understanding of what the fundamental building blocks of software interaction are and how they can be composed into more complex interactions [27]. This classification of software connectors identifies four services that are provided by software connectors namely *communication, coordination, conversion* and *facilitation*. Communication services are required for the transmission of data among components. Data transfer services are a primary building block of component interaction. Coordination services enable transfer of control among components.[1] Components interact by passing the thread of execution to each other. Conversion services transform the interaction required by one component to that provided by another. Conversion services allow components that have not been specifically tailored for each other to establish and conduct interactions. Facilitation services are required to mediate and streamline component interaction. They are required for facilitating and optimizing the interactions between heterogeneous components that have been designed to interoperate with each other.

Every connector provides services that belong to at least one of these categories. It is also possible to have multi-category connectors to satisfy the need for a richer set of interaction services. For example, it is possible to have a connector that provides both communication and coordination services.

2.3   Middleware

As already discussed, simple connectors such as memory access and procedure call are supported by programming languages; some languages also provide native thread management. However, support for more sophisticated interaction services and their composition is being studied through middleware, frameworks, and higher-level programming languages.

A middleware provides a degree of isolation between an application and the underlying hardware platform. Middleware is also used to hide other layers such as the network and the operating system variations from an application. Examples of middleware include JEDI [13], CORBA [30], COM [32], and Enterprise Java Beans [36]. Each of these technologies focuses on a particular form of component interaction, such as remote procedure calls, event registration, and distributed transactions. Ultimately, each middleware technology supports only a small set of interaction primitives that may not be universally applicable [14]. Furthermore, the use of these technologies can still lead to problems such as deadlocks within systems, and such problems can only be resolved by creating custom solutions [17].

Most existing middleware technologies do not allow alteration of their facilities. However, many distributed applications require middleware customization in order to manage system's evolution, thus creating a need for *adaptive middleware* [1]. Recently developed approaches for adaptive middleware [19], provide increased support for architectural evolution. Adaptive middleware can be customized to reduce resource usage, cope with network connectivity changes, or the mobility of components. Adaptive middleware also supports reflection so that an application can discover services available from the middleware and change them at run-time.

---

[1] In a concurrent setting, *transfer* of control from component A to component B does not necessitate the *loss* of control by A.

3 Example Application

To illustrate our approach, we use an application recently developed in collaboration with an external organization. The application supports distributed deployment of personnel, intended to deal with situations such as military crises and search-and-rescue efforts. The specific instance of this application depicted in Fig. 1 addresses military Troops Deployment and battle Simulations (TDS). A computer at *Headquarters* gathers information from the field and displays the current battlefield status in terms of the locations of friendly troops, enemy troops, and obstacles (e.g., mine fields). A *Headquarters* computer is networked to a set of devices used by *Commanders* in the field. Commanders can be connected directly to each other as well as to a number of *Soldiers*. Each commander controls his/her own part of the battlefield and can deploy troops, analyze a deployment strategy, and transfer troops to and from other commanders. Additionally, each commander can view the status of other parts of the battlefield. Soldiers only interact with commanders, and can view the status of the segment of the battlefield in which they are located, receive direct orders from their commanders, and report updates on their own status.

Fig. 1. TDS application distributed across multiple devices

Figure 2 illustrates the architecture of TDS consisting of three subsystems, one for each type of user. The *Map* component maintains a model of the system's overall resources—terrain, personnel, tank units, and mine fields. These resources are permanently stored inside the *Repository* component. The *StrategyAnalyzerAgent, DeploymentAdvisor*, and *SimulationAgent* components, respectively, (1) analyze the deployments of friendly troops with respect to enemy troops and obstacles, (2) suggest deployments of friendly troops based on their availability as well as positions of enemy troops and obstacles, and (3) incrementally simulate the outcome of the battle based on the current situation in the field. The *StrategyAnalysisKB* component stores strategy rules and the *SAKBUI* component provides the user interface for changing these rules. Combined, the *ResourceManager, CommanderManager, SoldierManager,* and *ResourceMonitor* components enable allocation and transfer of resources and periodically update the state of those resources. The *Weather* component provides local weather information and the *WeatherAnalyzer* component assesses the impact of those weather conditions. Finally, the *RenderingAgent* provides the main user interface of the application.

4 Approach

Architecture-based software development enables separation of components (data and processing elements) from connectors (interaction elements), thus minimizing inter-component dependencies [24]. We leverage this key property of architectures in supporting dependable system composition and evolution. Additionally, we make the following key observations about the problem space we are addressing:

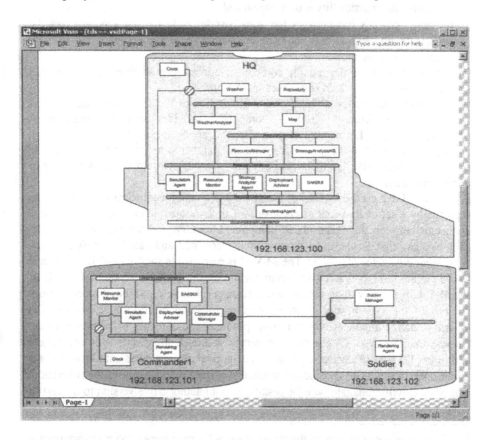

Fig. 2. Architecture of the TDS application. The unlabeled circles connecting components represent *peer* connectors

- real, OTS components can be of arbitrary granularity;
- an OTS component can have complex internal state that both influences the outcome of a given operation and changes as a result of that operation (e.g., the result of a stack *Pop* depends on the value of the stack's top element; a *Pop* also changes the state of the stack);
- a component can provide *non-terminal* operations;[2]
- components can assume various interaction protocols; and
- the data structures affected and possibly returned by the different components'operations may be arbitrarily complex.

When performing an upgrade of an existing component, one can encounter three possible relations between the old and new versions of the component:

1. the new version provides the same functionality, but better performance, security, reliability, and so forth;
2. the new version also provides additional functionality, but the basic approach for providing that functionality is unchanged; and
3. the new version's functionality has some overlap with the old version's, but the implementation approach is completely different (e.g., a novel algorithm or more efficient data structure).

Our approach supports dependable component upgrades in all three cases provided that certain assumptions hold (discussed in Section 5).

Figure 3 shows the partial architectural configuration of the TDS application. In this configuration, a *Strategy Analyzer* component provides several operations as illustrated in Fig. 4. Let us assume that, after this application is deployed, we obtain two new versions of *Strategy Analyzer* that are claimed to be improvements over the old version. We would like to assess both new versions before deciding which one to deploy in our system.

Figure 3 depicts the essence of our approach: a component (*Strategy Analyzer*) is replaced by a set of its versions encapsulated in a wrapper. The wrapper serves as a connector between the encapsulated component versions and the rest of the system [27]. We say that *Strategy Analyzer* is multi-versioned and call the wrapper *multi-versioning connector (M-V-C)*.[3] The M-V-C is responsible for "hiding" from the rest of the system the fact that a given component exists in multiple versions. The role of the M-V-C is to relay to all component versions each invocation that it receives from the rest of the system, and to propagate the generated result(s) to the rest of the system. Each component version may produce some result in response to an invocation. The M-V-C allows a system's architect to specify the component authority [12] for different operations. A component designated as authoritative for a given operation will be considered nominally correct with respect to that operation. The M-V-C will propagate *only* the results from an authoritative version to the rest of

---

[2] By *non terminal operation* we mean that the component will need to interact with other components in order to perform a requested operation. For example, operation *a* in component *A* may need to invoke operation *b* in component *B* to complete its task; in turn, *b* may need to invoke other components' operations *c* and *d*; and so forth.

[3] The term multi-version*ing* connector means that the connector facilitates the inclusion of and interactions with multi-version*ed* components.

the system. At the same time, the M-V-C will log the results of all the multi-versioned components' invocations and compare them to the results produced by the authoritative version.

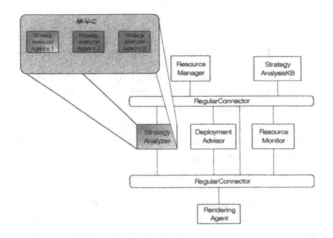

Fig. 3. Multi-versioning connector

We are also supporting authority specification at the level of individual operations (e.g., component version *v1* is authoritative for *analyzeStrategy*, while *v2* is authoritative for *calculateProbabilities*). For each possible invocation, we are assuming that there is going to be exactly one component designated as authoritative.

In addition to this "basic" functionality of insulating multi-versioned components from the rest of a system, and vice versa, the M-V-C provides several additional capabilities. The M-V-C allows component authority for a given operation to be changed at any point in time. It also allows insertion of a new component version into the system during runtime without removing the old versions or halting the system. However, if component authority for a given operation is changed or a new component version is inserted in the middle of a multi-versioned component's invocation, the change will take place after the completion of that invocation. The M-V-C can monitor the execution of the multiple component versions and perform comparisons of their performance (i.e., execution speed), correctness (whether they are producing the same results as the authoritative version) and reliability (number of failures). Furthermore, the M-V-C logs the execution history as a sequence of invocations of the multi-versioned component. In case a failure has occurred, this information can be used to determine which sequence of invocations has led to the failure. The M-V-C also periodically records the state of each component version. The execution history and the state "snapshots" can be used to roll back the execution of a multi-versioned component to any point in the past; this capability is further discussed in Section 5.

```
Component: StrategyAnalyzer
Operations:
  analyzeStrategy(int[][]):boolean;
  calculateProbabilities(int[][]):int[][];
  determineWinner(int[][]):String;
  fight(int[][]):int[][];
```

Fig. 4. Operations of the *Strategy Analyzer* component

M-V-C's monitoring mechanism (logging of component invocations, comparisons of their results, and component state "snapshots") can help an engineer make one of the following choices:

- replace the old version of the component with the new one,
- retain the old version (in case the new version introduces too many problems), or
- maintain both the old and new versions of the component.

In the first two cases, the M-V-C can be removed from the system to reduce the overhead introduced by its insertion, further discussed in Section 6.2. In the last case, the M-V-C will be retained and used to accomplish the desired functionality of a single conceptual component by simultaneously employing multiple implemented versions. In that case, the monitoring can be disabled to minimize the overhead.

To date, we have primarily focused on the use of our approach in the case of component upgrades. However, the same infrastructure can be used for improving system's dependability in cases when an entirely new component needs to be inserted into an application. The wrapped component can be inserted at the desired location in the system's architecture. The component's behavior can then be assessed with minimal disturbance to the rest of the system, since the M-V-C will be configured to intercept and "swallow" all the invocations the component tries to make. Once the new component is assessed in the context of the deployed system and it is established that the component produces satisfactory results, the wrapper around it (i.e., the M-V-C) may be removed.

5 Implementation

5.1 A Family of Architectural Middleware

In order to implement the approach outlined above, we needed an implementation infrastructure that supported not only component-based system composition, but also explicit implementation-level software connectors. Most existing component interoperability, or middleware, solutions (recall Section 2.3) support a single, though often quite powerful interaction facility (i.e., connector). On the other hand, our approach demanded multiple and varying numbers of lighter-weight connectors. For this reason, we elected to implement M-V-Cs using an existing family of architecture implementation frameworks, developed both in-house and by third parties [23]. In this subsection we describe the basic details of the frameworks, also referred to as *architectural middleware.* The next subsection will discuss how this infrastructure is used in the implementation of our M-V-C prototype.

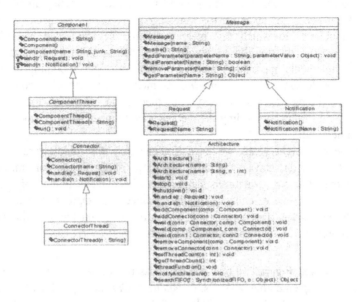

Fig. 5. UML class diagram of the middleware API

Middleware API. Figur 5 shows the external API of the architectural middleware, with classes that are used by application developers to implement an architecture. The *Architecture* class records the configuration of its constituent components and connectors. *Component* provides primitives to *send* and *handle* (i.e., receive) messages. *Connector* keeps track of attached components and dispatches messages to the appropriate components. Components and connectors may run in a shared thread of control (*Component* and *Connector*), or they may execute in their own threads (*ComponentThread* and *ConnectorThread*). *Component* and *ComponentThread* classes are abstract. Thus, it is necessary to subclass one of them in order to create application-specific components. On the other hand, since connectors provide application-independent interaction services, *Connector* and *ConnectorThread* are concrete classes and may be directly instantiated in an implementation.

In addition to the generic *Connector,* we have developed a library of connectors, such as those supporting various message routing protocols (e.g., broadcast, multicast, unicast), distribution of architectural elements [14], and security. Developers can select connectors that provide the needed interaction facilities from this library, and instantiate them directly into an architecture's implementation. At times when additional features are required or certain interaction behaviors need to be amended, the application architect can extend one or more connectors from this library to create the desired connector behavior [27]. We have, in fact, built M-V-Cs as simply another type of connector.

The middleware supports communication among components by sending and receiving *Messages* (*Requests* and *Notifications*). The middleware provides basic mechanisms for creating and exchanging messages. Components create messages and send them to connectors based on the components' internal processing algorithms and communication needs. In response to a message, a receiving connector selects its attached components to which this message should be forwarded based on the connector's internal distribution policy (e.g. broadcast, unicast, multicast). Each component implements application-specific processing of the incoming requests or notifications inside the corresponding *handle* method. In case of a connector-to-connector link, the messages are passed to another connector, which applies its own internal policy in further forwarding the messages on to its attached components (and possibly connectors).

Over the past eight years, we have implemented this middleware in several languages (C++, Ada, Java, Python), resulting in a family of middleware implementations. Various structural changes have been made to the middleware's internal design over time to enhance its performance and improve its extensibility. However, the external API, shown in Fig. 5, has remained unchanged, allowing full portability of applications across the middleware family.

Middleware Design. Figure 6 shows a UML class model of the middleware family member used in implementing M-V-Cs. *Component*, *Connector*, and *Architecture* are all sub-classed from *Brick* Each subclass of *Brick* implements a specific set of interfaces based on the type of architectural element to which it belongs. *IArchitecture* provides methods for managing the architectural configuration; *IConnector* provides methods for delivering messages; and *IComponent* provides the methods for processing messages. *Brick*s are attached to an *IScaffold* for providing execution and monitoring support. A class that implements *IScaffold* can selectively monitor messages flowing through the architecture based on their content. Scaffolds are also used to store messages and pool threads so that message dispatching can be done in a way most suitable to the application. This also allows us to separate the management of threads and messages from the *Architecture*, allowing one to easily compose many sub-architectures in a single application.

The middleware is symmetric in its support for components and connectors. This has allowed us to create a set of reusable connectors, with complex internal architectures. For example, we have composed a security connector to authenticate communicating components. We have also created modular "border" connectors to allow components across machine boundaries to communicate with each other and synchronous message connectors with procedure call-like semantics.

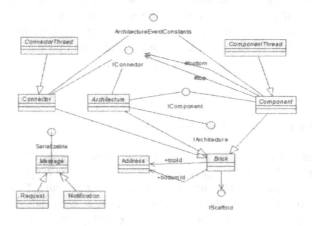

Fig. 6. Middleware design class model

We have been able to support various message routing techniques such as broadcast, multicast, and unicast by assigning an *Address* to each *Brick,* and then using these addresses for more targeted distribution of messages. The addresses are used during communication for identifying component(s) that are the intended to message recipients. It is the responsibility of sending components to specify message targets. This can be accomplished in a variety of ways: (1) hardwiring addresses into each component during development, (2) using a registry to record component types, and querying the registry to locate the target components; (3) broadcasting an initial message aimed at discovering the components with which communication is desired, and later using the discovered addresses for unicast distribution.

The middleware supports dynamism through operations for addition (*add*), removal (*remove*), connection (*weld*), and disconnection (*unweld*) of components and connectors in the *Architecture* class. Since the interaction among components is decoupled via flexible, first-class connectors, a high degree of dynamism is provided with minimal disturbance to the rest of the running system. The connectors are equipped with the capability to create and remove communication ports "on the fly" to accommodate dynamic changes to their attached components [29].

Call Dispatching. In order to optimize local component communication, the middleware uses a central FIFO message queue per each address space. A pool of *shepherd* threads is kept ready to handle any calls or messages issued by any component in a given address space. The size of the thread pool is parameterized and, hence, adjustable. For communication that spans address spaces or machine boundaries, a message is transported via a special-purpose connector that encapsulates distribution to the recipient address space, and added to its message queue. A shepherd thread removes a message from the head of this queue as soon as it finishes processing the previous message. The shepherd thread is run through the connector attached to the sending component; the connector dispatches the message to relevant components using the same thread of execution for processing their *handle* methods (see Fig. 7). If a recipient component generates further messages, they are added to the end of the message queue, and different threads are used for dispatching those messages to their recipients. The control over the thread pool and the message queue is exercised from the *Architecture* class. The M-V-Cs implement a variation of this technique, as discussed below.

5.2   Multi-versioning Connectors

Our implementation of the multi-versioning connector (M-V-C) wrapper leverages the architectural middleware discussed above. The intrinsic support of the middleware connectors for runtime addition and removal of components [29] is leveraged in the context of the M-V-C to add and remove component versions during runtime. In the course of developing the M-V-C, we have extended the middleware with synchronous message passing connectors for the purpose of supporting a wider range of OTS components. In particular, we have implemented two special-purpose, reusable software connectors, called M-V-C-Top and M-V-C-Bottom. As shown in Fig. 8, these two collaborating connectors encapsulate multiple versions of a component, allowing their parallel execution and monitoring as discussed in Section 4.

When a message is sent to a multi-versioned component (e.g., *Strategy Analyzer* in Fig. 8) from any component below the *M-V-C-Bottom* or above the *M-V-C-Top* connectors, the corresponding connector invokes within each component version the operation that is responsible for processing that message. Even though the operation is invoked on all the installed versions, only the messages generated by the authoritative version are propagated by the two M-V-C connectors to the rest of the system. In our example, whenever a *determineWinner* request message is sent from the *Rendering Agent* component, M-V-C-Bottom will return to *Rendering Agent* only the result produced by (the authoritative) version *v2*; the results produced by versions *v1* and *v3* are compared with those of *v2* and logged, but are not propagated to the rest of the system.

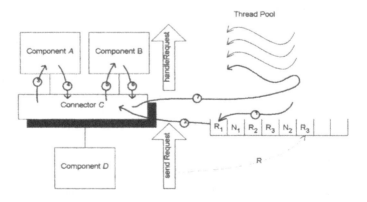

Fig. 7. Message dispatching in the architectural middleware

The GUI of our implementation of the M-V-C is shown in the bottom window of Fig. 9. This window is separate from an application's UI, such as that of TDS, partially depicted in the top window. The M-V-C window shows the list of component versions in the upper left frame. The table in the upper right frame shows the current authority specification and the total (cumulative) execution time, in milliseconds, for each invoked operation of a selected component version (in this case, version *v1* of *Strategy Analyzer*).

The table in the middle frame displays the execution statistics for the selected component version. For each operation, the table shows the number of times the operation has been invoked, the average execution time for that operation (-1 if the operation is not implemented by the component version), and the number of times the operation produced identical and different results in comparison to the authoritative version. The table also displays the number of times an error (an exception or a failure) occurred during the execution of the operation, and whether the invoked operation is implemented by the component version.

The bottom two frames in the M-V-C window display the call and result logs as sequences of generated messages. Using these logs, the *Undo* button can revert the states of a given set of multi-versioned components to any point in the past. This capability is achieved by taking "snapshots" of and storing the versions' states at regular intervals[4] and by logging each message sent to a multi-versioned component. The undo capability of the M-V-C is enabled by the event-based nature of the middleware and its support for explicit connectors. It is important to note that the undo operation can only be performed on the multi-versioned components. Rolling back the state of the rest of the system is not supported by our current implementation; the primary reason for this is the large overhead such a capability would introduce to an application's size and speed. The undo operation determines whether an architectural change (i.e., addition or removal of a component version) occurred between the application's past state to which we want to revert and its current state. The M-V-C restores the application's previous architecture if necessary (e.g., by removing the added component versions) and restores the desired states of all component versions. The state of a given component is restored to any point in the past in a six-step process:

1. *Select a Past State:* The engineer selects the desired (target) state to which she wants to revert by selecting a particular message in the call log (the bottom left frame of the M-V-C window in Fig. 9). As depicted in Fig. 10, the selected message corresponds to a point (msg $_{i+k}$) in the multi-versioned component's execution. Since the component states are recorded by the M-V-C only at discrete intervals, note that there may be no recorded state corresponding to the exact point in time signified by the selected message. This issue is addressed in step 4 below.

---

[4] To implement the "snapshots" we have experimented both with Java's serialization mechanism and cloning (deep copy) of objects in memory. Even though we consider this issue to be outside the scope of the paper, we should note that the current version of the M-V-C implements deep copy of objects as it proved much more efficient.

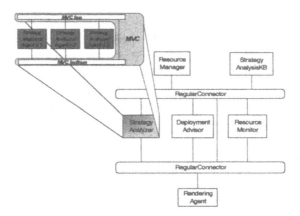

Fig. 8. Multi-versioning connector realization

2. *Insulate the Multi-Versioned Component:* M-V-C-Top and M-V-C-Bottom continue logging all messages arriving from outside components, but temporarily stop relaying them to the multi-versioned components.

3. *Remove the Existing Component Versions:* Each component version (e.g., the three versions of *StrategyAnalyzer*) is disconnected from M-V-C-Top and M-V-C-Bottom (using the middleware's *unweld* operation [29]) and unloaded from the application.

4. *Roll Back the Clock in Large Increments:* The desired past, recorded states of all component versions, selected in step 1 above, are retrieved, loaded, and attached to M-V-C-Top and M-V-C-Bottom (using the middleware's *weld* operation). Since the component states are recorded only at *discrete* intervals, the state restored in this step should be the nearest recorded state *preceding* the desired state. For example, Fig. 10 shows that the desired state is between the states recorded at times N-9 and N-10; in that case, the retrieved and restored state should be the one recorded at time N-10.

5. *Advance the Clock in Small Increments:* If the component state restored in step 4 above precedes the target state, as shown in the example in Fig. 10, the recorded message log is used by M-V-C-Top and M-V-C-Bottom to send messages to the reinserted component and thus rapidly advance its state to the *exact* desired point in the (more recent) past.

6. *Re-Join the Application:* Finally, M-V-C-Top and M-V-C-Bottom reopen the communication between the multi-versioned component and the rest of the application.

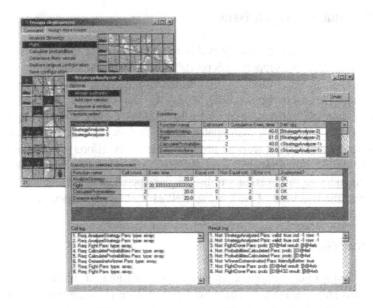

Fig. 9. M-V-C monitoring window (bottom) and a screenshot of the TDS application (top)

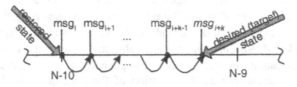

Fig. 10. Restoring a component's state to a point *between* two recorded states

Our implementation of the M-V-C allows the user to change the authority of a given operation at runtime (signified by the highlighted menu option in the bottom window of Fig. 9). This change may be reflected in the running application, since different component versions may provide different implementations of the operation. Finally, we leverage our middleware's support for explicit, multiple connectors to enable the use of the M-V-C in different locations in a *single* architecture. Our middleware's reliance on asynchronous message-based interaction directly support dependable *simultaneous* upgrades of multiple components. In the example architecture shown in Fig. 3, the *Deployment Advisor* component may be multi-versioned at the same time as the *Strategy Analyzer* component.

6 Evaluation and Open Issues

Our approach has been successfully evaluated on a number of examples [16,25]. We have also evaluated our support to dependable component upgrade in the context of system deployment and evolution [28]. Furthermore, we have also performed a series of benchmarks to assess the overhead of M-V-C. Our approach has shown a lot of promise to date and appears better suited to supporting systems involving realistic, large-scale OTS components than related approaches (e.g., [10]). At the same time, we consider this research a work in progress. Our future efforts will address several unresolved issues and eliminate the simplifying assumptions we have made thus far. In the remainder of this section we discuss our approach in the context of system deployment, the overhead of M-V-C, as well as a number of open issues that will frame our future work.

6.1   Deployment

Software deployment comprises activities for installing or updating an already implemented software system. These activities include (1) deployment of a system onto a new host, (2) component upgrade in an existing system, (3) static analysis of the proposed system configuration, and (4) dynamic analysis of the configuration after the deployment.

As described in [28], we leverage explicit connectors, our architectural analysis tools [25], and the family of architectural middleware in supporting these activities. Specifically, in support of tasks 1 and 3 above, we provide a special purpose component, called *AdminComponent* that is able to (1) send and receive messages containing application elements (i.e., components and connectors) and the accompanying information (i.e., the location of these elements in the destination configuration), and (2) effect the changes contained in the message (e.g., addition, removal, connection and disconnection of architectural elements) to the running system via its pointer to the *Architecture* object. In order to deploy the desired architecture onto a host (or a set of hosts) we assume that the host will contain an *Architecture* object with a preloaded *AdminComponent*. Additionally, in order to perform the static analysis of the proposed configurations, we provide a special purpose *ContinuousAnalysis* component that analyzes the (partial) architectural models during the application's execution in order to assess the validity of proposed run-time architectural changes, and possibly disallows the changes. *Continuous Analysis* component is built using a subset of our architectural analysis environment DRADEL [25].

The support described above provides assurance that the desired architectural configuration is valid according to its specification, and provides facilities for its deployment. However, implemented components may not preserve all the properties and relationships established at the architectural level (e.g., due to accidental coding errors) [26]. For this reason, in order to provide dependable system deployment and upgrade, the described deployment support is complemented with the use of M-V-C. M-V-C's role is to unintrusively assess the run-time effects of the proposed changes.

Our deployment support is used in concert with M-V-C to:(1) dynamically add the M-V-C wrapper and a set of component versions to be tested to the running system, and (2) dynamically remove the M-V-C wrapper and the set of obsolete component versions, once the behavior of the multiversioned component is assessed and the desired version of a multiversioned component is selected.

6.2   M-V-C Overhead

The memory overhead of a single M-V-C (i.e., without the GUI, where the results of the monitoring are stored in an external file) depends on three factors: the number of component versions being assessed, the number of operations of the multiversioned component, and the size of invocation history log. The overhead can be estimated using the following formula, obtained empirically:

$$Mem\_M\text{-}V\text{-}C \ (in \ KB) = 1.6 + 0.04 * num\_op + 0.1 * num\_ver + 0.008 * hist\_size$$

where *num_op* is the total number of operations provided by the multi-versioned component, *num_ver* is the total number of versions being tested, and *hist_size* is the size of invocation history log. For example, the overhead of a single M-V-C for 3 versions of the *Strategy Analyzer* component with 4 operations and a log history of 1,000 invocations with no GUI is around 10 KB. Additionally, the overhead of MVC's GUI is 402 KB since it uses an off-the-shelf GUI framework (Java Swing).

The performance overhead of M-V-C linearly depends on the number of versions being tested and the average operation execution time. The operation execution time directly depends on the algorithmic complexity involved.

6.3   Open Issues

We currently assume that different implementations of a multi-versioned component will be similar enough to allow comparisons of the results returned by the versions' operations. The comparisons are also predicated upon the existence of an "equal" method for the returned (arbitrarily complex) data structures. This is clearly inadequate in the case where fundamental differences exist between the different versions' implementations. In such a situation, a combination of the operations' results, different versions' internal states, and the message patterns they produce in the process of performing an operation may be needed to properly compare the components.

Furthermore, if an invoked operation of a multi-versioned component is non-terminal (recall Footnote 1), the M-V-C must decide which version's invocations to propagate. Note that this is different than propagating an operation's results: it may simply be that version 1 of component A needs to invoke an operation in component B, while version 2 needs to invoke an operation in component C. We are currently supporting this type of authority specification by assuming that the component designated as authoritative for performing a given non-terminal operation will also be authoritative for invoking any other operation. However, to more accurately assess the performance of different versions, both invocations (by versions 1 *and* 2) should be propagated. This is, in turn, likely to affect the application's functionality, so we clearly must develop a different solution to deal with this issue.

In our work to date, we have placed the burden of making the final decision regarding a component upgrade on the human engineer. The monitoring of the multi-versioned components can be used to aid automated decision-making. In this scenario, the engineer would just specify a set of criteria for removing a version (e.g., number of errors produced by a version over a given period of time) or for keeping only one version (e.g., if the version performs without any errors over a specific period of time). We can extend with minimal effort the current implementation of the M-V-C to support such automated decision making. One aspect of our future research will be to develop component upgrade heuristics that can then be used in automating this task.

7 Related Work

In addition to software architectures and middleware discussed in Section 2, this section outlines several other research areas and approaches from which our work has drawn inspiration.

Cook and Dage [12] have developed an approach to reliable software component upgrades that has directly influenced ours. Their component upgrade framework, HERCULES, treats only individual procedures as components, allows multiple such procedures to be executed simultaneously, and provides a means for comparing their execution results. Unlike our approach, HERCULES elaborates on the relationships among different versions (e.g., it supports explicit version trees). HERCULES allows the component authority to be specified at the level of a *subdomain*, an explicitly constrained subset of a procedure's domain.[5] Given that our components are coarser-grained and potentially much more heterogeneous, in our work to date specifying subdomains has shown to be of little practical use. Cook and Dage also propose voting as a mechanism for resolving situations in which there is no component version designated as authoritative. We are also considering such an approach. Finally, unlike our M-V-C, HERCULES does not provide any support for inserting and removing component versions at system runtime, or reverting a multi-versioned component to its past execution state.

Another related approach is Simplex [3], which supports fault-tolerant component upgrade through replacement units. Simplex provides analytic redundancy through co-existence of multiple components. The purpose of multiple component co-existence is the ability to use the replacement component in case the "leader" component fails. However, Simplex does not provide facilities for comparing the performance of these multiple versions.

The field of configuration management (CM) [7,9] deals with capturing the evolution of individual components and entire systems at the source code level. CM provides means for storing and relating different versions of a component. The goals

---

[5] A domain comprises the combined value spaces of a procedure's input parameters.

of CM are to properly facilitate simultaneous changes to a component and to track the evolution over time of each component, as well as of entire systems. CM systems typically do not ensure the preservation of desired functionality across different versions of the same component. We have thus recently integrated our implementation of M-V-C into an architecture-based CM system called Mae [13].

Recording the states of components in a distributed system is a difficult problem. The work of Chandy and Lamport [8] introduces an algorithm by which a set of cooperating operating system processes can determine and record the global state of a distributed system during execution. Similarly to our components, their approach assumes that the processes in a distributed system communicate by sending and receiving messages. Their approach also requires that each process be capable of recording its own state and the messages it sends and receives, and that any process in the system can send its state to the "main" process performing the system "snapshot".

Simultaneously using multiple ("N") versions of independently developed components has been investigated as a way of increasing the reliability of a software system [2,6,14]. Similarly to our approach, all components process the same requests and data during system execution, and voting mechanisms are used to determine the relative correctness and reliability of the different versions. In addition, our approach also assesses component performance and provides support for manipulating the deployed systems at runtime.

Finally, in our previous work we have performed extensive studies of our middleware's ability to support reuse of arbitrarily complex, heterogeneous OTS components and connectors [11,17,18,20]. In the process, we have developed a set of simple heuristics for reusing different classes of OTS components and connectors. These heuristics have been implemented in our architecture modeling, analysis, implementation, deployment, and evolution tools [13,19,22]. We consider the work described in this paper to be a complement to our previous work on reuse.

8 Conclusion

In the rapidly growing world of software development, releases of new components and component versions happen with increasing frequency. In such a setting, the dependability of a software system directly depends upon the key properties of those components (e.g., correctness, reliability, safety, efficiency, and so on). Our approach tries to maximize the benefits of the availability of many components, while, at the same time, minimizing the potential risks of relying on them (e.g., unknown reliability, difficulties with deploying the components in the running systems, and so on).

This paper presented an architecture-based approach to deploying and increasing the confidence in new versions of an OTS component. The essence of our approach is the use of explicit software connectors. We have built special purpose connectors (M-V-Cs) that allow multiple versions of a component to execute in parallel in the running system. The M-V-Cs also monitors component execution with minimal intrusion on the rest of the application. Our reliance on explicit multi-versioning connectors allows us to experiment with supporting some less common, but quite likely component upgrade and reuse situations. For example, we can utilize the behaviors of more than one component version in the same application, at the same time. M-V-Cs also allow us to "back out" of undesirable system states by reverting to a previous system state.

However, none of these features can be viewed as a component upgrade panacea and none come without a cost. M-V-Cs do induce overhead on an application's size. Processing performed by M-V-Cs also causes application slowdown. This is particularly the case if message logging is enabled in support of "architectural undo". Such overhead may be unacceptable in many applications. In addition, different versions of the same functionality may behave very differently and it may be difficult to meaningfully and efficiently compare their correctness or reliability. This is especially the case with non-terminal operations (recall Section 4). Therefore, while our current design and implementation of M-V-Cs has utility as is, it should be used judiciously, and recognized for what it does and does not do. The particular benefit of the M-V-Cs' current design, however, is its modularity, which will allow us to incrementally isolate and tackle many of the remaining issues.

References

1. G. Agha. Adaptive Middleware. Communications of the ACM. 45(6). June 2002.
2. R. Allen and D. Garlan. A Formal Basis for Architectural Connection. ACM Transactions on Software Engineering and Methodology, pp. 213–249, July 1997.
3. N.Altman et. al. Simplex in a Hostile Communications Environment: The Coordinated Prototype. Technical Report CMU/SEI-99-TR-016.
4. A. Avizienis. The N-Version Approach to Fault-Tolerant Software. IEEE Transactions on Software Engineering, 11(12):1491-1501, 1985.
5. D. Batory and S. O'Malley. The Design and Implementation of Hierarchical Software Systems with Reusable Components. ACM Transactions on Software Engineering and Methodology, 1(4), October 1992.
6. T.J. Biggerstaff. The Library Scaling Problem and the Limits of Concrete Component Reuse. IEEE International Conference on Software Reuse, November 1994.
7. T.J. Biggerstaff and A.J. Perlis. Software Reusability, volumes I and II. ACM Press/Addison Wesley, 1989.
8. S. Brilliant, J. Knight, and N. Leveson. Analysis of Faults in an N-Version Software Experiment. IEEE Transactions on Software Engineering, 16(2): 238-247, 1990.
9. C. Burrows and I. Wesley. Ovum Evaluates Configuration Management, Burlington, Massachusetts: Ovum Ltd., 1998.
10. K.M. Chandy and L. Lamport, Distributed Snapshots: Determining Global States of Distributed Systems, ACM Transactions on Computer Systems, 3(1):63-75, February 1985.
11. R. Conradi and B. Westfechtel. Version Models for Software Configuration Management. ACM Computing Surveys, 30(2): p. 232-282, 1998.
12. J. E. Cook and J. A. Dage, Highly Reliable Upgrading of Components. In Proceedings of the 1999 International Conference on Software Engineering (ICSE'99), pages 203-212, Los Angeles, CA, May 1999.

13. C. Cugola, E. Di Nitto, and A. Fuggetta. Exploiting an Event-Based Infrastructure to Develop Complex Distributed Systems. In Proceedings of the 20th International Conference on Software Engineering, Kyoto, Japan, April 1998.

14. E.M. Dashofy, N. Medvidovic, and R.N. Taylor. Using Off-the-Shelf Middleware to Implement Connectors in Distributed Software Architectures. In Proceedings of the 21st International Conference on Software Engineering (ICSE'99), pp. 3-12, Los Angeles, CA, May 16-22, 1999.

15. D. Garlan, R. Allen, and J. Ockerbloom. Architectural Mismatch, or, Why It's Hard to Build Systems out of Existing Parts. In Proceedings of the 17th International Conference on Software Engineering (ICSE 17), Seattle, WA, April 1995.

16. A. van der Hoek, M. Rakic, R. Roshandel, and N. Medvidovic. Taming Architectural Evolution. In Proceedings of ESEC/FSE 2001, Vienna, September 2001.

17. P. Inverardi and M. Tivoli, Automatic Synthesis of Deadlock Free Connectors for COM/DCOM Applications. In Proceedings of 8th European Software Engineering Conference held jointly with 9th ACM SIGSOFT International Symposium on Foundations of Software Engineering, Vienna, Austria, September 2001.

18. J. Knight and N. Leveson. An Experimental Evaluation of the Assumption of Independence in Multi-Version Programming. IEEE Transactions on Software Engineering, 12(1):96-109, 1986.

19. F. Kon, F. Costa, G. Blair, and R.H. Campbell. The Case for Reflective Middleware. Communications of the ACM. 45(6). June 2002.

20. G.E. Krasner and S.T. Pope. A Cookbook for Using the Model-View-Controller User Interface Paradigm in Smalltalk-80. Journal of Object-Oriented Programming, 1(3):26–49, August/September 1988.

21. C.W. Krueger. Software Reuse. ACM Computing Surveys, pages 131-183, June 1992.

22. N. Medvidovic, R.F. Gamble, and D.S. Rosenblum. Towards Software Multioperability: Bridging Heterogeneous Software Interoperability Platforms. In Proceedings of the 4th Interntl. Software Architecture Workshop (ISAW-4), Limerick, Ireland, June 4-5, 2000.

23. N. Medvidovic, N.R. Mehta and M. Mikic-Rakic, A Family of Software Architecture Implementation Frameworks, In Proceedings of the The Third Working IEEE/IFIP Conference on Software Architecture 2002, Montreal, Canada, August 2002.

24. N. Medvidovic, P. Oreizy, and R.N. Taylor. Reuse of Off-the-Shelf Components in C2-Style Architectures. In Proceedings of the 1997 Symposium on Software Reusability (SSR'97), pages 190-198, Boston, MA, May 17-19, 1997. Also in Proceedings of the 1997 International Conference on Software Engineering (ICSE'97), pages 692-700, Boston, MA, May 17-23, 1997.

25. N. Medvidovic, D.S. Rosenblum, and R.N. Taylor. A Language and Environment for Architecture-Based Software Development and Evolution. In Proc. of the 1999 International Conference on Software Engineering, pp. 44-53, Los Angeles, CA, May 1999.

26. N. Medvidovic and R.N. Taylor. Exploiting Architectural Style to Develop a Family of Applications. IEE Proceedings Software Engineering, vol. 144, no. 5-6, pages 237-248 (October-December 1997).

27. N.R. Mehta, N. Medvidovic, and S. Phadke. Towards a Taxonomy of Software Connectors. In Proceedings of the 22nd International Conference on Software Engineering (ICSE 2000), pages 178-187, Limerick, Ireland, June 4-11, 2000.

28. M. Mikic-Rakic and N. Medvidovic. Architecture-Level Support for Software Component Deployment in Resource Constrained Environments. In Proceedings of First International IFIP/ACM Working Conference on Component Deployment. Berlin, Germany, June 2002.

29. P. Oreizy, N. Medvidovic, and R.N. Taylor. Architecture-Based Runtime Software Evolution in Proceedings of the 20th International Conference on Software Engineering (ICSE'98), pp. 177-186, Kyoto, Japan, April 1998.
30. R. Orfali, D. Harkey, and J. Edwards. The Essential Distributed Objects Survival Guide. John Wiley & Sons, Inc., NY, 1996.
31. D.E. Perry and A.L. Wolf. Foundations for the Study of Software Architectures. ACM SIGSOFT Software Engineering Notes, pages 40-52, October 1992.
32. R. Sessions. COM and DCOM: Microsoft's Vision for Distributed Objects. John Wiley & Sons, Inc., NY, 1997.
33. M. Shaw. Architectural Issues in Software Reuse: It's Not Just the Functionality, It's the Packaging. In *Proceedings of IEEE Symposium on Software Reusability*, April 1995.
34. M. Shaw, R. DeLine, D. V. Klein, T. L. Ross, D. M. Young and G. Zelesnik. Abstractions for Software Architecture and Tools to Support Them. *IEEE Transactions on Software Engineering*, April 1995.
35. M. Shaw and D. Garlan. Software Architecture: Perspectives on an Emerging Discipline. Prentice-Hall, 1996.
36. Sun Microsystems, Inc. Java 2 Enterprise Edition Specification v1.2. http://java.sun.com/j2ee.
37. R. N. Taylor, N. Medvidovic, K. M. Anderson, E. J. Whitehead, Jr., J. E. Robbins, K. A. Nies, P. Oreizy, and D. L. Dubrow. A Component- and Message-Based Architectural Style for GUI Software. *IEEE Transactions on Software Engineering*, pages 390-406, June 1996.

Increasing System Dependability through Architecture-Based Self-Repair

David Garlan, Shang-Wen Cheng, and Bradley Schmerl

School of Computer Science
Carnegie Mellon University
5000 Forbes Ave, Pittsburgh, PA 15213
{garlan,zensoul,schmerl}@cs.cmu.edu

Abstract. One increasingly important technique for improving system dependability is to provide mechanisms for a system to adapt at run time in order to accommodate varying resources, system errors, and changing requirements. For such "self-repairing" systems one of the hard problems is determining when a change is needed, and knowing what kind of adaptation is required. In this paper we describe a partial solution in which stylized architectural design models are maintained at run time as a vehicle for automatically monitoring system behavior, for detecting when that behavior falls outside of acceptable ranges, and for deciding on a high-level repair strategy. The main innovative feature of the approach is the ability to specialize a generic run time adaptation framework to support particular architectural styles and properties of interest. Specifically, a formal description of an architectural style defines for a family of related systems the conditions under which adaptation should be considered, provides an analytic basis for detecting anomalies, and serves as a basis for developing sound repair strategies.

1. Introduction

One increasingly important technique for improving software-based system integrity is providing systems with the ability to adapt themselves at run time to handle such things as resource variability, changing user needs, and system faults. In the past, systems that supported such self-adaptation were rare, confined mostly to domains like telecommunications switches or deep space control software, where taking a system down for upgrades was not an option, and where human intervention was not always feasible. However, today more and more systems have this requirement, including e-commerce systems and mobile embedded systems. Such systems must continue to run with only minimal human oversight, and cope with variable resources (bandwidth, server availability, etc.), system faults (servers and networks going down, failure of external components, etc.), and changing user priorities (high-fidelity video streams at one moment, low fidelity at another, etc.).

Traditionally system self-repair has been handled within the application, and at the code level. For example, applications typically use generic mechanisms such as exception handling or timeouts to trigger application-specific responses to an observed

R. de Lemos et al. (Eds.): Architecting Dependable Systems, LNCS 2677, pp. 61–89, 2003.

fault or system anomaly. Such mechanisms have the attraction that they can trap an error at the moment of detection, and are well-supported by modern programming languages (e.g., Java exceptions) and run time libraries (e.g., timeouts for RPC). However, they suffer from the problem that it can be difficult to determine what the true source of the problem is, and hence what kind of remedial action is required. Moreover, while they can trap errors, they are not well-suited to recognizing "softer" system anomalies, such as gradual degradation of performance over some communication path, or transient failures of a server.

Recently a number of researchers have proposed an alternative approach in which system models – and in particular, architectural models – are maintained at run time and used as a basis for system reconfiguration and repair [32]. Architecture-based adaptation has a number of nice properties: As an abstract model, an architecture can provide a global perspective on the system, enabling high-level interpretation of system problems. This in turn allows one to better identify the source of some problem. Moreover, architectural models can make "integrity" constraints explicit, helping to ensure the validity of any system change.

A key issue in making this approach work is the choice of architectural style used to represent a system.[1] Previous work in this area has focused on the use of specific styles (together with their associated description languages and toolsets) to provide intrinsically modifiable architectures. Taylor et al. use hierarchical publish-subscribe via C2 [31, 36]; Gorlick et al. use a dataflow style via Weaves [14]; and Magee et al. use bi-directional communication links via Darwin [22].

The specialization to particular styles has the benefit of providing strong support for adapting systems built in those styles. However, it has the disadvantage that a particular style may not be appropriate for an existing implementation base, or it may not expose the kinds of properties that are relevant to adaptation. For example, different styles may be appropriate depending on whether one is using existing client-server middleware, Enterprise JavaBeans (EJB), or some other implementation base. Moreover, different styles may be useful depending on whether adaptation should be based on issues of performance, reliability, or security.

In this paper we show how to generalize architecture-based adaptation by making the choice of architectural style an explicit design parameter in the framework. This added flexibility allows system designers to pick an appropriate architectural style in order to expose properties of interest, provide analytic leverage, and map cleanly to existing implementations and middleware.

The key technical idea is to make architectural style a first class run time entity. As we will show, formalized architectural styles augmented with certain run time mechanisms provide a number of important capabilities for run time adaptation: (1) they define a set of formal constraints that allow one to detect system anomalies; (2) they are often associated with analytical methods that suggest appropriate repair strategies; (3) the allow one to link stylistic constraints with repair rules whose soundness is based on corresponding (style-specific) analytical methods; (4) they provide a set of operators for making high-level changes to the architecture; (5) they prescribe what aspects of a system need to be monitored.

---

[1] By "architectural style" we mean a vocabulary of component types and their interconnections, together with constraints on how that vocabulary is used.

In the remainder of this paper we detail the approach, focusing primarily on the role of architectural styles to interpret system behavior, identify problems, and suggest remediation. To illustrate the ideas we describe how the techniques have been applied to self-repair of an important class of web-based client-server systems, based on monitoring of performance-related behavior. As we will show, the selection of an appropriate architectural style for this domain permits the application of queuing-theoretic analysis to motivate and justify a set of repair strategies triggered by detection of architectural constraint violations.

2. Related Work

Considerable research has been done in the area of dynamic adaptation at an implementation level. There are a multitude of programming languages and libraries that provide dynamic linking and binding mechanisms, as well as exception handling capabilities (e.g., [8, 16, 18, 27]). Systems of this kind allow system self-repair to be programmed on a per-system basis, but do not provide external, reusable mechanisms that can be added to systems in a disciplined manner *per se*, as with an architecture-driven approach.

Our work is also related to distributed debugging systems, insofar as remotely monitoring a running system to locate problems [15]. However, those systems have focused on user-mediated monitoring, whereas our research is primarily concerned with automated monitoring and reconfiguration. Adaptive or reflective middleware attempts to provide some automated support for adaptation of distributed applications, through shared infrastructure for component integration. An adaptive middleware supports inspection and modification of its internal state, and enables high-level abstraction for greater ease in controlling the lower-level services provided by the middleware [1, 20]. This work is similar to ours in that the middleware maintains an explicit representation of its internal structure and uses that model to adjust its properties. While adaptive middleware technology gives an application greater flexibility to adapt to changing requirements and environments, it is focused at adapting shared infrastructure. Our work in contrast also allows adaptation of the applications running on *top* of such infrastructure.

The most closely related research is the work on architecture-based adaptation, mentioned earlier. As we noted, the primary difference between our work and earlier research in this area is the decoupling of style from the adaptive system infrastructure so that developers have the flexibility to pair an appropriate style to a system based on its implementation and the system attributes that should drive adaptation. To accomplish this we have to introduce some new mechanisms to allow "run time" styles to be treated as a design parameter in the run time adaptation infrastructure. Specifically, we must show how styles can be used to detect problems and trigger repairs. We must also provide mechanisms that bridge the gap between an architectural model and an implementation – both for monitoring and for effecting system changes. In contrast, for systems in which specific styles are built-in (as with [14, 35]) this is less of an issue because architectures are closely coupled to their implementations *by construction*.

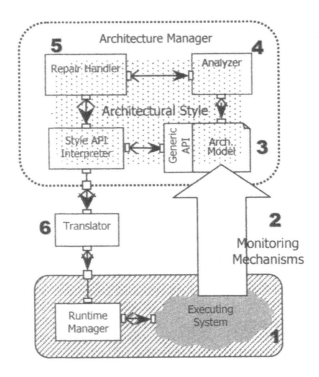

Fig. 1. Adaptation framework

Finally, there has been some work on formally characterizing architectural styles, and using them as a basis for system analysis [12, 35]. Our research extends this by showing how to turn "style as a design time artifact" into "style as a run time artifact". As we will see, this change requires two significant additions to the usual notion of style as a set of types and constraints: (1) style-specific repair rules, and (2) style-specific change operators. Some other efforts in this area have investigated formal foundations for dynamic architectures in terms of graph grammars and protocols, but have not attempted to use those formal descriptions as part of the run time adaptation infrastructure [3, 24, 40].

3. Overview of Approach

Our starting point is an architecture-based approach to self-adaptation, similar to [32] (as illustrated in Figure 1): In a nutshell, an executing system (1) is monitored to observe its run time behavior; (2) Monitored values are abstracted and related to architectural properties of an architectural model; (3) Changing properties of the architectural model trigger architectural analysis to determine whether the system is operating within an envelope of acceptable ranges; (4) Unacceptable operation causes repairs, which (5) adapt the architecture; (6) Architectural changes are propagated to the running system.

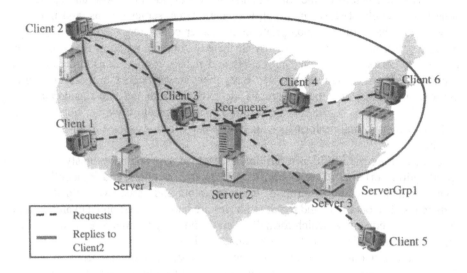

Fig. 2. Deployment architecture of example system

The key new feature in this framework is the use of style as a first class entity that allows one to tailor the framework to the application domain, and determines the actual behavior of each of the parts. Specifically, style is used to determine (a) what properties of the executing system should be monitored, (b) what constraints need to be evaluated, (c) what to do when constraints are violated, and (d) how to carry out repair in terms of high-level architectural operators. In addition we need to introduce a style-specific translation component to manage the transactional nature of repair and map high-level architecture operations into lower-level system operations.

To illustrate how the approach works, consider a common class of web-based client server applications that are based on an architecture in which web clients access web resources by making requests to one of several geographically distributed server groups (see Figure 2). Each server group consists of a set of replicated servers, and maintains a queue of requests, which are handled in FIFO order by the servers in the server group. Individual servers send their results directly to the requesting client.

The organization that manages the overall web service infrastructure wants to make sure that two inter-related system qualities are maintained. First, to guarantee quality of service for the customer, the request-response latency for clients must be under a certain threshold (e.g., 2 seconds). Second, to keep costs down, the set of currently active servers should be kept as loaded as possible, subject to the first constraint.

Since access loads in such a system will naturally change over time, the system has two built-in low-level adaptation mechanisms. First, we can activate a new server in a server group or deactivate an existing server. Second, we can cause a client to shift its communication path from one server group to another.

The challenge is to engineer things so that the system adapts appropriately at run time. Using the framework described above, here is how we would accomplish this.

First, given the nature of the implementation, we decide to choose an architectural style based on client-server in which we have clients, server groups, and individual servers, together with the appropriate client-server connectors (see Figure 3). Next, because performance is the key quality attribute of concern, we adapt that style so that it captures performance-related properties and makes explicit constraints about acceptable performance (see Figure 4). Here, client-server latency and server load are the key properties, and the constraints are derived from the two desiderata listed above. Furthermore, because of the nature of communication we are able to pick a style for which formal performance analyses exist – in this case M/M/m-based queuing theory.

To make the style useful as a run time artifact we now augment the style with two specifications: (a) a set of style-specific architectural operators, and (b) a collection of repair strategies written in terms of these operators and associated with the style's constraints. The operators and repair strategies are chosen based on an examination of the analytical equations, which formally identify how the architecture must change in order to affect certain parameters (like latency and load).

There are now only two remaining problems. First, we must get information out of the running system. To do this we employ low-level monitoring mechanisms that instrument various aspects of the executing system. We can use existing off-the-shelf performance-oriented "system probes," which we detail later. To bridge the gap between low-level monitored events and architectural properties we use a system of adapters, called "gauges," which aggregate low-level monitored information and relate it to the architectural model. For example, we have to aggregate various measurements of the round-trip time for a request and the amount of information transferred to produce bandwidth measurements at the architectural level.

The second problem is to translate architectural repairs into actual system changes. To do this we write a simple table-driven translator that can interpret architectural repair operators in terms of the lower level system modifications that we listed earlier. In the running system the monitoring mechanisms update architectural properties, causing reevaluation of constraints. Violated constraints (high client-server latencies, or low server loads) trigger repairs, which are carried out on the architectural model, and translated into corresponding actions on the system itself (adding or removing servers, and changing communication channels). The existence of an analytic model for performance (M/M/m queuing theory) helps guarantee that the specific modification operators for this style are sound. Moreover, the matching of the style to the existing system infrastructure helps guarantee that relevant information can be extracted, and that architectural changes can be propagated into the running system.

4. Style-Based Adaptation

In this section, we discuss in more detail each aspect of the architectural adaptation framework. We begin with an introduction on software architecture and architectural styles, and proceed to discuss the changes to these ideas necessary to make them available and useful for dynamic adaptation. We then discuss the techniques for observing and affecting the running system. In the next section, we give an example of the entire architectural style based on the example introduced in Section 3.

4.1 Architectural Models and Styles

The centerpiece of our approach is the use of stylized architectural models. Although there are many modeling languages and representation schemes for architecture, we adopt a simple approach in which an architectural model is represented as an annotated, hierarchical graph.[2] Nodes in the graph are *components*, which represent the principal computational elements and data stores of the system. Arcs are *connectors*, which represent the pathways of interaction between the components. Components and connectors have explicit interfaces (termed *ports* and *roles,* respectively). To support various levels of abstraction and encapsulation, we allow components and connectors to be defined by more detailed architectural descriptions, which we call *representations.*

To account for semantic properties of the architecture we allow elements in the graph to be annotated with extensible property lists. Properties associated with a connector might define its protocol of interaction, or performance attributes (e.g., delay, bandwidth). Properties associated with a component might define its core functionality, performance attributes (e.g., average time to process a request, load, etc.), or its reliability.

Representing an architecture as an arbitrary graph of generic components and connectors has the advantage of being extremely general and open ended. However, in practice there are a number of benefits to constraining the design space for architectures by associating a *style* with the architecture. An architectural style typically defines a set of types for components, connectors, interfaces, and properties together with a set of rules that govern how elements of those types may be composed .

Requiring a system to conform to a style has many benefits, including support for analysis, reuse, code generation, and system evolution [12, 35, 38]. Moreover, the notion of style often maps well to widely-used component integration infrastructures (such as EJB, HLA, CORBA), which prescribe the kinds of components allowed and the kinds of interactions that may take place between them.

As a result, a number of Architecture Description Languages (ADLs) and their toolsets have been created to support system development and execution for specific styles. For example, C2 [36] supports a style based on hierarchical publish-subscribe; Wright [2, 3] supports a style based on formal specification of connector protocols; MetaH [38] supports a style based on real-time avionics control components.

In our research we adopt the view that while choice of style is critical to supporting system design, execution, and evolution, different styles will be appropriate for different systems. For example, a client-server system, such as the one in our example, will most naturally be represented using a client-server style. In contrast, a signal processing system would probably adopt a dataflow-oriented pipe-filter style. While one might *encode* these systems in some other style, the mapping to the actual system

---

[2] This is the core architectural representation scheme adopted by a number of ADLs, including Acme [12], xArch [8], xADL [9], ADML [30], and SADL [27].

would become much more complex, with the attendant problems of ensuring that any observation derived from the architecture has a bearing on the system itself.

For this reason, two key elements of our approach are the explicit definition of style and its accessibility at run time for system adaptation. Specifically, we define a style as a system of types, plus a set of rules and constraints. The types are defined in Acme [12], a generic ADL that extends the above structural core framework with the notion of style. The rules and constraints are defined in Armani [26] a first-order predicate logic similar to UML's OCL [29], augmented with a small set of architectural functions. These functions make it easier to define logical expressions that refer to things like connectedness, type conformance, and hierarchical relationships.[3] We say that a system *conforms* to a style if it satisfies all of the constraints defined by the style (including type conformance).

An example of an architectural style is a pipe-filter style. Elements in this style include filter components, which receive data and transform that data, and pipe connectors, which transfer data between filters. In Acme, the definition of a filter component type looks like:

```
Component type Filter T = {
    Property throughput : float;
    Port stdIn : InputPortT;
    Port stdOut : OutputPortT;
}
```

This type definition would be instantiated in a given systems by creating specific filter components. Any component *conforming* to the FilterT type would have at least the throughput property, and the two ports stdIn and stdOut, which in turn need to conform to the port types InputPortT and OutputPortT.

Being able to define styles in Acme gives some reuse in our framework. We envision a suite of general styles (along with monitoring and repair capabilities) from which a style can be chosen to be plugged into our framework. An architect would then need to model the system according to this style, perhaps extending the style or utilizing other styles to model attributes of interest.[4]

4.2 Analytical Methods for Architectures

As we argued above, one of the main benefits of style-based architectural modeling is the ability to use analytical methods to evaluate properties of a system's architectural design. For example, MetaH uses real-time schedulability analysis, and Wright uses protocol model checking. Use of the appropriate analytical methods helps us to focus on the aspects of the architecture that we need to model, to identify the constraints of the style, and to guide the error resolution when constraints are violated. For instance,

---

[3] Details on Acme and Armani can be found elsewhere [12, 26]. Here we focus on how those representation schemes, originally developed as design-time notations, are extended and used to support run time adaptation.

[4] A style would also supply operators to modify the style, and perhaps repair facilities. These are discussed later in the section.

in a Service-Coalition style, cost analysis of the system indicates which services to monitor. Based on what factors drive cost—for example, performance—we can add to or refine cost-based constraints to take those factors into account. This can help guide us to the cause of error when a cost constraint fails. If performance were a factor, a cost violation in a particular component would suggest that we check the performance properties of that component for the cause. Furthermore, cost-benefit analysis would tell us how to trade-off cost with performance to find a better service during adaptation.

An analytical method can potentially be applied to several different styles. For example, one might use queuing theoretic analysis in a Client-Server style or a Pipe-Filter style, and cost-benefit analysis can be applied to almost any style. When applied to a particular style, however, the analytical method takes on the vocabulary of that style, and often augments elements of that style with analysis-specific properties. For example, queuing theoretic analysis augments a server component with properties such as load, service time, etc.

4.3   Using Styles to Assist Adaptation

The representation schemes for architectures and style outlined above were originally created to support design-time development tools. In this section we show how styles can be augmented to function as run time adaptation mechanisms. We then consider the supporting run time infrastructure needed to make this work out in practice (Section 4.4).

Two key augmentations to style definitions are needed to make them useful for run time adaptation: (1) the definition of a set of adaptation operators for the style, and (2) the definition of a set of repair strategies.

4.3.1   Adaptation Operators

The first extension is to augment a style description with a set of operators that define the ways one can change instances of systems in that style. Such operators determine a "virtual machine" that can be used at run time to adapt an architectural design.

Given a particular architectural style, there will typically be a set of natural operators for changing an architectural configuration and querying for additional information. In the most generic case, architectures can provide primitive operators for adding and removing components and connectors [31]. However, specific styles can often provide much higher-level operators that exploit the restrictions in that style and the intended implementation base. For example, a client-server style might support an operation to replicate a server to improve performance, whereas a pipe-filter style might support an operation to improve performance by adding a filer to compress the data on a pipe.

Two key factors determine the choice of operators for a style. First is the style itself – the kinds of components, connectors and configuration rules. Based on its constraints, a style can both limit the set of operations, and also suggest a set of higher-level operators. For example, if a style specifies that there must be exactly one instance of a particular type of component, such as a database, the style should not provide operations to add or remove an existing instance of this type. On the other hand, if another constraint says that every client component in the system must be attached to the (unique) database, it would make sense that a "new-client" operation would automatically create a new client-database connector and attach it between the new component and the database. These style-specific operators are defined in terms of style-neutral operators such as "add a component" or "remove a connector." The definition of these style-neutral operations can be based on [40] or [41].

The second factor is the feasibility of carrying out the change. To evaluate feasibility requires some knowledge of the target implementation infrastructure. It makes no sense to prescribe an architectural operator that has no hope of ever being carried out on the running system. For some styles, the relation is defined by construction (since implementations are generated from architectures). More generally, however, the style designer may have to make certain assumptions about the availability of implementation-changing operators that will be provided by the run time environment of the system. (We return to this issue in Section 7.)

It is important to note that, while it is necessary to write adaptation operators for each style, we anticipate that this will only need to be done once for each style. A style should provide all operations that make sense in changing the style, regardless of any particular adaptation that might occur. For example, for a Client-Server style, the moveClient operator will be the same regardless of the adaptation being performed.

While adaptation operators are specific to styles we can, however, describe some, commonly occurring operators. In general, every style would be expected to have some form of add and remove, as well as possibly activate and deactivate operators for component instances (e.g., addClient, removeFilter, activateServer, deactivateDB). A style would also be expected to have add/remove or connect/disconnect operators to setup connectors between components (e.g., addRPC, removeVideoStream, connectPipe, disconnectSQL). In addition, there will typically be operators to create, delete, and modify element properties (e.g., createLatencyProperty, deleteFrameRateProperty, modifyCompressionProperty). Finally, depending on the style, there might conceivably be operators for changing a component's behavior via modification of specific properties of the component, such as changing the internal behavioral protocol of a component.

4.3.2   Repair Strategies
The second extension to the traditional notion of architectural style is the specification of repair strategies that correspond to selected constraints of the style. The key idea is that when a stylistic constraint violation is detected, the appropriate repair strategy will be triggered.

Describing Repair Strategies
A repair strategy has two main functions: first to determine the cause of the problem, and second to determine how to fix it. Thus the general form of a repair strategy is a sequence of repair *tactics*. Each repair tactic is guarded by a pre-condition that determines whether that tactic is applicable. The evaluation of a tactic's pre-condition will usually involve the examination of various properties of the architecture in order to pinpoint the problem and determine applicability. If it is applicable, the tactic exe-

cutes a repair script that is written as an imperative program using the style-specific operators described above.

To handle the situation that several tactics may be applicable, the enclosing repair strategy decides on the policy for executing repair tactics. It might apply the first tactic that succeeds. Alternatively, it might sequence through all of the tactics, or use some other style-specific policy.

The final complication associated with repair strategies is the use of transactions. The body of a repair strategy is typically enclosed within a transactional scope so that if an error occurs during the execution of a repair, the system can abort the repair, leaving the architecture in a consistent state. Failure of a repair strategy can be caused by a number of factors. For example, it may be the case that none of the tactics have applicable firing conditions. Or, an applicable tactic may find that conditions of the actual system or its environment do not permit it to carry out its repair script. Transaction aborts cause the system to inform the user of a system error that cannot be handled by the automated mechanisms.

Choosing Tactics

One of the principal advantages of allowing the system designer to pick an appropriate style is the ability to exploit style-specific analyses to determine whether repair tactics are sound. By sound, we mean that if executed, the changes will help reestablish the violated constraint.

In general, an analytical method for an architecture will provide a compositional method for calculating some system property in terms of the properties of its parts. For example, a reliability analysis will depend on the reliability of the architectural parts, while a performance analysis will depend on various performance attributes of the parts. By looking at the constraint to be satisfied, the analysis can often point the repair strategy writer both to the set of possible causes for constraint violation, and for each possible cause, to an appropriate repair.

For instance, one type of analysis appropriate to the pipe-filter style is throughput analysis. Such an analysis allows one to characterize a batch-processing pipe-filter system by the ratio of the input quantity to the output quantity (say, in terms of records), and compose the overall ratio from the ratio of each individual filter based on connection topology. The administrator of this system might want to enforce a constraint on the system in terms of this input-output ratio. Violation of this throughput ratio constraint suggests congestion of processing within the system. The associated repair strategy can then use a more fine-grained throughput analysis to pinpoint the segment or the particular filter causing the congestion.

4.4 Bridging the Gap to Implementation

As we have argued, the use of style allows us to provide automated support for architectural adaptation *at the model level*. That is, we can use the constraints, operators, and analytical methods to determine how to modify the architecture.

The only catch is that we somehow have to relate all of that to the real world. There are two parts to this. The first is getting information out of the executing system

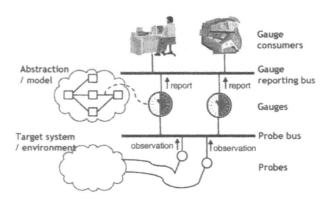

Fig. 3. Gauge infrastructure

so we can determine when architectural constraints are violated. The second is propagating architectural repairs into the system itself.

4.4.1   Monitoring

In order to provide a bridge from system level behavior to architecturally-relevant observations, we have defined a three-level approach illustrated in Figure 8. This monitoring infrastructure is described in more detail elsewhere [13]: here we summarize the main features, stressing the connection with style specifications.

The lowest level is a set of *probes*, which are "deployed" in the target system or physical environment.[5] Probes monitor the system and announce observations via a "probe bus." At the second level a set of *gauges* consumes and interprets lower-level probe measurements in terms of higher-level model properties. Like probes, gauges disseminate information via a "gauge reporting bus." The top-level entities in Figure 8 are *gauge consumers*, which consume information disseminated by gauges. Such information can be used, for example, to update an abstraction/model, to make system repair decisions, to display warnings and alerts to system users, or to show the current status of the running system.

The separation of the monitoring infrastructure into these parts helps isolate separable concerns. Probes are highly implementation-specific, and typically require detailed knowledge of the execution environment. Gauges are model-specific. They need only understand how to convert low-level observations into properties of more abstract representations, such as architectural models. Finally, gauge consumers are free to use the interpreted information to cause various actions to occur, such as displaying warnings to the user or automatically carrying out repairs.

In the context of architectural repair, we use the architectural style to inform us where to place gauges. Specifically, for each constraint that we wish to monitor, we must place gauges that dynamically update the properties over which the constraint is

---

[5] For monitoring, we utilize the terminology defined by the DASADA program, funded by DARPA.

defined. In addition, our repair strategies may require additional monitored information to pinpoint sources of problems and execute repair operations.

While it may be necessary to develop gauges for each different style, and probes for each specific implementation, we can gain some leverage by using general monitoring technologies. For example, if the concerns are bandwidth or latency then it is possible to use general network gauges (for example, those based on Remos [13]) to report the bandwidth, regardless of the adaptation. Similarly, it is possible to use general probe technology to ameliorate the task of writing probes for particular implementations. For example, while it might be necessary to *choose* which particular method calls need to be monitored in a particular implementation, it is possible to use existing technologies like ProbeMeister [39] to generate the actual probes, without writing any additional code.

4.4.2   Repair Execution

The final component of our adaptation framework is a translator that interprets repair scripts as operations on the actual system (Figure 1, item 6). As we noted earlier, we assume that the executing system provides a set of system-changing operations via a Runtime Manager. The nature of these operations will depend heavily on the implementation platform. In general, a given architectural operation will be realized by some number of lower level system reconfiguration operations. Each such operator can raise exceptions to signal a failure. The Translator then propagates them to the model level, where transaction boundaries can cause the repair strategy to abort.

Even though the system-changing operations are system specific, the mechanisms for propagating system changes can be fairly general, subject to the constraints of the implementation platform. These mechanisms can be as simple as socket communication, RPC, or Java RMI, or as complicated as mobile-code or an entire change propagation technology.

4.4.3   Putting the Pieces Together

Let us summarize how the parts work together, end-to-end, and how pieces of the framework in Figure 1 interact. While the system is running, relevant system properties are observed and collected by gauges in the Monitoring Mechanisms and updated on the Architectural Model. Whenever there is a change in a gauge value, the Analyzer in the Architecture Manager re-evaluates the architectural constraints to check for violation. Suppose that a latency constraint violation is detected in some Client role, then the Analyzer calls the Repair Handler to trigger a repair. The Repair Handler first signals the Analyzer to suspend all monitoring and captures a "snapshot" of the current state of the Architectural Model – doing so prevents other constraint violation from interfering with the present repair and preserves the property values at the time of constraint violation to facilitate decision-making. The Repair Handler then begins running the repair script.

The Repair Handler executes repair scripts, which involve calls to the style operators. These calls are executed by the Style API Interpreter, which interprets the calls as primitive architectural operators to update the Architectural Model (via the Generic API). The Style API Interpreter also passes the style operator calls to the Translator.

The Translator translates architectural style operations into implementation operations and passes them to the Runtime Manager, which executes it to make changes to the Executing System. The implementation operations have exceptions not shown that may be raised if execution fails. The Translator would then pass the exception signal back to the Repair Handler, which aborts the repair transaction. Whether the repair transaction commits or aborts the Repair Handler signals to the Analyzer to resume system monitoring and resets appropriate gauges.

At this point, as part of the dynamic verification to ensure that the repair was effective, the constraints are re-evaluated to determine whether any violations are now fixed, and the repair cycle completes. If a violation remains, or if a new violation is detected, the repair is triggered again and the process repeats.

5. Performance Adaptation of a Web-Based Server-Client System

In this section we give a detailed end-to-end description of how each of the elements in our adaptation framework come together to achieve runtime adaptation. We use the example described in Section 3 to illustrate our technique. The example is simple load balancing of a web-based client-server system. This is example is used simply to

```
Family PerformanceClientServerFam extends ClientServerFam with {
    Component Type PAClientT extends ClientT with {
        Properties {
            Requests : sequence <any>;
            ResponseTime : float;
            ServiceTime : float;
        };
    };
    Connector Type PALinkT extends LinkT with {
        Properties {
            DelayTime : float;
        };
    };
    Component Type PAServerGroupT extends ServerGroupT with {
        Properties {
            Replication : int <<default : int = 1;>>;
            Requests : sequence <any>;
            ResponseTime : float;
            ServiceTime : float;
            AvgLoad : float;
        };
        Invariant AvgLoad > minLoad;
    };
    Role Type PAClientRoleT extends ClientRoleT with {
        Property averageLatency : float;
        Invariant averageLatency < maxLatency;
    };

    Property maxLatency : float;
    Property minLoad : float;
};
```

Fig. 4. Client/Server style extended for analysis

illustrate how our technique works; we are not proposing that this technique be applied to load-balancing of such systems – a technique that is already embedded in many systems.

5.1 Defining a Client-Server Architectural Style

Figure 4 contains a partial description of the style used to characterize the class of web-based systems of our example. The style is actually defined in two steps. The first step specifies a generic client-server style (called a *family* in Acme). It defines a set of component types: a web client type (ClientT), a server group type (ServerGroupT), and a server type (ServerT). It also defines a connector type (LinkT). Constraints on the style (appearing in the definition of LinkT) guarantee that the link has only one role for the server. Other constraints, not shown, further define structural rules (for example, that each client must be connected to a server).

```
Family ClientServerFam = {
    Component Type ClientT = {...};
    Component Type ServerT = {...};

    Component Type ServerGroupT = {...};

    Role Type ClientRoleT = {...};
    Role Type ServerRoleT = {...};

    Connector Type LinkT = {
        invariant size(select r : role in Self.Roles |
            declaresType(r, ServerRoleT)) == 1;
        invariant size(select r : role in Self.Roles |
            declaresType(r, ClientRoleT)) >= 1;
        Role ClientRole1 : ClientRoleT;
        Role ServerRole : ServerRoleT;
    };
};
```

Fig. 5. Client/Server style definition

There are potentially many possible kinds of analysis that one might carry out on client-server systems built in this style. Since we are particularly concerned with overall system performance, we augment the client-server style to include performance-oriented properties. These include the response time and degree of replication for servers and the delay time over links. This style extension is shown in Figure 5. Constraints on this style capture the desired performance related behavior of the system. The first constraint, associated with PAServerGroupT, specifies that a server group

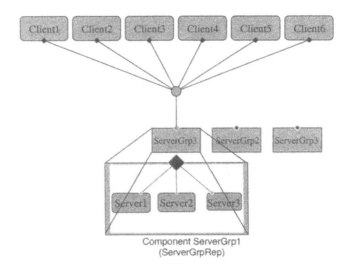

Fig. 6. Architectural model of example system

should not be under-utilized. The second constraint, as part of the PAClientRoleT, specifies that the latency on this role should not be above some specified maximum.

Having defined an appropriate style, we can now define a particular system configuration in that style, such as the one illustrated in Figure 6.

5.2   Using M/M/m Performance Analysis to Set Initial Conditions

The use of buffered request queues, together with replicated servers, suggests using queuing theory to understand the performance characteristics of systems built in the client-server style above. As we have shown elsewhere [35], for certain architectural styles queuing theory is useful for determining various architectural properties including system response time, server response time (T_s), average length of request queues (Q_s), expected degree of server utilization (u_s), and location of bottlenecks.

In the case of our example style, we have an ideal candidate for M/M/m analysis. The *M/M* indicates that the probability of a request arriving at component *s,* and the probability of component *s* finishing a request it is currently servicing, are assumed to be exponential distributions (also called "memoryless," independent of past events); requests are further assumed to be, at any point in time, either waiting in one component's queue, receiving service from one component, or traveling on one connector. The *m* indicates the replication of component *s*; that is, component *s* is not limited to representing a single server, but rather can represent a server group of *m* servers that are fed from a single queue. Given estimates for clients' request generation rates and servers' service times (the time that it takes to service one request), we can derive performance estimates for components according to Table 1. To calculate the expected system response time for a request, we must also estimate the average delay D_c

Table 1. Performance equations from [4]

(1)	Utilization of server group s	$u_s = \dfrac{R_s S_s}{m}$
(2)	Probability {no servers busy}	$p_0 = \left[\sum_{i=0}^{m} \dfrac{(mu_s)^i}{i!} + \dfrac{u_s(mu_s)^m}{m!(1-u_s)}\right]^{-1}$
(3)	Probability {all servers busy}	$P_Q = \dfrac{p_0(mu_s)^m}{m!(1-u_s)}$
(4)	Average queue length of s	$Q_s = \dfrac{P_Q u_s}{1-u_s}$
(5)	Average response time of s	$T_s = S_s + \dfrac{P_Q u_s}{R_s(1-u_s)} =$ $S_s + \dfrac{S_s(mu_s)^m}{mm!(1-u_s)^2 \sum_{n=0}^{m}\dfrac{(mu_s)^n}{n!} + (1-u_s)(mu_s)^{m+1}}$
(6)	System response time (latency)	$\sum T_s V_s + \sum D_c V_c$

imposed by each connector c, and calculate, for each component s and connector c, the average number of times (V_s, V_c) it is visited by that request. (Given V_s and the rates at which client components generate requests, we can derive rather than estimate R_s, the rate at which requests arrive at server group s.)

Applying this M/M/m theory to our style tells us that with respect to the average latency for servicing client requests, the key design parameters in our style are (a) the replication factor m of servers within a server group, (b) the communication delay D between clients and servers, (c) the arrival rate R of client requests and (d) the service time S of servers within a server group.

In previous work [35] we showed how to use this analysis to provide an initial configuration of the system based on estimates of these four parameters. In particular, Equation (5) in Table 1 indicates for each server group a design tradeoff between utilization (underutilized servers may waste resources, but provide faster service) and response time. Utilization is in turn affected by service time and replication. Thus, given a range of acceptable utilization and response time, if we choose service time then replication is constrained to some range (or vice versa). As we will show in the next section, we can also use this observation to determine sound run time adaptation policies.

We can use the performance analysis to decide the following questions about our architecture, assuming that the requirements for the initial system configuration are that for six clients each client must receive a latency not exceeding 2 seconds for each request and a server group must have a utilization of between 70% and 80%:

- How many replicated servers must exist in a server group so that the server group is properly utilized?
- Where should the server group be placed so that the bandwidth (modeled as the delay in a connector) leads to latency ŕŤot exceeding 2 seconds?

Given a particular service time and arrival rate, performance analysis of this model gives a range of possible values for server utilization, replication, latencies, and system response time. We can use Equation (5) to give us an initial replication count and Equation (6) to give us a lower bound on the bandwidth. If we assume that the arrival rate is 180 requests/sec, the server response time is between 10ms and 20ms the average request size is 0.5KB, and the average response size is 20KB, then the performance analysis gives us the following bounds:

  Initial server replication count= 3-5
  Zero-delay System Response Time = 0.013-0.026 seconds

Therefore,

  0 < Round-trip connector delay < 1.972 seconds, or
  0 < Average connector delay < .986 seconds

Thus, the average bandwidth over the connector must be greater than 10.4KB/sec. This analysis provides several key criteria for monitoring the running system. First, if latency increases undesirably, then we should check to ensure that the bandwidth assumption still holds between a client and its server. Second, if bandwidth is not the causing factor, then we should examine the load on the server.

5.3 Defining Adaptation Operators

The client-server architectural style suggests a set of style-specific adaptation operators that change the architectural while ensuring the style constraints. These operators are:

- **addServer**(): This operation is applied to a component of type ServerGroupT and adds a new component of type ServerT to its representation, ensuring that there is a binding between its port and the ServerGroup's port.
- **move**(to:ServerGroupT): This operation is applied to a client and first deletes the role currently connecting the client to the connector that connects it to a server group. It then performs the necessary attachment to a LinkT connector that will connect it to the server group passed in as a parameter. If no such connector exists, it will create one and connect it to the server group.
- **remove**(): This operation is applied to a server and deletes the server from its containing server group. Furthermore, it changes the replication count on the server group and deletes the binding.

The above operations all effect changes to the model. The next operation queries the state of the running system:

- **findGoodSGroup**(cl:ClientT,bw:float):ServerGroupT; finds the server group with the best bandwidth (above *bw*) to the client *cli*, and returns a reference to the server group.

These operators reflect the considerations just outlined. First, from the nature of a server group, we get the operations of adding or removing a server from a group. Also, from the nature of the asynchronous request connectors, we get the operations of adapting the communication path between particular clients and server groups. Second, based on the knowledge of supported system change operations, outlined in Section 4.4, we have some confidence that the architectural operations are actually achievable in the executing system.

5.4 Defining Repair Strategies to Maintain Performance

Recall that the queuing theory analysis points to several possible causes for why latency could increase. Given these possibilities, we can show how the repair strategy developed from this theoretical analysis. The equations for calculating latency for a service request (Table 1) indicate that there are four contributing factors: (1) the connector delay, (2) the server replication count, (3) the average client request rate, and (4) the average server service time. Of these we have control over the first two. When the latency is high, we can decrease the connector delay (by moving clients to servers that are closer) or increase the server replication count to decrease the latency. Determining which tactic depends on whether the connector has a low bandwidth (inversely proportional to connector delay) or if the server group is heavily loaded (inversely proportional to replication). These two system properties form the preconditions to the tactics; we have thus developed a repair strategy with two tactics.

Applying the Approach

We specify repair strategies using a repair language that supports basic flow control, Armani constraints, and simple transaction semantics. Each constraint in an architectural model can be associated with a repair strategy, which in turn employs one or more repair tactics.

Figure 7 (lines 1-3) illustrates the repair strategy associated with the latency threshold constraint. In line 2, "!→" denotes "if constraint violated, then execute." The top-level repair strategy in lines 5-17, fixLatency, consists of two tactics. The first tactic in lines 19-31 handles the situation in which a server group is overloaded, identified by the precondition in lines 24-26. Its main action in lines 27-29 is to create a new server in any of the overloaded server groups. The second tactic in lines 33-48 handles the situation in which high latency is due to communication delay, identified by the precondition in lines 34-36. It queries the running system to find a server group that will yield a higher bandwidth connection in lines 40-41. In lines 42-44, if such a group exists it moves the client-server connector to use the new group. The result of an instance of this repair on Figure 6 is depicted in Figure 8. The repair strategy uses a policy in which it executes these two tactics sequentially: if the first tactic succeeds it commits the repair strategy; otherwise it executes the second. The strategy will abort if neither tactic succeeds, or if the second tactic finds that it cannot proceed since there are no suitable server groups to move the connection to.

```
01 invariant r.averageLatency <= maxLatency
02 I→
03    fixLatency(r);
04
05 strategy fixLatency (badRole: ClientRoleT) = {
06    begin repair-transaction;
07    let badClient: ClienT =
08       select one cli: ClientT in self.Components |
09          exists p: RequestT in cli.Ports | attached(badRole, p);
10    if (fixServerLoad(badClient)) {
11       commit repair-transaction;
12    else if (fixBandwidth(badClient, badRole) {
13       commit repair-transaction;
14    } else {
15       abort(ModelError);
16    }
17 }
18
19 tactic fixServerLoad (client: ClientT) : boolean = {
20    let overloadedServerGroups: Set{ServerGroupT} =
21       { select sgrp: ServerGroupT in self.Components |
22          connected(sgrp, client) and
23          sgrp.AvgLoad > maxServerLoad };
24    if (size(overloadedServerGroups) == 0) {
25       return false;
26    }
27    foreach sGrp in overloadedServerGroups {
28       sGrp.addServer();
29    }
30    return (size(overloadedServerGroups) > 0);
31 }
32
33 tactic fixBandwidth (client: ClientT, role: ClientRoleT) : boolean = {
34    if (role.Bandwidth >= minBandwidth) {
35       return false;
36    }
37    let oldSGrp: ServerGroupT =
38       select one sGrp: ServerGroupT in self.Components |
39          connected(client, sGrp);
40    let goodSGrp: ServerGroupT =
41       findGoodSGrp(client, minBandwidth);
42    if (goodSGrp != nil) {
43       client.moveClient(oldSGrp, goodSGrp);
44       return true;
45    } else {
46       abort(NoServerGroupFound);
47    }
48 }
```

Fig. 7. Repair tactic for high latency

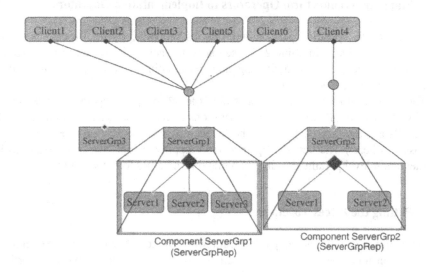

Fig. 8. Model of system after low bandwidth repair

5.5   Style-Based Monitoring

In our example above we are concerned with the average latency of client requests. To monitor this property, we must associate a gauge with the averageLatency property of each client role (see the definition of ClientRoleT in Figure 4). This latency gauge in turn deploys a probe into the implementation that monitors the timing of reply-request pairs. When it receives such monitored values it averages them over some window, updating the latency property in the architecture model when it changes. The latency gauge that we use is not specific to this style, or indeed to this implementation. The gauges utilizes probes that use the Remos network monitoring service, which in turn uses the SNMP to ascertain properties of the network.

But average latency is not the only architectural property that we need to monitor. The repair tactics, derived from queuing theoretic model of performance analysis, rely on information about two additional constraints: whether the bandwidth between the client and the server is low or whether the server group is overloaded (or both). Thus, to determine why latency is high in the architecture, we need to monitor these two properties. The gauge for measuring bandwidth uses the same probe used by the latency gauge for measuring the time it takes to receive a reply. An additional probe measures the size of the reply and calculates the bandwidth based on these values. Determining the load on the server can be done in a number of ways. We measure the size of a request queue to indicate whether the server group is overloaded.

5.6   Mapping Architectural Operators to Implementation Operators

To illustrate, the specific operators and queries supported by the Runtime Manager in our example are listed in Table 2. These operators include low-level routines for creating new request queues, activating and deactivating servers, and moving client communications to a new queue.

The Translator for our example maps the Style API Interpreter operations described in Section 4.3.1 to the Runtime Manager operations using the scheme summarized in Table 2. (Parameters passed between the levels also need to be translated. We do not discuss this here.) The actual map involves mapping model-level parameters to implementation level parameters, and mapping return values to model values.

5.7   Putting the Pieces Together

As an example of how the adaptation framework fits together in our implementation, we will consider one cycle of the repair, starting with a latency probe reporting a value, and ending with a client moving to a new server group. This cycle indicates how the architecture in Figure 6 is transformed into the architecture in Figure 8.

1. The bandwidth probe on the link between Client4 and ServerGroup1 reports a bandwidth of 18KB/sec to the probe bus.
2. The latency gauge attached to Client4's role combines this value with the average size of requests that it has seen, and calculates an average latency of 2.5secs, which it reports to the gauge bus. Similarly, the bandwidth gauge attached to Client4's role reports a bandwidth of 18KB/sec to the gauge bus.
3. The Architecture Manager, implemented as a gauge consumer, receives these values and adjusts the averageLatency and bandwidth properties of Client4's role.
4. The Analyzer, implemented using our Armani constraint analyzer, reevaluates constraints. The constraint averageLatency < maxLatency in Client4's role fails.
5. Tailor, the repair handler, is invoked and pauses monitoring before starting to execute the repair strategy in Figure 7, passing Client4's role as a parameter.

Table 2. Mapping between architecture and implementation operations

Model Level	Environment Level
addServer	**findServer** **activateServer** **connectServer**
moveClient	**createReqQue** **moveClient**
findGoodSGrp	Conditionals + multiple calls to **remos_get_flow**

6. The repair strategy first attempts to fix the server load, but returns false because no servers are overloaded.

7. The repair strategy attempts to fix the bandwidth. It examines the bandwidth property of the role, and determines that it is larger than 10.4KB/sec (line 34). It then calls the architectural operator findGoodSGrp to find the server group with the best bandwidth. This invokes queries to remos_get_flow.

8. The operator findGoodSGrp returns ServerGroup2 now has the best bandwidth and initiates the moveClient operator (line 43). This in turn invokes the change interface for the application to effect the move.

6. Implementation Status

In terms of the adaptation framework in Figure 1, our implementation contains the following pieces:

Monitoring Mechanisms: Our approach is general enough to be used with existing technologies for monitoring systems and their environments. To connect with the infrastructure described in Section 4.4.1, a wrapper needs to be written for these technologies that allows events to be generated according to the probe infrastructure, mentioned in Figure 8, turning the technology into a probe. We have developed prototype probes for gathering information out of networks, based on the Remos system [21]. We have developed general-purpose gauges that can be used to report data about expected and observed bandwidth and latencies based on data from this system.

Other technology has also been successfully integrated into our infrastructure, most notably the ProbeMeister system for unobtrusively monitoring Java classes [39], and the Event Packager and Event Distiller systems for monitoring temporal events from executing systems [17]. In addition, we have produced gauges that monitor the adherence of elements of the architecture to protocols expressed in FSP [23].

Architectural Models: AcmeStudio, a design environment that allows architectures to be described in Acme, has been modified so that it provides run time observation of a software architecture [34]. A general library has been developed that can be integrated with other architectural tools to associate gauge information with architectural models.

Architectural Analysis: We have modified our tool for evaluating Armani constraints at design times so that it evaluates constraints dynamically at run time.

Repair Handler: The Armani constraint evaluator has been augmented so that it supports the specification and execution of repairs.

Translator and **Runtime Manager:** Currently, we have hand-tailored support for these components that need to be changed for each implementation. Our work in this area will concentrate on providing more general mechanisms where appropriate, and perhaps using off-the-shelf reconfiguration commands for commercial systems. In fact, we are actively investigating how to utilize the Workflakes system for a more general solution to the problem of mapping between architecture and implementation.

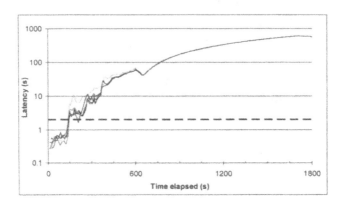

Fig. 9. Average Latency for Control (No Repair).

7. Experience

Thus far we have experimented with architectural adaptation for two kinds of system properties: (1) performance for web-based systems, illustrated earlier, and (2) protocol conformance.

To evaluate the effectiveness of our adaptation framework for performance-oriented adaptation, we conducted an experiment to test system adaptation using a dedicated, experimental testbed consisting of five routers and eleven machines communicating over 10 Mbps lines. The implementation that we used for our experiment was based on the example presented in this paper – that of a client-server system using replicated server groups communicating over a distributed system. System loads were fabricated in three segments over 30 minutes so that we could observe the self-repair behavior of the system.

The results showed that for this application and the specific loads used in the experiment, self-repair significantly improved system performance. Figures 9 and 10 show sample results for the system performance without adaptation, and with, respectively. (See [7] for details.) However, it also revealed, perhaps not unexpectedly, that externalized repair introduces some significant latency. In our system it took several seconds for the system to notice a performance problem and several more seconds to fix it. Although we can imagine speeding up the roundtrip repair time, this does indicate that the approach is best suited for repair that operates on a global scale, and that handles longer term trends in system behavior.

The second application of the approach has been to monitor and check protocols of interaction between components. Connectors are associated with protocol constraints that indicate the allowed order of communication events. These are defined in a process algebra, FSP [23], and then used by "protocol gauges" at run time to detect when communicating components fail to respect the specified protocols. For example, a protocol error might occur when a component attempts to write data to a pipe after it has closed that pipe, or if a client attempts to communicate with a server without first initializing its session.

8. Discussion

We have described an approach in which architecture-based self-adaptation is supported by the incorporation of styles as an explicit design choice in the adaptation framework. The flexibility inherent in this approach permits the system maintainer to pick a style that matches well to existing implementation bases, provides a formal basis for specifying constraints, and can permit the definition of repair policies that are justified by analytic methods.

However, this flexibility also introduces several new complexities over other approaches in which the choice of architectural style is hardwired into the framework. In particular, at least three critical questions are raised: First, is it always possible to map architectural repairs into corresponding system changes? Second, is it always possible to monitor relevant run time information? Third, is it reasonable to expect that analytical techniques can address a sufficiently broad set of concerns to inform our repair strategies? We address each issue in turn.

Model-Implementation Map: In our approach the ability to map architectural changes to corresponding implementation reconfigurations is moderated by two factors. First is an assumption that systems provide a well-defined set of operations for modifying a running system. Of course, in general this may not be true. Some systems are inherently not reconfigurable, in which case our approach would simply not work.

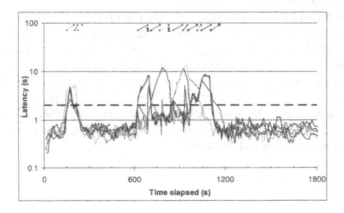

Fig. 10. Average latency under repair

However, many systems do in fact embody changing operations – such as the ability to load dynamic libraries and remote code, to redirect communications to alternative pathways, or to do dynamic resource management. Moreover, we would argue that such capabilities are going to be increasingly prevalent in modern systems that are intended to function in a connected, service-based universe. For example, modern frameworks like Jini provide as a fundamental building block the notion of allocation and deallocation of resources, and location-independence of services.

The other moderating factor is an assumption that architectural style is not chosen arbitrarily. Obviously, attempting to pair an arbitrary style with an arbitrary implementation could lead to considerable difficulty in relating the two. However, one of the hallmarks of our approach is that it encourages one to match an appropriate style to an implementation base. Hence, in fact, the flexibility of choosing a style can actually help reduce the gap between system implementations and architectural models.

Implementation-Model Map: For our approach to work it must be possible to reflect dynamic system state into an architectural model. To do this we provide a multi-leveled framework that separates concerns of low-level system instrumentation from concerns of abstracting those results in architecturally meaningful terms. What makes us think that either part will be feasible in the general case?

The ability to monitor systems is itself an active research area. Increasingly systems are expected to provide information that can be used to determine their health. Moreover, there is an increasingly large number of non-intrusive post-deployment monitoring schemes. For example, to deal with network performance we were able to use a monitoring infrastructure developed completely independently. It in turn relies on the standard protocol SNMP. Other researchers and practitioners are developing many other schemes such as the ability to place monitors between COM components, the ability to monitor network traffic to determine security breaches, the ability to monitor object method calls, and various probes that determine whether a given component is alive.

In terms of mapping low-level information to architectural information, the capability will certainly depend on the distance between the architectural and implementation styles. As we argued earlier, our approach encourages developers to pick styles where that mapping will be straightforward.

Analytical Methods: A key feature of our approach is the notion that repair strategies should leverage architectural analyses. We demonstrated one such analysis for performance. What makes us think that others exist? In fact, there is considerable work recently on finding good architecture-based analyses. For example, Klein et al. [19] provide a method of reasoning about the behavior of component types that interact in a defined pattern. In earlier work we showed how to adapt protocol analysis to architectural modification [3]. Others have shown how real-time schedulability can be applied [38]. Although far from providing a complete repertoire of analytical techniques, the space is rich, and getting richer.

9. Conclusion and Future Work

In this paper we have presented a technique for using software architectural styles to automate dynamic repair of systems. In particular, styles and their associated analyses
- make explicit the constraints that must be maintained in the face of evolution
- direct us to the set of properties that must be monitored to achieve system quality attributes and maintain constraints
- define a set of abstract architectural operators for repairing a system
- allow us to select appropriate repair strategies, based on analytical methods

We illustrated how the technique can be applied to performance-oriented adaptation of certain web-based systems.

For future research we see opportunities to improve each of the areas mentioned in Section 7. We need to be able to develop mechanisms that provide richer adaptability for executing systems. We need new monitoring capabilities, and reusable infrastructure for relating monitored values to architectures. We need new analytical methods for architecture that will permit the specification of principled adaptation policies.

Additionally we see a number of other key future research areas. First is the investigation of more intelligent repair policy mechanisms. For example, one might like a system to dynamically adjust its repair tactic selection policy so that it takes into consideration the history of tactic effectiveness: effective tactics would be favored over those that sometimes fail to produce system improvements. Second is the link between architectures and requirements. Systems may need to adapt, not just because the underlying computation base changes, but because user needs change. This will require ways to link user expectations to architectural parameters and constraints. Third is the development of concrete instances of our approach for some of the common architectural frameworks, such as EJB, Jini, and CORBA.

Acknowledgements
The research described in this paper was supported by DARPA, under Grants N66001-99-2-8918 and F30602-00-2-0616. Views and conclusions contained in this document are those of the authors and should not be interpreted as representing the official policies, either expressed or implied, of DARPA.

References

[1]   Agha, G. A. Adaptive Middleware. Communications of the ACM 45(6):30-32, Jun. 2002.

[2]   Allen, R.J. A Formal Approach to Software Architecture. PhD Thesis, published as Carnegie Mellon University School of Computer Science Technical Report CMU-CS-97-144, May 1997.

[3]   Allen, R.J., Douence, R., and Garlan, D. Specifying Dynamism in Software Architectures. Proc. the Workshop on Foundations of Component-Based Software Engineering, Sept. 1997.

[4]   Allen, R.J and Garlan, D. A Formal Basis for Architectural Connection. ACM Transactions of Software Engineering and Methodology, Jul. 1997.

[5] Bertsekas, D. and Gallager, R. Data Networks, Second Edition. Prentice Hall, 1992. ISBN 0-13-200916-1.

[6] Carzaniga, A., Rosenblum, D.S., and Wolf, A.L. Achieving Expressiveness and Scalability in an Internet-Scale Event Notification Service. Proc. 19th ACM Symposium on Principles of Distributed Computing (PODC 2000), Portland OR, Jul. 2000.

[7] Cheng, S-W., Garlan D., Schmerl, B.R., Steenkiste, P.R., Hu. N. Software Architecture-based Adaptation for Grid Computing. Proc. 11th IEEE Conference on High Performance Distributed Computing (HPDC 2002), Edinburgh, Scotland, July 2002.

[8] Dashofy, E., Garlan, D., van der Hoek, A., and Schmerl, B. http://www.ics.uci.edu/pub/arch/xarch/.

[9] Dashofy, E., van der Hoek, A., and Taylor, R.N. A Highly-Extensible, XML-Based Architecture Description Language. Proc. Working IEEE/IFIP Conference on Software Architecture, Amsterdam, The Netherlands, Aug. 2001.

[10] Gantenbien, R.E. Dynamic Binding in Strongly Typed Programming Languages. *Journal of Systems and Software* **14**(1):31-38, 1991.

[11] Garlan, D., Allen, R.J., and Ockerbloom, J. Exploiting Style in Architectural Design. Proc. SIGSOFT '94 Symposium on the Foundations of Software Engineerng, , New Orleans, LA, Dec. 1994.

[12] Garlan, D., Monroe, R.T., and Wile, D. Acme: Architectural Description of Component-Based Systems. Foundations of Component-Based Systems. Leavens, G.T., and Sitaraman, M. (eds). Cambridge University Press, 2000 pp. 47-68.

[13] Garlan, D., Schmerl, B.R., and Chang, J. Using Gauges for Architecture-Based Monitoring and Adaptation. Proc. 1st Working Conference on Complex and Dynamic System Architecture. Brisbane, Australia, Dec. 2001.

[14] Gorlick, M.M., and Razouk, R.R. Using Weaves for Software Construction and Analysis. Proc. 13th International Conference on Software Engineering, IEEE Computer Society Press, May 1991.

[15] Gorlick, M.M. Distributed Debugging on $5 a day. Proc. California Software Symposium, University of California, Irvine, CA, 1997 pp. 31-39.

[16] Gosling, J. and McGilton, H. The Java Language Environment: A White Paper. Sun Microsystems Computer Company, Mountain View, California, May 1996. Available at http://java.sun.com/docs/white/langenv/.

[17] Gross, P.N, Gupta, S., Kaiser, G.E., Kc, G.S., and Parekh, J.J. An Active Events Model for Systems Monitoring. Proc. 1st Working Conference on Complex and Dynamic Systems Architecture, Brisbane, Australia, Dec. 2001.

[18] Ho, W.W. and Olsson, R.A. An Approach to Genuine Dynamic Linking. *Software – Practice and Experience* **21**(4):375—390, 1991.

[19] Klein, M., Kazman, R., Bass, L., Carriere, J., Barbacci, M., Lipson, H. Attribute-Based Architecture Styles. Software Architecture Proc. 1st Working IFIP Conference on Software Architecture (WICSA1), (San Antonio, TX), Feb. 1999, 225-243.

[20] Kon, F., Romn, M., Liu, P., Mao, J., Yamane, T., Magalh, C.,Campbell, R.H. Monitoring, security, and dynamic configuration with the dynamic TAO reflective ORB. IFIP/ACM International Conference on Distributed Systems Platforms, 2000, New York, New York.

[21] Lowekamp, B., Miller, N., Sutherland, D., Gross, T., Steenkiste, P., and Subhlok, J. A Resource Query Interface for Networr-aware Applications. Cluster Computing, 2:139-151, Baltzer, 1999.

[22] Magee, J., Dulay, N., Eisenbach, S., and Kramer, J. Specifying Distributed Software Architectures. Proc. 5th European Software Engineering Conference (ESEC'95), Sitges, Sept. 1995. Also published as Lecture Notes in Computer Science 989, (Springer-Verlag), 1995, pp. 137-153.

[23] Magee, J., and Kramer, J. Concurrency: State Models and Java Programs. Wiley, 1999.

[24] Métayer, D.L. Describing Software Archtiecture Styles using Graph Grammars. *IEEE Transactions on Software Engineering*, **24**(7):521-553, Jul. 1998.

[25] Miller, N., and Steenkiste, P. Collecting Network Status Information for Network-Aware Applications. IEEE INFOCOM 2000, Tel Aviv, Israel, Mar. 2000.

[26] Monroe, R.T. Capturing Software Architecture Design Expertise with Armani. Carnegie Mellon University School of Computer Science Technical Report CMU-CS-98-163.

[27] Moriconi, M. and Reimenschneider, R.A. Introduction to SADL 1.0: A Language for Specifying Software Architecture Hierarchies. Technical Report SRI-CSL-97-01, SRI International, Mar. 1997.

[28] Morrison, R., Connor, R.C.H., Cutts, Q.I., Dunstan, V.S., and Kirby, G.N.C. Exploiting Persistent Linkage in Software Engineering Environments. *The Computer Journal* **38**(1):1—16, 1995.

[29] Object Management Group. The OMG Unified Modeling Language Specification, Version 1.4. Sep. 2001. Available at http://www.omg.org/technology/documents/formal/uml.htm.

[30] The OpenGroup. Architecture Description Markup Language (ADML) Version 1. Apr. 2000. Available at http://www.opengroup.org/publications/catalog/i901.htm.

[31] Oriezy, P., Medvidovic, N., and Taylor, R.N. Architecture-Based Runtime Software Evolution. Proc. International Conference on Software Engineering 1998 (ICSE'98). Kyoto, Japan, Apr. 1998, pp. 11—15.

[32] Oriezy, P., Gorlick, M.M., Taylor, R.N., Johnson, G., Medvidovic, N., Quilici, A., Rosenblum, D., and Wolf, A. An Architecture-Based Approach to Self-Adaptive Software. *IEEE* Intelligent *Systems* **14**(3):54-62, May/Jun. 1999.

[33] Shaw, M. and Garlan, D. Software Architectures: Perspectives on an Emerging Discipline. Prentice Hall, 1996.

[34] Schmerl, B.R., and Garlan, D. Exploiting Architectural Design Knowledge to Support Self-repairing Systems. Proc. 14th International Conference on Software Engineering and Knowledge Engineering, Ischia, Italy, Jul. 15-19, 2002.

[35] Spitznagel, B. and Garlan, D. Architecture-Based Performance Analysis. Proc. 1998 Conference on Software Engineering and Knowledge Engineering, Jun. 1998.

[36] Taylor, R.N., Medvidovic, N., Anderson, K.M., Whitehead, E.J., Robbins, J.E., Nies, K.A., Oriezy, P., and Dubrow, D.L. A Component- and Message-Based Architectural Style for GUI Software. *IEEE Transactions on Software Engineering* **22**(6):390-406, 1996.

[37] Valetto, G., and Kaiser, G. A Case Study in Software Adaptation. Proc. 1st ACM SIGSOFT Workshop on Self-Healing Systems (WOSS 2002), Charleston, SC, Nov. 2002.

[38] Vestel, S. MetaH Programmer's Manual, Version 1.09. Technical Report, Honeywell Technology Center, Apr. 1996.

[39] Wells, D., and Pazandak, P. Taming Cyber Incognito: Surveying Dynamic / Reconfigurable Software Landscapes. Proc. 1st Working Conference on Complex and Dynamic Systems Architectures,, Brisbane, Australia, Dec 12-14, 2001.

[40] Wermelinger, M., Lopes, A., and Fiadeiro, J.L. A Graph Based Architectural (Re)configuration Language. Proc. Joint 8th European Software Engineering Conference and the 9th ACM SIGSOFT Symposium on the Foundations of Software Engineering. Vienna, Austria, Sep. 2001, pp. 21—32.

[41] Wile, D.S. AML: An Architecture Meta-Language. Proc. Automated Software Engineering Conference, Cocoa Beach, FL, Oct. 1999.

Dependability in the Web Services Architecture

Ferda Tartanoglu[1], Valérie Issarny[1],
Alexander Romanovsky[2], and Nicole Levy[3]

[1] INRIA Rocquencourt
78153 Le Chesnay, France
{Galip-Ferda.Tartanoglu,Valerie.Issarny}@inria.fr
http://www-rocq.inria.fr/arles/
[2] University of Newcastle upon Tyne
School of Computing Science, NE1 7RU, UK
Alexander.Romanovsky@newcastle.ac.uk
[3] Laboratoire PRiSM, Université de Versailles Saint-Quentin-en-Yvelines
78035 Versailles, France
Nicole.Levy@prism.uvsq.fr

Abstract. The Web services architecture is expected to play a promi-
nent role in developing next generation distributed systems. This chapter
discusses how to build dependable systems based on the Web services architecture. More specifically, it surveys base fault tolerance mechanisms,
considering both backward and forward error recovery mechanisms, and
shows how they are adapted to deal with the specifics of the Web in the
light of ongoing work in the area. Existing solutions, targeting the development of dependable composite Web services, may be subdivided into
two categories that are respectively related to the specification of Web
services composition and to the design of dedicated distributed protocols.

1 Introduction

Systems that build upon the Web services architecture are expected to become
a major class of wide-area distributed systems in the near future. The Web services architecture targets the development of applications based on XML-related
standards, hence easing the development of distributed systems through the dynamic integration of applications distributed over the Internet, independently of
their underlying platforms.

A Web service is a software entity deployed on the Web whose public interface is described in XML. A Web service can interact with other systems by
exchanging XML-based messages, using standard Internet transport protocols.
The Web service's definition and location (given by a URI) can be discovered by
querying common Web service registries. Web services can be implemented using
any programming language and executed on heterogeneous platforms; as long
as they provide the above features. This allows Web services owned by distinct
entities to interoperate through message exchange.

Although the modularity and interoperability of the Web services architecture enable complex distributed systems to be easily built by assembling several

R. de Lemos et al. (Eds.): Architecting Dependable Systems, LNCS 2677, pp. 90–109, 2003.
© Springer-Verlag Berlin Heidelberg 2003

component services into one composite service, there clearly is a number of research challenges in supporting the thorough development of distributed systems based on Web services. One such challenge relates to the effective usage of Web services in developing business processes, which requires support for composing Web services in a way that guarantees dependability of the resulting composite services. This calls for developing new architectural principles of building such composed systems, in general, and for studying specialized connectors "glueing" Web services, in particular, so that the resulting composition can deal with failures occurring at the level of the individual component services.

Several properties of the Web services architecture must be taken into account while addressing the above issues. Web services are decentralized in architecture and in administration. Therefore, individual Web services can have different characteristics (e.g., transactional supports, concurrency policies, access rights), which may not be compliant with each other. Moreover, Web services use Internet transport protocols (e.g., HTTP, SMTP) and interacting with them requires dealing with limitations of the Internet such access latency, timeouts, lost requests and security issues. These specifics of Web services require special care for supporting dependability of complex distributed systems in integrating them. The provision of effective support for the dependable integration of Web services is still an open issue, which has led to tremendous research effort over the last couple of years, both in industry and academia, as surveyed in the following.

This chapter is organized as follows. Section 2 introduces base Web services architecture, and discusses Web services composition and related dependability requirements. Then, proposed fault tolerance mechanisms for composite Web services are surveyed: Section 3 overviews transaction protocols for the Web based on backward error recovery, and Section 4 presents how forward error recovery can be applied to Web services composition processes. Finally, Section 5 summarizes our analysis, and sketches our current and future work.

2   The Web Services Architecture

Although the definition of the overall Web services architecture is still incomplete, the base standards have already emerged from the W3C[1], which define a core middleware for Web services, partly building upon results from object-based and component-based middleware technologies. These standards relate to the specification of Web services and of supporting interaction protocols. Furthermore, there already exist various platforms that are compliant with the Web services architecture, including .NET[2], J2EE[3] and AXIS[4]. Figure 1 depicts the technology stack of the base Web services architecture, each layer being defined with common protocol choices. Main standards for the Web services architecture

---

[1] World Wide Web Consortium, http://www.w3.org.

[2] Microsoft .NET, http://www.microsoft.com/net/.

[3] Java 2 Platform, Enterprise Edition, http://java.sun.com/j2ee.

[4] Apache AXIS, http://xml.apache.org/axis.

being defined by the W3C Web Service Activity[5] and the Oasis Consortium[6] are the following:

- **SOAP** (Simple Object Access Protocol) defines a lightweight protocol for information exchange that sets the rules of how to encode data in XML, and also includes conventions for partly describing the invocation semantics (either synchronous or asynchronous) as well as the SOAP mapping to an Internet transport protocol (e.g., HTTP) [24].
- **WSDL** (Web Services Description Language) is an XML-based language used to specify: (i) the service's abstract interface that describes the messages exchanged with the service, and (ii) the concrete binding information that contains specific protocol-dependent details including the network end-point address of the service [23].
- **UDDI** (Universal Description, Discovery and Integration) specifies a registry for dynamically locating and advertising Web services [18].

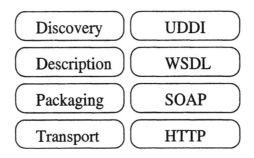

Fig. 1. Web services architecture

Composing Web services then relates to dealing with the assembly of autonomous components so as to deliver a new service out of the components' primitive services, given the corresponding published interfaces. We use the travel agent case study to illustrate a composite Web service. The travel agent service assists the user in booking complete trips according to his/her requests and is built by composing several existing Web services (e.g., accommodation and flight booking, and car rental Web services) located through a public Web services registry (see Figure 2). Each Web service is an autonomous component, which is not aware of its participation into a composition process. A typical scenario for the travel agent service is as follows:

- The user interacts only with the travel agent whose internal computations are hidden from the user.
- The user sends a query to the travel agent with the date for the travel and the itinerary.

---

[5] http://www.w3.org/2002/ws/.

[6] http://www.oasis-open.org.

- The travel agent proposes to the user complete trips satisfying his/her request, after querying appropriate accommodation, flight and car rental Web services.
- The travel agent makes all the respective bookings and reservations on Web services, according to the user's choices, and returns him/her a confirmation.
- If a full trip cannot be found, the travel agent tries to offer the user some replacement trips but no action can be taken without his/her approval.

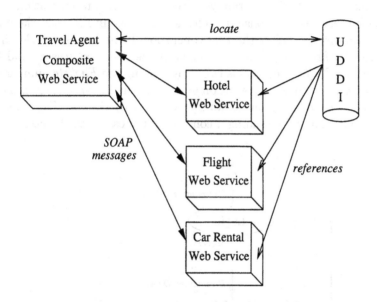

Fig. 2. A composite Web service example: The travel agent service

In the current Web services architecture, interfaces are described in WSDL and published through UDDI. However, supporting composition requires further addressing: (i) the specification of the composition, and (ii) ensuring that the services are composed in a way that guarantees the consistency of both the individual services and the overall composition. This calls for the abstract specification of Web services behaviors (see Section 2.1) and of their composition (see Section 2.2) that allows reasoning about the correctness of interactions with individual Web services. In addition, the composition process must not only define the functional behavior of the composite service in terms of interactions with the composed services, but also its non functional properties, possibly exploiting middleware-related services (e.g., services relating to WS-Security [14] for enforcing secure interactions). Various non-functional properties (e.g., availability, extendibility, reliability, openness, performance, security, scalability) should be accounted for in the context of Web services. However, enforcing dependability of composite Web services is one of the most challenging issues due to the concern for supporting business processes, combined with the fact that the composition process deals with the assembly of loosely-coupled autonomous components (see Section 2.3).

2.1 Specifying Conversations

To enable a Web service to be correctly integrated in a composition process, Web services conversations (also referred as to choreography) are to be provided in addition to WSDL interfaces for describing the observable behavior of a Web service by specifying the protocol in terms of message exchanges that should be implemented for correct interaction with the service. As an illustration, a flight booking Web service can publish its behavior as shown in Figure 3: the booking process starts with the call of the *Login* operation. If the login succeeds, the user can call the *FlightRequest* operation. Then, if the result returns a valid list of flights, the *BookFlight* operation is called by sending the *FlightId* number of the corresponding flight. The conversation ends if (i) the *Login* operation fails, (ii) the user calls *Logout* during the booking process or (iii), the *BookFlight* operation terminates successfully by sending a confirmation message to the user.

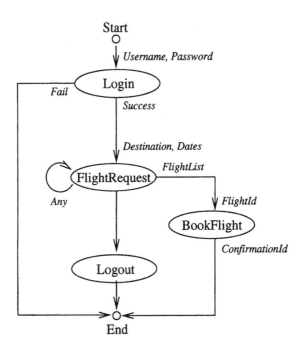

Fig. 3. A conversation for the flight booking Web service

The W3C Choreography Working Group[7] aims at extending the Web services architecture with a standard for specifying Web services conversations. Existing proposals to the W3C for specifying conversations include WSCL (Web Services

---

[7] http://www.w3.org/2002/ws/chor/.

Conversation Language) [26] and WSCI (Web Service Choreography Interface) [25]. In addition, WSCI can be used to describe additional properties related to the service behavior (e.g., transactional properties and exceptional behavior). Note that the specification of conversations, which enriches the definition of Web services interfaces, should be accounted for, for the definition of Web services registries like UDDI. Instances of Web services should be retrieved with respect to the definition of both the service's interfaces, observable behaviors and non-functional properties (e.g., transactional behavior). WSDL extensibility elements allow the Web service interface definition to be extended and can be, for example, used to add information describing conversations and other properties. In addition, WSCL can further be published in UDDI registries for retrieving Web services with respect to the conversations that the services support [1].

2.2   Specifying Composition Processes

Web services are integrated according to the specification of a composition process. Such a process may be specified as a graph (or process schema) over the set of composed Web services (see Figure 4). It is worth noting that if some Web services used in a composition process have associated conversation descriptions (e.g., WSCL or WSCI) for the operations they support, the overall composition must conform to all these descriptions. The specification of a composition graph may be:

1. Automatically inferred from the specification of individual services as addressed in [16].
2. Distributed over the specification of the component Web services as in the XL language [7].
3. Given separately with XML-based declarative languages as BPEL, BPML, CSDL and SCSL [11, 2, 4, 28], or in the form of state-charts as undertaken in [6].

The first approach is quite attractive but restricts the composition patterns that may be applied, and cannot thus be used in general. The second approach is the most general, introducing an XML-based programming language. However, this limits the re-usability and evolution of (possibly composite) Web services due to the strong coupling of the specification of the composition process with that of the composed services. The third approach directly supports reuse, openness, and evolution of Web services by clearly distinguishing the specification of component Web services (comprising primitive components that are considered as black-box components and/or inner composite components) from the specification of composition. Hence, although there is not yet a consensus about the best approach for specifying composite Web services, it may be anticipated that this will most likely rely on the XML-based specification of a graph over Web services that is decoupled from the specification of the composed Web services. The main reasons that lead to this conclusion include compliance and complementarity with established W3C standards (i.e., WSDL and SOAP), thus providing reusability, openness and extensibility, but also the fact that it is the approach undertaken by most industrial consortia.

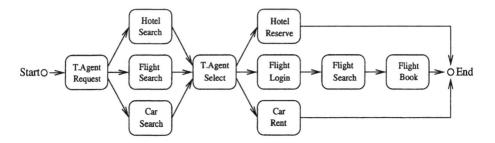

Fig. 4. Composition graph for the travel agent service

2.3   Dependability Requirements

Composite Web services have high dependability requirements that call for dedicated fault tolerance mechanisms due to both the specifics of the Web services architecture and limitations of the Internet, which is not a reliable media [9]. The autonomy of component Web services raises challenging issues in specifying composition processes and in particular exceptional behaviors of composite services when dealing with faults. These faults include but are not limited to (i) faults occurring at the level of the Web services, which may be notified by error messages, (ii) faults at the underlying platform (e.g., hardware faults, timeouts), and (iii) faults due to online upgrades of service components and/or of their interfaces.

In general, the choice of fault tolerance techniques to be exploited for the development of dependable systems depends very much on the fault assumptions and on the system's characteristics and requirements. There are two main classes of error recovery [10]: backward (based on rolling system components back to the previous correct state) and forward error recovery (which involves transforming the system components into any correct state). The former uses either diversely-implemented software or simple retry; the latter is usually application-specific and relies on an exception handling mechanism [5]. It is a widely-accepted fact that the most beneficial way of applying fault tolerance is by associating its measures with system structuring units as this decreases system complexity and makes it easier for developers to apply fault tolerance [20]. Structuring units applied for both building distributed systems and providing their fault tolerance are well-known: they are *distributed transactions* and *atomic actions*[8]. Distributed transactions [8] use backward error recovery as the main fault tolerance measure in order to satisfy completely or partially the ACID (atomicity, consistency,

---

[8] also referred to as conversations, but we will not use this term to avoid confusion with Web services conversations.

isolation, durability) properties. Atomic actions [3] allow programmers to apply both backward and forward error recovery. The latter relies on coordinated handling of action exceptions that involves all action participants. Backward error recovery has a limited applicability, and in spite of all its advantages, modern systems are increasingly relying on forward error recovery, which uses appropriate exception handling techniques as a means [5]. Examples of such applications are complex systems involving human beings, COTS components, external devices, several organizations, movement of goods, operations on the environment, real-time systems that do not have time to go back. Integrated Web services clearly fall into this category.

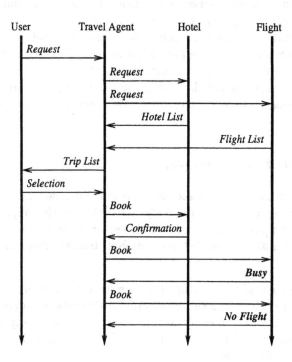

Fig. 5. Sequence diagram for the travel agent service

A typical example that shows the need for a specialized fault tolerance mechanism for the Web services architecture is the issue of running distributed transactions over several autonomous Web services. As an illustration, Figure 5 depicts a sequence diagram example associated with the travel agent service. We consider that for a given trip request (expressed by giving the journey dates and the location), the travel agent finds a list of available hotel rooms and flights to the destination. Then, the user selects a complete trip by choosing a hotel and a flight from the list of trips. Once the user has confirmed the booking, the travel agent makes the hotel reservation, which completes successfully and then, attempts for the flight booking. The flight booking Web service returns an error, informing that the server is busy, and after several attempts, the server returns a *NoFlightAvailable* error message. Several solutions can be applied to handle this type of faults:

1. The hotel reservation can be canceled –if possible. The user is then informed that this trip is no longer available and he/she can retry booking by selecting another trip (e.g., by changing the dates of the journey).
2. Alternative transport means instead of flight can be proposed to the user (e.g., a train ticket to a close city and renting a car).

These examples reflect two different fault tolerance mechanisms: (i) backward error recovery with cancellation/compensation and retry, and (ii) forward error recovery with an application-specific exception handler that handles the error without necessarily trying to restore the system state back.

Developing fault tolerant mechanisms for composite Web services has been an active area of research over the last couple of years. Existing proposals mainly exploit backward error recovery, and more specifically, transactions. However, the autonomy of Web services and the Web latency have led to exploit more flexible transactional models and forward error recovery techniques, as discussed in the next two sections.

3   Backward Error Recovery for the Web

Transactions have been proven successful in enforcing dependability in closed distributed systems and are extensively exploited for the implementation of primitive (non-composite) Web services. However, transactions are not suited for making the composition of Web services fault tolerant in general, for at least two reasons:

- The management of transactions that are distributed over Web services requires cooperation among the transactional supports of individual Web services, which may not be compliant with each other and may not be willing to do so given their intrinsic autonomy and the fact that they span different administrative domains.
- Locking resources (i.e., the Web service itself in the most general case) until the termination of the embedding transaction is in general not appropriate for Web services, still due to their autonomy, and also to the fact that they potentially have a large number of concurrent clients that will not stand extensive delays.

Enhanced transactional models have been considered to alleviate the latter shortcoming. In particular, the split model (also referred to as open-nested transactions) where transactions may split into a number of concurrent sub-transactions that can commit independently allows reduction of the latency due to locking [19]. Typically, sub-transactions are matched to the transactions already supported by Web services (e.g., transactional booking offered by a service). Hence, transactions over composite services do not increase the access latency as offered by the individual services. Enforcing the atomicity property over a transaction that has been split into a number of sub-transactions then requires using compensation over committed sub-transactions in the case of transaction abortion. However, to support this, Web services should provide compensating operations for all the operations they offer. Such an issue is in particular addressed by the BPEL [11] and WSCI [26] languages for specifying composite services, which allow compensating operations associated with the services operations to be defined. It is worth noting that using compensation for aborting distributed transactions must extend to all the participating Web services (i.e., cascading compensation by analogy with cascading abort). Such a concern is addressed in [15]. This paper introduces a middleware whose API may be exploited by clients of a composite service for specifying and executing a (open-nested) transaction over a set of Web services whose termination is dictated by the outcomes of the transactional operations invoked on the individual services. In addition to client-side solutions to the coordination of distributed open-nested transactions, work is undertaken in the area of distributed transaction protocols supporting the deployment of transactions over the Web, while not imposing long-lived locks over Web resources. We discuss here the two main proposals aimed at the Web services architecture: (i) the Business Transaction Protocol (BTP)[17], and (ii) Web Services Transaction (WS-Transaction) [13].

BTP introduces two different transaction models for the Web: (i) the *atomic business transactions* (or *atoms*), and (ii) the *cohesive business transactions* (or *cohesions*). A composite application can be built from both *atoms* and *cohesions* that can be nested. In the *atomic business transaction* model, several processes are executed within a transaction and either all complete or all fail. This is similar to distributed ACID transactions on tightly coupled systems. However, the isolation property is relaxed and intermediate committed values can be seen by external systems (i.e., systems not enrolled in the transaction). Figure 6 illustrates the *atomic business transaction* model using the travel agent service involving a flight booking Web service (*Flight*) and an accommodation booking Web service (*Hotel*). In this scenario, the hotel room booking fails while the flight booking succeeds, which leads to cancellation of the booked flight before the end of the transaction:

1. *Travel Agent* sends the request messages to *Flight* and to *Hotel* Web services.
2. *Flight* and *Hotel* respond (*Confirm* messages) with listings of available flights and hotel rooms.
3. *Travel Agent* orders the bookings by initiating commitments (*Prepare* messages).
4. *Flight* Web service returns *Prepared* and is ready to commit, while the *Hotel* Web service returns a *Fail* error message. Commit is no longer possible on the *Hotel* Web service for this transaction.
5. *Travel Agent* cancels the transaction on the *Flight* Web service by sending the *Cancel* order.
6. *Flight* Web service confirms cancellation with the *Canceled* message.

The *cohesive business transaction* model allows non-ACID transactions to be defined by not requiring successful termination of all the transaction's partic-

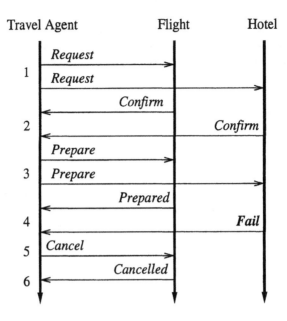

Fig. 6. BTP Atomic Business Transaction

ipants for committing. A travel agent service scenario example for illustrating *cohesive business transactions* is given in Figure 7, where the flight booking is performed on two distinct Web services. In this example, the transaction, which was originally initiated with three participants, ends with two commits and one abortion:

1. *Travel Agent* sends the request messages to the two flight booking Web services, *Air France* and *British Airways* and to the *Hotel* Web service.
2. Web services return response messages to the *Travel Agent*.
3. *Travel Agent* selects *Air France* for the flight booking, and therefore sends a *Cancel* message to *British Airways* Web service and a *Prepare* message to the two other Web services.
4. *Air France* and *Hotel* Web services acknowledge with the *Prepared* message and *British Airways* confirms the cancellation with the *Canceled* message.
5. *Travel Agent* confirms commits (*Confirm* messages).
6. Web services acknowledge (*Confirmed* messages).

WS-Transaction [13] defines a specialization of WS-Coordination [12], which is an extensible framework for specifying distributed protocols that coordinate the execution of Web services, and that can be used in conjunction with BPEL. Like BTP, it offers two different transaction models: (i) *atomic transactions* (AT) and (ii) *business activity* (BA). An *atomic transaction* adheres to the traditional ACID properties with a two-phase commit protocol. Note that as opposed to the BTP *atomic business transactions*, the isolation property is not relaxed in WS-Transactions, which as we mentioned before, is not suitable for the majority of Web service applications. The *business activity* protocol specifically serves

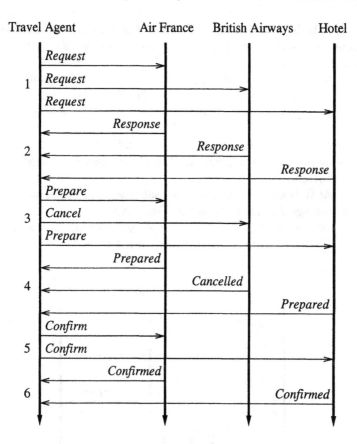

Fig. 7. BTP Cohesive Business Transaction

coordinating the execution of open-nested transactions over a set of activities, through a coordinator activity. If there is a need for a coordinated activity to be compensated, the coordinator sends *compensate* messages to all the participants involved in the activity. Then, each participant replies by sending back either a *compensated* or a *faulted* message, depending on whether the required compensation operation was successfully completed or not. However, there is no requirement for an agreement on the outcome, and any participant can leave the coordinated activity in which it is engaged, prior to the termination of peer participants. A WS-Transaction *business activity* example is shown in Figure 8, with an *Airline* Web service and an *Hotel* Web service:

1. The *Travel Agent* initiates the *Business Activity* with the *Flight* and *Hotel* participants by sending the *Request* messages.
2. The *Flight* and *Hotel* Web services enroll in the transaction (*Register* messages) by returning list of respective availabilities.
3. *Travel Agent* initiate booking on the *Flight* Web service (*Complete* message).

4. The *Flight* Web service returns *Completed* to confirm commitment, while the *Hotel* Web service returns an error message *Faulted* and can no longer commit the transaction.
5. In order to abort the whole transaction and restore the state, the *Travel Agent* sends a *Compensate* message to the *Flight* Web service which has already completed the (sub)-transaction and a *Forget* message to the *Hotel* Web service.
6. The *Flight* Web service compensates the committed transaction by canceling the booking order and confirms with the *Compensated* message sent back to the *Travel Agent*.
7. If the *Flight* Web service cannot compensate the booked operation, it returns an error message *Faulted* back to the *Travel Agent*.
8. In this case, the *Travel Agent* sends a *Forget* message to the *Flight* Web service. The flight has been booked and cannot be canceled.

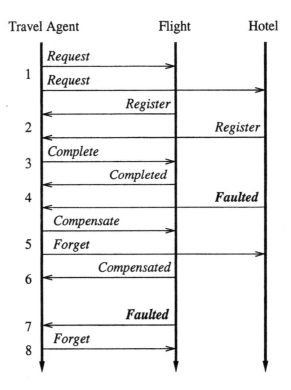

Fig. 8. WS-Transaction Business Activity

Although there is not yet a consensus on a standard protocol for managing transactions on the Web, various implementations of these protocols are already available: the JOTM transaction manager[9] and Cohesions[10] implement

---

[9] http://www.objectweb.org/jotm/.
[10] http://www.choreology.com/.

the BTP protocol, and the Collaxa Orchestration Server[11] permits the use of the WS-Transaction protocol when composing Web services with the BPEL language. However, solutions to the dependable composition of Web services that use primarily transactions do not cope with all the specifics of Web services. A major source of penalty lies in the use of backward error recovery in an open system such as the Internet, which is mainly oriented towards tolerating hardware faults but poorly suited to the deployment of cooperation-based mechanisms over autonomous component systems that often require cooperative application-level exception handling among component systems. Even with the use of *cohesions*, which does not necessarily roll back all participant states in case of abortion of one of them, they do not specify any specific way of providing fault tolerance, so everything is left to programmers. Moreover, cancellation or compensation does not always work in many real-life situations, which involve documents, goods, money as well as humans (clients, operators, managers, etc.) and which require application-specific error handling.

4 Forward Error Recovery for the Web

Forward error recovery, using an exception handling mechanism is extensively exploited in the specifications of composite Web services in order to handle error occurrences (e.g., [11], [2], [25]). For instance, in BPEL, exception handlers (referred to as fault handlers) can be associated to a (possibly nested) activity so that when an error occurs inside an activity, its execution terminates, and the corresponding exception handler is executed. However, when an activity is defined as a concurrent process and at least one embedded activity signals an exception, all the embedded activities are terminated as soon as one signaled exception is caught, and only the handler for this specific exception is executed. Hence, error recovery actually accounts for a single exception and thus cannot ensure recovery of a correct state. The only case where correct state recovery may be ensured is when the effect of all the aborted activities are rolled back to a previous state, which may not be supported in general, in the context of Web services, as discussed previously. The shortcoming of BPEL actually applies to all XML-based languages for Web services composition that integrate support for specifying concurrent activities and exception handling.

A solution to the above issue lies in structuring the composition of Web services in terms of *coordinated atomic actions*. The Coordinated Atomic Action (or CA action) concept [27] is a unified scheme for coordinating complex concurrent activities and supporting error recovery between multiple interacting components. Atomic actions are used to control cooperative concurrency and to implement coordinated error recovery whilst ACID transactions are used to maintain the consistency of shared resources. A CA action is designed as a set of participants cooperating inside it and a set of resources accessed by them. In the course of the action, participants can access resources that have ACID properties. Action participants either reach the end of the action and produce a

---

[11] http://www.collaxa.com/.

normal outcome or, if one or more exceptions are raised, they all are involved in their coordinated handling. If several exceptions have been raised concurrently, they are resolved [3] using a resolution tree imposing a partial order on all action exceptions, and the participants handle the resolved exception. If this handling is successful the action completes normally, but if handling is not possible then all responsibility for recovery is passed to the containing action where an external action exception is propagated. CA actions provide a base structuring mechanism for developing fault tolerant composite Web services: a CA action specifies the collaborative realization of a given function by composed services, and Web services correspond to external resources. However, as for transactions, ACID properties over external resources are not suited in the case of Web services. We have therefore introduced the notion of Web Services Composition Action (WSCA) that differs from CA actions in relaxing the transactional requirements over external resources (which are not suitable for wide-area open systems) and the introduction of dynamic nesting of WSCAs (i.e., nested calls of WSCAs for the sake of modularity) [22].

The travel agent service is used to illustrate how WSCAs can be applied for specifying the composition of Web services. We consider joint booking of accommodation and flights using separate hotel and airline Web services. Then, the composed Web service's operation is specified using WSCAs as follows. The top-level *TravelAgent* WSCA comprises the *User* and the *Travel* participants; the former interacts with the user while the latter achieves joint booking according to the user's request through call to the WSCA that composes the *Flight* and the *Hotel* participants[12]. Figure 9 depicts the software architecture of the travel agent service where rectangles represents components which can be either WSCA participants or Web services, and elliptical nodes represents connectors such as WSCAs connectors and SOAP connectors.

A diagrammatic specification of the WSCAs is shown in Figure 10. In *TravelAgent*, the *User* participant requests the *Travel* participant to book a flight ticket and a hotel room for the duration of the given stay. This leads the *Travel* participant to invoke the *JointBooking* WSCA that composes the *Hotel* Web service and the *Airline* Web service. The participants of the *JointBooking* WSCA respectively requests for a hotel room and a flight ticket, given the destination and departure and return dates provided by the user. Each request is subdivided into reservation for the given period and subsequent booking if the reservation succeeds[13]. In the case where either the reservation or the booking fails, the participant raises the *unavailable* exception that is cooperatively handled at the

---

[12] Such a workflow process is certainly not the most common since the user is in general requested for confirmation prior to booking. However, this scenario that applies most certainly to in-hurry-not-bother users enables concise illustration of the various recovery schemes that are supported.

[13] We assume here that all Web services understand and use term *unavailable* in the same way. To deal with the problem of meanings in a general fashion one could apply techniques that use ontology and standard ways of representing semantic information. Such an ontology for travel business partners can be found on http://opentravel.org.

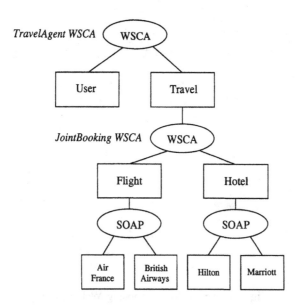

Fig. 9. WSCA architecture

level of the *JointBooking* WSCA denoted by the greyed box in the figure. If both participants signal the *unavailable* exception, then *Travel* signals the *abort* exception so that the exception gets handled by *TravelAgent* in a cooperation with the *User* (e.g., by choosing an alternative date). If only one participant raises the *unavailable* exception, cooperative exception handling includes an attempt by the other participant to find an alternative booking. If this retry fails, the booking that has succeeded is canceled and the abort exception is signaled to the calling *TravelAgent* WSCA for recovery with user intervention.

Compared to the solutions that introduce transactional supports for composed Web services, using WSCAs mainly differs in that it exploits forward error recovery at the composition level, while enabling exploitation of transactional supports offered by individual Web services – if available. Hence, the underlying protocol for interaction among Web services remains the one of the Web services architecture (i.e., SOAP) and does not need to be complemented with a distributed transaction protocol. Similarly to this solution, the one of [15] does not require any new protocol to support distributed open-nested transactions. An open-nested transaction is declared on the client side by grouping transactions of the individual Web services, through call to a dedicated function of the middleware running on the client. The transaction then gets aborted by the middleware using compensation operations offered by the individual Web services, according to conditions set by the client over the outcomes of the grouped transactions. The solution offered by WSCA is then more general since it allows forward error recovery involving several services to be specified at the composition level, enabling in particular to integrate non-transactional Web services while still enforcing dependability of the composite service and partial results of a nested action to be reported to the higher level action.

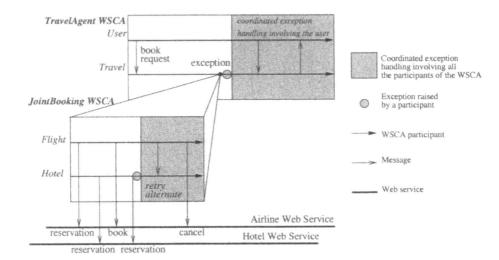

Fig. 10. WSCA for composing Web services

There is a number of Java and Ada implementations of CA actions developed for different platforms, environments and applications. A complete RMI Java framework was developed several years ago [29] and since then it has been applied in a number of industry-oriented case studies. It offers a number of classes (for defining actions, action participants, exception handlers) and a run-time support in a form of the action manager object. Recently it has been used for a preliminary experimental work on implementing a prototype Travel Agent system [21]. A Java-based local runtime support for WSCA is under development now. It is built as an adaptation of this extended CA action Java framework.

5   Conclusion

The Web services architecture is expected to play a major role in developing next generation distributed systems. However, the architecture needs to evolve to support all the requirements appertained to distributed systems. Addressing such requirements relates, in particular, in reusing solutions from the distributed system community. However, most solutions will not be reusable as is, mainly because of the openness of the Internet. Hence, making evolve the Web services architecture to support the thorough development of distributed systems raises a number of challenges.

This paper has addressed one of the issues raised in this context, which is the dependable composition of Web services, i.e., understanding how fault tolerance should be addressed in the Web services architecture. While dependability in closed distributed systems is conveniently addressed by transactions when concerned with both concurrency control and failure occurrences, it can hardly rely on such a mechanism in an open environment. A major source of difficulty lies in the use of backward error recovery which is mainly oriented towards tolerating hardware faults but poorly suited to the deployment of cooperation-based mechanisms over autonomous component systems that often require cooperative application-level exception handling among component systems. One solution to this concern lies in forward error recovery that enables accounting for the specific of Web services and that leads to structure Web services-based systems in terms of co-operative actions. In particular, we are able to address dependable service composition in a way that neither undermines the Web service's autonomy nor increases their individual access latency.

We are currently working on the formal specification of WSCAs for enabling rigorous reasoning about the behavior of composite Web services regarding both the correctness of the composition and offered dependability properties. The specification of composite Web services allows carrying out a number of analyzes with respect to the correctness and the dependable behavior of composite services. Except classical static type checking, the correctness of the composite service may be checked statically with respect to the usage of individual services. In addition, the same specification can be used for implementing executable assertions to check the composite service behavior online. Reasoning about the dependable behavior of composite Web services lies in the precise characterization of the dependability properties that hold over the states of the individual Web services after the execution of WSCAs. We are in particular interested in the specification of properties relating to the relaxed form of atomicity that is introduced by the exploitation of open-nested transactions within WSCA.

We are further implementing a base middleware support for WSCAs. The middleware includes the generation of composite Web services from WSCA specifications and a service for locating Web services that implements behavioral specification matching. In addition, we target development of related middleware support for improving the overall quality of composite Web services. We are in particular interested in developing a specialized caching support intended for reducing response time.

Acknowledgments

We would like to thank Marie-Claude Gaudel and Brian Randell for their helpful comments and discussions. This research is partially supported by the European IST DSoS (Dependable Systems of Systems) project (IST-1999-11585)[14].

References

1. D. Beringer, H. Kuno, and M. Lemon. Using WSCL in a UDDI Registry 1.02, 2001. UDDI Working Draft Technical Note Document,
   `http://www.uddi.org/pubs/wscl_TN_forUDDI_5_16_011.pdf`.
2. BPMI.org. Business Process Modeling Language (BPML), Version 1.0, 2002.
   `http://www.bpmi.org/bpml.esp`.

---

[14] `http://www.newcastle.research.ec.org/dsos/`.

3. R. H. Campbell and B. Randell. Error recovery in asynchronous systems. *IEEE Transactions on Software Engineering*, SE-12(8), 1986.
4. F. Casati, M. Sayal, and M-C. Shan. Developing e-services for composing e-services. In *Proceedings of CAISE 2001, LNCS 2068*, 2001.
5. F. Cristian. *Dependability of Resilient Computers*, chapter Exception Handling, pages 68–97. Blackwell Scientific Publications, 1989.
6. M-C. Fauvet, M. Dumas, B. Benatallah, and H-Y. Paik. Peer-to-peer traced execution of composite services. In *Proceedings of TES'2001, LNCS 2193*, 2001.
7. D. Florescu, A. Grunhagen, and D. Kossmann. XL: An XML language for Web service specification and composition. In *Proceedings of the WWW 2002 Conference*, 2002.
8. J. Gray and A. Reuter. *Transaction Processing: Concepts and Techniques*. Morgan Kaufmann, 1993.
9. M. Kalyanakrishnan, R.K. Iyer, and J.U. Patel. Reliability of Internet hosts: A case study from the end user's perspective. *Computer Networks*, (31):47–57, 1999.
10. P. A. Lee and T. Anderson. *Fault Tolerance Principles and Practice*, volume 3 of *Dependable Computing and Fault-Tolerant Systems*. Springer - Verlag, 2nd edition, 1990.
11. Microsoft and BEA and IBM. Business Process Execution Language for Web Services (BPEL4WS), Version 1.0, 2002.
    http://www.ibm.com/developerworks/library/ws-bpel/.
12. Microsoft and BEA and IBM. Web Services Coordination (WS-Coordination), 2002. http://www.ibm.com/developerworks/library/ws-coor/.
13. Microsoft and BEA and IBM. Web Services Transaction (WS-Transaction), 2002. http://www.ibm.com/developerworks/library/ws-transpec/.
14. Microsoft and IBM and VeriSign. Web Services Security (WS-Security), Version 1.0, 2002. http://www.ibm.com/developerworks/library/ws-secure/.
15. T. Mikalsen, S. Tai, and I. Rouvellou. Transactional attitudes: Reliable composition of autonomous Web services. In *DSN 2002, Workshop on Dependable Middleware-based Systems (WDMS 2002)*, 2002.
16. S. Narayanan and S. McIlraith. Simulation, verification and automated composition of Web services. In *Proceedings of the WWW 2002 Conference*, 2002.
17. Oasis Committee. Business Transaction Protocol (BTP), Version 1.0, 2002. http://www.oasis-open.org/committees/business-transactions/.
18. Oasis Committee. Universal Description, Discovery and Integration (UDDI), Version 3 Specification, 2002. http://www.uddi.org.
19. C. Pu, G. Kaiser, and N. Hutchinson. Split-transactions for open-ended activities. *Proceedings of the 14th VLDB Conference*, 1988.
20. B. Randell. Recursive structured distributed computing systems. In *Proc. of the 3rd Symp. on Reliability in Distributed Software and Database Systems*, pages 3–11, Florida, USA, 1983.
21. A. Romanovsky, P. Periorellis, and A.F. Zorzo. Structuring integrated Web applications for fault tolerance, 2003. To be presented at the 6th Int. Symposium on Autonomous Decentralised Systems. Pisa, Italy, April 2003. (a preliminary version: Technical Report CS-TR-765, University of Newcastle upon Tyne).
22. F. Tartanoglu, V. Issarny, N. Levy, and A. Romanovsky. Dependability in the web service architecture. In *Proceedings of the ICSE Workshop on Architecting Dependable Systems*, Orlando, USA, May 2002.
23. W3C. Web Services Description Language (WSDL) 1.1, W3C Note, 2001. http://www.w3.org/TR/wsdl (W3C Working Draft for version 1.2 is available at http://www.w3.org/TR/wsdl12).

24. W3C. Simple Object Access Protocol (SOAP) 1.2, W3C Candidate Recommendation, 2002. http://www.w3.org/TR/soap12-part0/.
25. W3C. Web Service Choreography Interface (WSCI) 1.0, W3C Note, 2002. http://www.w3.org/TR/wsci/.
26. W3C. Web Services Conversation Language (WSCL) 1.0, W3C Note, 2002. http://www.w3.org/TR/wscl10/.
27. J. Xu, B. Randell, A. Romanovsky, C. M. F. Rubira, R. J. Stroud, and Z. Wu. Fault tolerance in concurrent object-oriented software through coordinated error recovery. In *Proceedings of the Twenty-Fifth IEEE International Symposium on Fault-Tolerant Computing*, 1995.
28. J. Yang and P. Papazoglou. Web component: A substrate for Web service reuse and composition. In *Proceedings of CAISE 2002*, 2002.
29. A.F. Zorzo and R. J. Stroud. An object-oriented framework for dependable multi-party interactions. In *proc. of Conf. on Object-Oriented Programming Systems and Applications (OOPSLA'99), ACM Sigplan Notices 34(10)*, pages 435–446, 1999.

A Component Based Real-Time Scheduling Architecture

Gerhard Fohler, Tomas Lennvall, and Radu Dobrin

Departement of Computer Science and Engineering
Mälardalen University, Sweden
{gerhard.fohler,tomas.lennvall,radu.dobrin}@mdh.se

Abstract. Functionality for various services of scheduling algorithms is typically provided as extensions to a basic paradigm, intertwined in the kernel architecture. Thus, scheduling services come in packages around single paradigms, fixed to a certain methodology and kernel architecture. Temporal constraints of applications are addressed by a combination of scheduler and system architecture. Consequently, changing system architecture results in a complete rescheduling of all tasks, calling for a new cycle of analysis and testing from scratch, although a schedule meeting all temporal constraints already existed.

We propose a component based architecture for schedule reuse. Instead of tying temporal constraints, scheduler, and system architecture together, we provide methods which allow for the reuse of existing schedules on various system architectures. In particular, we show how a schedule developed for table driven, dynamic or static priority paradigm can be reused in the other schemes.

We address an architecture to disentangle actual scheduling from dispatching and other kernel routines with a small interface, suited for a variety of scheduling schemes as components. ...

1 Introduction

Historically, the choice of scheduling paradigm has been a central design decision when building real-time systems. Systems were typically custom design for particular application, choosing the type of system architecture and scheduling paradigm to best suit application demands was acceptable. As real-time systems are becoming increasingly general (real-time) purpose, such limiting choices are no longer acceptable, as a variety of applications with diverse demands have to be handled in an efficient way.

The same application may be required to execute on a different system than originally conceived: a complete redesign, as is often necessary when platforms or technologies change, including changes of scheduling paradigm, is a costly process, in particular when trusted and proven applications have to undergo the entire testing and maturing process from scratch.

Furthermore, scheduling algorithms have been typically developed around central paradigms, such as earliest deadline first (EDF)[15], fixed priority scheduling (FPS)[15], or off-line schedule construction. Additional functionality, such as

R. de Lemos et al. (Eds.): Architecting Dependable Systems, LNCS 2677, pp. 110–125, 2003.

aperiodic task handling, guarantees, etc., is typically provided as extensions to a basic algorithm. Over time, scheduling packages evolved, providing sets of functionality centered around a certain scheduling methodology.

EDF or fixed priority scheduling (FPS), for example, are chosen for simple dispatching and flexibility. Adding constraints, however, increases scheduling overhead or requires new, specific schedulability tests which may have to be developed yet.

Off-line scheduling methods can accommodate many specific constraints as time is available even for sophisticated methods. They can expand the range of constraints handled by adding functions, e.g., checks in search algorithms. All this, however, comes at the expense of limited runtime flexibility, in particular the inability to handle activities with parameters not completely known beforehand, such as aperiodic and sporadic tasks.

A similar approach dominates operating system functionality: implementation of the actual real-time scheduling algorithm, i.e., take the decisions which task to execute at which times to ensure deadlines are met, are intertwined with kernel routines such as task switching, dispatching, and bookkeeping to form a scheduling/dispatching package. Additional real-time scheduling functionality is added by including or "patching" this module. Replacement or addition of only parts is a tedious, error prone process.

Given this scheduling centric approach, a designer given an application composed of mixed tasks and constraints has to choose which constraints to focus on in the selection of scheduling algorithm; other constraints have to be accommodated as good as possible. Along with the choice of algorithm, operating system modules are chosen early in the design process.

A designer using a scheduling driven approach, given an application composed of mixed tasks and constraints, faces the choice of which constraints to focus on, i.e., those directly supported by the scheduling algorithm efficiently, and which to try to fit into the scheduler assumptions, i.e., handled only inefficiently, or not at all. Along with the choice of algorithm, operating system modules are selected early on in the design process.

We propose the use of scheduling components to reuse existing scheduling schemes and provide for easy replacement at the operating system level. We identify a "temporal interface" to express temporal behavior of an application and show its use in the transformation between scheduling schemes. We present an architecture to disentangle actual real-time scheduling from dispatching and other kernel routines with a small interface, suited for a variety of scheduling schemes as plug-ins.

The rest of the paper is organized as follows: in section 2 we introduce scheduling centric design and three fundamental real-time scheduling schemes. In section 3 we present issues of schedule reuse from the design and analysis perspective. In section 4 we introduce the real-time scheduling component and discuss a number of practical issues in section 5. Section 6 concludes the paper.

2   Scheduling vs. Application Centric Design

In this section, we discuss the consequences of scheduling centric design and briefly introduce three fundamental real-time scheduling schemes.

2.1   Scheduling Centric Design

Early real-time system design focused on approaches, in which a single application exhibiting simple temporal constraints was controlled by a dedicated, custom built real-time computing system. As input/output management and scheduling were the main operating system services, the selection of scheduler was a central design decision. The temporal demands of applications such as simple control loops suited directly simple, period/deadline type of temporal constraints, which could be used by the scheduler directly. Thus, such monolithic, scheduler centric approaches were appropriate.

As both applications and operating systems gained in complexity such approaches become tedious and costly: temporal demands do no longer fit directly into schedulers, but design needs to decompose applications into tasks and transform temporal application demands to derive timing constraints individually. Various design choices influence temporal feasibility (schedulability) testing, introducing an iterative process. As constraints handled by schedulers no longer match those of applications directly, artifacts are introduced to suit the scheduler: the design process is determined by the choice of scheduler and the types of constraints it handles.

From the operating system perspective, monolithic approaches involve close coupling of scheduler and operating system: implementation of the actual real-time scheduling algorithm, i.e., take the decisions which task to execute at which times to ensure deadlines are met, are an integral part of the kernel routines such as task switching, dispatching, and bookkeeping to form scheduling/dispatching module. As costly custom designs are replaced with more general purpose (real-time) operating systems, changes to schedulers or even their replacement is hindered by scheduler and kernel being closely intertwined. Usually, changing scheduler results in redesign of system and application.

Consequently, design process become *scheduler centric* (figure 1), as the choice of scheduling paradigm and algorithm determine both the design process with its decomposition and refinement of temporal constraints, as well as choice of operating system.

Rather, system design should focus on an application and its demand, taking system and scheduler specific decisions as late as possible. In an *application centric* approach (figure 2), temporal characteristics of an application are identified first and then decomposed into a temporal representation without consideration for the scheduling paradigm used. An example for such an intermediate representation is proposed here, *target windows*. These represent the temporal demands of an application by constraints on task executions, as opposed to scheduler specific constraints. Design and in particular decomposition and derivation of temporal constraints will not be biased by a particular scheduling scheme. By providing

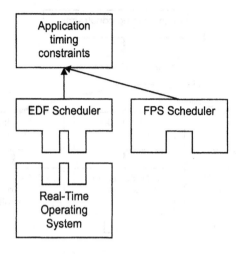

Fig. 1. Scheduler Centric Design

techniques to transform target windows into constraints and attributes suitable to a number of scheduling algorithms, temporal application demands can be met by each of these algorithms, enabling not only late scheduler selection, but also reuse of existing schedules. Furthermore, by disentangling, kernel and scheduler, the monolithic operating system approach can be replaced by a component architecture: the actual routines to perform scheduler specific functions, such as priority handling are separated from kernel activities such as dispatching.

Here we specifically propose a design approach addressing three fundamental scheduling schemes, *fixed priority based (FPS)*, *dynamic priority based (EDF)*, and off-line scheduled *table-driven (TD)*. First, an off-line scheduler transforms temporal application demands into target windows. We provide transformation techniques to transform target windows into task constraints and attributes for FPS and EDF. On the operating system side, we present an based architecture for scheduling components, which can be replaced to handle diverse scheduling algorithms.

2.2   Fundamental Real-Time Scheduling Paradigms

In real-time systems there are two major scheduling strategies: off-line and on-line scheduling. On-line scheduling is priority based and is additionally divided in fixed priority scheduling (FPS) and dynamic priority scheduling, e.g., earliest deadline first (EDF). In this section we present a brief introduction to each of them.

Off-Line Scheduling. The off-line, table-driven, scheduler allocates tasks to the processors and resolves complex constraints by determining windows for tasks to execute in, and sequences, usually stored in scheduling tables. At run-time, a simple dispatcher selects which task to execute from the scheduling tables,

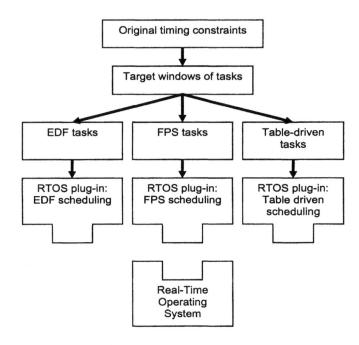

Fig. 2. Application Centric Design

ensuring tasks execute within the windows and thus meet their constraints. For off-line scheduled task, typically, the runtime dispatcher is invoked at regular time intervals, *slots*, and performs table lookup for task selection. The off-line scheduler assigns absolute points in time for the execution of all tasks.

Off-line scheduling for time-triggered systems provides determinism, as all times for task executions are determined and known in advance. In addition, complex constraints can be solved off-line, such as distribution, end-to-end deadlines, precedence, jitter, or instance separation. However, as all actions have to be planned before startup, run-time flexibility is lacking. While the times for temporal constraints have to be kept, e.g., a task cannot execute after its deadline, order constraints are relative, i.e., tasks can execute earlier provided the execution order of the schedule is maintained. The off-line schedule, however, prevents tasks from executing at a different time, even if resources become available earlier, e.g., by early termination of a task, i.e., the schedule is over constrained.

Fixed Priority Scheduling (FPS). FPS has been widely studied and used in a number of applications, mostly due its simple run-time scheduling, small overhead, and good flexibility for tasks with incompletely known attributes. Modifications to the basic scheme to handle semaphores [20], aperiodic tasks [21], static [23] and dynamic [17] offsets, and precedence constraints [10], have been presented. Temporal analysis of FPS algorithms focuses on providing guarantees that all instances of tasks will finish before their deadlines. The actual start and completion times of execution of tasks, however, are generally not known and depend largely on run-time events, compromising predictability.

The tasks to be scheduled by FPS policy can be either periodic or non-periodic. The periodic tasks are characterized by periods, offsets, deadlines, and same priorities for all invocations of the same task. Non-periodic tasks can be either aperiodic or sporadic. While the aperiodic tasks attributes are unknown, i.e., arrival time and deadline, sporadic tasks have minimum inter-arrival times, i.e., the time interval in which at most one task instance can be released.

A real time system running according to the fixed priority scheduling strategy provides for flexible task executions since the scheduling decision, i.e., the choice of which task to execute at each time point is made at run-time. Additionally, FPS has the ability to handle on-line events with incompletely known attributes, such as aperiodic and sporadic events. However, FPS is limited with respect to the ability to handle multiple complex constraints, such as jitter, end-to-end deadlines or instance separation. For example, additional tasks or constraints added to an existing fixed priority based system require new schedulability tests which may not have been developed yet, or may find the system unschedulable in the new configuration.

Dynamic Priority Scheduling. In dynamic priority scheduling, e.g., earliest dead-line first (EDF), the priorities of tasks change dynamically during runtime. As for FPS, EDF has a fairly simple run-time mechanism, the tasks must be executed in earliest absolute deadline order, and EDF also provides good flexibility to tasks whose attributes are not completely known.

Additions to the basic EDF algorithm to efficiently handle aperiodic tasks by using server mechanisms have been presented in [22], and in [1]. Normal EDF does not behave well if there is overload in the systems, but in [3] the authors extend EDF, called Robust EDF (RED), to handle overload in a predictable way.

The schedulability analysis for the EDF algorithm is very simple compared to the FPS schedulability test. If the total task utilization is kept under 100% a simple test is sufficient to determine if the task set is schedulable or not. Compared to FPS where the situation becomes more complex if the task set has a high utilization an exact analysis is needed.

Tasks that are scheduled by EDF are similar to the FPS tasks, as they can be periodic or non-periodic (aperiodic or sporadic). The difference is that EDF tasks do not have a fixed priority attribute, the priority is dynamically derived from the absolute deadline.

3   Schedule Reuse

In this section, we discuss issues of schedule reuse from the design and analysis perspective. We introduce target windows as temporal interface between temporal demands of an application and actual algorithms and present methods to transform target windows into tasks attributes and constraints suitable for fixed priority and dynamic priority based scheduling.

3.1   Temporal Interface

For a set of tasks with complex constraints, the ideal scenario would be to have a set of methods that would map the constraints directly into attributes for all scheduling strategies, i.e., off-line, EDF and FPS. However, different scheduling strategies have different abilities to handle complex constraints. Off-line scheduling, for example, can solve more complex constraints then FPS or EDF, while mapping complex constraints directly into FPS attributes may not be possible or NP-hard.

A way to reduce the complexity of the attribute assignment problem is to derive a common temporal interface between the original complex constraints and the different scheduling strategies. The basic idea is to derive temporal windows, i.e., *target windows*, for each task, representing the time intervals in which the tasks have to execute and complete, regardless from the scheduling algorithm, in order to ensure the original timing constraints. Then, by analyzing the overlapping between the target windows, attributes specific for each scheduling strategy are derived, i.e., priorities and offsets for FPS or deadlines for EDF. While guaranteeing the original constraints when scheduling the tasks by the different scheduling algorithms, the approach leads to an suboptimal solution in terms of reduced flexibility, as tasks are constrained to execute within reduced time intervals.

By selectively adjusting the target windows for each task, a strict execution behavior of selected tasks can be guaranteed, while flexibility is provided for the rest. Thus, more flexibility can be exploited while maintaining the constraints resolved by the off-line schedule.

Selectively Reduced Runtime Flexibility. While desirable in general, additional flexibility may be harmful for some tasks, e.g., those sampling and actuating in a control system. For such tasks, the deterministic execution provided by the off-line schedule has to be pertained.

To do so, joining of target windows can be prevented, or the length of some windows can be reduced selectively to keep the strict execution behavior of selected tasks, while providing flexibility for the rest. Thus, the approach allows the amount of run-time flexibility of a task to be set off-line in a predictable way.

3.2   Transforming Off-Line Schedules to Attributes for Dynamic Priority Scheduling

The goal is to transform the target windows into independent EDF tasks with start times, deadline pairs. Our transformation method is based on the preparations for on-line scheduling in slot shifting, as described in [7].

The transformation method should be flexible to include new types of constraints, to accommodate application specific demands and engineering requirements. A number of general methods for the specification and satisfaction of constraints can be applied for real-time tasks, e.g., [12]. Runtime scheduling has to ensure that tasks execute according to their constraints, even in the presence of additional tasks or overload situations.

We propose to use the off-line transformation and on-line guarantee of complex constraints of the slot-shifting method [7]. Due to space limitations, we cannot give a full description here, but confine to salient features relevant to our new algorithms. More detailed descriptions can be found in [6], [7], [11]. It uses standard off-line schedulers, e.g., [18], [6] to create schedules which are then analyzed to define start-times and deadlines of tasks.

First, the off-line scheduler creates scheduling tables for the selected periodic tasks with complex constraints. It allocates tasks to nodes and resolves complex constraints by constructing sequences of task executions. The resulting off-line schedule is one feasible, likely suboptimal solution. These sequences consist of subsets of the original task set separated by allocation. Each task in a sequence is limited by either sending or receiving of inter-node messages, predecessor or successor within the sequence, or limits set by the off-line scheduler. Start times and deadline are set directly to the times of inter-node messages or off-line scheduler limits, or calculated recursively for tasks constrained only within sequences. A more detailed description can be found in [7]. The final result is a set of independent tasks on single nodes, with start-times and deadlines, which can be scheduled by EDF at run-time. The resulting feasible schedules represent the original complex constraints.

3.3   Transforming Off-Line Schedules to Attributes for Fixed Priority Scheduling

The goal of the transformation is to derive FPS attributes for a set of tasks with complex constraints such that the FPS tasks at run time will execute feasibly while fulfilling the original constraints. To do so, target windows are derived for each instance of each task. Then, by analyzing the target windows, attributes for FPS have to be assigned to the tasks such that their run-time execution, when scheduled by FPS will reenact the off-line schedule and, thus, fulfill the original constraints. However, FPS cannot resolve all types of constraints with the same priorities for all task instances directly. The constraints may require different task sequences for instances of the same tasks, as, e.g., by earliest deadline first, leading to inconsistent attributes (i.e., priorities) for different instances of the same task. We solve this issue by splitting the task with the inconsistent attributes into a number of new periodic tasks, *artifacts* [5, 4], each of them with fixed attributes suitable for FPS. The instances of the new tasks comprise all instances of the original task. Since a priority assignment conflict involves more than one task, there is typically the choice of which task to split. A key issue is the number of new created artifacts needed to achieve consistent task attributes suitable for fixed priority scheduling. Depending on which task instances are first transformed into artifacts, when performing the attribute assignment, the final number of tasks with fixed consistent attributes for FPS may vary. Our goal is to find the splits which yield the smallest number of FP tasks.

Integer Linear Programming (ILP). In order to find a feasible priority assignment and, at the same time, to minimize the number of eventually new created artifacts, the overlapping between the different target windows are analyzed. Then, *sequences of execution*, representing the order of execution of the tasks to fulfill precedence constraints, are derived within the time intervals delimited by the starts and ends of the target windows. The sequences of execution are transformed directly into priority inequalities that must hold between the original task instances such that the original constraints are fulfilled at run time when scheduling the tasks by FPS. The priority inequalities will serve as constraints to an integer linear programming solver with a goal function that will yield a feasible priority ordering for a minimum number of tasks suitable for FPS. The flexibility of the ILP solver allows for simple inclusion of other criteria via goal functions.

Periods and Offsets. Since the priorities of the FPS tasks have been assigned by the ILP-solver, we can now focus on the assignment of periods and offsets. At this point we have a set of tasks with priorities produced by the LP-solver, consisting of a subset of the original task-set, and a set of artifact tasks. Based on the information provided by the LP-solver, periods and offsets are assigned to each task, in order to ensure the run time execution within their respective target windows. The artifact tasks will be assigned periods equal to the last common multiple (LCM) of the task periods, and offsets equal to the earliest start time of the original task instances, to guarantee the run-time execution within the original target windows.

By using an ILP solver for the derivation of priorities, additional demands such as reducing number of preemptions levels can be added by inclusion in the goal function.

The method does not introduce artifacts or reduce flexibility unless required by constraints: a set of FPS tasks, scheduled off-line according to FPS and transformed by the method, will execute in the same way as the original FPS tasks.

In same cases, additional splits may be performed, due to violation of the periodicity in the off-line schedule, which gives different offsets for different instances of the same task. By minimizing the number of artifact tasks, the method minimizes the number of offsets in the system as well, since the offsets are not changed unless tasks have to split.

4   Real-Time Scheduling Component in Operating Systems

In this section we describe the real-time scheduling component we propose to increase the flexibility for the designer. The purpose of the component is to schedule tasks that are part of a real-time application. Figure 3 shows how the component interacts with the system, i.e., the operating system and the application (consisting of tasks).

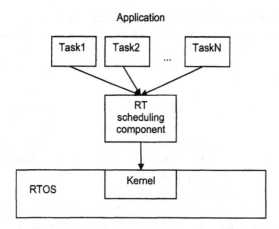

Fig. 3. Component and System Interaction

We have based our design on previous work [14] where we define and describe a minimum interface needed for a plug-in scheduling component. The scheduling component is designed to support different scheduling algorithms, such as fixed priority, dynamic priority, or table driven scheduling.

4.1 Component Architecture

The proposed architecture consists of a scheduling component that interacts with the tasks in an application. The scheduling component consists of four subcomponents, *the plug-in scheduler*, the *dispatcher*, the *execution sequence table*, and the *wake-up calendar* as shown in the figure 4.

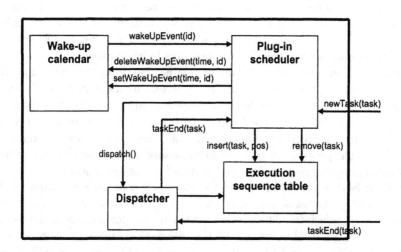

Fig. 4. Internal Component Architecture

Component Interface. The purpose of the interface to the scheduling component is to be as small and intuitive as possible so that it does not incur a big overhead when writing real-time applications that uses this scheduling component. The interface consists of only two operations that both deal with the life-cycle of a task:

new Task() is used when new tasks are created, *new Task* in turn redirects the call to the *plug-in scheduler* subcomponent. The *plug-in scheduler* executes an acceptance test on the new task to see if it schedulable or not, depending on the result (yes or no) further actions are taken respective to the algorithm implemented in the subcomponent.

taskEnd() is used to indicate that a task has finished its execution and the call is redirected to the *dispatcher* subcomponent. The *dispatcher* sends an event to the *plug-in scheduler* that in turn will remove the finished task from the *execution sequence table*.

Subcomponents. As detailed in figure 4 there are four subcomponents in the scheduling component, each of them is detailed here. The subcomponents also communicate through interfaces, thus making it possible to replace one subcomponent without affecting any of the other subcomponents. This gives the system designer a wider choice of which configuration to use, and to tune it more easily to the application that will run.

Plug-In Scheduler. The *plug-in scheduler* encapsulates a specific scheduling algorithm behind a common interface. This makes the rest of the scheduling component decoupled from the scheduling and it also makes it possible to change the other subcomponents without affecting the *plug-in scheduler*.

The *plug-in scheduler* contains the handles to all tasks that it schedules at the moment and it inserts tasks into the *dispatcher* when they are ready to execute. The interface to the *plug-in scheduler* is; *new Task()* which handles the arrival of a new task, this function executes a guarantee test to see if the task can be executed or not. *wakeUpEvent()* is used by the *wake-up calendar* to activate the *plug-in scheduler* at a certain point in time. *taskEnd()* is used by the *dispatcher* to signal that a task has finished execution.

Dispatcher. The *dispatcher* is responsible for handling the execution of the tasks, only one task can be executing at one moment in time. To get the task to execute the dispatcher first suspends any currently executing tasks, then it gets the next task to execute from the *execution sequence table*, and finally it activates the new task. The *dispatcher* is also responsible for notifying the *plug-in scheduler* of *taskFinished()* events so that it can do the bookkeeping associated with the ending of a tasks execution.

Execution Sequence Table. The *execution sequence table* contains all /linebreak the ready tasks, sorted in the order determined by the algorithm in the *plug-in scheduler*. The *plug-in scheduler* component has exclusive modification rights to this table, and the interface is; *insert()* to insert a task into the table at a certain position, and *remove()* to remove a task from the table.

Wake-Up Calendar. The *wake-up calendar* contains a set of timers needed
by the *plug-in scheduler*, this might be deadline timers, to catch deadline
misses, reactivation points for the *plug-in scheduler* and so on. The interface
for the *wake-up calendar* is; *setWakeUpPoint()* used to set a wake-up point
for the *plug-in scheduler* and *deleteWakeUpPoint()* which is used to remove
wake-up points. To handle multiple wake-up points each is associated with
an unique id, which enables the *plug-in scheduler* to recognize the specific
event.

4.2   Component Diversity and Applicability

The scheduling component was designed with diversity and applicability in mind,
as we wanted the possibility of using any scheduling algorithm. The different
behavior of scheduling paradigms are hidden behind the common scheduling
component interface.

We will discuss how this architecture would be applied to three different
scheduling paradigms, and we also detail the behavior of the components for the
different paradigms.

Earliest Deadline Scheduling Component. This component implements
the Earliest Deadline First (EDF) algorithm. EDF tasks are characterized by
start times, worst case execution times (WCET), and deadlines. Task can either
be periodic (requiring an extra period parameter) or aperiodic (requiring no
extra parameter).

When the system starts the tasks executing will call the component using
newTask(). The first thing that happens is that the *plug-in scheduler* suspends
all tasks. Then all the "arrived" tasks are subject to an acceptance test, and if
accepted they are inserted into the *execution sequence table* and sorted according
to the EDF algorithm. But before inserting accepted tasks into the table, the
plug-in sets a wake-up event corresponding to the deadlines of the tasks in the
wake-up calendar. This is done for all arriving and accepted tasks to be able to
cope with possible deadline misses.

After this, the *plug-in scheduler* is suspended and the *dispatcher* is activated.
The dispatcher does its job and suspends. If no new tasks arrive the currently
executing task will execute until it finishes when it calls the component using *taskEnd()*. This activates the *dispatcher* which in turn activates the *plug-in
scheduler*. The *plug-in scheduler* removes the task from the *execution sequence
table* and the it activates the *dispatcher* again. Depending on if the task is periodic or aperiodic it is treated differently, periodic tasks are stored internally in a
waiting queue until its activated again the next period. Then, the task is again
inserted into the correct position (according to EDF) in the *execution sequence
table*. Aperiodic tasks are simply removed since a reactivation of the task will use
the *newTask()* interface and it requires a new acceptance test to be executed.

If a "new" task is activated when the system is running, it will behave as the
other tasks and call the component. The component executes the acceptance test

(after suspending the task) and if the task is accepted it will be inserted into the *execution sequence table*. After this, the *dispatcher* is activated (as usual) and it checks if the running task is the same as the first one in the *execution sequence table*. If they are not the same, the running task is suspended (preempted), the first task in the table is activated, and the *dispatcher* suspends. Otherwise the *dispatcher* just suspends.

If a deadline miss is detected the *plug-in scheduler* will remove the task from the *execution sequence table* then the dispatcher is activated. The dispatcher will notice that the running task is not the first one in the table, suspend it, and then activate next task.

Fixed Priority Scheduling Component. This component implements Fixed Priority Scheduling (FPS), where tasks have start time, WCET, priority, and deadline parameters. As for EDF tasks can be periodic or aperiodic and have a period parameter or not. This component behaves similar to the EDF component during runtime, but it differs in how the *execution sequence table* is sorted and how tasks are guaranteed in the acceptance test.

When the system starts, the component does the same thing as the EDF component; suspend all new tasks and executes the acceptance test for these tasks. The accepted tasks are inserted into the *execution sequence table*, after all deadline wake-up events are set.

The runtime behavior is like the EDF component; the *plug-in scheduler* activates the *dispatcher* and suspends, the dispatcher activates the first task and suspends. New tasks are subject to the acceptance test, deadline wake-up events are set for accepted tasks, then they are inserted into the *execution sequence table*. Preemption might occur if the new task ends up first in the table, otherwise the running task will continue to execute. Tasks that have finished their execution are treated like in the EDF component, and deadline misses are also treated in the same manner.

Table-Driven Scheduling Component. A system using off-line generated (table-driven) [18] schedules usually has more stringent task requirements than tasks used in on-line scheduled systems. In table-driven schedules tasks has fixed start and finishing times (stored in a table). This means that not all the tasks (possibly no one) will be ready to execute at the start of the systems, instead they are activated according to the table. For table-driven systems that are purely off-line scheduled, there is no dynamic activity, e.g., no new tasks arrive during the execution of the system. This makes the runtime behavior of a table-driven scheduler easier than both the EDF and FPS schedulers.

Before the start of the system the *plug-in scheduler* needs to do some preparations. Internally the plug-in stores the table created by the off-line scheduler, containing the start and finishing times of all the tasks.

When the system starts all tasks in the internal table are suspended and only the tasks with a starting time equal to the current time is inserted into the *execution sequence table*. As with EDF and FPS, plug-in wake-up events are also set for the finishing times of the tasks in the internal table. The plug-in also sets a wake-up event (one at a time) for every time slot as in the MARS system [13]. Then the plug-in activates the *dispatcher* and suspends itself. The *dispatcher* checks if there are any tasks in the *execution sequence table* and activates the first task if any, and then it suspends. The plug-in will be activated every slot and will take the same actions every time, it also wakes up if tasks misses deadlines. If a task finishes execution in a timely manner it is removed from the *execution sequence table* and inserted when it's start time corresponds to the current time again.

5   Practical Issues

We envision our approach to be applied in dedicated real-time systems, providing for modifications to the kernel, such as small, embedded systems. Then, the effort to disentangle scheduler from kernel is similar to that of implementing the scheduler itself.

As mentioned before, the efforts to introduce our approach in operating systems can range from including a middle-ware layer to changes in run-time scheduler and interface.

The middle-ware approach necessary for general purpose operating systems, such as Windows NT, will require efforts on one hand to provide for some real-time behavior, e.g., [9] [16], and for the middle-ware itself.

Some dedicated real-time operating systems such as Shark [8] are designed with exchanging scheduling modules in mind. Others, such as Marte [19], provides application specific scheduling, i.e., applications can provide schedulers themselves. In both types of systems, our approach will not be executed directly on the operating system kernel, but on-top, potentially in coexistence with others. More general real-time systems, such as RT Linux [2] demand a broader adaptation of our approach for implementation. While not a full fledged middle-ware layer, our approach does not go into the core directly.

The amount of run-time overhead of the propose approach depends on the type of system it is implemented on: *general purpose operating systems* requires a middle-ware layer which is located between the applications and the actual kernel primitives. Consequently, the overhead introduced can be high, and issues such as granularity have to be given consideration.

By changing the scheduler in *dedicated real-time operating systems* following our approach, the introduction of the new API will introduce only small overheads. Instead of entangled, potentially optimized calls, invocations and data access go via the API.

6   Summary

We have addressed issues in the design of real-time system, in particular related to the impact of scheduling. Scheduling centric approaches, in which the choice of scheduling paradigm is a central architectural decision taken early in the design process, pose limitations as they bias the derivation of temporal constraints and intertwine scheduling and operating system functions. Consequently, changing scheduling paradigm or operating system usually results in costly redesign of applications.

Application centric design, as proposed here, focusing on application demands first. Instead of tailoring the decomposition and derivation of timing constraints to suit a particular scheduling paradigm, this approach expresses such constraints in a scheduler independent, intermediate way. Transformation techniques then provide scheduler specific task constraints and attributes. A runtime scheduling component approach on the operating system side disentangles kernel activities and scheduling functions. Depending on the scheduling scheme used, the appropriate component interacts with the operating system via a small interface and can be replaced easily.

Consequently, the choice of scheduling paradigm in the proposed application centric approach can be taken late in the design process, providing for scheduling independent design and replacement and reuse of schedulers for applications and operating systems.

Specifically, we introduced target windows to represent intermediate temporal information, which are determined by an off-line scheduler. We presented methods to transform target windows into task attributes and constraints suitable for fixed priority, dynamic priority based, and table driven scheduling. On the operating system side, we presented a small interface and minimum kernel functionality to support runtime scheduling components for these scheduling themes. Thus, our methods allow temporal constraints expressed via target windows to be kept independent of actual scheduling component chosen.

References

1. L. Abeni and G. Buttazzo. Integrating Multimedia Applications in Hard Real-Time Systems. In *In Proceedings of International Real-Time Systems Symposium*, 1998.
2. M. Barabanov and V. Yodaiken. Introducing Real-Time Linux. *Linux Journal*, February 1997.
3. G. Buttazzo and J. Stankovic. RED: A Robust Earliest Deadline Scheduling Algorithm. In *In Proceedings of 3rd International Workshop on Responsive Computing Systems*, September 1993.
4. R. Dobrin, G. Fohler, and P. Puschner. Translating off-line schedules into task attributes for fixed priority scheduling. In *Proceedings of the 22nd IEEE Real-Time Systems Symposium*, London, UK, Dec. 2001.
5. R. Dobrin, Y. Ozedmir, and G. Fohler. Task attribute assignment of fixed priority scheduled tasks to reenact off-line schedules. In *Proceedings of the 7th IEEE Conference on Real-Time Computing Systems and Applications*, Korea, Dec. 2000.
6. G. Fohler. *Flexibility in Statically Scheduled Real-Time Systems*. PhD thesis, Wien, Österreich, April 1994.
7. G. Fohler. Joint scheduling of distributed complex periodic and hard aperiodic tasks in statically scheduled systems. In *Proceedings of the 16th Real-Time Systems Symposium*, Pisa, Italy, Dec. 1995.

8. P. Gai, L. Abeni, M. Giorgi, and G. Buttazzo. A New Kernel Approach for Modular Real-Time Systems Development. In *In Proceedings of the 13th IEEE Euromicro Conference on Real-Time Systems*, June 2001.

9. O. Gonzalez, K. Ramamritham, C. Shen, and G. Fohler. *Building Reliable Component-Based Systems*, chapter Building Real-Time Systems with Commercial-Off-The-Shelf Components, Ivica Crnkovic and Magnus Larsson (editors). Artech House Publishers, 2001.

10. M. Gonzalez Harbour and J.P. Lehoczky. Fixed Priority Scheduling of Periodic Task Sets with Varying Execution Priority. In *Proceedings of Real-Time Systems Symposium*, pages 116–128, Dec. 1991.

11. D. Isovic and G. Fohler. Handling Sporadic Tasks in Statically Scheduled Distributed Real-Time Systems. In *Proceedings of the 10th Euromicro Conference on Real-Time Systems*, June 1999.

12. F. Jahanian, R. Lee, and A. Mok. Semantics of modechart in real time logic. In *Proc. of the 21st Hawaii International Conference on Systems Sciences*, pages 479–489, Jan. 1988.

13. H. Kopetz, A. Damm, Ch. Koza, M. Mulazzani, W. Schwabl, Ch. Senft, and R. Zainlinger. Distributed Fault-Tolerant Real-Time Systems: The MARS Approach. *IEEE Micro*, February 1989.

14. T. Lennvall, G. Fohler, and B. Lindberg. Handling Aperiodic Tasks in Diverse Real-Time Systems via Plug-ins. In *International Symposium on Object-Oriented Real-Time Distributed Computing*, 2002.

15. C. L. Liu and J. W. Layland. Scheduling Algorithms for Multiprogramming in a Hard-Real-Time Environment. *Journal of the ACM*, 20(1):46–61, Jan. 1973.

16. I. Mizunuma, C. Shen, and M. Takegaki. Middleware for Distributed Industrial Real-Time Systems on ATM Networks. In *In Proceedings of International Real-Time Systems Symposium*, December 1996.

17. J.C. Palencia and M. Gonzalez Harbour. Schedulability Analysis for Tasks with Static and Dynamic Offsets. In *Proceedings of Real-Time Systems Symposium*, 1989.

18. K. Ramamritham. Allocation and scheduling of complex periodic tasks. In *International Conference on Distributed Computing Systems*, pages 108–115, 1990.

19. M. A. Rivas and M. Gonzalez Harbour. MaRTE OS: An Ada Kernel for Real-Time Embedded Applications. In *In International Conference on Reliable Software Technologies - Ada-Europe'2001*, May 2001.

20. L. Sha, R. Rajkumar, and J.P. Lehoczky. Task Period Selection and Schedulability in Real-Time Systems. *IEEE Transactions on Computer*, 39(9):1175–1185, Sept 1990.

21. B. Sprunt, L. Sha, and J.P. Lehoczky. Aperiodic Task Scheduling for Hard Real-Time Tasks. *The Journal of Real-Time Systems*, 1989.

22. M. Spuri and G.C. Buttazzo. Scheduling Aperiodic Tasks in Dynamic Priority Systems. *The Journal of Real-Time Systems*, March 1996.

23. K. Tindell. Adding Time Offsets to Schedulability Analysis. Technical report, Departament of Computer Science, University of York, 1994.

Fault Tolerance in Software Architectures

A Fault-Tolerant Software Architecture for Component-Based Systems

Paulo Asterio de C. Guerra[1], Cecília Mary F. Rubira[1], and Rogério de Lemos[2]

[1] Instituto de Computação
Universidade Estadual de Campinas, Brazil
{asterio,cmrubira}@ic.unicamp.br
[2] Computing Laboratory
University of Kent at Canterbury, UK
r.delemos@ukc.ac.uk

Abstract. Component-based software built from reusable software components is being used in a wide range of applications that have high dependability requirements. In order to achieve the required levels of dependability, it is necessary to incorporate into these complex systems means for coping with software faults. However, the problem is exacerbated if we consider the current trend of integrating off-the-shelf software components, from independent sources, which allow neither code inspection nor changes. To leverage the dependability properties of these systems, we need solutions at the architectural level that are able to guide the structuring of unreliable components into a fault-tolerant architecture. In this paper, we present an approach for structuring fault-tolerant component-based systems based on the C2 architectural style.

1 Introduction

Modern computer systems are based on the integration of numerous existing software components that are developed by independent sources [6]. The source code and internal design of these components are generally not available to the organization using the component. Moreover, a component's configuration, environment, and dependencies can be changed at integration or deployment time. Thus, many of the challenges of using component-based software in critical applications cannot be effectively addressed via traditional software assurance technologies [29]. This means that new and improved approaches have to be sought in order to obtain trustworthy systems out of unreliable components that are not built under the control of the system developers. In this scenario, fault tolerance, which is associated with the ability of a system to deliver services according with its specification in spite the presence of faults [13], is of paramount importance as a means to dependability.

Our aim is to structure, at the architecture level, fault-tolerant component-based systems that use off-the-shelf components. For that, we define an idealised architectural component with structure and behaviour equivalent to the idealised fault-tolerant component concept [1]. This concept provides a means of system structuring

R. de Lemos et al. (Eds.): Architecting Dependable Systems, LNCS 2677, pp. 129-149, 2003.

which makes it easy to identify *what* parts of a system have *what* responsibilities for trying to cope with *which* sorts of fault. A system is viewed as a set of components interacting under the control of a design. Components receive requests for service and produce responses. When a component cannot satisfy a request for service, it will return an exception. An idealised fault-tolerant component should in general provide both normal and abnormal (i.e. exception) responses in the interface between interacting components, in a framework that minimizes the impact of these provisions on system complexity [19]. Moreover, this idealised architectural component can be used as a building block for a system of design patterns that implement the idealised fault-tolerant component for concurrent distributed systems [5].

For representing software systems at the architectural level, we have chosen the C2 architectural style for its ability to incorporate heterogeneous off-the-shelf components [17]. However, this ability of combining existing components is achieved through rules on topology and communication between the components that complicate the incorporation of fault tolerance mechanisms into C2 software architectures. For example, basic communication mode between C2 components is based on asynchronous messages broadcasted by connectors, which causes difficulties for both error detection and fault containment[7][11].

Research into describing software architectures with respect to their dependability properties has gained attention recently [20][25][26]. Nonetheless, rigorous specification of exception handling models and of exception propagation at the architecture level remains an open issue [12]. The work on exception handling has focused on *configuration exceptions*, which are exceptional events that have to be handled at the configuration level of software architectures [12]. In terms of software fault tolerance, the traditional principles used for obtaining software diversity have also been employed in the reliable evolution of software systems, specifically, the upgrading of software components. The *Hercules framework* [8] employs concepts associated with *recovery blocks* [19]. The notion of *multi-versioning connectors* (MVC) [18], in the context of C2 architectures, is derived from concepts associated with *N-version programming* [3].

The architectural solution presented in this paper is distinct from the works referred above since its focus is on more fundamental structuring concepts, to be applied in a broader class of exceptional conditions, not only configuration exceptions, and for structuring specialized fault tolerance mechanisms, including those for reliable upgrade. The rest of this paper is structured as follows. Section 2 gives a brief overview of fault tolerance and the C2 architectural style. Section 3 describes the proposed architectural solution of the idealised component, which is then formalised in Section 4. An illustrative case study is presented in Section 5 to demonstrate the feasibility of the proposed approach. Final conclusions are given in Section 6.

2   Background

2.1   Fault Tolerance

The causal relationship between the dependability impairments, that is, faults, errors and failures, is essential to characterise the major activities associated with fault tolerance [13]. A *fault* is the adjudged or hypothesized cause of an error. An *error* is the part of the system state that is liable to lead to a subsequent failure. A *failure* occurs when a system service deviates from the behaviour expected by the user. The basic strategy to achieve fault tolerance in a system can be divided into two steps [14]. The first step, called *error processing*, is concerned with the system internal state, aiming to detect errors that are caused by activation of faults, diagnose the erroneous states, and recover to error free states. The second step, called *fault treatment*, is concerned with the sources of faults that may affect the system, including fault localization and fault removal.

The *idealised fault-tolerant component* is a structuring concept for the coherent provision of fault tolerance in a system. Through this concept, we can allocate fault tolerance responsibilities to the various parts of a system in an orderly fashion, and model the system recursively. Each component can itself be considered as a system on its own, which has an internal design containing further sub-components [1].

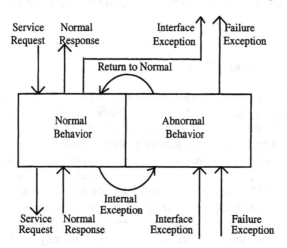

Fig. 1. Idealised fault-tolerant component

The communication between idealised fault-tolerant components is only through request/response messages (Figure 1). Upon receiving a *service request*, an idealised component will react with a *normal response* if the request is successfully processed or an *abnormal response*, otherwise. This abnormal response may be due to an invalid service request, in which case it is called an *interface exception*, or due to a failure in processing a valid request, in which case it is called a *failure exception*. The internal structure of an idealised component has two distinct parts: one that implements its *normal behaviour*, when no exceptions occur, and another that implements its *abnormal behaviour*, which deals with the exceptional conditions. This separation of concerns, applied recursively to components, subsystems and the overall system, greatly simplifies the structuring of fault tolerance systems, allowing their complexity to be manageable. An *internal exception* is associated with an error detected within the n*ormal behaviour* part of a component, switching the control flow of the idealised component to its *abnormal behaviour* part. This error may be recovered, allowing the operation to be completed successfully *(return to normal)* or, alternatively, an *external exception* is propagated to the caller component. An idealised component should provide appropriate handlers for all kinds of exceptions it may raise internally or may receive from a server component.

To draw a more complete view of an idealised fault-tolerant component we should consider also a few additional messages, not explicitly represented in Fig. 1. During error recovery, the *abnormal behaviour* part may also send service requests to other components and receive the corresponding responses, which may be either normal responses or new external exceptions. Moreover, both *normal behaviour* and *abnormal behaviour* parts must have access to the component internal state, either by means of shared memory or additional internal request / response messages, to allow error recovery by the *abnormal behaviour* part.

The present work is based on the following assumptions: (i) the synchronicity between requests and responses between components; and (ii) a single thread of control for each component, not allowing concurrent requests to be processed by the same component.

2.2   The C2 Architectural Style

A software architecture is an abstract representation of a software system described as a set of connected components in a specific configuration, which ignores implementation details [22]. The basic elements of software architecture are components and connectors. By architectural style we mean a set of design rules that identify the kinds of components and connectors that may be used to compose a system or subsystem, together with local or global constraints on the way the composition is done [23].In particular, the C2 architectural style is a component-based style directed at supporting large grain reuse and flexible system composition, emphasizing weak bindings between components [27]. In this style, components of a system may be completely unaware of each other. This may be the case when one integrates various commercial off-the-shelf components (COTS), possibly with heterogeneous styles and implementation languages. The components communicate only through asynchronous messages mediated by connectors that are responsible for message routing, broadcasting and filtering. Interface and architectural mismatches are dealt with by using wrappers for encapsulating each component [9].

Both components and connectors in the C2 architectural style (Figure 2) have a *top interface* and a *bottom interface*. Systems are composed in a layered style. The *top interface* of a component may be connected to the *bottom interface* of a single connector. The *bottom interface* of a component may be connected to the *top interface* of another single connector. Each side of a connector may be connected to any number of components or connectors. When two connectors are attached to each other, it must be from the bottom of one to the top of the other. [27]

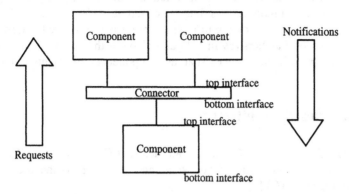

Fig. 2. C2 style basic elements

There are two types of messages in C2: *requests* and *notifications*. By convention, *requests* flow up through the system's layers and *notifications* flow down. This C2 convention is in reverse of the usual sense of "upper" and "lower" components in a client/server style, as is the case of the idealised fault-tolerant component shown in Fig. 1. In response to a request, a component may emit a notification back to the components below, through its bottom interface. Upon receiving a notification, a component may react, as if a service was requested, with the implicit invocation of one of its operations.

2.3   Software Architecture and Fault Tolerance

Dependable architectures demonstrably possess properties such as reliability, availability and security, which are achieved through fault tolerance mechanisms [26]. A fault-tolerant software architecture allows us to reason about whether a specified set of dependability properties is being satisfied, under the assumptions of a fault model. Examples of fault-tolerant software architectures can be found in [21][25][26].

The level of abstraction in which a fault-tolerant software architecture is described plays an important role in its applicability. Lower levels of abstractions simplify the instantiation of concrete configurations with the desired dependability properties but restrict the range of software systems where they may be applied. The Simplex architecture [21] and the Distributed Component Framework [30] are examples of such lower level architectures. Higher levels of abstractions, as in the CAATS approach [25], may be applied to a wider range of software systems, at the cost of greater design and implementation effort and, consequently, causing difficulties in obtaining assurances of its conformance to the fault-tolerant abstract architecture. Architecture description hierarchies [26] provides a strategy for refining a fault-tolerant architecture, to a more concrete level and down to implementation, using only verified refinement patterns which guarantee that those fault-tolerant properties are preserved.

Existing fault-tolerant software architectures also differ with respect to their underlying fault model. The simplest and most common fault model is restricted to fail-stop failures of nodes in a network, which are tolerated by means of groups of replicated software components residing in different nodes, as in [30]. Software design faults are far more complex to tolerate, requiring added redundancy through specialized exception handlers, as in [21] and [25]. In this work we are concerned mainly with design faults that may exist at the components implementation level.

3   The Proposed Architecture

The objective of this section is to define an idealised C2 component (iC2C), which should be equivalent, in terms of behaviour and structure, to the idealised fault-tolerant component (iFTC) [1].

3.1   Overall Structure of the Idealised C2 Component

The implementation of an iC2C (section 2.1) should be able to use any C2 component with minimum restrictions. It is also desirable to integrate idealised C2 components into any C2 configurations to allow the interaction of iC2Cs with other idealised and/or regular C2 components.

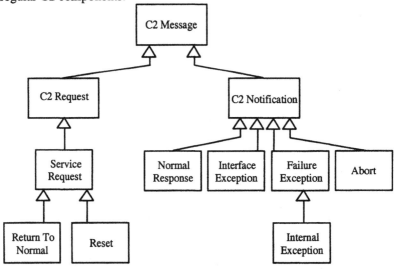

Fig. 3. Message types defined for the iC2C

The first task is to extend the C2 message type hierarchy to represent the different message types defined by the idealised fault-tolerant component concept (iFTC). Service requests and normal responses of an iFTC are directly mapped as requests and notifications in the C2 architecture, respectively. As interface and failure exceptions of an iFTC flow in the same direction as a normal response, they are considered subtypes of notifications in the C2 architecture (Figure 3).

In order to minimize the impact of fault tolerance provisions on the system complexity, we model the normal behaviour and abnormal behaviour parts of the iFTC as separated sub-components of the iC2C. This outcome leads to an overall structure for the iC2C that has two components and three connectors, as shown in Fig. 4.

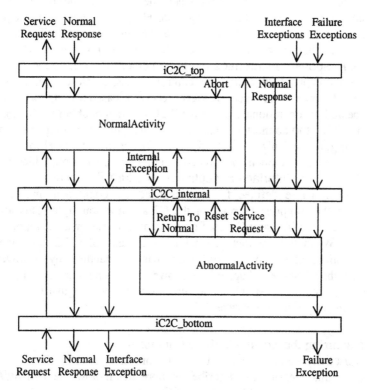

Fig. 4. Idealised C2 component (iC2C)

The NormalActivity component implements the normal behaviour, processing *service requests* from client components and sending back *normal responses*. It is also responsible for error detection during this processing, and the signalling of *interface exceptions* and *internal exceptions*. The AbnormalActivity component is responsible for error recovery, and the signalling of *failure exceptions*. For consistency, internal exceptions are mapped as a subtype of notification, and, the ReturnToNormal, flowing in the opposite direction, are mapped as a request (Figure 3). During error recovery, the AbnormalActivity component may also send service requests and receive the corresponding notifications to / from the NormalActivity component or any server components above the iC2C in the architecture.

Two additional message types that may be sent to the NormalActivity component complete the full set of messages within the iC2C: Abort notifications and Reset requests. An Abort notification terminates the NormalActivity component after an external exception is received and before the internal control flow of the iC2C is switched to the AbnormalActivity component. A Reset request switches the control flow back to the NormalActivity component, and is sent by the AbnormalActivity component when it terminates an unsuccessful recovery, after an external exception is sent to the client component.

The connectors of our iC2C shown in Fig. 4 are specialized, reusable, C2 connectors with the following roles:

(i)   The iC2C_bottom connector connects the iC2C with the lower components of a C2 configuration, and serializes the Service Requests received. Once a request is accepted, this connector queues new requests that are received until completion of the first request. When a request is completed, a notification is sent back, which may be a Normal Response, an Interface Exception or a Failure Exception.

(ii)   The iC2C_internal connector controls message flow inside the iC2C, selecting the destination of each message received based on its originator, the message type and the operational state of the iC2C (normal or abnormal state).

(iii)   The iC2C_top connector connects the iC2C with other components above it in the C2 configuration. This connector synchronizes each Service Request sent by the iC2C to a server component with its corresponding notification, which may be a Normal Response, an Interface Exception or a Failure Exception.

The overall structure defined for the idealised C2 component makes it fully compliant with the component's rules of the C2 architectural style. This allows an iC2C to be integrated into any C2 configuration and interact with components of a larger system. When this interaction establishes a chain of iC2C components the external exceptions raised by a component can be handled by a lower level component (in the C2 sense of "upper" and "lower") allowing hierarchical structuring of error recovery activities. An iC2C may also interact with a regular C2 component, either requesting or providing services.

3.1.1   Structuring the NormalActivity Component

The NormalActivity component can be built from scratch or reusing an existing component. In this section, we describe in more detail how the NormalActivity component can be implemented from existing C2 components.

As previously mentioned, the NormalActivity component is responsible for the implementation of the normal behaviour of the idealised C2 component. It is also responsible for detecting errors that may affect the normal behaviour. In the case of a NormalActivity component to be built from existing C2 components that do not have error detection capabilities, there is a need to add error detection capabilities to them. A possible architectural solution for structuring the NormalActivity component is shown in Fig. 5. The BasicNormal component is an existing C2 component implementing the services provided by the iC2C to its client components. The CollaboratingComponent is another C2 component implementing additional error detection functions that may be required by the iC2C. A pair of special-purpose connectors (normal_top and normal_bottom) wraps these two components, following the pattern of the *multi-versioning connector* (MVC) [18]. The normal_bottom coordinates the collaboration between the BasicNormal and CollaboratingComponent components, providing the NormalActivity component with capabilities for error detection. Errors are detected by checking the pre- and post-conditions, and invariants associated to each service provided by the BasicNormal component [25]. The proposed approach was inspired by the concepts of *coordination contracts* [2] and *co-operative connectors* [16].

The Normal Activity component can also interact with other components outside the scope of the iC2C. In this case, the CollaboratingComponent should be placed higher in the C2 configuration, and the normal_top connector should act as a proxy of the component in the context of the NormalActivity component.

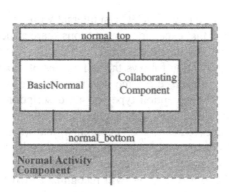

Fig. 5. A composite NormalActivity component

3.1.2   Structuring the AbnormalActivity Component

The AbnormalActivity component is responsible for both error diagnosis and error recovery. Depending on the complexity of these tasks, it may be convenient to decompose it into more specialized components for error diagnosis and error handling.

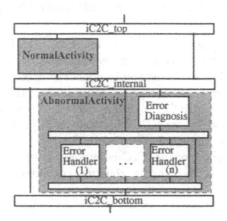

Fig. 6. Decomposition of the AbnormalActivity component

Figure 6 presents a possible architectural solution for structuring the AbnormalActivity component. In this solution, the responsibility for coordinating the exception handling is allocated to the ErrorDiagnosis component that may propagate a new exceptional notification to a specialized ErrorHandler.

3.2   Integration of the iC2C into C2 Configurations

In this section, we describe how an iC2C can interact with other C2 components in an architecture. We assume that exception notifications share a special type name, which distinguishes them from any possible normal notification. Apart from its unique type name, an exception notification follows the same rules of a normal notification, that is, "a statement of what interface routine was invoked and what its parameters and return values where". The exception type and its description are part of the return values of an exception notification, which are represented as a set of data objects [10]. A regular C2 component (rC2C) is a C2 component that: (i) does not send exception notifications, and (ii) does not recognize an exception notification received as being the signalling of an exception. An exception notification's type name and its return values are meaningless to a rC2C, that will recognize an exception as a notification sent in response to a given interface routine invoked.

These assumptions are valid for C2 component built without knowledge of the iC2C concept. We will not consider special cases, such as a C2 component capable to send a forged exception notification or built to recognize exception notifications but not behaving as an iC2C.

Next we analyse the various kinds of interaction between an iC2C and other iC2Cs or rC2Cs:

Case 1. An iC2C requesting services to another iC2C. A request can either result in a normal notification or an external (interface or failure) exception notification. In the case of an exception notification the client should handle it in a predicable way.

Case 2. An iC2C requesting services to an rC2C. The iC2C should be able to translate notifications that may be sent by the rC2C, to notify its clients about abnormal conditions, into exception notifications. The iC2C top connector should act as a domain translator of exception notifications. This includes translating notifications sent by an rC2C signalling abnormal conditions into exception notifications understood by the iC2C abnormal activity component and recognize exception notifications that can be handled by the normal activity component. The normal activity component of the iC2C is responsible for preventing and detecting errors that may be caused by any other abnormal condition not properly signalled by the rC2C.

Case 3. An rC2C requesting services to an iC2C. We have two distinct cases here: *Case 3.1. The iC2C does not send exceptional notifications.* This would be possible if an iC2C could be able to completely mask every possible exception. A request will always result in a normal (and fault-free) notification to the rC2C.

Case 3.2. The iC2C may send exceptional notifications. In this case, the iC2C may reply with a normal notification or an exception notification. The problem is that the behaviour of the rC2C cannot be predicted when the request results in an exception notification. To solve this, we may either (i) promote the rC2C to an iC2C and proceed as in case 1, or (ii) extend the fault tolerance capabilities of the iC2C in order to mask every possible exception notification sent by it and proceed as in case 3.1.

For promoting an rC2C to an iC2C, the rC2C may be wrapped into a normal activity component, which adds error detection capabilities to it (Figure 7). This normal activity component is inserted into an iC2C with a new abnormal activity component responsible for handling exceptions raised by the normal activity component or by other iC2C providing services to it.

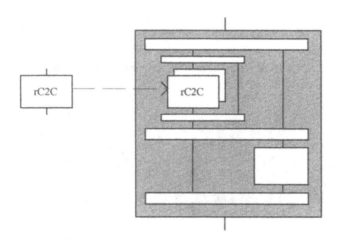

Fig. 7. Promoting an rC2C to an iC2C

The fault tolerance capabilities of an existing iC2C may be extended in two ways:

a) Wrapping the existing iC2C as the normal activity component of a new iC2C (the wrapper) and providing an abnormal activity component responsible for handling some (or all) failure exceptions of that existing iC2C[1] and / or external exceptions not handled by it (Figure 8); or

b) Adapting the bottom interface of the existing iC2C through a new iC2C (the adaptor) responsible for handling some (or all) interface and failure exceptions sent by that existing iC2C (Figure 9). The adaptor's normal activity component acts as a simple redirector, delegating all requests to the existing iC2C.

The extensions described in items (a) and (b) above produce a new interface, provided by the wrapper or adaptor, which is a specialization of the existing iC2C interface, as in a subtype relationship.

---

[1]The normal activity component may send interface exceptions and failure exceptions. It is the internal connector that classifies the failure exceptions as being "internal" or "external", depending on the port that receives the notification.

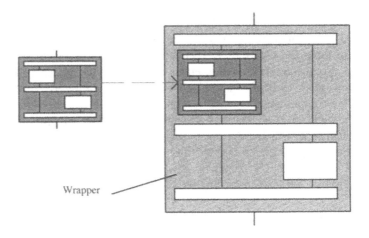

Fig. 8. Wrapping an iC2C to improve fault tolerance

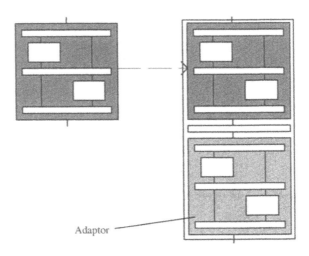

Fig. 9. Adapting an iC2C interface to improve fault tolerance

A C2 architecture (or configuration) may itself be treated as a component, allowing us to use the iC2C structure to build an "ideal C2 architecture (iC2A)". In such configuration the AbnormalActivity component of this iC2A is responsible for handling exceptions that may propagate through all levels of the architecture, including reconfiguration of the architecture (configuration exceptions) [12].

3.3   From an Ideal Component to an Ideal C2 Connector

In distributed systems, connectors may be as complex and fault-prone as components. In our proposed approach, a fault-tolerant connector should be able to detect and recover from three kinds of errors: (i) errors in the messages received from other connectors or components; (ii) errors in the communication between it and the components connected to it, and (iii) errors in its internal logic.

Figure 10 shows a C2 configuration for an idealised fault-tolerant connector, derived from the iC2C configuration (Figure 4). The TopConnector and BottomConnector are simple, more reliable, connectors, providing low-level communication services between the surrounding components and connectors. The NormalActivityConnector provides the more specialized and complex services, such as message filtering and multicasting, and implements the error detection mechanisms. The AbnormalActivityConnector implements the error recovery procedures.

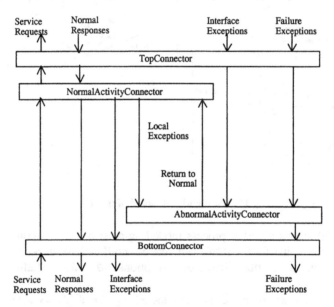

Fig. 10. The idealised C2 connector

4   Formal Representation of the iC2C

In order to demonstrate that C2 architectures can be built using iC2C, we have developed a formal model for the iC2C. Our formal is based on the UPPAAL tool [15], which allows the precise specification and verification of the iC2C protocols. The basis of the UPPAAL is the notion of timed automata extended with data variables, such as integer and Boolean variables. The automata consist of a collection of control nodes connected by edges. The control nodes of the automata are decorated by invariants that are conditions expressing constraints on the clock values. The edges of the automata are decorated with guards that express a condition to be satisfied for the edge to be taken, synchronisation actions that are performed when the edge is taken, and clock resets and assignments to integer variables.

The first model developed (Figure 11) was a high-level representation of the iC2C, consisting of three very simple automata, modelled as *processes* in UPPAAL.

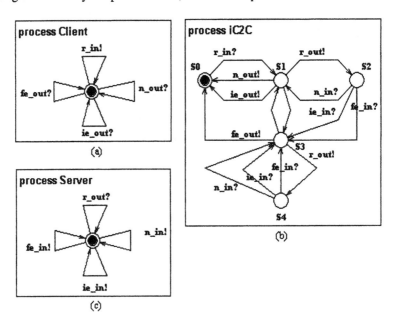

Fig.11. The high-level model of the iC2C

Figure 11(a) shows a Client process modelling a set of C2 components that send service requests (r_in) to the iC2C and receive notifications back, which may be normal notifications (n_out), interface exceptions (ie_out) or failure exceptions (fe_out);

Figure 11(b) shows an iC2C process modelling the iC2C as a whole, with 5 internal states: (i) S0 - its initial state where the iC2C is idle and ready to accept a new request (r_in); (ii) S1 - where the iC2C is processing a request with normal behaviour; (iii) S2 - where the iC2C is idle, after sending a service request (r_out) to a server component while processing with normal behaviour a service request from a client, and is waiting for a notification, which may be a normal notification (n_in), an interface exception (ie_in) or a failure exception (fe_in), (iv) S3 - where the iC2C is recovering from an exception (abnormal behaviour); and (v) S4 - where the iC2C is idle, after sending a service request (r_out) to a server component while recovering from an exception and is waiting for a notification to arrive;

Figure 11(c) shows a Server process that models a set of C2 components that accept the service requests sent by the iC2C and send the corresponding notifications back (n_in).

This high-level model of the iC2C only represents the flow of messages crossing the iC2C external boundaries. All these messages were modelled as synchronous events corresponding to a message being sent/taken by the iC2C at/from one of its external ports. The transitions from/to state S1 to/from state S3 represents, respectively, an internal exception, and the return to normal behaviour.

This high level model was further refined in two steps. An intermediate level model was created replacing the iC2C process by three separate processes representing the NormalActivity component, the AbnormalActivity component and the iC2C_top connector. At this intermediate level we abstracted the roles of the iC2C_bottom and iC2C_internal connectors, allowing the NormalActivity, AbnormalActivity and Client processes to communicate directly through synchronous messages.

Finally, a low-level model was developed that adds two new processes to model the iC2C_bottom and iC2C_internal connectors. Figure 12 shows the NormalActivity process at this level.

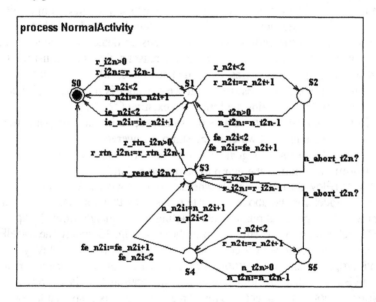

Fig.12. The low-level model for the NormalActivity component

With exclusion of the Reset and Abort control signals, all the messages within the iC2C were modelled as asynchronous events using UPPAAL variables representing message queues between two communicating elements. Sending and receiving a message in such a queue is represented by incrementing and decrementing the corresponding variable, respectively. The variable names are composed by (i) a prefix indicating the message type, which can be "r_" for requests, "n_" for notifications, "fe_" for failure exceptions, "ie_" for interface exceptions, "eie_" for external interface exceptions, and "efe_" for external failure exceptions; (ii) a suffix indicating the message sender and receiver, in the form "_x2y" where x and y can be one of the initials a, b, i, n or t for respectively the AbnormalActivity component, iC2C_bottom connector, iC2C_internal connector, NormalActivity component or iC2C_top connector; and (iii) an optional message subtype, as "rtn" (return-to-normal), "reset" or "abort".

The properties verified for this models were: (i) it never deadlocks; (ii) when the iC2C accepts a new request all its internal elements are in their initial states; (iii) while the NormalActivity component is processing a request with normal behaviour (states S1 or S2 in Fig. 12) then the AbnormalActivity component is idle (initial state); and (iv) while the AbnormalActivity component is active (not in it initial state) the NormalActivity component is not processing a request with normal behaviour.

5   Case Study

In order to illustrate the structuring concepts presented in this paper, we refer to a small example extracted from the Mine Pump Control System [24]. The basic problem is to control the amount of water that collects at the mine sump, switching on the pump when the water level rises above a certain limit and switching it off when the water has been sufficiently reduced. Two sensors detect the water level: a high water sensor and a low water sensor. For safety reasons, the pump must not be turned on when the atmosphere contains too much methane, which concentration is also monitored by a sensor. The subsystem that we consider is responsible for controlling the physical pump, and contains the following existing C2 components:

(i)   PumpControlStation - drains the sump, activating the pump and turning it off when the level of water in the sump is lowered.

(ii)   LowWaterSensor - signals when the level of water is low.

(iii)   Pump - commands the pump to be turned on/off.

(iv)   WaterFlowSensor - signals whether water flows from the sump.

The fault model for the above subsystem assumes that transient faults can affect the operation of the physical pump when reacting to commands from Pump.

The C2 architecture of the subsystem is shown in Fig. 13, where the IdealPump is implemented as an idealised C2 component (iC2C). The NormalActivity component of IdealPump, which is PumpNormal, consists of components Pump and WaterFlowSensor that are joined into a collaboration that is coordinated by the PumpNormal_bottom connector. This same connector is responsible for detecting errors in IdealPump, checking the WaterFlowSensor status after a pump on/off requested, and raising an internal exception when the expected condition is not met.

The AbnormalActivity component (PumpAbnormal) is responsible for processing the error, by issuing retry requests to the Pump until either the normal operation is resumed or the exception is propagated to PumpControlStation.

In the configuration shown in Fig. 13 the PumpNormal component is structured as discussed in Section 3.1.1, encapsulating the WaterFlowSensor inside the IdealPump as a CollaboratingComponent of Pump. This decision relies on the assumption that the WaterFlowSensor has a single role in the system, which is to aid in the detection of errors in the Pump component. In case the WaterFlowSensor should provide services to other components as well, the solution would be to place it higher in the C2 configuration, above the IdealPump, as shown in Fig. 14.

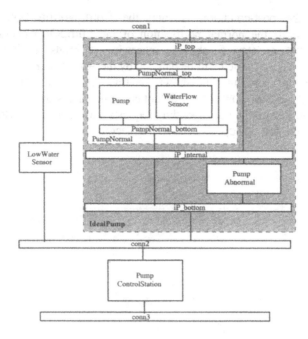

Fig. 13. The C2 Configuration for fault-tolerant PumpControlStation

In both cases operations pumpOn() and pumpOff(), provided by the IdealPump, will be implemented as a collaboration between Pump and WaterFlowSensor, coordinated by the PumpNormal_bottom connector. For example, the main steps in processing the pumpOn() service request are:

1. The PumpNormal_bottom connector sends a getPumpState() to the Pump.
2. The Pump component processes this request and sends back a notification of its current state (on/off).
3. The PumpNormal_bottom connector receives this notification and check if the pre-condition for the pumpOn() operation is satisfied (the Pump must be off).
4. If the pre-condition holds, the PumpNormal_bottom connector sends the pumpOn() request to the Pump, otherwise it sends a FailureException notification, to be handled by the AbnormalPump component.
5. The Pump processes this request to activate the physical pump and sends back a normal notification of its processing.
6. Before forwarding this normal notification down the architecture, the PumpNormal_bottom connector sends a readWaterFlow() request to the WaterFlowSensor.
7. The WaterFlowSensor processes this request and sends back a notification of its current status (active / inactive).
8. The PumpNormal_bottom receives this notification and check if the post-condition for the pumpOn() operation is met (the sensor must be activated).

9. If the post-condition is met, the PumpNormal_bottom connector forwards the normal notification of the pumpOn() operation (sent by Pump at step 5 above), otherwise it sends a FailureException notification, which will be handled by the AbnormalPump component.

In the alternate configuration shown in Fig. 14, the PumpNormal_bottom connector and the WaterFlowSensor do not communicate with each other directly in steps 1, 3, 6 and 8, with the corresponding requests and notifications flowing through the PumpNormal_top, ipTop, and conn1 connectors.

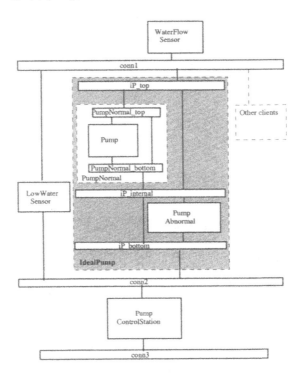

Fig. 14. Alternate configuration for the Pump subsystem

6   Conclusions

In this paper, we have investigated the structuring of fault-tolerant component-based systems at the architectural level. For the purpose of our work, we have employed the C2 architectural style [27], which promotes the development of component-based systems using off-the-shelf components. The intent was to provide an idealised C2 component with structure and behaviour equivalent to the idealised fault-tolerant component [1].

The communication rules between components in the C2 style, based on the broadcasting of asynchronous messages, is desirable from the point of view of component-based design. However, they complicate the incorporation of fault tolerance mechanisms into architectures that are instantiations of this style[7][11]. Another difficulty that we encountered was the restrictions imposed by the C2 topology rules. For solving these problems we employed constructs similar to multi-versioning connector [18], consisting of pairs of collaborating connectors to define fault containment boundaries within the system, and synchronized communications within the idealised C2 component using notifications as acknowledgments of requests. In addition to the work describe above, we have also defined an idealised C2 connector. This fault-tolerant architectural element is especially useful considering that connectors in the C2 architectural style are more than simple communication primitives, and that the architectural approach advocated in this paper requires connectors to be also a place of computation.

Our results demonstrate the feasibility of the proposed approach for the C2 architectural style, and suggest their application to other architectural styles also belonging to the *interacting processes style* category, which are styles dominated by communication patterns among independent, usually concurrent, processes [23]. In the future, after being applied to and validated by real-world fault-tolerant applications, the proposed approach may be generalized as an architectural pattern.

Our ongoing work includes extending an existing C2 Java framework [28] to aid in the implementation of the iC2C abstraction and its integration into C2 architectural configurations. Another ongoing work is to evolve the protocols defined for iC2C internal elements to relax the restriction imposed on the synchronicity between requests and notifications flowing from/to the iC2C to/from server components, to allow an iC2C to send concurrent requests and receive notifications asynchronously. In a later stage, we plan also to study in more depth the problem of an iC2C processing concurrent requests and/or notifications with implicit invocation, to avoid the serialization of requests received by the iC2C.

Acknowledgments

Paulo Guerra is partially supported by CAPES/Brazil. Cecília Rubira and Paulo Guerra are supported by the FINEP/Brazil "Advanced Information Systems" Project (PRONEX-SAI-7697102200). Cecília Rubira is also supported by CNPq/Brazil under grant no. 351592/97-0.

References

[1]   T. Anderson and P.A. Lee. *Fault Tolerance: Principles and Practice*. Prentice-Hall, 1981.
[2]   L.F. Andrade and J.L. Fiadeiro. Feature modeling and composition with coordination contracts. In *Proceedings Feature Interaction in Composed System (ECOOP 2001)*, pages 49-54. Universitat Karlsruhe, 2001.
[3]   A. Avizienis. The N-Version Approach to Fault-tolerant Software. *IEEE Transactions on Software Engineering*, 11(2):1491-1501, December 1995.
[4]   L. Bass, P. Clements, and R. Kazman. *Software Architecture in Practice*. Addison-Wesley, 1998.
[5]   D. M. Beder, B. Randell, A. Romanovsky, and C.M.F. Rubira. On Applying Coordinated Atomic Actions and Dependable Software Architectures for Developing Complex Systems. In *Proceedings of the 4th IEEE International Symposium on Object-Oriented Real-Time Distributed Computing (ISORC 2001)*, Magdeburg, Germany, May 2-4, 2001, pp. 103-112, IEEE Computer Society Press.
[6]   A.W. Brown and KC. Wallnau. The current state of CBSE. *IEEE Software*, 15(5):37-46, September / October 1998.
[7]   T.D. Chandra. Unreliable failure detectors for reliable distributed systems. *Journal of the ACM*, 43(2):225-267, March 1996.
[8]   J.E. Cook and J.A. Dage. Highly reliable upgrading of components. In *Proceedings of the 21st International Conference on Software Engineering (ICSE'99)*, pages 203-212, New York, NY, May 1999. ACM Press.
[9]   D. Garlan, R. Allen, and J. Ockerbloom. Architectural mismatch: Why reuse is so hard. *IEEE Software*, 12(6):17-26, November 1995.
[10] A.F. Garcia, C.M.F. Rubira, A. Romanovsky, and J. Xu. A Comparative Study of Exception Handling Mechanisms for Building Dependable Object-Oriented Software. *In Journal of Systems and Software*, Elsevier, Vol. 59, Issue 2, November 2001, pp. 197-222.
[11] F.C. Gärtner. Fundamentals of fault-tolerant distributed computing in asynchronous environments. *ACM Computing Surveys*, 31(1):1-26, March 1999.
[12] V. Issarny and J.-P. Banatre. Architecture-based exception handling. In Proceedings of the *34th Annual Hawaii International Conference on System Sciences (HICSS'34)*. IEEE, 2001.
[13] J.C. Laprie. *Dependability: A Unifying Concept for Reliable Computing and Fault Tolerance*, chapter 1, pages 1-28. Blackwell Scientific Publications Ltd., 1989.
[14] J.C. Laprie. Dependability: Basic concepts and terminology. In *Special Issue of the Twenty-Fifth International Symposium on Fault-Tolerant Computing (FTCS- 25)*. IEEE Computer Society Press, 1995.
[15] K.G. Larsen, P. Petersson, and W. Yi. UPPALL in a Nutshell. In *International Journal on Software Tools for Technology Transfer*. 1997.
[16] R. de Lemos. Describing evolving dependable systems using co-operative software architectures. In *Proceedings of the IEEE International Conference on Software Maintenance (ICSM 2001)*, pages 320-329. 2001.
[17] N. Medvidovic, P. Oreizy, and R.N. Taylor. Reuse of off-the-shelf components in C2-style architectures. In *Proceedings of the 1997 Symposium on Software Reusability (SSR'97)*, 1997.
[18] M. Rakic and N. Medvidovic. Increasing the confidence in o-the-shelf components: A software connector-based approach. In *Proceedings of the 2001 Symposium on Software Reusability (SSR 2001)*, pages 11-18. ACM/SIGSOFT, May 2001.

[19] B. Randell and J. Xu. The evolution of the recovery block concept, In *Software Fault Tolerance*, chapter 1. John Wiley Sons Ltd., 1995.

[20] T. Saridakis and V. Issarny. Developing Dependable Systems using Software Architecture. Technical report, INRIA/IRISA, 1999.

[21] L. Sha, R. Rajkumar, and M. Gagliardi. Evolving Dependable Real-Time Systems. In *1996 IEEE Aerospace Applications Conference Proceedings*. 1996.

[22] M. Shaw and D. Garlan. *Software Architecture: Perspectives on an Emerging Discipline*. Prentice Hall. 1996.

[23] M. Shaw and P. Clements. A Field Guide to Boxology: Preliminary Classification of Architectural Styles for Software Systems. In *Proceedings of the COMPSAC97, First International Computer Software and Applications Conference*, 1997.

[24] M. Sloman and J. Kramer. *Distributed Systems and Computer Networks*. Prentice Hall, 1987.

[25] D. Sotirovski. Towards fault-tolerant software architectures. In R. Kazman, P. Kruchten, C. Verhoef, and H. Van Vliet, editors, *Working IEEE/IFIP Conference on Software Architecture*, pages 7-13, Los Alamitos, CA, 2001.

[26] V. Stavridou and R.A. Riemenschneider. Provably dependable software architectures. In *Proceedings of the Third ACM SIGPLAN International Software Architecture Workshop*, pages 133-136. ACM, 1998.

[27] R.N. Taylor, N. Medvidovic, K. M. Anderson, E. J. Whitehead Jr., J. E. Robbins, K. A. Nies, P. Oreizy, and D. L. Dubrow. A component- and message-based architectural style for GUI software. *IEEE Transactions on Software Engineering*, 22(6):390-406, June 1996.

[28] UCI. Archstudio 3 - Foundations - c2.fw, http://www.isr.uci.edu/projects/archstudio/c2fw.html, accessed November, 2002.

[29] G. Vecellio, and W.M. Thomas. Issues in the assurance of component-based software. In *Proceedings of the 2000 International Workshop on Component-Based Software Engineering*. Carnegie Mellon Software Engineering Institute, 2000.

[30] S.S. Yau and B. Xia. An Approach to Distributed Component-Based Real-Time Application Software Development. In *The First IEEE International Symposium on Object-Oriented Real-Time Distributed Computing (ISORC'98)*. 1998.

The Role of Event Description in Architecting Dependable Systems

Marcio Dias and Debra Richardson

School of Information and Computer Science
University of California, Irvine
Irvine, CA 92697-3425 USA
{mdias,djr}@ics.uci.edu

Abstract. Software monitoring is a technique that is well-suited to supporting the development of dependable system. It has been widely applied not only for this purpose but also for other purposes such as debugging, security, performance evaluation and enhancement, etc. However, there is an inherent gap between the levels of abstraction of the information that is collected during software monitoring (the implementation level) and that of the software architecture level where many design decisions are made. Unless an immediate structural one-to-one architecture-to-implementation mapping takes place, we need a specification language to describe how low-level events are related to higher-level ones. Although some specification languages for monitoring have been proposed in the literature, they do not provide support up to the software architecture level. In addition, these languages make it harder to link to (and reuse) information from other event-based models often employed for reliability analysis. In this paper, we discuss the importance of event description as an integration element for architecting dependable systems.

1 Introduction

Architectural representations of systems have been shown to be effective in assisting the understanding of broader system concerns by abstracting away from details of the system implementation [17-19,21]. The software architecture level of abstraction helps the developer in dealing with system complexity, and it is a more appropriate level for analysis, because components, connectors, and their configuration are better understood and are more intellectually tractable at that level [12,21,26].

Building dependable systems requires additional management services, which impose still more complexity on the system [24]. These services include fault-tolerance, safety, security (intrusion detection), and resource management, among others. An underlying service to all these services is software monitoring.

Software monitoring is a well-known technique for observing and understanding the dynamic behavior of programs when they are executed, and it can be applied for many different purposes [13,23,25]. In addition to promoting dependability, software monitoring can be used for testing, debugging, correctness checking, performance

R. de Lemos et al. (Eds.): Architecting Dependable Systems, LNCS 2677, pp. 150-174, 2003.

evaluation and enhancement, security, control, program understanding and visualization, ubiquitous computing, and dynamic documentation.

Software monitoring consists of collecting information from the system execution, detecting particular events or states using the collected data, analyzing and presenting relevant information to the user, and possibly taking some preventive or corrective actions. As the information is collected from the execution of the program implementation, there is an inherent gap between the level of abstraction of the collected events (and states) and of the software architecture. Unless the implementation was generated from the software architectural description or there is an easily identifiable one-to-one architecture-to-implementation mapping [3,19,26], there must be a description of how those (primitive) events are related to higher-level (composed) events.

Many monitoring systems were developed so that the user could specify composed events from primitive ones, using provided specification languages [1,4,5,9,11,16,24,25]. However, in general, these specification languages either are restricted to a single monitoring system [1,4,5,11,24], are not generic enough to serve many different purposes [4,5,9,11,16,25], or cannot associate specified events to the software architecture [1,4,5,9,11,16,24,25].

There is no monitoring system able to provide for all these different purposes. One problem occurs when a user is interested in applying monitoring for more than one purpose (for instance, dependability, performance evaluation, and program visualization). In this case, he or she would need to run different monitoring systems and, consequently, need to describe the same events multiple times using different specification languages.

To put it simply, software monitoring is a technique well-suited to supporting the development of dependable systems, and it has been widely applied for this purpose. However, monitoring systems suffer in their ability to associate collected information to the software architecture level.

In this paper, we discuss how software monitoring can be applied at the software architectural level to support dependability. In this context, we present some requirements for event description languages, as well as our ongoing work on xMonEve, an XML-based language for describing monitoring events, and how xMonEve addresses the problem of performing software monitoring at different levels of abstraction.

Section 2 introduces concepts related to event-based software monitoring, including types of software monitoring, and classifications for events. Section 3 presents some of the features of xMonEve language, and how event types can be described in it. In section 4, we discuss, with examples, how the association between events and elements at different levels of abstraction (from implementation to architecture, to requirements) can help to bridge the gap between implementation and architecture in the context of developing dependable systems. Related work is discussed in section 5, and section 6 presents our conclusions and plans for future work.

2   Event Monitoring

There are basically two types of monitoring systems based on information collection: sampling (time-driven) and tracing (event-driven). By sampling, information about the execution state is collected either synchronously (at a specific time rate), or asynchronously (through direct request of the monitoring system). With tracing, on the other hand, information is collected when an event of interest occurs in the system [20].

Tracing allows a better understanding of system behavior than does sampling. However, tracing monitors also generate a much larger volume of data than do sampling monitors. In order to alleviate this data volume problem, some researchers have been working on encoding techniques [22]. A more common and straightforward way to reduce data volume is to collect interesting events only, rather than all events that happen during program execution [14,16]. However, this second approach may limit the analysis of events and conditions unforeseen previously by program execution.

Both state information and event information are important for understanding program execution [24]. Since a tracing monitor collects information when events occur, state information can be obtained by collecting the events associated with state changes. With a hybrid approach, sampling can represent the action of collecting state information into an event for the tracing monitoring. As with other events, not all events with state information should be collected, but rather only those events that are of interest. Integrating sampling and tracing monitors and collecting the state information through events reduces the complexity of the monitoring task.

A monitoring system needs to know which events are of interest—i.e., which events should be collected. Therefore, it provides an event specification language for the user. In addition, it needs to know the kind of analysis it should perform on the collected information. The user may, for example, provide a specification of the correct behavior of the system, and the monitoring system then checks for correct behavior and indicates when the system did not perform according to the specification. Another approach is to have the user specify the conditions of interest, with the monitoring system identifying when these conditions are detected and notifying the user. A third approach, which is not frequently used by monitoring systems, is to characterize (i.e., build a model of) the system behavior from the program execution. This approach is mainly useful for program understanding and dynamic documentation, in a fashion similar to the work of Cook and Wolf [6] and Wolf and Rosenblum [27] in the context of software processes.

Since analysis is so intrinsic to the monitoring activity, it has become normal to have monitoring specification languages with which the user describes not only the events but also the analysis to be performed. As a consequence, monitoring specification languages today are generally biased toward the kind of analysis performed by the monitoring system. However, monitoring systems can be used to perform many types of analyses, and possibly to take different actions depending on its purpose. For example, one monitoring system being used for performance enhancement may take actions such as commands for program reconfiguration (modifications on the program to improve performance). On the other hand, a monitoring system applied for software testing could have analyses such as conformance verification and coverage-criteria evaluation, and actions such as test-case generation and selection. Therefore, although specific actions can be associated to events (e.g., satisfying conditions or by pattern matching), this association should not be described in the event description language - external descriptions for analyses and actions for monitoring systems are required.

To the best of our knowledge, there is no specification method for monitoring systems that separates event type description from analysis and action description. As further discussed in section 5, many monitoring specification languages and event languages have been proposed, but they present some limitations for the description of event types for monitoring systems, and/or do not provide support for the requisite separation of concerns (event types vs. analyses vs. actions). Independent treatment (and possibly description) is necessary for questions such as: "What are the events (event types) of interest of the system?"; "What is(are) the purpose(s) for monitoring the system?" (e.g. performance, reliability, etc.); "What kinds of analysis should be performed?" (e.g. condition detection, correctness checking or comparison, or model characterization); and "What actions should be performed when a specific situation (e.g. an event, event sequence, or condition) is identified?" (e.g. generation a new event, execute OS command, modify dynamically the structure of the program, start a new program, etc).

In the current step of our research, we are focusing on the first question for monitoring specification languages — i.e., "What are the events of interest of the system?" We are defining an extendable and flexible language (xMonEve) for describing monitoring events independently of the system implementation, the purpose of analysis, and the monitoring system.

2.1   Events in the Software Monitoring Context

Before presenting the requirements for event languages for monitoring systems, we need to understand the kinds of events with which monitoring systems deal. Basically, an event is an atomic, instantaneous action that occurs during system execution. The literature has presented some classifications for event [23,11], and a more common and generic classification groups events into three different categories [23]:

- **Hardware-level events** are low-level activities such as page faults, sampling of a cache miss counter, and I/O channel activity. For example, events can include exceeded threshold on corrupt packets, exceeded threshold on stuck links, or excessive violations occurring from such things as static on a network line.
- **Process-level events** are events observable external to the process. Communication between a program and file (or device) is evident by observing communication between the application and the file subsystem (in a Unix-based system). Communication between processes is similarly visible by observing activity occurring between an application and the interprocess communication subsystem. Process state information is available in the process control subsystem.

- **Application-dependent events** describe activity internal to an application. The types of application-dependent events that a monitoring system defines for use depend on the monitoring system's purpose. Defining just the right event set can be difficult. What set of events is sufficient to capture the desired behavior in the application? Is it enough to capture changes to selected variables and messages passed between processes, or is a higher-level view needed to observe, for example, changes to the membership of a group of processes?

Although monitoring can be performed at all these categories, specific hardware instrumentation is needed for the first category hardware-level events. Software monitoring systems deal with events at those other two categories, process-level and application-dependent events.

Application-dependent events can be associated to many different elements in the program, such as simple statements (e.g., assignment and expressions), procedures and functions, classes and objects, modules, components and subsystems. Each of these elements appears on different levels of abstraction. Naturally, events associated to statements and procedures are at a lower-level than events associated to components and subsystems. While the former kind of event is closer to the implementation code, the latter is more related to the architecture of the system.

One of the main purposes for an event description language is to describe what are the types of events of interest in a program, what are the relationship between those types of events, and how lower-level and higher-level events are associated to each other. From this point on, the term "event" is used to represent an event instance, while the term "event type" or "type of event" is to reference the semantics and structure of an event.

Table 1. Events of interest for monitoring may not exist explicitly in the application code.

	Application code snippet and statement of interest (underlined)	Explicit event in the application statement	Example of possible events (types) of interest for the monitoring system
1.	`balance = -10;`	none	• assign (var=balance; val= -10) • Account_negative_state
2.	`alertStatus = orange;`	none	• assign (var=alertStatus; val= orange) • high_risk_of_attack
3.	`socket.write("LOAD xyz.txt");`	none (but implicitly leads to a network message event)	• net_comm (ip,sock,msg) • File_Request ("xyz.txt")
4.	`event = new WindowEvent(...);` `fireWindowEvent(event);`	GUI event	• *WindowEvent* • GUI_Event_Fired • Window_Closing_Request
5.	`event = new OpenAccountEvent(...);` `AccountManager.handle(event);`	application domain event	• *OpenAccountEvent* • AccMgr_Handle_Entered • AccMgr_Handle_Exited
6.	`event=new Event("New Account",...);` `publish(event);`	publish-subscribe event	• *Event("New Account",...)* • Request_Open_Account

2.2 The Relationship between Event Types and the Application Code

As mentioned before, a monitoring system can observe and analyze different kinds of events associated to the application code elements. However, it is important to understand that, depending on its purpose, the monitoring system should be able to observe events from the program execution that are not explicit events for the application. For example, the execution of a simple assign statement or a function call in the code may represent (or generate) an event for the monitoring system.

Table 1 shows some examples of how event types of interest for the monitoring system can be associated to the application code, independently of an explicit event element in the program. In examples 1 to 3, there is no explicit event present in the application code, while it is explicit for example 4 to 6.

In example 1, the statement "balance = -10" is not an event in the application context, but it can represent (generate) different types of events for the monitoring system, such as the implementation level event "assign (...)" and the architecture-level event "Account_negative_state" (if it is associated to an architectural component Account). For a monitoring system, the statement in example 2 could represent (or generate) the requirement level event "high_risk_of_attack", if this is associated to a property requirement. In examples 4 to 6, the monitoring system can observe the events as they exist in the application, and also create other events based on the code statement. For example 5, the monitoring system could observe the "OpenAccountEvent" (possibly an architecture level event), as well as events with timing information before and after the method "AccountManager.handle()" is called (for performance purpose).

As we discuss later, the event description language needs to capture the information about how events for the monitoring system is mapped to the code. In other words, it should describe what is (are) the statement(s) in the code that will generate events of a specific type, and how to assign properties to these events from the code. This is what we call "mapping" between event type and implementation. This information can be used by the monitoring system to properly instrument the application or configure its mechanisms to capture the events (when instrumentation occurs not in the application code, but in the interpreter, virtual machine, or operating system). Events mapped to code are known as primitive events.

It is important to note here that the mapping information between event types and program code does not exist in the context of publish-subscriber systems, once they deal with events that are explicitly created in the application.

2.3 Primitive vs. Composed Events, and their Relation to Event Level

Events that are associated directly to an element in the code are so called primitive events. Although many primitive events may even be low-level (implementation level) events, this is far from a rule. If the element in code to which a primitive event is associated corresponds to a component or a specific interprocess communication, this event would possibly be at the architectural level. For example, an event at the architectural level between components A and B could be associated to a specific invocation from a class A' of a method of class B', given that classes A' and B' represent façades [7] of components A and B, respectively. Although this primitive event is mapped to a method invocation between classes A' and B', it is associated to the architectural elements A and/or B.

A composed event type is one that is described in terms of the composition of other (one or more) events, either primitive or composed. Although a composed event may represent an association or aggregation of other events, that is not necessarily a higher-level event than those from which it is composed. For example, two events (e1 and e2) associated to a class C can compose another event (e3) that is also associated to class C. Therefore, events e1, e2 and e3 would be at the same level in relation to the system, or we can simply say that those events are associated to the same element, the abstraction known as "class C".

In order to associate types of events to different levels of the application, the event language should describe more than just the origin of an event, that is, if it is primitive (mapped directly to the code) or composed (indirectly to the code, associated through the composition of other events). An event language should also associate an event type to the element (abstraction) of the application to which it is associated.

From the examples mentioned in the previous paragraphs, we can notice that event types, independently of being primitive or composed, can be associated to lower-level or higher-level abstractions of the program. As mentioned earlier, these abstractions can be as low-level as simple statements and procedures, and also as high-level as components, connectors and subsystems. In addition, events can also be associated to other kinds of abstractions, such as those elements present on requirement specification models.

As we discuss later in the paper, although these elements (or abstractions) may be structurally related to each other (for example, an architectural component may represent a composition of services – methods – provided by different classes), the event description language is not the right place to have structural information of the application described (this kind of description is supported by other models, such as UML models or ADLs). The main problem is that different abstractions may not have a direct structural association between them, in the sense that, for example, one class can be part of two or more different components at the architectural level. With the concept of abstractions and the association provided by the composition of events, the relationship between abstractions of different levels is defined based not on the application structure, but on the behavioral association between event types.

2.4   Abstractions and Viewpoints

The main idea of associating event types to the program element was originally influenced by the concept of viewpoints proposed by Bates [4], but with the purpose of complimenting its capabilities. An informal definition for a viewpoint is a set of event types of an application that are of interest to be monitored at a specific time (or execution). Similar to a program slicing technique, a viewpoint would serve to define the events of interest that should be monitored, including also other events based on the dependencies between those event types.

In our context, an architectural viewpoint of the program execution could be defined as a viewpoint with the set of all event types associated to all architectural abstractions. For example, all event types associated to every component and connector (i.e., the architecture abstractions) of one application would compose a global architectural viewpoint and could be monitored. Naturally, a global viewpoint of the architecture may not be appropriated to our needs given the volume of possible events observed. Therefore, more purpose oriented viewpoints (for example, the architecture performance viewpoint, a component security viewpoint, etc) can help us (and the monitoring system) to focus on those events of interest in a specific moment.

3   The xMonEve Language

3.1   Requirements for xMonEve

Initially, we identified new requirements for event description languages. Some of the requirements that are guiding us through the development of xMonEve are as follows.

- **Generality of purpose**: It needs to be flexible enough to accommodate event description for multiple monitoring purposes (i.e., independent of the analysis to be performed).
- **Independence of the monitoring system**: It must allow generic description of events, both primitive and composed, not restricted to a specific monitoring system (or environment).
- **Implementation independence**: It needs to provide mechanisms that separate the conceptual event from the implementation mapping.
- **Reusability**: Event descriptions should be reusable independently of the implementation and monitoring system.
- **Extensibility**: Extension of event descriptions should be supported, so that more specific information can be associated with events. For instance, one extension could be the association of monitoring events with software architectural elements.

Like most monitoring specification languages, with xMonEve we can represent the types of both primitive and composed events. Primitive events are events that occur in a specific moment in time—i.e., an instantaneous occurrence. Composed events are events composed of other events (primitive or composed ones) that have specific moments of starting and ending. While a composed event's starting time is defined by the first event to happen, the last event determines its ending time.

Composed events provide a higher-level abstraction for the system execution. Primitive events may be filtered out and abstracted into composed events, allowing unneeded details to be thrown away.

One important advantage of event description is that it is well-suited to bridging the gap between software architecture and implementation (mapping). For multiple reasons, including reuse, maintainability, performance, security, etc., the implementation structure may not exactly correspond to the conceptual architectural structure. Events imply a behavioral/functional mapping for associating architecture with implementation, instead of a structural mapping. A behavioral/functional mapping between implementation and any previous software specification document (software architecture, requirements, etc.) should always be possible. If the system behavior/functionality cannot be associated with implementation actions (independently of how hard it may be for a human being to do this association), then this behavior/functionality was not implemented in the first place.

Therefore, although events play an important role in the mapping between architecture and implementation, event specification languages have often ignored this role and have not provided any mechanism for associating these different abstraction levels with each other.

3.2   Key Features of xMonEve

After discussing some of the issues of event monitoring and the requirements for xMonEve, some of the key features of xMonEve are:

- **Event types associated to application abstractions.** The abstraction is the element of the application that defined the context of the event. An abstraction can be an implementation element (such as procedures, classes and objects), an architectural element (such as components and connectors), or any other kind of element associated to the application, such as a requirement element.

- **Primitive event types being externally mapped to the application code.** The advantage of having the mapping between event type and the code described externally to the code, in the event language, is that it does not enforce the use of one specific type of instrumentation by the monitoring system. For example, while one monitoring system could insert snippets of code into the application source code to capture the events, another monitoring system could have the instrumentation happening not in the application source code, but in the application binary code, in the interpreter, or even in the operating system. For this reason, the event type can be associated to multiples mapping descriptions, since one mapping description may not be adequate to all different instrumentation mechanisms.

- **Cross-cutting description of composed event types.** The description of composed event types separates three main aspects of event composition: (1) dependent composing events (the events that may compose the event), (2) event correlation (temporal relation between events for composition), and (3) event condition (conditions between event properties that need to be satisfied for the composition). It is important to note that not every composed event type will contain all those three aspects. For example, if the occurrence of events A and B characterizes an event C independently of their properties, the condition aspect is not present. An advantage of the separation of those aspects is that each aspect can have its own semantics without interfering with the other aspects. For example, while one composed event type may have its event correlation described as regular expression, another composed event could have it described as a binary tree, DAG, FSM, or another semantics for event correlation.

- **Flexibility for refinement of event type description.** The description of an event type can be done in progressive refinements, given that parts of the description is not enforced. For example, a primitive event type et_1 may be defined initially with no mapping to the code. Although the monitoring system would not be able to capture events et_1 during the execution until a mapping is provided, other event types could be described as composition of event type et_1 .

- **Extensibility inherently provided by XML.** Since xMonEve is a XML-based description, it inherits the capability of being extensible. When new elements or properties become required, or when a monitoring system is intended to be used for a purpose not previously supported, extensions to xMonEve can be straightforwardly added.

3.3 Describing Events With xMonEve

The purpose of this paper is not to provide a complete discussion of the xMonEve language, but rather to give an overview of its concepts and to emphasize some specific details relevant to the context of architecting dependable systems.

In xMonEve, every event type has a *name*, a *description*, and an *abstraction*. The abstraction field is used to associate the event with a context. For instance, while a primitive event "*Open*" may be associated with the "*File*" abstraction, a composed event "*Open*" may be associated with the "*CheckingAccount*" abstraction. It is important to note here that *CheckingAccount* may or may not represent a structure (e.g., a class or subsystem) of the system implementation. This mechanism allows multiple levels of abstraction, from the implementation level to the requirement level, passing through design and also software architecture. In the previous example, *CheckingAccount* may be a component abstraction at the software architectural level.

Example showing common features of every event

```
<event>
  <name>Open</name>
  <abstraction>File</abstraction>
  <description>opening file</description>
  (...)
</event>
```

In addition to the features that are common to every event, primitive and composed events also have distinct characteristics.

3.4   Primitive Events

A primitive event type may be of interest in more than one system and may appear on different implementations (multiple sources). In order to have a reusable definition for such an event type, multiple mappings between event and implementation should be allowed. For example, the event type "assign" (from examples 1 and 2 on Table 1) would be mapped to two different statements in source code. Thus, primitive event types may have zero, one, or multiple mappings. These event types will typically have no mapping description until the programmer specifies them, because he or she is the one with the appropriate knowledge. Naturally, monitoring systems (or instrumentation tools) will not be able to properly associate primitive event types to the source code if no mapping is provided.

Example mapping a primitive event to the implementation

```
<event>
  <name>Open</name>
  <abstraction>File</abstraction>
  (...)
  <primitive>

    <attributes>
      <field> <name>filename</name>
       <type>string</type> </field> (...)
    </attributes>

    <mapping>
      <language>Java</language>
      <classname>java.io.File</classname>
      <type><operation>File(String pathname)</operation></type>
      <when type=method_exit/>
      <assignments>
        <assign><field>filename</field>
          <parameter>pathname</parameter>
        </assign>
      </assignments>
    </mapping>
      (...)
  </primitive>
</event>
```

In this example, the event *Open* occurs when the "method" (actually the constructor) of java.io.File class returns and the event field filename has its value assigned from the pathname parameter. In other words, we have the event:

```
File.Open ( filename = "file.txt" )
```

whenever the following code is executed:

```
new java.io.File ( "file.txt" )
```

It is important to note that we are describing "what" the event is and how it is mapped to the code that is going to generate it. The issue of how the code is going to be instrumented in order to have this event generated is not addressed here because the installation of sensors and probes is dependent upon the monitoring system.

The extensibility of XML allows us to modify the mapping element in order to describe variant mapping to the code in cases in which the current mapping element may not be enough to adequately map the event to the code. Therefore, although the example shows the mapping of an event that happens every time a method is invoked, other XML elements allow different types of mapping, such as mapping events to specific statements in code (assignments, expressions, loop commands, etc).

3.5   Composed Events

When defining composed events, no mapping to the code is needed, because such events are composed of other events. In addition to the common event fields, composed events have three extra sections: *composition*, *correlation* and *conditions*.

Composition Section

In this section, the event types that may compose the event are described. That is, the composed event may depend upon the event types listed in this section. For example, if event A can be composed of either (B and C) or (B and D), this section will only state that event type A may depend on events B, C and D, even though no instance of event type A will depend on both events C and D.

Aliases have an important role in the event composition. Each composing event type can be associated to one or more aliases. The first advantage is encapsulation and information hiding, in the sense that other sections of the event type description will not reference external event types directly, what makes it simple to modify the event description. Another advantage is that alias works as an identifier for the instance of the event type. For example, if the composed event A is defined by a sequence of events B • C • B, we can have aliases b1 and b2 for the event type B to distingue between the first and the last event occurrence of composition (i.e., b1 being the alias for the first B occurrence, and b2 for the second and last occurrence of B). In this example, we could also assign only one alias (b) to the multiple occurrences of event type B if only the last occurrence of event type B should satisfy the set of conditions described in the Condition section.

Correlation Section

In this section, the temporal relational among the composing events (to generate the composed event) is given. A composed event can only be "created" (identified) from the composing events if their occurrence corresponds (respects) the correlation as described here.

Different semantics can be used here to describe the correlation, such as binary tree, regular expression, FSM, and DAG [1], although the examples in this paper are exclusively based on regular expressions. The flexibility of xMonEve allows other semantic descriptions being added when needed.

Condition Section

The condition section contains the conditions that have to be satisfied by the properties of the composing events. For example, a composed event A can defined as a sequence B • C, but only when properties of events B and C satisfy some conditions, which would be described in this section.

In the next example, we describe the event *AccountTransfer* for the abstraction *Client*. The abstraction *Client* may be an entity of either design (e.g., class), software architecture (e.g., Component), or an entity present on other software models.

Example of a composed event "AccountTransfer."

```
<event>
  <name>AccountTranfer</name>
  <abstraction>Client</abstraction>
  <composite>

  <composition>
    <alias> <name>request</name>
      <event>Bank.TransferRequest</event> </alias>
    <alias> <name>withdraw</name>
      <event>Account.Withdraw</event> </alias>
    <alias> <name>deposit</name>
      <event>Account.Deposit</event> </alias>
    <alias> <name>commit</name>
      <event>Bank.TranferCommit</event> </alias>
  </composition>

  <attributes>
    <field> <name>client</name>
      <value>request.client</value> </field>
    <field> <name>from</name>
      <value>withdraw.account</value> </field>
    <field> <name>to</name>
      <value>deposit.account</value> </field>
    <field> <name>amount</name>
      <value>withdraw.amount</value></field>
  </attributes>
```

> Composition
> request = Bank.TransferRequest
> withdraw = Account.Withdraw
> deposit = Account.Deposit
> commit = Bank.TransferCommit

```
                              Correlation
                            Regular Expression
<correlation>        request • { withdraw • deposit | deposit • withdraw } • commit
    <regexp>
       <sequence min=1 max=1>
          <event min=1 max=1>request</event>
          <parallel min=1 max=1>
            <event>withdraw</event>
            <event>deposit</event>
          </parallel>
          <event min=1 max=1/>commit</event>
       </sequence>
    </regexp>
  </correlation>
                                  Conditions
                    request.client = withdraw.client = deposit.client = commit.client
                              withdraw.amount = deposit.amount
  <condition>               withdraw.account != deposit.account
     <and>
        <equals> <value>request.client</value>
          <value>withdraw.client</value>
          <value>deposit.client</value>
          <value>commit.client</value> </equals>
        <equals> <value>withdraw.amount</value>
          <value>deposit.amount</value> </equals>
        <not><equals><value>withdraw.account</value>
          <value>deposit.account</value></equals></not>
     </and>
    </condition>
   </composite>
 </event>
```

The *Client.AccountTranfer* event is composed of four other events, and for each of them an alias (with local scope) is associated in the *composition* section:

- *Bank.TransferRequest* event associated with the alias *request*;

- *Account.Withdraw* event associated with the alias *withdraw*;

- *Account.Deposit* event associated with the alias *deposit*, and

- *Bank.TransferCommit* event associated with the alias *commit*.

The *attributes* section describes the fields of the *Client.AccountTranfer* event and the value that is going to be assigned to each of these fields. For example, the *AccountTransfer* event contains the field "from," and the value assigned to it is the value of the attribute "account" from the event *withdraw*.

In the *correlation* section, different correlation semantics could be used. In the example, a regular expression is used to describe the following correlation (the symbol '•' represents sequence, and the symbol '|' represents choice):

request • (withdraw • deposit | deposit • withdraw) • commit

Finally, the *condition* section defines the constraints for the composition. For instance, the events must be associated with the same client, the amounts withdrawn and deposited have to be the same, and the withdrawing and depositing accounts should be different for the event to be considered a transfer event.

4   Architecting Dependable Systems

With xMonEve, events can be described using both top-down and bottom-up approaches, because the language is independent of the development process. However, in the context of architectural development of dependable software, a top-down approach would be more natural (though not the only possible approach). The architect would describe (incomplete composed) events at the architectural level, while the designer and/or programmer would decompose these events into lower-level events, until they could be completely defined in terms of primitive events only.

In this section, we first discuss the role of events as the integration element for the development of dependable systems from software architecture to program execution. Then, we present examples of top-down and bottom-up approaches to architecting such systems.

4.1   The Event as the Integration Element

According to Hofmann et al. [9], both monitoring and modeling rely on a common abstraction of a system's dynamic behavior—the event—and therefore they can be integrated into one comprehensive methodology for measurement, validation, and evaluation.

When considering modeling and analysis techniques that have been applied for designing dependable (reliable) systems, Markov models and simulations stand out [15]. It is important to note that the event abstraction is also common to these techniques. A Markov model has a state changed with the occurrence of an event, where time-to-occurrence is often modeled with a random exponential distribution. During simulation execution, event traces are generated, upon which analyses are performed.

Thus, the event abstraction can act as the basic element for integrating reliability models, architecture designs, system implementations, and analyses. In order to have this integration, an interchangeable (shared and canonical) representation of events should be available during the whole software development process. In this context, xMonEve represents an important step toward this integration.

4.2   Example of Top-Down Approach

Here, we informally describe a top-down approach to architecting dependable systems by using events as basic elements of integration.

When building Markov models for reliability analysis, architects and designers may associate information about the model with the events. In this case, the event would include the information about the state change, as well as the random distribution of its occurrence. This event definition could be used for running a reliability analysis prior to system development.

For example, suppose the software architect describes a Markov model to represent the states of a component in relation to the occurrence of failure. Although Markov cannot be considered itself an architectural model, it is associated to the architectural element "Component A" in this example. A simple model could be the one in **Fig 1**. When Component A enters an overload state, it is supposed to regulate itself and return to a normal state in a period of time. If it cannot normalize its state during this time, it is considered a failure, and some action may have to be taken to keep the system stable.

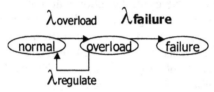

Fig 1. Markov model for Component A

With the Markov model for Component A, the event of this component entering into a failure state can be described in xMonEve with an appropriate extension to the Markov model. A simple extension for this support would include information about state transition and the random distribution of the event occurrence.

Extension of an event description with information for the Markov model.

```
<event>
  <name>enterFailureState</name>
  <abstraction>ComponentA</abstraction>
  <markov>
    <transition>
      <from>overload_state</from>
      <to>failure_state</to>
    </transition>
    <distribution (...) />
    (...)
  </markov>
  (...)
</event>
```

The information about the Markov model is being added in the event description with the only purpose of providing the origin of the event, as a rationale, so the event can be traced back to the requirements, in this case. As stated in the beginning, the event description should not contain any information the analysis that the monitoring system should perform. Thus, by associating the event to its original Markov model does not imply that the monitoring system is going to perform an analysis over the application events based on the Markov semantics.

In the example, the event was defined from the Markov model applied to the software component at the architectural level. However, when the event was defined, the software developers may not have had the implementation. Therefore, no mapping or decomposition of this event would be defined.

During further development (design, implementation, testing...) of the system, independently of having or not having Markov (or other) extensions to an event definition, software architects, designers, and programmers may decompose (or compose) an event into (from) other events by defining and associating these new events. Thus, multiple levels of event abstraction can be created, from requirements and software architecture abstractions to implementation primitive events.

In the previous example, the event definition will have further information added by software architects, designers, and/or programmers. The event *ComponentA.enterFailureState* could be described (in the <composition> section) as a composition of two events: a *ComponentA.enterOverloadState* (with alias *eos*) and *BufferA.loadAverageSampling* (with alias avg). Notice that BufferA may be an implementation abstraction, such as an object, class, or data structure.

In the <correlation> section, it is described that an *eos* event must happen exactly once before 1 or many *avg* events. Although this is described with an extended semantics of regular expression (<regexp> section), extended support to other semantics (such as petri-nets, directed acyclic graphs, and boolean trees, for example) could be used instead.

Finally, in the <condition> section, the developer would describe the conditions that should be satisfied for the composition of the event. In this case, the conditions are: (1) Component A should be in running status when it enters into the overload state (i.e., eos.status == running), (2) the load average of Buffer A has to be greater that 100, and (3) the elapsed time since Component A entered into the overload state must be greater than 500 milliseconds.

Description of event ComponentA.enterFailureState with its decomposition

```
<event>
  <name>enterFailureState</name>
  <abstraction>ComponentA</abstraction>
  <markov>...</markov>

  <composite>
    <composition>
      <alias><name>eos</name>
        <event>ComponentA.enterOverloadState</event></alias>
      <alias><name>avg</name>
        <event>BufferA.loadAverageSampling</event></alias>
    </composition>
```

Composition
eos =ComponentA.enterOverloadState
avg = BufferA.loadAverageSampling

```
<attributes>
  <field><name>status</name><value>eos.status</value><field>
  <field><name>loadaverage</name>
      <value>avg.la</value></field>
</attributes>

<correlation>
  <regexp>
    <sequence min=1 max=1>
      <event min=1 max=1>eos</event>
      <event min=1 max=unbound>avg</event>
    </sequence>
  </regexp>
</correlation>

<condition>
  <and>
    <equals><value>eos.status</value>
      <const>running</const></equals>
    <gr><value>avg.la</value><const>100</const></gr>
    <gr><exp>ellapsedTime(eos.timestamp.end,
                        avg.timestamp.end)</exp>
      <const>500</const></gr>
  </and>
</condition>
  </composite>
</event>
```

After the implementation of the application, with the event description represented in xMonEve, a monitoring system can observe the application execution and analyze its behavior at multiple abstraction levels, depending upon the purpose and interest of the user. For instance, analysis can happen at the implementation level for debugging, performance evaluation, testing, etc., as well as at the architectural level for dependability, performance evaluation, validation, etc.

4.3   Example of Bottom-Up Approach

Once we have the detailed design and/or implementation of the application, higher level events can be composed from lower level (and possibly primitive) events identified in the application. In this section, we present an example of using event definition with a bottom-up approach when architecting dependable systems. The example described here is related to the availability of system parts based on exchange of heartbeat messages.

Let the application be a distributed system that contains multi-process communication between processes A and B. In Process A, the class AvailabilityReporter sends a heartbeat message to Process B every 30 seconds.

In process B, the class HeartbeatReceiver receives heartbeats from process A. It is supposed to receive one heartbeat before every 60 seconds. If process B does not receive any heartbeat message from process A in 60 seconds, process A is considered to not be available.

In this example, the lower level (primitive) event of receiving a heartbeat from any process in the `HeartbeatReceiver` would be associated to the invocation of method `handleHBEvent` of an instance object of `edu.uci.rel.HeartbeatReceiver`. The value of `e.getSenderName` would be assigned to attribute `sender_process_name`.

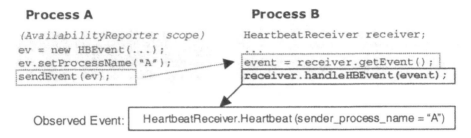

Fig.2. Event "HeartbeatReceiver.Heartbeat" being observed from system execution. Note that this event is associated to the class abstraction *HeartbeatReceiver*, and, therefore, may not be an architecture-level event

Description of primitive event HeartbeatReceiver.Heartbeat

```
<event>
   <name>Heartbeat</name>
   <abstraction>HeartbeatReceiver</abstraction>

   <primitive>
      <attributes>
         <field><name>sender_process_name</name>
            <type>String</type></field>
      </attributes>

      <mapping>
         <language>Java</language>
         <classname>edu.uci.rel.HeartbeatReceiver</classname>
         <type>
            <operation>handleHBEvent(Event e)</operation>
         </type>
         <when type=method_entry/>
         <assignments>
            <assign>
               <field>sender_process_name</field>
               <parameter>e.getSenderName()</parameter>
            </assign>
         </assignments>
      </mapping>
   </primitive>
</event>
```

Considering the process A being represented by a component A in the architecture of our application, we can describe the higher level event of not having component A available from the previously described HeartbeatReceiver.heartbeat event. In order to describe the ComponentA.IsNotAvailable event, we can use a Timer.Tick event to verify the elapsed time since the last Heartbeat event received. When the heartbeat from process "A" is followed (not necessarily immediate) by one or more tick events, and the time elapsed between them is greater than 1 min (60000 milliseconds), the event ComponentA.IsNotAvailable is fired.

Event Trace
[millis]: <event>

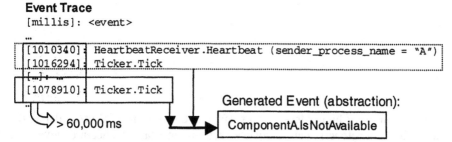

Fig. 3. Event "IsNotAvailable" (associated to the architectural element "ComponentA") being generated from lower-level events

Description of event ComponentA.IsNotAvailable

```
<event>
    <name>IsNotAvailable</name>
    <abstraction>ComponentA</abstraction>

    <composite>

        <composition>
            <alias> <name>heartbeat</name>
                <event>HeartbeatReceiver.Heartbeat</event> </alias>
            <alias> <name>tick</name>
                <event>Timer.Tick</event> </alias>
        </composition>

        <attributes/>

        <correlation>
            <regexp>
                <sequence min=1 max=1>
                    <event min=1 max=1>heartbeat</event>
                    <event min=1 max=unbound>tick</event>
                </sequence>
            </regexp>
        </correlation>
```

```
<condition>
    <and>
        <equals><value>heartbeat.sender_process_name</value>
            <const>A</const></equals>
        <gr><exp>ellapsedTime(heartbeat.timestamp.end,
                           tick.timestamp.end)</exp>
            <const>60000</const></gr>
    </and>
</condition>

</composite>
</event>
```

With the definition of higher-level events, such as ComponentA.IsNotAvailable, the architects and developers can associate actions at the architecture level for reconfiguration and adaptation of the system for dependability purpose. As mentioned before, it is easier and more efficient the management of such dependability action at the architecture level than at the implementation level.

5   Related Work

Many specification languages have been proposed in the literature for describing events (and states) for use in monitoring techniques. The definition of xMonEve is influenced by characteristics present in most of them.

Some specification languages were developed based upon extended regular expressions, such as EBBA [3]. These languages put more emphasis on temporal ordering, and thus they generally have limited capability to specify states, and events are assumed to occur instantaneously. These languages influenced xMonEve in the specification of the correlation of composed events, although in xMonEve we also considered non-instantaneous events.

Snodgrass [25] developed a query language for a history database, using it to specify events and states. Although this work has had a large influence on monitoring techniques, the language has a limited set of operators from relational algebra with a limited representational power. One important influence of Snodgrass' work upon ours is that in because of his use of relational algebra the language delineates the derived information that is desired and not how it is derived.

PMMS [16] uses a specification language based on relational calculus to form descriptions of events and user questions. A big contribution of this work was in providing an automatic technique for instrumenting the program code to collect only the events needed to answer explicit user questions. This technique removed the burden of code instrumentation from the programmer. The PMMS language, however, has limitations for specifing events, and this is linked to the fact that PMMS supports tracing only, and not sampling.

Shim et al. [24] proposed a language based on classical temporal logic for specifying events and states. This work influenced us to consider non-instantaneous events. However, they did not provide any mechanism for creating different levels of abstraction (to associate, for instance, events with software architecture elements). Nor did they provide an extensible way to associate more semantics with the event specification.

With FLEA [5], the user expresses his or her requirements and assumptions for monitoring. The main idea behind this is to be able to monitor programs that were not developed with monitoring in mind and to check software requirements through events. In a similar way, xMonEve is meant to be independent of implementation, and this also includes its structure. In addition, we also think it is important to bridge different abstractions, such as requirements and implementation, and any other possible abstraction.

The ActEvent model proposed by P. Gross et al. [8] presents an XML-based language (SmartEvents) for event description. This language associates event instances to their syntactic and semantic model. This language is proposed primarily for primitive events, those events with a direct association (or mapping) to the application, directly collected by probes. In our case, xMonEven is used to describe the types for primitive and composed events. In the context of ActEvent research, xMonEve could be used for the installation of the probes in the target application and to partially help in the construction of Gaugents [8].

Another kind of related work is the application of software monitoring at the architecture level [3,26]. It is worth mentioning that both of these cited works propose the instrumentation of connectors for collecting the information, instead of the components. Also, the basic element for analysis is the event at the architectural level. In these works, the mapping problem between software architecture and implementation is simplified because the implementation and software architecture design present a one-to-one structural correspondence.

6   Conclusions

The event and its definition play a major role in the integration of development techniques for architecting dependable systems, because this is an abstraction common to multiples techniques. However, to have an effective integration, events also have to be described in a common way. xMonEve is an event description language designed for this integration purpose. We are currently working on xMonEve definition and refinement. xMonEve does not describe how the event is going to be collected, but rather what that event is or represents. xMonEve is not intended to substitute for other event specification languages but to promote integration of techniques by providing an interchangeable description of events.

In this position paper, we presented the problem of mapping implementation to software architecture, we discussed the importance of the event description in the context of developing complex and reliable systems, we presented requirements for event description languages, we presented our current work in xMonEve, we showed how xMonEve can support the integration of reliability techniques and software architectures, we proposed a top-down approach for reliability, and we compared our work with other specification languages from the literature.

In our discussion, on some occasions we say "the developer would describe the event," or something similar. However, this is a hard task by itself and should be supported by tools. Event definitions could and should be generated/extracted from many system documents, such as requirement specifications, architectural and design models, testing documents, source code, etc. This type of tool support is also an important step toward establishing the usefulness and success of monitoring techniques, as well as event specification languages. Tools can also help during the description task by providing the user with intuitive GUI, in a way that the developer need not even to visualize the xMonEve description for the event types. Our future work plans include the development of tools to extract event descriptions from specific software documents and providing a proper GUI for the developer.

At this stage, we have not yet addressed analysis and action description — i.e., how to describe what types of analyses and actions a monitoring system should perform, and for what purpose. It is important right now, however, for us to understand better how different purposes may affect monitoring systems. Since a major part of the functionality of monitoring systems is the same in multiple situations, we will need a family of monitoring systems with customizable components, so that the configuration of monitoring systems can move another step forward. Instead of configuring sensors and probes, configuration would represent the tailoring of the whole monitoring system to fulfill specific developer needs. We are currently working on a framework for development of dynamic and configurable monitoring systems based on architectural customizable services and components.

Acknowledgements

We would like to acknowledge Professor David Redmiles, Professor Henry Muccini, Cleidson de Souza, Roberto Silva and members of the ROSATEA group, especially Marlon Vieira, for discussions on research efforts associated with this work. We also appreciate the feedback from the reviewers and the efforts of the editors in putting together this special issue.

We are very grateful to the agencies that have supported this work in part, including the Brazilian Research Agency (CNPq award #200256/98-2), the National Science Foundation (NSF award #0083099), and the University of California and Conexant Systems via the UC MICRO program.

References

[1]   E. Al-Shaer, H. Abdel-Wahab, and K. Maly, "HiFi: A New Monitoring Architecture for Distributed Systems Management", IEEE 19th International Conference on Distributed Computing Systems (ICDCS'99), pp. 171-178, Austin, Texas, May 1999.

[2]   J. Bailey, A. Poulovassilis, and P. Wood, "An Event-Condition-Action Language for XML", in Procceedings of the Eleventh International World Wide Web Conference (WWW 2002), May 7-11, 2001, Honolulu, Hawaii, USA.

[3]   R. Balzer, "Instrumenting, Monitoring, & Debugging Software Architectures", 1997. [http://citeseer.nj.nec.com/411425.html] (accessed on Nov 15th, 2002).

[4]   P.C. Bates, "Debugging heterogeneous distributed systems using event-based models of behavior", ACM Trans Computer System, vol. 13, n. 1, Feb. 1995, pp. 1 - 31

[5]   D. Cohen, M. Feather, K. Narayanaswamy, and S. Fickas, "Automatic Monitoring of Software Requirements", Proc Int'l Conf Software Engineering (ICSE) 1997, pp. 602-603.

[6]   J. Cook and A. Wolf, "Automating Process Discovery through Event-Data Analysis", in Proceedings of the 17th International Conference on Software Engineering (ICSE17), pages 73-82, Seattle, WA, April 1995.

[7]   E. Gamma et al., "Design Patterns: Elements of Reusable Object-Oriented Software", Addison-Wesley, 1995.

[8]   P. Gross, S. Gupta, G. Kaiser, G. Kc, and J. Parekh, "An Active Events Model for Systems Monitoring", in Proc Working Conference on Complex and Dynamic Systems Architecture, December, 2001.

[9]   R. Hofmann, R. Klar, B.Mohr, A. Quick, and M. Siegle, "Distributed Performance Monitoring: Methods, Tools, and Applications", IEEE Trans. Parallel and Distributed Systems, vol. 5, n. 6, June 1994, pp.585-598.

[10]   Y. Huang and C. Kintala, "Software Implemented Fault Tolerance: Technologies and Experience", Proc. 23rd Int'l Symp on Fault Tolerance Computing, 1993, pp. 2-9.

[11]   D. Hilbert and D. Redmiles. "Extracting Usability Information from User Interface Events". ACM Computing Surveys, vol. 32, n. 4, December 2000.

[12]   P. Inverardi and A. Wolf, "Formal Specification and Analysis of Software Architectures Using the Chemical Abstract Machine Model", IEEE Transactions on Software Engineering, vol. 21, no. 4, April 1995, pp. 373-386.

[13]   C. Jeffery, "Program Monitoring and Visualization: An Exploratory Approach", Springer-Verlag, 1999.

[14]   J. Joyce, G. Lomow, K. Slind, and B. Unger. "Monitoring Distributed Systems". ACM Transactions on Computer Systems, vol. 5, no. 2, May 1987.

[15]   J.F. Kitchin, "Practical Markov Modeling for Reliability Analysis", Proc Annual Reliability and Maintainability Symposium, 1988, Jan. 1988, pp. 290-296.

[16]   Y. Liao and D. Cohen, "A Specification Approach to High Level Program Monitoring and Measuring", IEEE Trans. Software Engineering, vol. 18, n. 11, Nov. 1992.

[17]   D. Luckham, and J. Vera, "An Event-Based Architecture Definition Language", IEEE Transactions on Software Engineering, Vol 21, No 9, pp.717-734. Sep. 1995, 21 pages.

[18]   Jeff Magee, Naranker Dulay, Susan Eisenbach, and Jeff Kramer, "Specifying Distributed Software Architectures", Proc. of 5th European Software Engineering Conference (ESEC'95), Sitges, September 1995, LNCS 989, (Springer-Verlag), 1995, 137-153.

[19]   N. Medvidovic, D. Rosenblum, and R. Taylor, "A Language and Environment for Architecture-Based Software Development and Evolution", Proc Int'l Conf on Software Engineering, May 1999, pp. 44 -53

[20]   D.M. Ogle, K. Schwan, and R. Snodgrass, "Application-Dependent Dynamic Monitoring of Distributed and Parallel Systems", IEEE Trans. Parallel and Distributed Systems, vol. 4, n. 7, July 1993, pp. 762-778.

[21]   D. Perry and A. Wolf, "Foundations for the Study of Software Architecture", ACM SIGSOFT Software Engineering Notes, vol. 17, no. 4, October 1992, pp. 40-52.

[22]   S. Reiss and M. Renieris, "Encoding Program Executions", Proc Int'l Conf Software Engineering, May 2001.

[23]   B. Schroeder, "On-Line Monitoring: A Tutorial", IEEE Computer, vol. 28, n. 6, June 1995, pp.72-77.

[24]   Y.C. Shim and C.V. Ramamoorthy, "Monitoring and Control of Distributed Systems", Proc. 1st Int'l Conf on System Integration, Apr. 1990, pp. 672-681.

[25]   R. Snodgrass, "A Relational Approach to Monitoring Complex Systems", ACM Trans. Computer Systems, vol. 6, n. 2, May 1988, pp.156-196.

[26]   M. Vieira, M. Dias, and D. Richardson, "Analyzing Software Architecture with Argus-I", Proc Int'l Conf on Software Engineering, June 2000, pp. 758 -761.

[27]   A. Wolf and D. Rosenblum, "A Study in Software Process Capture and Analysis", in Proceedings of the Second International Conference on the Software Process (ICSP2), pages 115-124, Berlin, Germany, February 1993.

Architectural Mismatch Tolerance

Rogério de Lemos[1], Cristina Gacek[2], and Alexander Romanovsky[2]

[1]Computing Laboratory
University of Kent at Canterbury, UK
r.delemos@ukc.ac.uk
[2]School of Computing Science
University of Newcastle upon Tyne, UK
{cristina.gacek,alexander.romanovsky}@ncl.ac.uk

Abstract. The integrity of complex software systems built from existing components is becoming more dependent on the integrity of the mechanisms used to interconnect these components and, in particular, on the ability of these mechanisms to cope with architectural mismatches that might exist between components. There is a need to detect and handle (i.e. to tolerate) architectural mismatches during runtime because in the majority of practical situations it is impossible to localize and correct all such mismatches during development time. When developing complex software systems, the problem is not only to identify the appropriate components, but also to make sure that these components are interconnected in a way that allows mismatches to be tolerated. The resulting architectural solution should be a system based on the existing components, which are independent in their nature, but are able to interact in well-understood ways. To find such a solution we apply general principles of fault tolerance to dealing with architectural mismatches.

1   Introduction

Software architecture can be defined as the structure(s) of a system, which comprise software components, the externally visible properties of those components and the relationships among them [18][20]. A software architecture is usually described in terms of its components, connectors and their configuration [15]: components represent computation units, connectors correspond to the communication protocols, and configurations characterize the topology of the system in terms of the interconnection of components via connectors.

As a result of combining several architectural elements using a specific configuration, architectural mismatches may occur [11]. *Architectural mismatches* are logical inconsistencies between constraints of various architectural elements being composed. An architectural mismatch occurs when the assumptions that a component makes about another component, or the rest of the system, do not match. That is, the assumptions associated with the service provided by a component are different from the assumptions associated with the services required by a component for behaving as specified [15]. These assumptions can be related to the nature of components and connectors (control and data models, and synchronization protocols), the global

R. de Lemos et al. (Eds.): Architecting Dependable Systems, LNCS 2677, pp. 175-194, 2003.
© Springer-Verlag Berlin Heidelberg 2003

system structure, or the process of building the system [11][20]. Traditionally, mismatches have been dealt with statically [8][10], by means of analysis and removal. For example, a formal approach has been advocated to uncover architectural mismatches in the behavior of components, in particular, deadlocks [4][12].

There are many reasons to support our claim that it is usually non-practicable to statically localize and correct all possible architectural mismatches, and because of this, we believe that it is vital to be able to build systems that can tolerate such mismatches. This is mainly due to the complexity of modern systems and restricted applicability of the static methods of correcting mismatches (c.f. software design faults). First of all, complex applications have complex software architectures in which components are interconnected in complex ways and have many parameters and characteristics to be taken into account, and they have to meet many functional and non-functional requirements that often have to be expressed at the level of software architecture. Secondly, architects make mistakes while defining software architectures, in general, and while dealing with mismatches, in particular. Thirdly, there is a strong trend in using off-the-shelf elements while building complex applications and because of the very nature of such elements some information about their architectural characteristics may be unavailable. Lastly, modern software systems are to be open, flexible and adaptive, and they may undergo dynamic reconfiguration (often by incorporating new components knowledge about which is not available offline), adding uncertainty about the various architectural elements present at any point in time.

Instead of dealing with architectural mismatches during development time, which is the conventional approach, this paper shows how these mismatches can be tolerated during runtime at the architectural level. The rest of the paper is structured as follows. Section 2 discusses architectural mismatches in the context of features that are associated either with the architectural elements or the application being represented by these elements. In Section 3, we present some basic dependability concepts that provide the basis for the following discussion (in Section 4) on architectural mismatches from the perspective of system dependability. In Section 5, we address the notion of mismatch tolerance by discussing in more detail its basic activities. Section 6 presents several simple examples that demonstrate the proposed approach. Finally, Section 7 concludes with a summary of the contribution and a perspective of future research.

2   Architectural Mismatches and Features

To understand better the ways of tolerating architectural mismatches we will look first into specific characteristics of the individual architectural elements to be composed into a system, as well as into the reoccurring architectural solutions (i.e. architectural styles) applied for building system architectures.

2.1   Architectural Features

The architectural mismatches occur because of inconsistencies among given architectural elements. These inconsistencies can be stated in terms of the features (i.e. characteristics or properties relevant to system composition) exhibited by the architectural elements to be integrated into the system. Such features have proven to be very useful for static mismatch detection [10].

A considerable number of such features have been determined while studying system composition from the viewpoint of detecting architectural mismatches during system development to allow systems to be corrected by removing mismatches [10]. Concurrency, distribution, supported data transfers (e.g. via shared data variables, explicit data connectors, shared repositories, etc.), dynamism (system ability to change dynamically its topology), encapsulation (provision of well-defined interfaces), layering, backtracking, and reentrance are some of the examples of the architectural features relevant to possible mismatches. A very useful source of such features can be found in research on online system upgrading, where, for example, additional (meta-) information describing component behavior is used to deal with component interface upgrades [13].

Another dimension of the analysis proposed in [10] is relevance of such features to the particular architectural styles (such as pipe-and-filter, blackboard, etc.) employed in building system architecture: it is clear that some of these features are not applicable to some particular styles. For example, the pipe-and-filter style assumes multithreaded concurrency, no backtracking or reentrance, while the blackboard style assumes backtracking, imposes no restrictions on types of concurrency and assumes no reentrance. The overall idea here is that by analyzing the characteristics of the architectural elements to be integrated and the styles from which these elements were derived, the system architects are able to localize architectural mismatches earlier in the life cycle.

Some examples of architectural mismatches that can be detected by analyzing the architectural features are [10]:

- *Data transfer from a component that may later backtrack* – this mismatch may cause undesired side effects on the overall composed system state.
- *Call to a non-reentrant component* - this mismatch may happen when system composition is achieved via a bridging (triggered) call, and the callee is not reentrant and is already running at the time of the call.
- *Sharing or transferring data with different underlying representations* - this mismatch happens when sharing or transferring data with different underlying representations, including differences in data formats, units and coordinate systems.

2.2   Style-Specific and Application-Specific Mismatches

Architectural features of architectural elements and their groupings may be inherent to the architectural style(s) used, or specific to the application at hand. This occurs because architectural styles impose constraints on the kinds of architectural elements that may be present and on their configurations [20], yet they do not prescribe all the features that may be present in an application [10]. During software development, the software architecture is incrementally refined following the refinement of the system definition. Initially, the software architecture is defined in terms of architectural styles, thus binding the style-specific features. Subsequently, as the architecture is further refined towards the life-cycle architecture, application-specific features are bound. This is exemplified on Table 1 (adapted from [9]). In the following we will refer to the architectural features pertinent to particular architectural styles as *style-specific features*. A set of such features is defined in [10]. The features that are defined by the characteristics of the application to be developed but not by the architectural styles employed are called *application-specific features*.

Every time an architectural feature is bound, there is a potential for an architectural mismatch to be introduced. Hence, we refer to architectural mismatches as being:

- *style-specific* - if their presence is brought about by some architectural feature(s) that the style(s) imposes, or
- *application-specific* - if their presence is due to architectural decisions imposed by the application at hand but not the particular style(s) used.

Table 1. Refinement of software architecture under a Spiral Model Development

	Early Cycle 1	End of Cycle 1	Cycle 2	Cycle 3
Definition of operational concept and system requirements	Determination of top-level concept of operations	Determination of top-level concept of operations	Determination of detailed concept of operations	Determination of IOC requirements, growth vector
Definition of system and software architecture	System scope/ boundaries/ interfaces	System scope/ boundaries/ interfaces	Top-level HW, SW, human requirements	Choice of life-cycle architecture
Elaboration of software architecture	*No explicit architectural decision*	*Small number of candidate architectures described by architectural styles*	*Provisional choice of top-level information architecture*	*Some components of above TBD (low-risk and/or deferrable)*
Binding of architectural features	*No architectural features explicitly defined*	*Fixed architectural features that are defined by architectural styles, others are unknown*	*Architectural features defined by architectural styles are fixed as are some application specific ones, others are unknown*	*Most architectural features are fixed, the few unknown ones relate to parts of the architecture still to be defined*

Identification of the nature of the architectural mismatches, as well as the nature of the architectural features causing these inconsistencies among architectural elements plays a vital role in developing approaches to tolerating such mismatches.

3   Dependability

Dependability is a vital property of any system justifying the reliance that can be placed on the service it delivers [14]. The causal relationship between the dependability impairments, that is, faults, errors and failures, is essential for characterizing the major activities associated with the dependability means (fault tolerance, avoidance, removal and forecasting). A *fault* is the adjudged or hypothesized cause of an error. An *error* is the part of the system state that is liable to lead to the subsequent failure. A *failure* occurs when a system service deviates from the behavior expected by the user.

Fault tolerance is a means for achieving dependability working under assumptions that a system contains faults (e.g. ones made by humans while developing or using systems, and caused by aging hardware) and aiming at providing the required services in spite of them. Fault tolerance is carried by error processing, aiming at removing errors from the system state before failures happen, and fault treatment, aiming at preventing faults from being once again activated [14].

Error processing typically consists of three steps: error detection, error diagnosis and error recovery. *Error detection* identifies an erroneous state in the system. *Error diagnosis* assesses the damage caused by the detected error, or the errors propagated before detection. *Error recovery* transforms a system state that contains errors into an error free state. Recovery typically takes forms of either backward error recovery or forward error recovery. When the former is applied the system is returned to a previous (assumed to be correct) state; the typical techniques used are application-independent and often work transparently for the application (e.g. atomic transactions and checkpoints). Forward error recovery intents to move the system into a correct state using knowledge about the current erroneous state; this recovery is application-specific by its nature. The most general means for achieving it is exception handling [5].

Fault treatment consists of two steps: fault diagnosis and system repair. *Fault diagnosis* determines the causes of the error in terms of both location and nature. *System repair* consists of isolating the fault to avoid its reactivation, reconfiguring the system either by switching on spare components or reassigning tasks among non-failed components, and reinitializing the system by checking, updating and recording the new configuration [1]. The process of repairing the system usually modifies its structure in order for the system to continue to deliver an acceptable service.

Providing system fault tolerance plays an ever-growing role in achieving system dependability as there are many evidences proving that it is not possible to rid the system and system execution from faults. These include the growing complexity of software causing programmers' bugs, operators' mistakes, and failures in the environment in which the system operates.

4   Dependability and Mismatches

In the context of dependability, an architectural mismatch is an undesired, though expected, circumstance, which must be identified as a *design fault* (in the terminology from [14]). When a mismatch is activated, it produces an *error caused by mismatch* (ECM) that can either be latent or detected. Similarly to errors, only a subset of ECMs can be detected as such (see Figure 1). Additional information is needed to allow an error to be associated with a mismatch. Eventually, there is a system failure when the ECM affects the service delivered by the system.

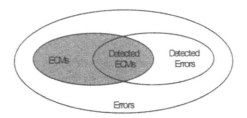

Fig. 1. Detected errors caused by mismatches

For describing the means for dealing with architectural mismatches, we draw an analogy with faults, which can be avoided, removed or tolerated. Faults are tolerated when they cannot be avoided, and their removal is not worthwhile or their existence is not known beforehand. The same kind of issues happens with architectural mismatches. Mismatches can be *prevented* by imposing strict rules on how components should be built and integrated. Mismatches can be *removed* when integrating arbitrary components by using static analysis methods and techniques [10]. However, this does not guarantee the absence of mismatches since risk and cost tradeoffs may hinder their removal, or system integrators may not be aware of their existence (similarly, research has shown that residual faults in software systems are inevitable). Consequently, mismatches should be *tolerated* by processing ECMs and treating mismatches, otherwise the system might fail.

In the following, before presenting mismatch tolerance, we discuss in more detail what is mismatch prevention and mismatch removal.

4.1   Mismatch Prevention

The approaches associated with mismatch prevention attempt to protect a component, or the context of that component, against potential mismatches by adding to the structure of the system architectural solutions. The assumption here is that the integrators are aware of all incompatibilities between system components. For example, if the architectural style of a particular component does not fit the style of the system in which is to be integrated, then a specialized wrapper can be developed as a means of fixing architectural incompatibilities [18].

There are three classes of structuring techniques for dealing with architectural mismatches, all of which are based on inserting code for mediating the interaction between the components [7]:

- *Wrappers* – which are a form of encapsulation whereby some component is enclosed within an alternative abstraction, thus yielding to an alternative interface to the component;

- *Bridges* – which translate some of the assumptions of the components interfaces. Different from a wrapper, a bridge is independent of any particular component, and needs to be explicitly invoked by an external component;
- *Mediators* – which exhibit properties of both wrappers and bridges. Different from a bridge, a mediator incorporates a planning function that results in the runtime determination of the translation. Similar to wrappers, mediators are first class software architecture entities due to their semantic complexity and runtime autonomy.

4.2   Mismatch Removal

The approaches associated with mismatch removal are those that aim at detecting architectural mismatches during the integration of arbitrary components [10]. Existing approaches for identifying architectural mismatches are aimed for the development of software, either during the composition of components while evaluating the architectural options [10], or during architectural modeling and analysis [8]. The Architect's Automated Assistant (AAA) approach uses automatic static analysis for performing early risk assessment for the purpose of detecting mismatches during component composition [10]. It is an approach that supports rapid evaluation of components with respect to potential incompatibilities among them. The software integrator gathers the information for the analysis, known as architectural features, from the system requirements and the specification of the components. On the other hand, the technique for architectural modeling relies on the specification of component invariants and services for analyzing the architectural conformance of its components. For example, the behavioral conformance of the pre- and post-conditions of two components can be analyzed using a model checking tool [8] [15]. The above two techniques, evaluation of architectural options and architectural modeling, are argued to be complementary because the former is able to detect mismatches very early during development, while the latter performs a more detailed and precise analysis of component mismatch.

The techniques being proposed by these approaches are so specific to the context of software development that they cannot be transposed for runtime detection of error caused mismatches (ECMs). For example, how can we detect during runtime whether components have single or multiple threads, and how can we identify inconsistencies between the pre- and post-conditions among operations of interacting components? However, although it is difficult, in general terms, to relate the detection of errors to specific architectural mismatches that have caused them, it is nevertheless feasible to associate some (detectable) errors to architectural mismatches that may occur in the components' behavior, their interfaces, or interaction protocols. For example, a mismatch may occur in the naming of an operation or message, or in the number, ordering, type, and units of parameters [21].

5   Architectural Mismatch Tolerance

The main motivation for specifying mechanisms for tolerating architectural mismatches at the architectural level, instead of the implementation level, for example, is that the nature of mismatches and the context in which they should be fixed would be lost at the later stages of software development. Making an analogy with fault tolerance, it has been shown that the same type of problem exists when exception handling is not considered in the context of the software life cycle [6]. Moreover, we cannot expect that a general runtime mechanism would be able to handle a wide range of architectural mismatches, in the same way as there is no sufficiently general fault tolerance mechanism that can handle all classes of faults. It is envisaged that different classes of architectural mismatches will require different types of detection mechanisms and fixes that have to be specified at the architectural level.

Although the goal is to tolerate architectural mismatches at the architectural level, it is nevertheless necessary to deal with two levels of abstraction: the architectural level, where the mismatches are actually introduced, and the execution level, where ECM processing and mismatch treatment take place. *ECM processing* comprises three steps [14]:

- *Detection of ECMs*, which identifies erroneous states that are caused by mismatches;
- *Diagnosis of ECMs*, which assesses the system damages caused by the detected ECMs;
- *Recovery from ECMs*, which brings the system to an ECM-free state.

However, ECM processing is not sufficient if we would like to avoid the recurrence of the same architectural mismatch, so there is the need to treat mismatches, in the same way as faults are treated [14]. *Mismatch treatment* involves two major steps:

- *Mismatch diagnosis*, which determines the cause (localization and nature) of the ECM;
- *System repair*, which prevents a new activation of the architectural mismatch; it is performed by isolating the mismatch, and reconfiguring and reinitializing the system, in order to continue to provide an adequate, perhaps degraded, service.

The intent of fault tolerant techniques is to structure systems to inhibit the propagation of errors, and to facilitate their detection and the recovery from them. Similarly, when dealing with architectural mismatches, there is the need to structure systems at the architectural level in a way that prevents propagation of ECMs, facilitates ECM detection and recovery, and makes it difficult for the architectural mismatches to be reactivated.

In addition to system structuring, there is also the need for documenting architectural features of the system, as discussed in Section 2. This information is fundamental for distinguishing ECMs from other system errors, architectural mismatches from faults, and for choosing features suitable for tolerating style- and application-specific architectural mismatches. If little or no information is made available at the architectural level, either as interface properties of architectural elements or error codes, then this distinction cannot be characterized. For example, if there is no information about the types of data transferred between two architectural elements but the producer and the consumer assume different types (e.g. measurement units) the following situations are possible:

- An error is detected by the consumer but because there is not enough information it cannot be identified as an ECM, so unsuitable fault tolerance measures are applied (e.g. rollback);
- An error is further propagated outside the consumer and detected by other components. In this case without additional information it is impossible to identify the damage area to be recovered;
- The ECM is not detected and the system fails to deliver the service.

In order to provide the basis for defining an architectural solution for tolerating mismatches, in the rest of this section we present in more detail the activities associated with ECM processing and mismatch treatment. For each of the activities, we take into consideration whether architectural features, both style- and application-specific, are incorporated into the architectural description of a system.

5.1   ECM Processing

As previously discussed, the detection of an ECM implies the presence of an architectural mismatch. The activation of a mismatch causing a system error depends on whether some conditions are satisfied, these conditions are related to inconsistencies in architectural features. In the following, we present in more detail the different activities associated with ECM processing.

5.1.1   ECM Detection

Upon error detection, one must first determine whether that particular error can be identified as an ECM. For an error to be detected as an ECM we need additional information at runtime about the system states and the features of the relevant architectural elements that would enable to identify this particular error as an ECM. This ought to be done based on the detected error and on the presence of the conditions required for activating the architectural mismatch.

The identification of an error as an ECM will facilitate the process of error recovery, in particularly if the error can be differentiated as being either caused by an application- or style-specific mismatch. For both types of ECMs, error codes should be provided as an outcome of a failed operation, and these codes should be related to architectural features of the system (as it will be seen in the examples in Section 6). Provision of an error code to an error caused by a style-specific mismatch could be related to the execution of an operation that violates the properties of an architectural notation, for instance, when in a non-reentrant pipe-and-filter architecture a filter sends data to another filter that is already processing data from other source. On the other hand, provision of an error code to an error caused by an application-specific mismatch could be related, for example, to the semantic discrepancy of data received from other component; this error code should help, for instance, identify that the data received has the wrong type, such as, instead of receiving a value in meters, the value is in feet.

Identification of a system error as an ECM is not essential if provisions are made in the later stages of mismatch tolerance for processing the error and treating the fault accordingly. However, the later an error is identified as an ECM or a fault as a mismatch, the more costly and more uncertain (mainly in its successful outcome) the respective processes of recovery and repair are. One of the techniques that can be used for detecting ECMs is executable assertions.

5.1.2   ECM Diagnosis

The purpose of ECM diagnosis is to assess the damages caused by the detected ECM. During damage assessment it is necessary to identify all the erroneous states of the system before initiating recovery from the ECM, for this purpose there is no need to differentiate system errors from ECMs. If an ECM is not detected close to where it is activated, the propagation can render impossible the error recovery. This is usually the case for errors caused by an application-specific mismatch. The propagation of such ECM to other architectural elements depends on the encapsulation properties of the architectural language used to describe the system. Ideally the error should be contained within the component where the mismatch is activated. On the other hand, an error caused by a style-specific mismatch is more capable of affecting the whole architectural configuration of a system than a single component due to the lack of diversity in the style-specific features of the architecture. For example, in a blackboard architecture where only some of the components are able to backtrack, the impact of a component backtracking has to be assessed in the context of the whole system architecture to identify which components' states might have been affected by the backtracking. For both style- and application-specific mismatches, the process of damage assessment can be performed either by using static or dynamic techniques [1].

5.1.3   ECM Recovery

The purpose of ECM recovery (which can be one of the form: backward, forward or compensation, as well as their combination) is to replace at the architectural level an ECM state by an error-free state. The level of difficulty encountered for recovering from ECMs very much depends on the specific characteristics of the ECM, the application, and the error containment capabilities of the architectural style.

In general terms, the type of ECM, whether style- or application-specific, should dictate the choice of recovery form. For errors caused by style-specific mismatches, backward recovery is more appropriate because they are application independent and require general approaches for recovering. If the architecture provides adequate error containment capabilities, ECM recovery may consist of eliminating existing erroneous states within an architectural element, this can be done by rolling back to an error-free state that the element had prior to the detection of the ECM. For example, if a component semantically checks the information it provides to other components for potential errors then it can be assumed that errors that might occur within the component are not propagated to the rest of the system. On the other hand, if the architecture does not provide adequate error containment capabilities, then the recovery at the architectural element level might not be sufficient, and there is the need to have a coordinated recovery involving several system components and connectors. For example, if a component needs to rollback and there are other components in the system that cannot rollback then some system coordination might be needed to rid the system of the ECMs.

For errors caused by application-specific mismatches, forward recovery is more appropriate since knowledge about the application allows bringing the system into a new (correct) state from which the processing can resume. In particularly forward recovery in the form of exception handling can be used for dealing with those errors that are anticipated. For example, if a component detects a semantic discrepancy in the value of a variable that is transferred by other component with a different underlying representation, then the component can calculate a new value (assuming it knows the correct underlying context, which, again, can be documented in a form of corresponding architectural features), and resume normal processing.

In those cases where we cannot distinguish whether the ECM is either style- or application specific, or even an error cannot be identified as an ECM, error recovery should follow a general approach based on backward error recovery. In these situations, as in all those in which not enough information is provided for supporting process of tolerating a mismatch, error recovery often becomes intrinsically complex.

5.2   Mismatch Treatment

The treatment of mismatches aims to avoid mismatches from being further activated once their nature and location have been identified. As an activity following ECM processing, mismatch treatment attempts to avoid the re-activation of mismatches. If enough information regarding architectural features is made available as the interface properties of architectural elements, the process of tolerating mismatches might be reduced to mismatch repair. This can be achieved if, before any operation, architectural elements check for potential mismatches by requesting information about the architectural features of the other elements. After a potential mismatch is localized it should be repaired. For example, in a pipe-and-filter architecture, if a filter before sending its data checks for the status of the other filter and detects that the other filter is already receiving data from other source, then an alternative filter that is able to provide the same kind of services could be sought in the system.

As we have already seen in the descriptions of previous activities, the treatment of mismatches depends on whether the relevant architectural features are style- or application-specific. For example, as we will show later, mismatches caused by incompatibilities in the style-specific features of an architecture often require more fundamental changes to the system architecture at hand. In the following, we present in more detail the different activities associated with mismatch treatment, considering again style- and application-specific mismatches.

5.2.1   Mismatch Diagnosis

The purpose of mismatch diagnosis is to determine the cause of ECMs, in terms of both location and nature, which, in particular, means identification of the architectural elements that failed and the way they failed. This activity is fundamental for the process of mismatch repair since a clear identification of the mismatch is needed before any changes are made on the system architecture. The activity of diagnosis is complicated by the fact that it often requires a lot of information from the system and elaborate means to process this information. The types of information that are necessary: the detected erroneous state (which presumably is cause by a mismatch), the overall state of the system when the ECM is detected, the configuration of the architecture, together with the available information on architectural features. The latter, in particular, provides the means for identifying the nature of the architectural mismatches. Although it is important to known whether a mismatch is style- or application-specific, the identification of the type of mismatch among a list of potential mismatches [10] is equally necessary for selecting the appropriate repair for the architecture.

5.2.2   Mismatch Repair

The purpose of mismatch repair is to prevent mismatches from being activated again. Since each mismatch is caused by incompatibilities between features of architectural elements (mainly components), the repair of this mismatch can be performed by modifying the system structure. This architectural reconfiguration is performed in runtime, and it is not a simple task as in most cases it requires redundant architectural elements that are intrinsically diverse[1] in the way they provide architectural features (both application- and style-specific), since mismatches are design faults. The reconfiguration can be performed in various forms: removal or/and addition of a single component, removal of all the components involved in a mismatch (e.g., a particular architectural style-specific mismatch), replacement of the connector linking the problematic components with a new connector with additional functionalities aiming at avoiding mismatches. For example, in the case of a component that is not able to rollback, this component can be replaced by other component that allows rollback, or an alternative connector can be provided that allows information to be buffered.

The dichotomy between style- and application-specific mismatches for system repair is difficult to observe since for repairing some style-specific mismatches it is necessary to rely on application level mechanisms and techniques. In these cases, simple replacing an architectural element is not a viable option due to the lack of diversity in the features of the architectural style, which creates inherent difficulties in repairing some style-specific mismatches. In terms of application-specific mismatches, the repair mechanisms and techniques are essentially application related and as such should exploit available redundancies at the application level.

Although the general aim of mismatch repair is to find and employ mechanisms and techniques that are sufficiently general to allow dealing with a wide range of mismatches, in real systems this is difficult to achieve because of three main reasons: mismatches of different types require different ways of reconfiguration and different types of redundant elements, very often not enough system redundancies can be made available, and the most effective way of performing repair is application dependent.

Summarizing, in order for the system to tolerate architectural mismatches, it is crucial that the information associated with the architectural features (either style- or application-specific) is documented and encoded in the system in different forms, either as error codes for performing activities associated with ECM processing, or as interface properties for the activities associated with mismatch treatment. If enough information is made available, then the process of tolerating architectural mismatches becomes less complex and less prone to faults. In the following, we demonstrate

---

[1] By diverse elements we mean here architectural elements that provide the same functionality but have different designs and implementations.

through examples the different activities associated with mismatch tolerance, including the cases in which the whole process can be improved, sometimes by suppressing some of the activities, when suitable architectural features are exploited during runtime.

6 Examples

This section demonstrates how mismatches can be tolerated following the framework discussed above. From the whole set of potential architectural mismatches discussed in [10], we have selected three mismatches, which are representative of the different types of mismatches and allow us to show different ways of tolerating them. In order to analyze the particularities associated with style-specific mismatches, the examples will be presented in the context of three architectural styles [20]: pipe-and-filter, blackboard, and client-server.

Our assumption here is that some of the non-functional properties/attributes of components (in particular, ones related to the architectural features) are published at their interfaces. Depending on the information available and on the way it is processed, we can distinguish three general scenarios in which architectural mismatches can be tolerated.

1. The first scenario falls into the category in which mismatch tolerance is restricted to mismatch repair. The basis for this scenario is the above assumption that features of the architectural elements are provided at their interfaces. The availability of this information allows for a component before engaging into an interaction, trying to identify potential mismatches. If an architectural mismatch is localized, then the activities associated with error processing and mismatch diagnosis can be ignored.
2. The second scenario falls into the category in which mismatch tolerance starts with ECM detection. During the interaction between two components when one of them returns an error diagnosed as an ECM, there is no need for the system to perform error diagnosis. Once again, for this to be possible it is necessary that additional information, about its architectural features, be made available at the interface of the architectural components.
3. The third scenario falls into the category in which mismatch tolerance starts with detection of a system error. In this scenario, there is no additional information available about the architectural features. Hence, there is a need to perform error diagnosis to identify the nature of the error as being an ECM, for that, additional information is needed about the state of the system.

In the following, we discuss how three different mismatches can be tolerated in the context of the above three scenarios. For each example of architectural mismatch, we present the type of mismatch, the characteristics of the architectural styles being used, and provide a small architectural configuration capturing the mismatch being discussed. Within this context, we proceed to explain, in detail, the different steps associated with the process of tolerating architectural mismatches.

6.1   Style-Specific Mismatch

As a style-specific mismatch, we consider the mismatch "*call to a non-reentrant component*". This mismatch happens when a component calls another component, and the latter may already be performing the requested execution and this execution is not reentrant [10]. This mismatch will be analyzed in the context of the pipe-and-filter style in which data is transformed by successive components. The components are the filters, which have almost no contextual information and retain no state between executions, and the connectors are the pipes, which are stateless [20].

An example of the pipe-and-filter architectural configuration in which the above mismatch can occur is shown in Figure 2(a), when FilterA calls FilterC without waiting until the currently executed request from FilterB is completed. In this example we assume that a Unix environment is used, which can provide a runtime documentation related to the appropriate style-specific features. For implementing the first scenario we have to ensure that the resources/ports become exclusive before executing any interaction between the filters. Implementation of the second scenario assumes that FilterB always executes additional (application) code before connecting to FilterC. The third scenario is not applicable here because FilterB always receives information based on the Unix error while accessing a busy filter, so we will not consider it any further.

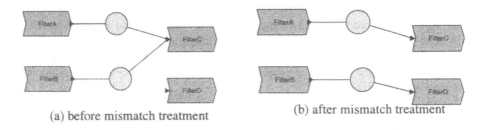

(a) before mismatch treatment   (b) after mismatch treatment

Fig. 2. A non-reentrant component in a pipe-and-filter architecture

This is how ECM processing and mismatch treatment (see Section 5) look like for the two remaining scenarios:

a) ECM Detection:
- for scenario 1, no detection needed;
- for scenario 2, such an ECM is detected using the error code generated by Unix.

b) ECM Diagnosis:
- for scenario 1, no diagnosis needed;
- for scenario 2, during damage assessment there is no need to identify the nature, since the error code provides enough information.

c) ECM Recovery:
- for scenario 1, no recovery required;
- for scenario 2, different ways of recovering are possible depending on the application (e.g., backward or forward recovery, compensation, and recovery employing time redundancy).

d) Mismatch Diagnosis:
- for both scenarios, the error code should provide enough information to identify the location and the nature of mismatch;

e) Mismatch Repair:
- for both scenarios, system reconfiguration involves the usage of alternative component or connector. The way of reconfiguring the system depends on the application characteristics. Some possible scenarios are as follows: FilterB can switch to using an alternate FilterD (as shown in Figure 2(b)); it can create another instance of FilterC and switch to using it; it can use a different type of pipe (e.g. a timed pipe); in the situation when FilterB has a higher priority than FilterA, FilterC could be killed. In Unix environments, a script can execute this repair.

6.2   Application-Specific Mismatch

As an application-specific mismatch, we consider the mismatch *"sharing or transferring data with differing underlying representations"*. This mismatch occurs when communication between two components concerning a specific data cannot happen because the data being shared or transferred has different underlying representations, which might include, different data formats, units and coordinate systems [10]. This mismatch will be analyzed in the context of the client-server style, which is representative of data abstract systems in which a component – the server, provides services to other components – the clients.

An example of the client-server architectural configuration in which the above mismatch can occur is shown in Figure 3(a), when Client1 requests a service from ServerA but provides a value in feet while the server requires it to be in meters. For implementing the two first scenarios, we assume that the application-specific features of both components contain information about the units being used. In the first scenario, this information is part of the interface of the server, while in the second scenario this information is part of the services provided by the server application. The implementation of the third scenario does not assume any additional information is provided.

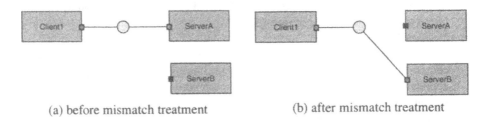

(a) before mismatch treatment   (b) after mismatch treatment

Fig. 3. Components with different underlying representations in a client-server architecture

This is how ECM processing and mismatch treatment look like for the three scenarios:

a) ECM Detection:
- for scenario 1, no detection needed;
- for scenario 2, an ECM is detected from the application-specific features of the component;
- for scenario 3, a system error is detected.

b) ECM Diagnosis:
- for scenario 1, no diagnosis needed;
- for scenario 2, during damage assessment there is no need to identify the nature, since the error provides enough information.
- for scenario 3, a full damage assessment is necessary.

c) ECM Recovery:
- for scenario 1, no recovery required;
- for scenarios 2 and 3, different ways of recovering are possible depending on the application (backward or forward recovery, or compensation).

d) Mismatch Diagnosis:
- for scenarios 1 & 2, the error should provide enough information to identify the location and the nature of mismatch;
- for scenario 3, a full mismatch diagnosis is necessary.

e) Mismatch Repair:
- for all the scenarios, system reconfiguration involves the usage of alternative component or connector. One of the ways to repair is for Client1 to request services of another ServerB (as shown in Figure 3(b)), which allows processing the request in feet. Another way to repair is to introduce a bridge that performs unit transformation.

6.3   Style- and Application-Specific Mismatch

As an application-specific mismatch, we consider the mismatch "*call or spawn from a subsystem that may later backtrack*". This mismatch occurs when after a component transfers data to other components, it backtracks, which might cause some undesired side effects. This mismatch will be analyzed in the context of the blackboard style, which allows building an active repository for sharing and transferring data between clients that run of independent threads [20]. Blackboard systems support backtracking, but they are neither reentrant nor preemptive.

An example of a blackboard architectural configuration in which the above mismatch can occur is shown in Figure 4, when Client1 attempts to backtrack, which is permitted by the BlackboardA, BlackboardB, and Client3, but not by Client2. For implementing the first and the second scenarios, it is necessary to have additional information on the ability of each component to backtrack, on the fact that backtracking is initiated by a component, and on a set of interconnected components to be involved in backtracking. In the first scenario, this information is part of the interfaces of the components, while in the second scenario this information is part of the services provided by the application. The implementation of the third scenario does not assume that any additional information is provided.

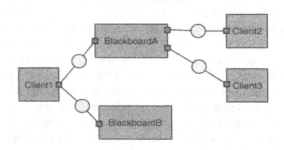

Fig. 4. Components that cannot backtrack in the blackboard architecture

This is how ECM processing and mismatch treatment look like for the three scenarios:

a) ECM Detection:
- for scenario 1, no detection needed;
- for scenario 2, an ECM is detected from the application-specific features of the components;
- for scenario 3, a system error is detected.

b) ECM Diagnosis:
- for scenario 1, no diagnosis needed;
- for scenario 2, during damage assessment there is no need to identify the nature, since the error provides enough information;
- for scenario 3, a full damage assessment is necessary, which might have affected all the system components.

c) ECM Recovery:
- for scenario 1, no recovery required;
- for scenarios 2 and 3, only forward recovery is possible because recovery is application dependent (backward recovery does not apply because one of the components is not able to backtrack).

d) Mismatch Diagnosis:
- for scenarios 1 and 2, the error should provide enough information to identify the location and the nature of mismatch;
- for scenario 3, a full mismatch diagnosis is necessary.

e)   Mismatch Repair:
- for all the scenarios, system reconfiguration involves the usage of alternative component or connector; for example: an alternative component that allows backtracking, or a buffered connector to store data until there is no more risk of backtracking.

From the above exercise, we can draw several conclusions. If the appropriate information for dealing with potential mismatches (for example, documentation of the architectural features and availability of redundant architectural elements) is embedded into the system, right from its architectural conception, then the actual process of tolerating mismatches becomes much simpler. This includes both developing measures for mismatch tolerance and tolerating mismatches at runtime. The reasons for this are that on the one hand some of its activities, like diagnosis, that are complex, time consuming and prone to errors, cease to be necessary, but on the other hand important architectural information related to mismatches and their tolerance is lost during the following phases of the life cycle. Another conclusion is that, although the dichotomy for identifying the nature of mismatches (as style- or application-specific) is clear, the same cannot be said about the process of repairing them, since its techniques might require handling aspects that are particular to style and application. The assumption that architectural features should be part of the interfaces of the components can be weakened by employing other means for retrieving all information related to such properties, for example, using a reflective capability or a specialized registry for storing it.

7   Conclusions

The problem of tolerating architectural mismatches during runtime can be summarized as follows. When an error caused by mismatch (ECM) is detected in the system, mechanisms and techniques have to recover the state of the system to an error free state, otherwise the erroneous state of the system can propagate, eventually leading to a system failure. However, the detection and recovery of an error is not enough for maintaining the integrity of the system services because if the mismatch, which has caused the detected error, is not treated, it can yet again be activated and be the cause of other errors. Similarly to fault tolerance in which one cannot develop techniques that can tolerate any possible faults, it is difficult to develop techniques that are able to deal with all types of architectural mismatches, hence assumptions have to be made about the types of mismatches that caused the errors to be detected and handled during runtime.

In this paper, we have mainly stated the problems and outlined a general approach to handling architectural mismatches during runtime. Our preliminary analysis shows that a number of particular mismatch tolerance techniques can be developed depending on the application, architectural styles used, types of mismatches, redundancies available, etc. It is clear for us that there will always be situations when mismatches should be avoided or removed rather than tolerated. Beyond the working examples discussed in the paper, the applicability of the proposed approach to real systems still remains an open issue. However, since the paper advocates application of general fault tolerant mechanisms and techniques for handling architectural mismatches, the potential limitations of our approach are the same as those associated with traditional fault tolerance when applied to the systems of the same scale and complexity. This, in particular, concerns scalability of the techniques and the ways the systems are structured.

In our future work we will be addressing these issues, trying to define in a more rigorous way the applicability of the approach and to develop a set of general mismatch tolerance techniques. Some of the possible approaches are to modify how existing architectural styles are applied, to design a set of connectors capable of tolerating typical mismatches, to extend existing components and connectors with an ability to execute exception handling, and to develop a number of handlers that are specific for mismatches of different types.

Acknowledgements. Alexander Romanovsky is supported by IST DSoS project (IST-1999-11585).

References

1. T. Anderson and P. Lee. *Fault-Tolerance: Principles and Practice*. Prentice-Hall Int. Englewood Cliffs, NJ. 1981.
2. A. Avizienis, J.-C. Laprie, and B. Randell. *Fundamental Concepts of Dependability*. Technical Report 739. Department of Computing Science. University of Newcastle upon Tyne. 2001.
3. L. Bass, P. Clements, and R. Kazman. *Software Architecture in Practice*. Addison-Wesley. 1998.
4. D. Compare, P. Inverardi, and A.L. Wolf. "Uncovering Architectural Mismatch in Component Behavior". *Science of Computer Programming (33)2*. 1999. pp. 101-131.
5. F. Cristian. "Exception Handling". *Dependability of Resilient Computers*. T. Anderson (Ed.). Blackwell Scientific Publications. 1989. pp. 68-97.
6. R. de Lemos and A. Romanovsky. "Exception Handling in the Software Lifecycle". *International Journal of Computer Systems Science & Engineering 16(2)*. March 2001. pp. 167-181.
7. R. DeLine. "A Catalog of Techniques for Resolving Packaging Mismatch". *Proceedings of the 5th Symposium on Software Reusability (SSR'99)*. Los Angeles, CA. May 1999. pp. 44-53.
8. A. Egyed, N. Medvidovic, and C. Gacek. "Component-Based Perspective on Software Mismatch Detection and Resolution". *IEE Proceedings on Software 147(6)*. December 2000. pp. 225-236.
9. C. Gacek, A. Abd-Allah, B. Clark, and B. Boehm, "On the Definition of Software Architecture". *Proceedings of the First International Workshop on Architectures for Software Systems – In Cooperation with the 17th International Conference on Software Engineering*. D. Garlan (Ed.). Seattle, WA, USA. April 1995. pp. 85-95.
10. C. Gacek. *Detecting Architectural Mismatches during System Composition*. PhD Dissertation. Center for Software Engineering. University of Southern California. Los Angeles, CA, USA. 1998.
11. D. Garlan, R. Allen, and J. Ockerbloom, "Architectural Mismatch: Why Reuse is so Hard". *IEEE Software 12(6)*. November 1995. pp. 17-26.

12. P. Inverardi, A.L. Wolf, and D. Yankelevich. "Checking Assumptions in Component Dynamics at the Architectural Level". *Proceedings of the 2nd International Conference on Coordination Models and Languages.* Lecture Notes in Computer Science 1282. Springer, Berlin. September 1997. pp. 46-63.

13. C. Jones, A. Romanovsky, and I. Welch. A Structured Approach to Handling On-Line Interface Upgrades. *Proceedings of the 26th Annual International Computer Software and Applications Conference (COMPSAC 2002).* Oxford, UK. August 2002. IEEE CS Press. pp. 1000-1005.

14. J.-C. Laprie. "Dependable Computing: Concepts, Limits, Challenges". *Special Issue of the 25th International Symposium On Fault-Tolerant Computing.* IEEE Computer Society Press. Pasadena, CA. June 1995. pp. 42-54

15. N. Medvidovic, D.S. Rosenblum, and R.N. Taylor. "A Language and Environment for Architecture-Based Software Development and Evolution". *Proceedings of the 21st International Conference on Software Engineering (ICSE'99).* Los Angeles, CA. May 1999. pp. 44-53.

16. N. Medvidovic and R.N. Taylor. "A Classification and Comparison Framework for Software Architecture Description Languages". *IEEE Transactions on Software Engineering 26(1).* 2000. pp. 70-93.

17. P. Oberndorf, K. Wallnau, and A.M. Zaremski. "Product Lines: Reusing Architectural Assets within an Organization". *Software Architecture in Practice.* Eds. L. Bass, P. Clements, R. Kazman. Addison-Wesley. 1998. pp. 331-344.

18. D.E. Perry and A.L. Wolf. "Foundations for the Study of Software Architecture". *SIGSOFT Software Engineering Notes 17(4).* 1992. pp. 40-52.

19. D.S. Roseblum and R. Natarajan. "Supporting Architectural Concerns in Component Interoperability Standards". *IEE Proceedings on Software 147(6).* December 2000. pp. 215-223.

20. M. Shaw and D. Garlan. *Software Architecture: Perspectives on an Emerging Discipline.* Prentice-Hall. 1996.

21. R.N. Taylor, N. Medvidovic, K.M. Anderson, E.J. Whitehead, J.E. Robbins, K.A. Nies, P. Oreizy, and D.L. Dubrow "A Component- and Message-Based Architectural Style for GUI Software". *IEEE Transactions on Software Engineering 22(6).* June 1996. pp. 390-406.

Dependability Analysis in
Software Architectures

Quality Analysis of Dependable Systems: A Developer Oriented Approach

Apostolos Zarras[1], Christos Kloukinas[2], and Valérie Issarny[3]

[1] Computer Science Department, University of Ioannina, Greece
zarras@cs.uoi.gr
[2] VERIMAG, Centre Équation, 2 avenue de Vignates, 38610 Gières, France
Christos.Kloukinas@imag.fr
[3] INRIA, Domaine de Voluceau, B.P. 105, 78 153 Le Chesnay Cédex, France
Valerie.Issarny@inria.fr

Abstract. The quality of dependable systems (DS) is characterized by a number of non-functional properties (e.g., performance, reliability, availability, etc.). Assessing the DS quality against these properties imposes the application of quality analysis and evaluation. Quality analysis consists of checking, analytically solving, or simulating models of the system, which are specified using formalisms like CSP, CCS, Markov-chains, Petri-nets, Queuing-nets, etc. However, developers are usually not keen on using such formalisms for modeling and evaluating DS quality. On the other hand, they are familiar with using architecture description languages and object-oriented notations for building DS models. Based on the previous and to render the use of traditional quality analysis techniques more tractable, this paper proposes an architecture-based environment that facilitates the specification and quality analysis of DS at the architectural level.

1 Introduction

Nowadays, there exists a clear trend for business, industry, and society to place increasing dependence on systems, consisting of the integration of numerous, disparate and autonomous components. Consequently, users have strong non-functional requirements on the quality of these systems. To satisfy these demands, quality analysis must be performed during the lifetime of the system. The quality of dependable systems (DS) is characterized by a number of attributes (e.g., security, performance, reliability, availability, etc.), whose values are, typically, improved by using certain means (e.g., encryption, load balancing, fault tolerance mechanisms). Two different kinds of quality analysis can be performed:

- *Qualitative analysis*, which aims at facilitating and verifying the correct use of certain means for improving the DS quality.
- *Quantitative analysis*, which aims at predicting the values of the quality attributes characterizing the overall DS quality.

R. de Lemos et al. (Eds.): Architecting Dependable Systems, LNCS 2677, pp. 197–218, 2003.
© Springer-Verlag Berlin Heidelberg 2003

The above kinds of quality analysis are complementary. In particular, the results of quantitative analysis are most probably affected by certain means, whose correct use is verified by the qualitative analysis. On the other hand, the use of certain means is guided by the results of the quantitative analysis at early design stage.

Performing quality analysis is not a new challenge and several techniques have been proposed and used for quite a long time [1–4]. Techniques for qualitative analysis are mainly based on theorem proving and model checking. Typically, models specifying the system's behavior are built using formalisms like CSP, CCS, Pi-Calculus, TLA, etc. Then, these models are checked against properties that must hold for the system to behave correctly. Techniques for quantitative analysis can be analytic, simulation, or measurement-based. Again models specifying the system's behavior are built using formalisms like Markov-chains, Petri-nets, Queuing-nets, etc. Certain model parameters (e.g., failure rates of the system's primitive elements) are obtained using measurement-based techniques. Then, the models are analytically solved, or simulated, to obtain the values of the attributes that characterize the overall system's quality. The main problem today is that building good quality models requires lots of experience and effort. Developers use Architecture Description Languages (ADLs) [5, 6], and object oriented notations (e.g., UML [7]) to design the system architecture. It is a common case that they are not keen on building quality models using CSP, CCS Markov chains, Petri-nets, Queuing-nets, etc. Hence, the ideal would be to provide the developers with an environment, which enables the specification of DS architectures and further provides adequate tool support that facilitates the specification of models suitable for DS quality analysis.

In this paper, we investigate the above issue and we present a developer-oriented, architecture-based environment for the specification and quality analysis of dependable systems. The specification of DS architectures is based on an extensible ADL, which is defined in Section 2. Section 3, then, presents an approach that facilitates the qualitative analysis of DS at the architectural level. Similarly, Section 4 discusses an approach that facilitates the quantitative analysis of DS at the architectural level. Finally, Section 5 concludes this paper with a summary of the contributions to DS quality analysis, the lessons learned, and the future directions of this work.

2   Architecture Description Language

2.1   Background and Related Work

Architecture description languages are notations enabling the rigorous specification of the structure and behavior of systems. ADLs come along with tools that facilitate the analysis and the construction of systems, whose architecture is specified using them. Several ADLs have been proposed in the past years and they are all based on the same base principles [6]. In particular, the structure of systems is specified using *components*, *connectors* and *configurations*. It is worth noticing that existing ADLs have concise semantics and are widely known and used in academia, but their use in the industry is quite limited. Industrials, nowadays, tend to use object-oriented notations for specifying the architecture of their software systems. UML, in particular, is becoming an industrial standard notation for the definition of a family of languages (i.e., UML profiles) for modeling software. However, there is a primary concern regarding the imprecision of the semantics of UML. To increase the impact of ADLs in the real world, and to decrease the ambiguity of UML, we propose an ADL defined in relation to standard UML elements. Our main objective is the definition of a set of core extensible language constructs for the specification of components, connectors and configurations. This core set of extensible constructs shall further facilitate future attempts for mapping existing ADLs into UML. Our effort relates to the definition of architecture meta-languages like ACME [5] and AML [8]. Our work also compares to the recent XML-based, extensible ADL [9]. Our approach can be the basis for the definition of a standard UML profile for ADLs, while [9] can be the basis for a complementary standard DTD used to produce textual specifications from graphical ADL models.

2.2 Basic Concepts

To define ADL components, connectors, and configurations in relation to standard UML model elements, we undertook the following steps: (i) identify standard UML element(s), whose semantics are close to the ones needed for the specification of ADL components, connectors and configurations; (ii) if the semantics of the identified element(s) do not exactly match the ones needed for the specification of components, connectors, and configurations, extend them properly and define a corresponding UML stereotype(s) [1]; (iii) If the semantics of the identified element(s) match exactly, adopt the element(s) as a part of the core ADL language constructs.

A *component* abstracts a unit of computation or a data store. As discussed in the literature [10, 11], various UML modeling elements may be used to specify an ADL component. The most popular ones are the Class, Component, Package, and Subsystem elements. From our point of view, the UML Component element is semantically far more concrete compared to an ADL component, as it specifically corresponds to an executable software module. Moreover, the UML Class element is often considered as the basis for defining architectural components. However, a UML class does not directly support the hierarchical composition of systems. It is true that the definition of a UML Class may be composite, consisting of a number of constituent classes. However, the class specification can not contain the interrelationships among the constituent classes. Consequently, if an ADL composite component is mapped into a UML class, its definition may comprise a set of constituent components for which we have no means to describe the way they are connected through connectors. Technically, to achieve

---

[1] A UML stereotype is a UML element whose base class is a standard UML element. Moreover, a stereotype is associated with additional constraints and semantics.

the previous we would need to define a Package containing the UML class definitions and a static structure diagram showing how they are connected. However, packages cannot be instantiated or associated with other packages. Hence, they are not adequate for specifying ADL components. This leads us to use the UML Subsystem element to model ADL components. A UML Subsystem is a subtype of both the UML Package and Classifier element, which may be instantiated multiple times, and associated with other subsystems. Precisely, we define an ADL component as a UML Subsystem, that may provide and require standard UML interfaces. The ADL component is further characterized by a property, named *"composite"*, which may be true, or false depending on whether, or not a component is built out of other components and connectors.

A *connector* is an association representing the protocols through which components may interact. Hence, the natural choice for specifying it in UML is by stereotyping the standard UML Association element. A connector role corresponds to an association end. Moreover, the distinctive feature of a connector is a non-empty set of interfaces, named *"Interfaces"*, representing the specific parts of components' functionality playing the roles. Each interface out of the set must be provided by at least one associated component. Equally, each interface out of the set must be required by at least one associated component. So far, we considered connectors as associations representing communication protocols. However, we must not ignore the fact that, in practice, connectors are built from architectural elements, including components and more primitive connectors. Taking CORBA for example, a CORBA connector can be seen as a combination of functionalities of the ORB and of CORBA services (i.e., COSs). Hence, it is necessary to support hierarchical composition of connectors. At this point, we face a technical problem: UML Associations can not be composed of other model elements. However, there exists a standard UML element called Refinement defined as *"a dependency where the clients are derived by the suppliers"* [7]. The refinement element is characterized by a property called mapping. The values of this property describe how the client is derived by the supplier. Hence, to support the hierarchical composition of connectors, we define a stereotype, whose base class is the standard UML Refinement element and is used to define the mapping between a connector and a composite component that realizes the connector.

A *configuration* specifies the assembly of components and connectors. In UML, the assembly of model elements is specified by a model. The corresponding semantic element of a model is the standard UML Model element, defined as *"an abstraction of a modeled system specifying the system from a certain point of view and at a certain level of abstraction...the UML Model consists of a containment hierarchy where the top most package represents the boundary of the modeled system"* [7]. Hence, a configuration is actually a UML model, consisting of a containment hierarchy where the top-most package is a composite ADL component. The given definition of configuration is weak in that it enables the description of any architectural configuration provided it complies with the well-formedness rules associated with the component and connector elements. This results from our concern of supporting the description of various architectural styles, which possibly come along with specific ADLs as is the case with the C2 style [6]. Constraints that are specific to a style are introduced through the definition of a corresponding extension of the ADL configuration element, possibly combined with extension of the UML elements for component and connector definition.

2.3   Tools

The basic ideas described so far for the specification of software architectures are realized into a prototype implementation of the architecture-based development environment, which makes use of an existing UML modeling tool. More specifically, we use the Rational Rose tool [2] for the graphical specification of software architectures. The Rational Rose tool allows the definition of user specific add-ins that facilitate the definition and use of stereotyped elements. Given the aforementioned facility, we implemented an add-in that eases the specification of architectural descriptions using the elements defined in the previous subsection. Moreover, we use an already existing add-in, which enables generating XMI textual specifications of architectures specified graphically using the Rational Rose tool; these textual specifications shall serve as input to the tools we use for qualitative and quantitative analyses of architectures. We further developed an OCL verifier that can be used to verify architectural constraints expressed in OCL. Note that we could have used an already existing verifier implemented in Java [3]. However, given that the expected complexity of our models is high, we preferred developing a more efficient implementation based on OCAML [4], which has been successfully used to efficiently develop large applications like the COQ theorem prover [5].

2.4   Example

To illustrate the use of our environment, we employ examples taken from a case study we are investigating in the context of the DSoS IST project [6]. The case study is a travel agent system (TA). TA offers services for flight, hotel, and car reservations. It consists of the integration of different kinds of existing systems supporting air companies, hotel chains, and car rental companies. Figure 1 gives a screen shot of the actual architecture of the TA as specified using the UML modeling tool, which we customized. The TA comprises the *TravelAgent-FrontEnd* component, which serves as a GUI for potential customers wanting

---

[2] http://www.rational.com. Notice that the use of the Rational Rose tool was mainly motivated by pragmatic consideration that is the ownership of a license and former experience with this tool. However, our specific developments may be integrated within any extensible, UML-based tool that processes XMI files.

[3] http://www.db.informatik.uni-bremen.de/projects/USE.

[4] http://www.caml.inria.fr/ocaml/.

[5] http://www.coq.inria.fr.

[6] http://www.newcastle.research.ec.org/dsos.

to reserve tickets, rooms, and cars. The TA further includes the *HotelReservation, FlightReservation, CarReservation* components, which accept as input individual parts of a customer request for hotel, ticket and car reservation, and translate them into requests for services provided by specific hotel, air company and car company components. The set of the hotel components is represented by the Hotels composite component. Similarly, the sets of air company and car company components are represented by the *AirCompanies* and *CarCompanies* composite components. Two different kinds of connectors are used in our architecture. The HTTP connectors (e.g., see the specification relating to HTTP in Figure 1) represent the interaction protocol among customers and the TA front end component, and among components translating requests and existing component systems implementing Web servers. The RPC connector represents the protocol used among the front end component and the components that translate requests. Note that multi-party connectors abstract complex connector realizations, which may actually be refined into various protocols, depending on the intended behavior. For instance, the RPC connector may be refined into a number of bi-party connectors as well as into a complex transactional connector.

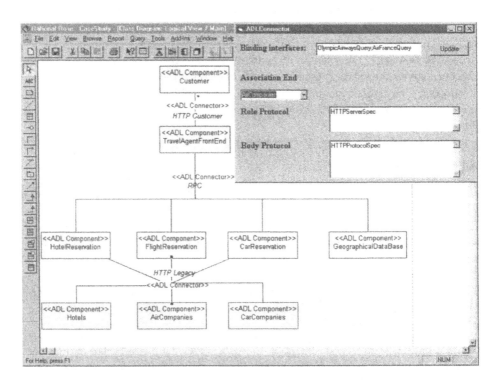

Fig. 1. The architecture of the travel agent DS

3   Qualitative Analysis

3.1   Background and Related Work

Since the early work on ADL definition, there has been a significant effort for defining ADLs that ease the qualitative analysis of software architectures. Specifically, a number of existing ADLs come along with tools like theorem provers and model-checkers, allowing the specification of the functional behavior of components and connectors making up a system, and the verification of properties that must hold for the system against the system's functional behavior [1, 4]. In existing ADLs, the specification of the system's behavior is, typically, done using formalisms like logic or process algebras. Hence, to perform qualitative analysis, developers have to learn these formalisms and tools. They further have to derive mappings between the basic architectural concepts (e.g., components, connectors, ports, roles, etc.) they use to specify software architectures and the basic constructs provided by the formalism that is to be used for specifying the system's functional behavior (e.g., processes, channels, etc.), if these mappings are not already provided by the ADL itself. Neither of the previous tasks is straightforward for everyday developers who are very experienced and educated on the use of object-oriented modeling methods (e.g., UML methods), and several programming languages like C, C++, Java, but are not experts in logic and process algebras. An evidence of this is provided in the Web site of PVS [7], a well-known theorem-prover, where the following warning is given: *"...PVS is a large and complex system and it takes a long while to learn to use it effectively. You should be prepared to invest six months to become a moderately skilled user (less if you already know other verification systems, more if you need to learn logic or unlearn Z)..."*

A number of approaches have recently been proposed to try to alleviate the previous complexities towards rendering the use of qualitative analysis more tractable to nowadays developers. For instance, in [12], the authors propose a tool for model checking UML models. Developers have to specify these using state-chart diagrams, which are then used for generating models that serve as input to the SPIN model checker [13]. However, state-chart specifications of system behavior are quite low level and certainly not easy to produce. Take for instance the usual case where developers need to specify loops, procedure calls, synchronization and communication using state-charts. In this case, developers would prefer using a modeling language, which resembles a real programming language instead of using automata such as state-charts. We thus consider that the approach proposed in [12] is not a solution. Another approach is proposed in [14], which introduces stereotypes that are formally specified using Finite State Processes (FSP). FSP models may then be generated from UML models annotated with the stereotypes, for analysis using the Labelled Transition System Analyzer (LTSA) tool. This solution alleviates the limitations of the previous but it requires specifying formal models in FSP, which is not known by the vast majority of developers.

---

[7] http://pvs.csl.sri.com/whatispvs.html.

From the above discussion and from a pragmatic point of view, it is not possible to completely avoid using a tool-specific formalism for performing qualitative analysis in the general case. Hence, our basic requirement becomes to integrate into our environment an existing tool for qualitative analysis, whose formalism for behavioral modeling is as natural as possible for the developers. This has led us to exclude, in the first place, theorem provers. In consequence, we are left with the option of integrating into our framework a model-checking tool. The second requirement, for rendering the qualitative analysis simpler, comprises providing an automated procedure that maps basic architectural concepts into basic constructs of the behavioral modeling formalism assumed by the selected model-checking tool. This allows the automated generation of formal behavioral models from DS architectural descriptions.

3.2   Basic Concepts

Support for the specification of the functional behavior of the basic architectural elements that constitute a DS, is provided by our environment as follows:

- ADL components are characterized by a property, called *"Body Behavior"*, whose value can be assigned to a textual specification, given in any behavioral modeling formalism, describing the components' behavior.
- UML interfaces provided/required by ADL components are characterized by a property, called *"Port Behavior"*, whose value describes in some textual specification, the particular protocol used at that point of interaction.
- ADL connectors are characterized by:
  - A property, named *"Body Protocol"* (see Figure 1), whose value specifies the role-independent part of the interaction protocol.
  - A set of properties (see Figure 1), named *"Role Protocol"*. Each one of these corresponds to an association end, i.e., a role. The value of each property specifies the role-dependent part of the interaction protocol represented by the connector.

3.3   Tools

We identified 3 widely used model checking tools that could be integrated into our environment, i.e., FDR2 [8], SMV [9] and SPIN [13]. Among them, we have chosen SPIN because: (i) it is based on a C-like language for modeling system behavior, which is more familiar to DS developers compared to other modeling languages, and (ii) it has built-in channels, i.e., constructs used for modeling message-passing, with which we can easily model parts of the ADL connectors. A model in the SPIN modeling language, i.e., PROMELA, consists of a number of independent processes, i.e., each one has its own thread of execution, which communicate either through global variables or through special communication channels by message-passing, as is done in CSP, at least in its machine

---

[8] http://www.formal.demon.co.uk/fdr2manual.
[9] http://www.cs.cmu.edu/~modelcheck.

readable version. Therefore, the mapping of our basic architectural elements to the constructs of PROMELA can be done in a way analogous to the mapping used by the Wright ADL for CSP [1]. In particular in [1], for each component, connector, port/interface and role, a corresponding process is generated. Each generated process shall communicate with the rest through channels generated as prescribed by the configuration of the DS. However, such a mapping results in the generation of a large number of processes and requires a substantial amount of resources for model checking.

Table 1. Generating PROMELA Models

Component	For each component c:
	- Create a PROMELA process type, *"proctype"*, named after the component, whose behavior is given by the value of *"Body Behavior"*
	- For each port p of c, create an *"inline"* procedure whose name is the catenation of the component's and the port's name, i.e., c_p. This procedure contains the *Port Behavior* of the respective port p. For interacting with its environment, c_p uses a channel named after the port's name, i.e., p.
Connector	For each connector c:
	- Create a *"proctype"*, named after the connector, whose behavior is given by the value of *"Body Protocol"*. Unlike the processes corresponding to ADL components that take no arguments, these processes receive as arguments at initiation time the channels they will be using for their respective roles. These channels are named after the roles themselves.
Configuration	Create a special process called *"init"* in PROMELA, which will be responsible for instantiating the rest of the architecture. More specifically:
	- The *"init"* process creates as many instances of the processes corresponding to particular ADL components, as there are instances of these components in the configuration.
	- Afterwards, it does the same for each instance of an ADL connector but it uses the attachments of component ports to connector roles to deduce the specific channels that should be passed as arguments to the processes corresponding to the connector.

To alleviate the above problem, we have chosen to generate independent processes for each component and connector specified in a DS architectural description, while for each port and role we generate PROMELA inline procedures. This inline procedure construct of PROMELA allows us to define new functions that can be used by processes, but do not introduce their own threads of execution. In this manner, we keep to a minimum the number of different processes that the model-checker will be asked to verify, thus enabling the verification of large architectures. Then, for each port of an ADL component we declare in the PROMELA description of the component, a communication channel named after that port. This channel will be used by the process related to the ADL component for communicating through that specific port. Since ports of ADL components are bound to specific roles of ADL connectors, their channels are passed as arguments to the processes created for these connectors, at the time of their initiation. Thus, messages sent from a process of an ADL component at a channel corresponding to a port of it, will be received by a process of an ADL connector. Similarly, messages sent from a process of an ADL connector to a channel it has received as argument at initiation time, will be in fact received by a process of an ADL component, whose port was mapped to that channel. Even though the proposed mapping may seem as depriving the architect from the possibility to describe complex cases, e.g., multi-threaded components, it is not so. Indeed, it is always possible to describe a component as a composite one, i.e., one that consists of a number of simpler components and connectors, which will be subsequently modeled as a number of independent processes. The steps that are followed for generating a complete PROMELA model from an architectural description are given in Table 1.

3.4   Example

To exemplify the qualitative analysis of DS, we get back to the TA case study. A typical property that is often required over RPC and HTTP connectors is for reply messages to be received by the client in the order it sent the corresponding request messages. Meeting the previous is usually under the responsibility of the connector realization, possibly in association with the server. For instance, the HTTP/1.0 and HTTP/1.1 realizations of the HTTP connector differ in that the latter supports persistent connections and allows pipelining of request messages, which leads to explicitly require for the server to ensure that it sends back reply messages in the order it received the corresponding request messages. In the TA case study, we consider both realizations of HTTP. Moreover, we consider two realizations of the *TravelAgentFronEnd* component and the rest of the Web servers supporting the hotel, car and flight reservations. In the first case, the components process HTTP requests sequentially, while in the second case they use multi-threading to process multiple HTTP requests in parallel.

The processes corresponding to the RPC and the HTTP/1.0 connectors are similar in functionality; they iterate constantly, doing the following: (i) they receive a request from the component assuming the role of the RPC caller/Web client, (ii) deliver it to the component assuming the role of RPC callee/Web server, (iii) receive the reply from the callee/server, and (iv) forward it to the caller/client. The HTTP/1.1 connector works differently; it can receive multiple requests and forward them to the callee/server, or decide to read one (or more) replies and deliver them to the caller/client. For instance, the following is the specification of the RPC connector:

Role Protocol: *caller(RPC_channel, request, reply)*
        { *RPC_channel ! request; RPC_channel ? reply* }
Role Protocol: *callee(RPC_channel, request, reply)*
        { *RPC_channel ? request; RPC_channel ! reply* }
Body Protocol:
        { *Msg request, reply;*
        do
            :: caller ? request; callee ! request;
            :: callee ? reply; caller ! reply;
        od }

The *Customer* component initiates requests to the *TravelAgentFrontEnd* and waits for responses. The reservation components get requests from the RPC connector and diffuse them, through the HTTP connector, to the existing Web servers supporting the hotel, car and flight reservations. In the sequential versions of the *TravelAgentFrontEnd* component and of the Web servers supporting reservations, the corresponding PROMELA processes process each request and send the corresponding reply before serving a new request. Their concurrent versions are based on a pool of threads. For illustration, the following is the specification of the Web servers that handle requests sequentially:

Port Behavior: *HTTP_Request(HTTP_channel, request, reply)*
        { *HTTP_channel ? request; HTTP_channel ! reply* }
Body Behavior:
        { *chan HTTP_channel ; Msg request, reply;*
        do
            :: HTTP_Request(HTTP_channel, request, reply)
        od }

Four different PROMELA models were generated. These models result from the combination of the different HTTP and Web server versions. More specifically, for all components and connectors, corresponding processes were generated. The realizations of the generated processes consist of the *Body Behavior* and *Body Protocol*, for components and connectors respectively. These processes were connected via channels generated for each port of the various components, according to the configuration given in Figure 1. SPIN was then used to assess the TA against ordered delivery of reply messages to the customers for all the 4 cases resulting from the combination of the different HTTP and Web server versions. Checking of the models resulted in identifying an erroneous architecture for the TA that is the case where Web components interact via HTTP/1.1 and the Web servers handle concurrently the request messages. The full source code of the TA PROMELA model used in this case study can be found in [15].

4 Quantitative Analysis

4.1 Background and Related Work

Pioneer work on the quantitative analysis of software systems at the architectural level includes Attribute-Based Architectural Styles (ABAS) [16]. In general, an architectural style includes the specification of types of basic architectural elements (e.g., pipe and filter) that can be used for specifying a software architecture, constraints on using these types of architectural elements, and patterns describing the data and control interaction among them. An ABAS is an architectural style, which additionally provides modeling support for the quantitative analysis of a particular quality attribute (e.g., performance, reliability, availability). More specifically, an ABAS includes the specification of:

- *Quality attribute measures* characterizing the quality attribute (e.g., the probability that the system correctly provides a service for a given duration, mean response time).
- *Quality attribute stimuli*, i.e., events affecting the quality attribute of the system (e.g., failures, service requests).
- *Quality attribute parameters*, i.e., architectural properties affecting the quality attribute of the system (e.g., faults, redundancy, thread policy).
- *Quality attribute models*, i.e., traditional models that formally relate the above elements (e.g., a Markov model that predicts reliability based on the failure rates and the redundancy used, a Queuing network that enables predicting the system's response time given the rate of service requests and performance parameters like the request scheduling and the thread policies of the various system elements).

In [17], the authors introduce the Architecture Tradeoff Analysis Method (ATAM) where the use of an ABAS is coupled with the specification of a set of scenarios, which roughly constitutes the specification of a service profile. ATAM has been tested for analyzing quality attributes like performance, availability, modifiability, and real-time. In all these cases, quality attribute models (e.g., Markov models, queuing networks) are manually built given the specification of a set of scenarios and the ABAS-based architectural description. However, in [17], the authors recognize the complexity of the aforementioned task; the development of quality analysis models requires about 25% of the time spent for applying the whole method. ATAM is a promising approach for doing things right. However, nowadays, there is a constant additional requirement for doing things fast and easy.

Our environment supports the automated generation of quality attribute models from architectural descriptions embedding quality attributes. In particular, the environment currently supports the generation of performance and reliability models aimed at analysis tools that have been recognized successful for handling complex models associated with real systems. Note that there is no unique way to model systems. A model is built based on certain assumptions. Thus, the model generation procedures supported by our environment are customizable. Customization is done according to certain assumptions that can be made by the developer for the quality stimuli and parameters affecting the value of the particular quality attribute that is assessed. Due to the lack of space, we provide hereafter details regarding only the case of reliability. The interested reader is referred to [18] and [15] for details regarding the case of performance, where the former concentrates on performance analysis of workflow-based systems.

4.2   Basic Concepts

To perform quantitative analysis, we have to specify a service profile, i.e., a set of scenarios, describing how the inspected system is used. In our environment, scenarios are specified using UML collaboration diagrams. A scenario then specifies the interactions among a set of component and connector instances, structured as prescribed by the configuration of the inspected system. Moreover, the definitions of the base ADL elements have been extended to support the specification of reliability measures, parameters, and stimuli, as defined below.

The basic *reliability measure* is the probability that a scenario successfully completes within a given time duration. A scenario may fail if instances of components, nodes [10], and connectors used in it, fail because of faults causing errors in their state. The manifestations of errors are failures. Hence, faults are the basic *parameters*, associated with components/connectors/nodes, which affect the reliability of an inspected system. Failures are the *stimuli*, associated with components/connectors/nodes, causing changes in the value of the reliability measure. According to [19], faults and failures can be further characterized by the properties given in Tables 2 and 3. Different combinations of the values of these properties can be used to customize properly the generation procedure of quality attribute models, which is detailed in Subsection 4.3.

Except for faults and failures, another parameter affecting reliability is redundancy. Redundancy schemas can be defined using the base ADL constructs defined in Section 2. More specifically, a redundancy schema is a configuration of redundant architectural elements, which behave as a single fault tolerant unit. According to [20], a redundant schema is characterized by the kind of mechanism used to detect errors, the way the constituent elements execute towards serving incoming requests, the confidence that can be placed on the results of the error detection mechanism and the number of component and node faults that can be tolerated. The properties characterizing a redundancy schema are summarized in Table 4. A re-configurable/repairable redundancy schema may be characterized by additional properties (e.g. repair rate, number of spares, state of the spares), whose values reflect the particular re-configuration/repair policy used.

Table 2. Properties of Failures

Failure Properties	Range	Associated ADL Element
domain	time/value	Component/Connector/Node
perception	consistent/inconsistent	

---

[10] Since an ADL component is by definition an extension of the standard UML Subsystem element, it is associated with a set of UML nodes on top of which it executes.

Table 3. Properties of Faults

Fault Properties	Range	Associated ADL Element
nature	intention/accident	Component/Connector/Node
phase	design/operational	
causes	physical/human	
boundaries	internal/external	
persistence	permanent/temporary	
arrival-rate	Real	
active-to-benign	Real	
benign-to-active	Real	
disappearance	Real	

Table 4. Properties of Redundancy Schemas

Redundancy Properties	Range	Associated ADL Element
error-detection	vote/comp./acceptance	Component
execution	parallel/sequential	
confidence	absolute/relative	
service-delivery	continuous/suspended	
no-comp-faults	Integer	
no-node-faults	Integer	

4.3   Tools

The quantitative analysis of DS is supported by our environment with automated procedures, which take as input, architectural specifications defined using the basic concepts discussed so far, and generate traditional quality attribute models. The specific tool integrated into our environment for reliability analysis is called SURE-ASSIST [21]. The tool calculates reliability bounds given a state space model describing the failure and repair behavior of the inspected system. The tool was selected because it is very highly rated compared to other reliability tools [2] and because it is available for free. However, the automated support provided by our environment for reliability analysis can be coupled with any other tool that accepts as input state space models.

A state space model consists of a set of transitions between states of the system. A state describes a situation where either the system operates correctly, or not. In the latter case the system is said to be in a *death state*. The state of the system depends on the state of its constituent elements. Hence, it can be seen as a composition of sub states, each one representing the situation of a constituent element. A state is constrained by the range of all possible situations that may occur. A state range can be modeled as a composition of sub state ranges, constraining the state of the elements that constitute the system. A transition is characterized by the rate by which the source situation changes into the target situation. If, for instance, the difference between the source and the target situation is the failure of a component, the transition rate equals to the failure rate of the component. The specification of large state-space models is often too complex and error-prone. The approach proposed in [22] alleviates this problem. In particular, instead of specifying all possible state transitions, the authors propose specifying the following: (i) the state range of the system, (ii) transition rules between sets of states of the system, (iii) the initial state of the system, and (iv) a death state constraint. In a transition rule, the source and the target set of states are identified by constraints on the state range (e.g., if the system is in a state where more than 2 subsystems are operational, then the system may get into a state where the number of subsystems is reduced by one). A complete state space model can then be generated using the algorithm described in [22]. Briefly, the algorithm takes as input an initial system state. Then, the algorithm applies recursively the set of transition rules. During a recursive step, the algorithm produces a transition to a state derived from the initial one. Depending on the rule that is applied, in the resulting state, one or more elements are modeled as being failed, or operational, while in the initial state they were modeled as being operational or failed, respectively. If the resulting state is a death state, the recursion ends.

Complete state space models are automatically generated from DS architectural descriptions embedding the specification of reliability stimuli and parameters, by following the steps below.

First, a state range definition for each collaboration belonging to a given service profile is generated. The state of a collaboration is composed of the states of the component and connector instances used within the collaboration and the state of nodes on top of which the component instances execute. If a component is composite, its state is composed of the states of the constituent elements. The range of states for a component/connector/node depends on the kind of faults that may cause failures. At this point, the generation procedure is customized accordingly. In the case of permanent faults for instance, a component/connector/node may be either in an OPERATIONAL, or in a FAILED state. In the case of intermittent faults, a component/connector/node may be in an OPERATIONAL state, or it may be in a FAILED-ACTIVE or in a FAILED-BENIGN state. The range of states for a component further depends on the kind of redundancy used. Again, the generation procedure is customized accordingly.

After generating the state range definition for a collaboration *collab*, the step that follows comprises the generation of transition rules for components/connectors/nodes used in the collaboration. These rules depend on the kinds of faults of the corresponding architectural element. For instance, for permanent faults, the rules follow the pattern given in Table 5. What is left at this point is to generate the definition of the initial state of the collaboration, and the definition of the death state constraint. The initial state is a state where all of the elements used in the collaboration are operational. A collaboration is in death state if any of the architectural elements used within it is not operational. Hence, the death state constraint consists of the disjunction of base predicates, each one of which defines the death state constraint for an individual element used in the collaboration. More specifically, the base predicate for a component, connector, or a node states that the element is in a FAILED state. The base predicate for a redundancy schema is the disjunction of two predicates. The first one states that the number of failed redundant component instances is greater than the number component faults that can be tolerated. Similarly, the second one states that the number of failed redundant nodes is greater than the number of node faults that can be tolerated.

Table 5. Transition Rules for Permanent Faults

ADL Element	Rule
Component	For all instances of primitive components, c:
	− If *collab* is in a state where c is in an OPERATIONAL state st, then *collab* may get into a state st' where c is FAILED. The rate of these transitions is equal to the arrival rates of the faults that cause the failure of c, $c.Faults.arrival\text{-}rate$ (see Table 3).
	For all instances of composite components, c:
	− If *collab* is in a state st where c is OPERATIONAL, then *collab* may get into a state st' where c is FAILED due to a failure of a constituent element c'. The rate of these transitions is equal to the arrival rates of the faults that cause the failure of c', $c'.Faults.arrival\text{-}rate$.
	For all instances of composite components rc representing a redundancy schema of k components:
	− If *collab* is in a state st where rc is OPERATIONAL, and the number of failed redundant component instances if fc, then *collab* may get into a state st' where the number of failed components of rc is $fc + l$. The difference between st and st' is l redundant component instances of the same type t, which in st were OPERATIONAL and in st' are FAILED. The rate of these transitions is equal to the fault arrival rate specified for t. This rule captures failure dependencies among redundant component instances of the same type. These components are used in the same conditions and with the same input. Hence, if one of them fails due to a design or an operational fault, all of them will fail.
Connector	For all instances of primitive connectors see the case of primitive components. For all instances of composite connectors, see the case of composite components.
Node	We assume that nodes fail independently from each other. Hence, for all nodes in *collab*:
	− If *collab* is in a state st where a node n is in an OPERATIONAL state, then *collab* may get into a state st' where n is in a FAILED state.
	− Moreover, in st', all instances of components c deployed on n are in a FAILED state.
	− Finally, in st' all instances of redundancy schemas rc, built out of m components deployed on n, have $fc + m$ failed components and $fn + 1$ failed nodes.
	The rate of these transitions is equal to the arrival rate of the faults that caused the failure of n, $n.Faults.arrival\text{-}rate$.

4.4 Example

To demonstrate the automated quantitative analysis detailed in the previous subsection, we use the TA case study. The goal of our analysis is not to obtain precise values of the reliability measure since this would require to precisely model the Internet, which in general is considered as rather unrealistic [23]. For that reason, we concentrate on comparing different scenarios towards improving the design of our system, while assuming certain invariants for modeling issues related to the Web. Our objective is to try to improve the reliability of TA while keeping the cost of the required changes in the TA system low.

The scenario shown in Figure 2 gives a typical use case of TA. This scenario constitutes the basic service profile used for the reliability analysis, i.e., the provided scenario is processed for the automatic generation of the state space model analyzed by the SURE-ASSIST tool. According to the scenario, one or more customers use an instance, *ta*, of the *TravelAgentFrontEnd* to request the reservation of a flight ticket, a hotel room and a car. The *ta* component instance breaks down such a request into 3 separate requests. The first one relates to the flight ticket reservation and is sent to an instance, *fr*, of the *FlightReservation* component. The *fr* component instance uses this request to generate a new set of requests, each one of which is specific to an air company that collaborates with the TA system. The set of specific requests are finally sent to an instance, *ac*, of the *AirCompanies* composite component, which represents the current set of collaborating air companies. Similarly, the second and the third requests are related to the hotel and the car reservations, respectively. These requests are sent to instances of the *HotelReservation* and *CarReservation* components, which reproduce them properly and send them to the current sets of collaborating hotels and car companies.

The component instances used in the scenario may fail to give answers to customers. Component failures are manifestations of design faults. We assume that these faults are accidental, created by the component developers. Moreover, component faults are all permanent and their arrival rates vary depending on the type of the components. More specifically, the fault arrival rates for the components that represent component systems supporting hotels, air companies and car companies are much smaller compared to the faults arrival rates of the rest of the components that make up the TA system. The reason behind this is that the component systems supporting hotels, air companies and car companies have already been in use and their implementations are quite stable. On the other hand, the TA front end and reservation components are still under development. The nodes used in our scenario may fail because of permanent faults. HTTP and RPC connectors may also fail, however, in this case it is more pragmatic to assume that we deal with temporary faults, which may disappear with a certain rate. The arrival rates of node faults are much smaller than the arrival rates of component faults. This also holds for the RPC connector. On the contrary, the HTTP connector is expected to be quite unreliable, with a failure rate greater than that of the components used in the TA (specific failure rates for the individual entities that constitute the DS can be obtained using measurement based techniques; for the ones we assume here we rely on measures presented in [24, 25]). For illustration, Figure 2 shows the detailed specification of the reliability stimuli and parameters that are given for the *FlightReservation* component.

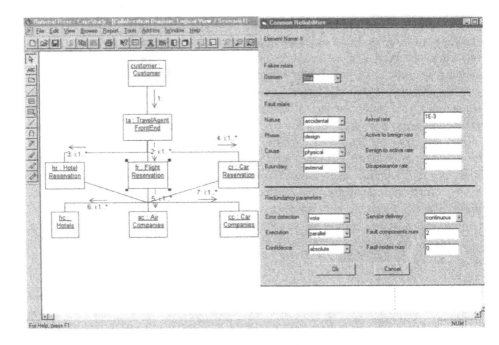

Fig. 2. A generic scenario for TA

By taking a closer look at the architecture of the TA system, we can deduce that some sort of redundancy is used. In particular, the *Hotels*, *AirCompanies* and *CarCompanies* components are composite, consisting of k components that represent the dependable systems supporting hotels, air companies and car companies. The reservation components request from them, room, ticket and car reservations. For the scenario to be successful, we need answers from at least one hotel, one air company, and one car company. Hence, *Hotels*, *AirCompanies*, and *CarCompanies* can be seen as ad hoc redundancy schemas with the following properties: the execution of redundant elements is parallel (*redundancy.execution = parallel*), the number of component and node faults that can be tolerated is $k - 1$ (*redundancy.no-comp-faults* and *redundancy.no-node-faults* $= k - 1$).

To further improve the architecture regarding the provided reliability, we designed three additional redundancy schemas. The first one contains k different versions of the *HotelReservation* component. Upon the instantiation of the schema, k component instances are created, one of each version. These instances execute in parallel and are deployed on k different nodes. The second schema contains k versions of the *FlightReservation* component, the instances of which are also deployed on the k nodes, on top of which the instances of the *Hotel-Reservation* component execute. Finally, the last schema contains k versions of the *CarReservation* component, the instances of which are also deployed on the nodes used to execute the instances of the *HotelReservation* component. At runtime, a customer request is broken down by the instance of the *TravelA-gentFrontEnd* component into individual requests for flight ticket, hotel room and car reservation. Each one of these requests is replicated and sent to all the redundant instances of the corresponding reservation component. Each instance of the reservation component translates the request into specific requests for the corresponding available component systems and sends them. When the instance of the *TravelAgentFrontEnd* starts receiving offers for flight tickets, hotel rooms and cars, it removes identical reply messages and combines them into replies that are returned to the customer. We tried our scenario for $n = 1, 2, 3$ redundant versions. Given the aforementioned scenario and reliability parameters and, three complete state space models were generated and analytically solved. The results obtained are summarized in Figure 3. For further detail about the scenario, including complexity of the generated state space models, the interested reader is referred to [15].

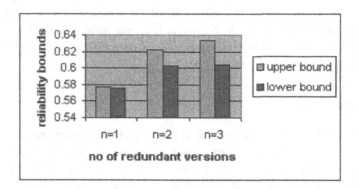

Fig. 3. Results produced by the reliability analysis of TA

The main observation we make is that the reliability of TA does increase. However, the improvement when we use redundant versions is certainly not spectacular. The explanation for this is simple. In our scenario, the most unreliable element used is the HTTP connector. This is the main source causing the reliability measure to have small values. Any improvement in the rest of the architectural elements used shall not cover this problem, which unfortunately can not be easily alleviated. Hence, using multiple versions does not bring much gain. However, the good news are that regarding the cost of using multiple versions, we do not lose much. The elements for which we produced multiple versions just translate TA specific requests into component systems' specific requests. Since the functionality of these components is quite simple, re-implementing them differently (e.g., using different developers) is not a complex, neither a time-consuming task. Note here that the fact that the functionality of the redundant components is simple does not mean that there can be no bugs in their implementation. Actually, mistakes in the mapping of TA requests into component systems' specific requests can be quite often. Furthermore, the cost of developing multiple versions is low since we did not really use any strong synchronization among the different versions.

5   Conclusion

5.1   Summary

In this paper, we presented an environment for the quality analysis of DS. The overall design and realization of our environment is guided by the needs of its current and potential users, imposing the simplification of certain extremely important and inevitable development activities related to the quality analysis and assurance of the DS. The quality analysis of systems is traditionally based on methods and tools that have a strong formal basis. We believe that the proposed environment brings everyday developers closer to such methods and tools. The environment relies on an architecture description language for the specification of DS architectures, which is defined based on UML, a standard and widely accepted notation for modeling software. Our environment further provides a certain level of automation that eases the development of traditional quality models from architectural descriptions.

5.2   Evaluation

Having reached into a stable prototype implementation of our environment, we now concentrate on testing it on real world case studies. So far, we used it successfully in the context of the DSoS IST project for the quality analysis of the Travel Agent system. Parts of the analysis was presented here in the form of demonstrating examples. We further used the basic ideas of our environment in the context of the C3DS IST [11] project for the performance and reliability analysis of workflow based dependable systems [18]. The experimentation with the aforementioned systems led us into several useful remarks, which can become the milestones of a more concrete evaluation process which we plan as future work.

More specifically, in the case of quantitative analysis, a high level of automation can be achieved since the developer is requested only to specify quality attributes within the DS architecture specification. Formal models, processed by existing analysis tools are, then, automatically generated from the architecture specification. However, an important question is: to what extend the generated models are representative of the system. Our experience with the performance

---

[11] http://www.newcastle.research.ec.org/c3ds/.

and reliability analysis of workflow-based systems showed that the model generation procedures we propose are helpful but quite generic. In order to generate models of good quality for workflow-based systems, we had to refine the architecture description language we use, so as to provide constructs for modelling tasks and task dependencies. Moreover, we had to revise the model generation procedures to take into account specificities of the standard platform [18], on top of which the workflow-based systems were built. Hence, the lesson learned here is that the ADL must serve as a base for the specification of different architectural styles for different families of systems. Moreover, it is more realistic to build different model generation procedures for different families of systems. Those procedures are still reusable and produce more concrete models for quality analysis.

In the case of qualitative analysis, the automation that can be achieved is more limited since the developer is requested to formally specify the behavior of architectural elements. This led us to carefully select an existing qualitative analysis method and associated tool whose use is natural to the developers. Besides, we showed that there are benefits from automating the mapping between the basic ADL constructs used for software architecture specification, into constructs of the formal notation used for behavioral analysis.

Acknowledgments

This work has been partially funded by the IST DSoS project.

References

1. Allen, R., Garlan, D.: Formalizing architectural connection. In: Proceedings of the 16th ACM-SIGSOFT-IEEE International Conference on Software Engineering (ICSE'94). (1994) 71–80
2. Geist, R., Trivedi, K.: Reliability estimation of fault tolerant systems: Tools and techniques. IEEE Computer **23** (1990) 52–61
3. Kobayashi, H.: Modeling and Analysis: An Introduction to System Performance Evaluation Methodology. Addison-Wesley (1978)
4. Magee, J., Kramer, J., Giannakopoulou, D.: Behavior analysis of software architectures. In: Proceedings of the 1st IFIP Working Conference on Software Architectures (WICSA-1). (1999) 35–49
5. Garlan, D., Monroe, R., Wile, D.: ACME: An architectural description interchange language. In: Proceedings od CASCON'97. (1997)
6. Medvidovic, N., Taylor, R.: A classification and comparison framework for software architecture description languages. IEEE Transactions on Software Engineering **26** (2000) 70–93
7. OMG: UML semantics 1.3 (1997)
8. Wile, D.: AML: An architecture meta-language. In: Proceedings of the 14th IEEE International Conference on Automated Software Engineering (ASE-99). (1999)
9. Dashofy, E., Van Der Hoek, A., Taylor, R.: An infrastructure for the rapid development of XML-based architecture description languages. In: Proceedings of the 24th International Conference on Software Engineering (ICSE 2002). (2002) 266–276

10. Garlan, D., Kompanec, J., Pinto, P.: Reconciling the needs of architectural description with object-modeling notations. In: Proceedings of the 3rd International Conference on the Unified Modeling Language (UML-2000). (2000)
11. Medvidovic, N., Rosenblum, D.S., Robbins, J.E., Redmiles, D.F.: Modeling software architectures in the unified modeling language. ACM Transactions on Software Engineering and Methodology ((to appear))
12. Lilius, J., Paltor, I.P.: vUML: A tool for verifying UML models. In: Proceedings of the 14th IEEE International Conference on Automated Software Engineering (ASE'99). (1999) 255–258
13. Holzmann, G.J.: The SPIN model checker. IEEE Transactions on Software Engineering **23** (1997) 279–295
14. Kaveh, N., Emmerich, W.: Deadlock detection in distributed object systems. In: Proceedings of the 8th European Software Engineering Conference (ESEC) / 9th ACM SIGSOFT Symposium on the Foundations of Software Engineering (FSE). (2001)
15. Zarras, A., Kloukinas, C., Issarny, V., Nguyen, V.K.: An Architecture-based Environment for the Development of DSoS. In: IC2 Report: Initial Results on Architectures and Dependable Mechanisms for Dependable SoSs. (2001) Available at URL: http://www.newcastle.research.ec.org/dsos/deliverables.
16. Klein, M., Kazman, R., Bass, L., Carriere, S.J., Barbacci, M., Lipson, H.: Attribute-based architectural styles. In: Proceedings of the 1st IFIP Working Conference on Software Architecture (WICSA-1). (1999) 225–243
17. Kazman, R., Carriere, S.J., Woods, S.G.: Toward a discipline of scenario-based architectural engineering. Annals of Software Engineering **9** (2000) 5–33
18. Zarras, A., Issarny, V.: Automating the performance and reliability analysis of enterprise information systems. In: Proceedings of the 16th IEEE International Conference on Automated Software Engineering (ASE 2001). (2000)
19. Laprie, J.C.: Dependable computing and fault tolerance: Concepts and terminology. In: Proceedings of the 15th International Symposium on Fault-Tolerant Computing (FTCS-15). (1985)
20. Laprie, J.C., Arlat, J., Beounes, C., Kanoun, K.: Definition and analysis of hardware and software fault-tolerant architectures. IEEE Computer **23** (1990) 39–51
21. Butler, R.W.: The SURE approach to reliability analysis. IEEE Transactions on Reliability **41** (1992) 210–218
22. Johnson, S.C.: Reliability analysis of large complex systems using ASSIST. In: Proceedings of the 8th AIAA/IEEE Digital Avionics Systems Conference. (1988) 227–234
23. Floyd, S., Paxson, V.: Difficulties in simulating the internet. ACM/IEEE Transactions on Networking (2001)
24. Chandra, B., Dahlin, M., Gao, L., Nayate, A.: End-to-end wan service availability. In: Proceedings of the 2nd USENIX Symposium on Internet Technologies and Systems. (2001) 97–108
25. Kaâniche, M., Kanoun, K., Martinello, M., Simache, C. In: CSDA3 Report: SoS Dependability Assessment : Modelling and Measurement. (2002) Available at URL: http://www.newcastle.research.ec.org/dsos/deliverables.

Stochastic Dependability Analysis of System Architecture Based on UML Models

István Majzik[1], András Pataricza[1], and Andrea Bondavalli[2]

[1] DMIE, Budapest University of Technology and Economics
Magyar Tudósok krt. 2, H-1117 Budapest, Hungary
[2] DSI, University of Firenze, Via Lombroso 6/17, I-50134 Firenze, Italy
{majzik,pataric}@mit.bme.hu, a.bondavalli@dsi.unifi.it

Abstract. The work in this paper[1] is devoted to the definition of a dependability modeling and model based evaluation approach based on UML models. It is to be used in the early phases of the system design to capture system dependability attributes like reliability and availability, thus providing guidelines for the choice among different architectural and design solutions. We show how structural UML diagrams can be processed to filter out the dependability related information and how a system-wide dependability model is constructed. Due to the modular construction, this model can be refined later as more detailed information becomes available. We discuss the model refinement based on the General Resource Model, an extension of UML. We show that the dependability model can be constructed automatically by using graph transformation techniques.

1 Introduction

Standardized design methods and tools are available for the designers of complex computer systems in order to increase the effectiveness of the design. UML (Unified Modeling Language [26]), UML based methods and CASE (Computer-Aided Software Engineering) tools are widely used for the design of various systems from small embedded controllers to large information infrastructures.

An effective design process should include an early validation of the architectural choices and concepts underlying the design. The more earlier the bottlenecks and insufficiencies are highlighted, the less is the loss due to the necessary corrections and re-design. Dependability is among the properties to be validated during the system design, especially in the case of critical systems.

Our earlier ESPRIT project HIDE[2] aimed at the creation of an integrated design environment that augmented UML based design tools with mathematical analysis techniques [7]. Model based dependability evaluation was supported by elaboration of an automatic transformation from UML diagrams to Timed Petri Nets (TPN) that

---

[1] This work was supported partially by ESPRIT Open LTR 27439 'HIDE', the Italian-Hungarian Bilateral Cooperation project I-37/2000, Hungarian NSF T-038027 and the Hungarian Ministry of Education under contract FKFP 0103/2001.

[2] HIDE - High-level Integrated Design Environment for Dependability was carried out by FAU Erlangen, PDCC Pisa, TU Budapest, Intecs Sistemi Pisa and MID GmbH Nuremberg.

R. de Lemos et al. (Eds.): Architecting Dependable Systems, LNCS 2677, pp. 219–244, 2003.

could be solved by off-the-shelf analysis tools to get reliability and availability attributes of the system under design. This transformation, together with its extensions and implementation techniques elaborated since that time are the subjects of our paper.

The idea of translating design models into reliability models can be found in several papers. [13] converts UML models to dynamic fault trees. However, in this work the basis of the translation is not the functional design since UML is used mainly as a language to describe error propagation and module substitution. Here also a translator is reported that converts UML descriptions into reliability block diagrams. Similarly, OpenSESAME [34] uses high-level (graphical) diagrams to express dependencies, error propagation and redundancy structure. In this case analysis of availability is performed by a transformation to Generalized Stochastic Petri Nets. In [18], Markov chains are used to derive reliability of middleware architectures described in extended UML.

In our transformation we applied a modular and hierarchical approach. In the early architectural design phase the relevant information is captured from UML structural views and a system-wide dependability model is constructed. Here we use UML as a standard architecture description language (note that our method can be adapted to other architectural languages as well). The critical parts of the model (as shown by the analysis) are extended as the design gets refined and relevant information becomes available. These ideas are also widely accepted in the related literature. It is agreed that architecture evaluation based on analytical dependability modeling deserves attention in the early design phase [14], the modeling approach should be modular [22] and the model should be refined hierarchically as the design includes more and more information [4]. It is observed that the separation of architectural and service concerns allows the dependability analysis from the perspective of different users [29].

The paper is organized as follows. Sect. 2 motivates the model based dependability analysis. Sect. 3 introduces the design conventions and the extensions necessary to include local dependability related parameters in the early phases of the design. Sect. 4 describes the model transformation from the structural view of UML to the TPN dependability model. Sect. 5 discusses the ways of model refinement concentrating especially on the modeling of resources and faults related to the resources. Sect. 6 presents how the model transformation is implemented while Sect. 7 provides assessment of the approach. Sect. 8 concludes the paper.

2   Dependability Modeling and Analysis

This section motivates the need for model-based dependability evaluation, gives the rationale of dependability modeling and introduces a hierarchical and modular modeling approach.

2.1   Purpose of the Model Based Dependability Analysis

Evaluation of *availability* and *reliability* (two attributes of system dependability as defined in [19]) is necessary to assess whether the system being developed satisfies its targets. Analytical modeling has proven to be useful and versatile to evaluate these attributes in the design phase. Dependability models allow comparing different architectural solutions and design choices and to run sensitivity analysis identifying both dependability bottlenecks and critical parameters to which the system is sensitive.

In our approach, dependability modeling is to be performed in addition to the architectural design based on the extensions of the architectural model of the target system by the parameters needed for the analysis. This approach avoids to build a dependability model from scratch, thus the consistency between the designers' model and the dependability model is guaranteed by the process.

2.2 Components of a Dependability Model

The abstraction of a dependability model consists of the following general parts:
- *Fault activation processes*, which model the fault occurrences in basic system components (especially physical resources).
- *Propagation processes*, which model the consequences of fault occurrences and result in derived failure events. E.g. a failure of a network card results in the failure of an information retrieval service.
- *Repair processes*, which model how basic or derived events are removed from the system. Repair can be implemented by fault treatment and/or error recovery depending on the type of the component.
- *Mapping from architectural level to service level*, which gives how the failures of software and/or hardware components and subsystems result in the failure of a system service (as observable by the user). Different mappings can be used to take into account different service needs (ways of usage).

The fault activation processes are determined by environmental conditions, and physical or computational properties of the elements of the system. The propagation processes are influenced by the structure of the system (e.g. interactions, redundancy, and fault tolerance schemes). The repair processes are determined by the (physical or) computational policy implemented in the system.

2.3 Formalisms and Tools for Dependability Analysis

Among the various formalisms and tools developed for dependability modeling and analysis, Petri nets have been widely accepted because of their expressiveness and powerful solution techniques. Timed and stochastic extensions of Petri nets encompass the class of Generalised Stochastic Petri Nets (GSPN) [2], Deterministic and Stochastic Petri Nets (DSPN) [1] and Markov Regenerative Stochastic Petri Nets (MRSPN) [9]. Many automated tools based on Petri nets are available, e.g. UltraSAN [30], PANDA [3], GreatSPN [8], SPNP [10], SURF2 [31]. In certain cases (e.g. exponential transition firing times) analytic solution is possible, otherwise simulation has to be performed.

2.4 Mastering Complexity

Dependability modeling and analysis of complex systems pose serious problems due to the complexity of the dependability model, which may be out of the range existing tools can deal with. This complexity is due to the large number of components as well as the complex interactions among (redundant) hardware and software entities.

Small systems can be analyzed by modeling the behavior at a fine granularity, e.g. at UML statechart level. However, as the complexity of the system increases, another approach has to be followed. *Modular modeling* and *hierarchic refinement* of a rough (structural) dependability model are typical ways of mastering complexity. First only the relevant aspects of the system are modeled and analyzed, which enables the computation of numerical results and at the same time allows the estimation of the sensitivity of system-level attributes to the parameters of specific components. In this way those components and design decisions can be identified that need a refined analysis. Modular modeling allows replacing components of a rough dependability model with more detailed ones.

In our approach, first we build a quite abstract model, which concentrates on the structure of the system and, accordingly, takes information from the structural UML diagrams. It has the following advantages:

- It results in a system-wide (but less detailed) representation of the dependability characteristics of the system in its entirety.
- The size of the model and thus the time and resource needs of the analysis can be controlled.
- Preliminary evaluations of the system dependability during the early phases of the design can be provided. Usually, the structural UML models, that is the class, object, and deployment diagrams, are available before the detailed low level ones, and the analysis on models derived from the structural view provides indications about the critical parts of the system that require a more detailed representation.

By using appropriate interfaces, the structural dependability models can be augmented by inserting more detailed information coming from refined UML models of the identified critical parts of the system. This way we can deal with various levels of details ranging from very preliminary abstract UML descriptions up to the refined specifications of the last design phases.

Accordingly, dependability modeling and analysis can be performed in several steps. The first step has the fundamental task of extracting the relevant dependability information from the mass of information available in the UML description. In this step, the structural dependability model is built, in which we can fix the fault activation, error propagation and repair processes as well as the mapping to the service level. The dependability model is formalized by a Timed Petri Net (TPN) that can be translated to the input format of the specific Petri net tool selected for performing the analysis.

The subsequent steps can refine the structural model by replacing modules of the structural dependability model (i.e. the corresponding TPN) with sub-models constructed on the basis of the refined UML models (e.g. also behavioral diagrams like statecharts and message sequence charts that describe the interaction of components more precisely. For the purpose of this sub-model construction, other methods of processing UML diagrams are provided (Section 5).

In this paper we will show the construction of the structural dependability model, identify the interfaces to extend this model and make reference to approaches available to construct the refined sub-models.

2.5 Model Parameters and Validation of the Dependability Model

Dependability modeling - especially in the case of rough structural models constructed in the early design phases - should be based on a number of assumptions and simplifications. Since the assumptions and simplifying hypotheses may lead to wrong approximation of the system behavior, the resulting error should always be estimated either through sensitivity analysis or by comparing the results obtained by the model containing the assumption and by a model where it has been released.

Another problem is that models need many (aggregate) parameters whose meaning is not always intuitive for the designers. Obviously, values for such parameters may be difficult to provide in early phases of design. The ideal source would be to provide them through experimental tests on prototypes (unlikely to be available). Alternatives are data from similar systems (modules) or data derived from designers' experience.

Experimental results have to be provided at later stages to validate the numerical results gained by the solution of the dependability model. It has however to be emphasized that instead of the concrete numerical dependability measures, the outcomes of the sensitivity analysis and the comparison of design choices are the most beneficial results of a model based dependability evaluation.

3 System Modeling in the Early Phases of Design

In the early phases of the design we assume that an architectural description of the system is available. The software architecture is specified by class, object and collaboration diagrams. The allocation of the software elements to hardware units and resources is described by static deployment diagrams, no dynamic resource utilization is specified. The dependability-related attributes of components are aggregate ones that combine performance-related and dependability-related attributes (like component activation probability and error detection coverage are aggregated to error propagation probability).

In the subsequent design steps the model of the system is to be refined. From the point of view of the dependability modeling, the management of redundancy and the specification of dynamic resource usage play a crucial role. Accordingly, more refined UML models are assumed that separate usage (conformant with the corresponding UML resource modeling profile [25]) and fault activation/error propagation. The aspects of this kind of model refinement are detailed in Sect. 5.

3.1 Attributes of the System and Its Components

The system-level dependability attributes, i.e. availability and reliability are computed by the solution of the dependability model based on the *local dependability attributes* of the various components of the system. In the abstract structural model, the local (aggregate) attributes of basic components are values characterizing fault activation, error propagation and repair processes (Sect. 2.2) as follows:

- Fault activation is characterized by the *fault occurrence* (random variable representing the time needed for the activation of a fault), the *error latency* (random variable representing the time needed to bring the component to a failure after the fault generates an erroneous internal state) and the *ratio of permanent and transient faults*. Naturally, in stateless (purely functional) components there is no error latency, while in software components only permanent (design) faults occur.

- Error propagation is characterized by the *error propagation probability* which is assigned to a pair of interconnected components whenever the failure of a server-like component results in the failure of the another, client-like component. Two components can be connected in terms of failure propagation bi-directionally if any one of them may influence the failure of the other component. In this case error propagation probability is assigned in both directions.
- Repair is characterized by the *repair delay* (random variable representing the time needed to perform the repair). Note that error propagation prescribes a constraint for the repair of a component: the repair of a component can not be completed until all the used components are fully operational.
- Mapping from architecture to service levels is characterized typically by Boolean logic expressions describing what combinations of component failures can constitute the failure of the service. These combinations are visualized by a *fault tree*.

The structure of this dependability model is inspired by the approach presented in [20]. We have slightly modified that model: we use a more reduced hierarchy and, for the sake of convenience, we distinguish between stateless and stateful components. The distinction between them is important from the point of view of the potential erroneous state, error latency and propagation. Similarly, the distinction of hardware components is necessary from the point of view of the transient faults.

As it partially turns out from the above set of relevant attributes, we have introduced a set of general assumptions for the dependability model:

- Solid software failures are not taken into account (assuming that they were removed before execution by a thorough debugging and fault removal).
- There are no failures that compensate the effects of other ones.
- "Repair" is implicit if the fault disappears after activation (transient hardware faults and all software faults). Repair of a derived failure is implicit if it disappears as soon as the underlying faults and failures have been repaired.
- Explicit repair refers to the actions that are planned and scheduled by the designer. Explicit repair may remove (permanent) faults from the system or restore the service of system components.

In the following we detail the restrictions to be imposed on the UML designer to allow translating the specification into a dependability model. These restrictions are mainly related to the introduction of redundancy into the system, for which particular structures are to be utilized to permit the identification of the crucial points. Since the information on dependability aspects is typically not included into a UML design, we prescribe a set of extensions of the standard UML in order to create controlled interface towards the designer for the input of parameters, the selection of desired measures, and the choice of the fault-tolerance structures to be included into the system.

3.2   Redundancy Structures

One fundamental choice has been made in defining the way redundancy has to be expressed in the UML design. We opted for the so called "class based" redundancy which prescribes that elements of a redundancy structure must be defined as instances of specific classes (based on templates and stereotypes) [35]. It is important to notice that this choice supports the use of design patterns collected in a fault-tolerance library. Moreover, the construction of such library can be integrated with the dependability modeling in the sense that it will be possible to associate to the elements of the library their dependability sub-models which will be derived only once, thus building at the same time a library of dependability sub-models.

In general, a system component is redundant if its service can be delivered by another component in a coordinated way, without the interaction of the client(s). Accordingly, operation of redundant components presumes the existence of a coordinator (called here *redundancy manager*) and some type of *adjudicator*. A given service is provided by a set of redundant components called here *variants*, which are coordinated by the redundancy manager: the service is available through the redundancy manager and the redundant components can not be used separately. A component may be a participant in a single redundancy structure only. Other, non-redundant components can not be included in a redundancy structure (but the variants may use the service of another components).

Accordingly, redundancy structures must be composed of objects instantiated from the following types of classes: redundancy manager, variant, and adjudicator (which can be further refined by various subtypes e.g. tester, voter or comparator).

The specific conditions of the failure of the redundancy structure (which can be quite complex) are either available in the library of dependability-related design patterns or they have to be derived by analyzing the UML diagrams describing the behavior of the redundancy structure.

It has to be emphasized that the construction of the structural dependability model relies on behavioral diagrams only in the case of redundancy managers. Otherwise, behavioral diagrams are used only in the subsequent phases to refine the structural dependability model (Sect. 5).

3.3   Specifying Dependability Related Properties and Requirements

Basic UML focuses on capturing the complex functionality of the system but neglects non-functional aspects such as quality of service (QoS). To allow dependability analysis of designs, UML has to be extended with a notation for describing the quantitative properties of model elements and the required properties of the system to be analyzed.

There are some ongoing activities to extend UML for dealing with such kind of data. The OMG proposal [25] describes a general approach to classify model elements by stereotypes and bind performance characteristics to them by using tagged values. We followed this approach, because this annotation does not change the UML meta-model and thus it is conformant with existing CASE tools. However, it may be inconvenient for working with a large number of elements (some of them having identical attributes). Because of its generality and object-oriented nature, the QoS specification language QML [12] is a potential extension. It was adapted to quantitative model analysis with respect to the OMG proposal in [17].

Accordingly, in our approach standard extensions of UML, i.e. stereotypes and tagged values are used to identify the elements of redundancy structures and to assign dependability attributes (Sect. 3.1) to components and relations.

The classes in redundancy structures, namely the redundancy manager, variant and adjudicator are stereotyped as `<<redundancy manager>>`, `<<variant>>` and `<<adjudicator>>`, respectively.

Stateless or stateful software and hardware components are stereotyped accordingly. The local dependability attributes are described by tagged values as follows:

- Fault occurrence: `FO=x`
- Error latency: `EL=y`
- Ratio of permanent faults: `PP=v`
- Repair delay: `RD=z`

The designer can assign a single value (here x, y, z, v are used to instantiate the parameter), two values (range for a sensitivity analysis), or no values (the parameter should be derived based on the parameters of underlying elements in the hierarchy). Different sets of tagged values are assigned to different types of components according to Table 1.

Table 1. Stereotypes and tagged values

Component type	Dependability attributes	Stereotypes	Tagged values
Stateless hardware	Fault occurrence, ratio of permanent faults, repair delay	`<<stateless>>`, `<<hardware>>`	FO, PP, RD
Stateful hardware	Fault occurrence, error latency, ratio of permanent faults, repair delay	`<<stateful>>`, `<<hardware>>`	FO, EL, PP, RD
Stateless software	Fault occurrence	`<<stateless>>`, `<<software>>`	FO
Stateful software	Fault occurrence, error latency, repair delay	`<<stateless>>`, `<<software>>`	FO, EL, RD

These stereotypes and corresponding tagged values can be applied to UML objects, classes (in this case all objects instantiated from the class should be assigned the same set of parameters), nodes and components.

Stereotype `<<propagation>>` indicates an error propagation path, with the tagged value `PP=x` to assign propagation probability. This stereotype can be applied to links between objects, associations between classes or nodes, deployment relations, dependencies, and generalization relationships.

In order to derive the non-trivial relations in redundancy structures automatically, further extensions are required. In statechart diagrams of the redundancy managers, failure states are distinguished by stereotypes. Similarly, stereotypes identify the specific types of adjudicators (e.g. testers and comparators). Tagged values are used to assign common mode fault occurrences to components. The detailed description of these extensions can be found in [5].

4   Construction of the Dependability Model

The structural dependability model is constructed first in the form of an intermediate model (IM) which is a hypergraph representing the components and their relations relevant from the point of view of the dependability analysis. In this way some peculiarities of UML (e.g. package hierarchy, composite objects and nodes, different types of dependencies) can be resolved which results in a simple and flat model with a limited set of elements and relations.

4.1   The Intermediate Model (IM)

The IM is a hypergraph G=(N,A), where each node in N represents an entity, and each hyperarc in A represents a relation between these entities. Both the nodes and the hyperarcs are labeled, that is they have attached a set of attributes completing their description. A generic node of the IM is described by a triple consisting of the fields `<name>`, `<type>` and `<attributes>`. We now give the semantic of the intermediate model by describing the sets N and A and what they represent.

Nodes represent the stateful or stateless hardware/software components described in the set of UML structural diagrams. Four types of nodes are used: SFE-SW (stateful software), SLE-SW (stateless software), SFE-HW (stateful hardware) and SLE-HW (stateless hardware). Attributes of the nodes characterize the fault activation and the repair processes according to Table 1.

The fault tolerance (redundancy) structures are represented by composite nodes FTS. The system service is represented by another specific node SYS to which the system-level attributes (measures of interest) are assigned. It has to be emphasized that these nodes represent the composite structures and not individual components.

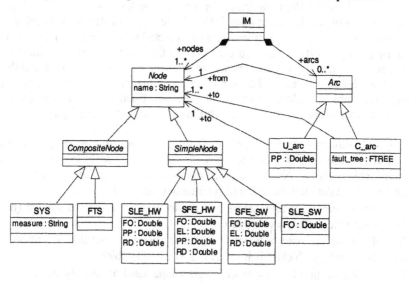

Fig. 1. Metamodel of the IM

Hyperarcs among the nodes represent two kinds of relations. "Uses-the-service-of" (U) type of hyperarc indicates an error propagation path between a server-like component (typically a resource) and a client-like component. A U hyperarch is a one-to-one relation directed from a node representing the client to the node representing the server. Error propagation may occur in the opposite direction, i.e. from the server to the client. The assigned attribute is the error propagation probability.

Another type of hyperarc represents the "is-composed-of" (C) relation in the case of fault tolerance (redundancy) structures, i.e. FTS nodes, and system services, i.e. SYS nodes. This type of hyperarc is a one-to-many relation directed from the FTS or SYS node to the nodes representing the constituent parts. The hyperarc is assigned a fault tree describing the conditions of error propagation from the parts to the composite structure.

The metamodel of the IM (in the form of class diagrams) is shown in Fig. 1.

4.2 Dependability Related Information in UML Diagrams

The dependability model is built by projecting the UML model elements into nodes, and the UML structural relations to hyperarcs of the IM. The types of nodes are determined by UML stereotypes, while the attributes are projected from tagged values of the corresponding UML model elements (Table 1). The types of hyperarcs are determined by the stereotypes assigned to the key elements of the composite structures (i.e. the redundancy managers).

According to the high-level approach, not only the "natural" software elements as objects, tasks, processes etc. can be identified but also higher-level, compound elements as use cases or packages. As the UML design is hierarchical, intermediate levels of the hierarchy can be represented by SYS nodes. The representation of a compound UML element (like a package) depends on the level of detail described or selected by the designer. If a compound UML element is not refined, or its refinement is not relevant for the dependability analysis (as selected by the designer) then it is represented by a simple software or hardware node in the IM. If it is refined and its refinement is relevant then its subcomponents are represented as simple nodes and the compound as a whole is represented by a SYS node. In the case of hyperarcs, all potential propagation paths are taken into account thus the structure of the model represents worst-case error propagation. The fine-tuning is left to the actual parameter assignment.

Now we summarize the role UML diagrams and elements considered in our model derivation. As already stated, we focus on the structural UML diagrams to construct the dependability model. Nevertheless, it may be necessary to use also behavioral diagrams for a more detailed modeling of redundancy structures.

- Use case diagrams identify actors and top-level services of the system (this way also identify the system level failure).
- Class diagrams are used to identify relations (associations) that are traced to objects. By default, each class is instantiated by a single object.
- Object, collaboration and sequence diagrams are used to identify objects (as basic components) and their relations. Messages identify the direction of the relations.
- Component diagrams are used to identify the relations among components, and in this way among objects realized by the components. Note that the components are instantiated on the deployment diagrams.
- Deployment diagrams are used to identify hardware elements and deployed-on (a specific case of "uses-the-service-of") relations among software and hardware ele-

ments. Relations among hardware elements (e.g. communication) are also described here.
- Statechart diagrams are used basically only in the case of redundancy structures, to derive the non-trivial relations among participants of the structure.

In the following we sketch the projection in the case of object and class diagrams. Other projections are described in [5].

4.3   Projection of the Model Elements of Object and Class Diagrams

Object diagrams (and also collaboration diagrams) include instances that are represented by nodes in the IM. Simple objects are projected into simple nodes of the IM. Composite objects are projected into a set of nodes, with unidirectional error propagation paths from the sub-objects to the composite one.

Since each object is a particular instance of a class, the relations of objects and their type information can be deduced by the analysis of the class diagrams. Model elements of class diagrams are utilized as follows.

Inheritance hierarchy of classes is utilized to identify the relationships: if an object is instantiated from a given class then the relationships of this class and also of its ancestors have to be taken into account.

Associations are binary or n-ary relations among classes. In general, associations mean that the objects instantiated from the corresponding classes know (i.e. can name) each other. Associations may be instantiated by links on object and collaboration diagrams, and communication among objects is possible along these links. Accordingly, an association indicates a potential bi-directional error propagation path among these objects thus it is projected into the IM. The following additional features might be taken into account.

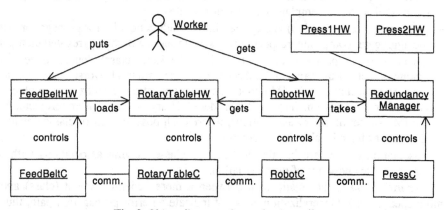

Fig. 2. Object diagram of a production cell

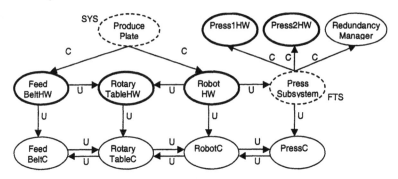

Fig. 3. Projection of the UML object diagram in Fig. 2. into the IM

- Navigability of an association end denotes whether the instance can be directly reached. However, it does not give precise information about the direction of the potential error propagation, since through return values also a unidirectional navigation may result in bi-directional error propagation. Accordingly, each association is projected by default to bi-directional error propagation.
- Or-associations (indicating a situation when only one of several possible associations may be valid) are all projected into the IM, in this way a worst case dependability model is constructed.
- Multiplicity of association ends are taken into account only when the classes are not instantiated on object diagrams. Indeed, in the early phases of the design the instantiation of the model may not be available. It might be useful for the designer to have a default instantiation in order to compute rough dependability measures. Accordingly, if a class has multiplicity specification then the value or the lower bound of its range can be taken into account. If it is missing or equal to zero then by default a single instance is taken into account. Metaclasses, type classes and parameterized classes (i.e. templates) are not instantiated.
- Aggregation (composition) is projected into a unidirectional error propagation path: the aggregate (composite, respectively) uses the service of the aggregated elements.
- Unary associations (both ends attached to the same class) denote associations among objects of the same class. According to the structural (worst case) approach, they are projected into the IM denoting error propagation paths from each object to each other. Reflexive paths are not considered. N-ary associations are projected into the IM as a set of binary associations, where each possible pair of classes included in the n-ary form is taken into account.
- Association classes are handled as separate classes having associations with the classes at the endpoints of the association.

Generalization is the relationship between a more general element (class) and a more specific one. Generalization does not indicate an error propagation path, thus it is not projected into the IM (but the inheritance of relations defined by generalizations is taken into account).

Dependency means a semantic relationship between classes. From the point of view of dependability modeling, those dependencies are relevant which relate also the instances (not only the classes themselves, like <<refine>> or <<trace>> relationships). This way in the set of the predefined types of dependencies, only the <<uses>> dependency (meaning that an element requires the presence of another element for its correct functioning) indicates an error propagation path, thus it is projected into the IM.

An example of an object diagram of a production cell (described in [6]) and the corresponding IM are shown in Fig. 2 and Fig. 3. Note that the objects Press1HW, Press2HW and RedundancyManager form a redundancy structure (Sect. 4.5). The external actor in Fig. 2 identifies the top level components providing the system service (Sect. 4.6).

4.4 Projection of Resource Usage

UML deployment diagrams show instances of hardware components (nodes) and the configuration of run-time components on them.
- *Nodes* are run-time physical objects, usually hardware resources. They are projected into hardware nodes in the IM.
- *Objects* realized by components are projected into software nodes of the IM.
- *UML components* represent pieces of run-time software. If a component is refined, i.e. the set of objects realized by the component is given then the component is not projected into a separate software node of the IM. If a component is not refined then it is projected into a single software node of the IM.
- *Deployment relations* among nodes and components and realization relations among components and objects (both shown by graphical nesting or composition associations) indicate potential error propagation paths with direction from the nodes to the objects. They are projected into the IM.

Note that the conventions introduced in the General Resource Model (GRM [25]) enable a more refined modeling of resource usage than in the case of deployment diagrams (see Sect. 5).

4.5 Projection of Redundancy

A redundancy structure (identified by the redundancy manager, Fig. 4) is projected into an FTS node of the IM connected, by using a C hyperarc, to the elements representing the redundancy manager, the adjudicators, and the variants.

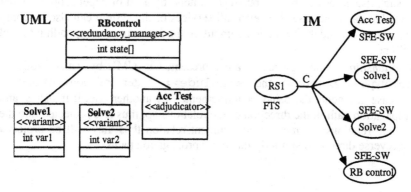

Fig. 4. Projection of a simple redundancy structure

In simple cases the error propagation is described by a fault tree. The construction of a fault tree corresponding to a redundancy structure (not included in the library of schemes) requires the analysis of the behavior, i.e. the statechart diagram, of the redundancy manager. This kind of analysis is supported by the designer, as he/she identifies (by stereotyping) the failure states and events in the statechart. The fault tree is constructed by a reachability analysis enumerating the paths in the statechart that can lead to failure states (i.e. failure of the redundancy structure) [5]. The incoming events on these paths identify the failures of variants and/or adjudicators that are considered as basic events in the fault tree. Repair is taken into account in a default way by using the dual counterpart of the fault tree.

In the case of sophisticated recovery and repair policies, the statechart of the redundancy manager is transformed directly to a TPN subnet (Sect. 5.1). This approach results in a more complex model but allows the analysis of non-trivial scenarios and temporal dependencies.

4.6   Mapping from Architectural to Service Level

In UML, the services of the system are identified on use case diagrams. Model elements of these diagrams include actors, use cases, communication associations among actors and use cases, and generalizations among use cases.

- A *use case* represents a coherent functionality of the system. Usually, each use case is refined by interactions of objects. However, it may happen that in the early phases of the design only some (important or critical) use cases are refined, the others are not. Accordingly, if a use case is not refined or the refinement is not relevant then it is projected into a simple IM node, otherwise it is projected into a SYS node of the IM, which relates the nodes resulting from the projection of the other UML diagrams belonging to this use case.
- *Actors* represent (roles of) users or entities that interact directly with the system. Being external entities from the point of view of a given service, actors are not projected into the IM.
- *Communication associations* among actors and use cases identify the services of the system. If a use case is connected directly to external actor(s) then it is projected into a top-level SYS node of the IM. Usually, a real system is composed of several use cases, more of them being connected directly to actors. Dependability measures of such use cases can be computed separately, by a set of dependability models assigned to each use case. However, all services of the system can also be composed in a single dependability model, computing the measures corresponding to multiple SYS nodes.
- *Relationships* among use cases are represented in UML by generalizations with stereotype <<extend>> and <<include>>. Extend relationships mean that a use case augments the behavior implemented by another one. It indicates an error propagation path in the direction of the relationship, thus it is projected into the IM. Include relationships mean a containment relation thus they will be projected (in the reverse direction) similarly into error propagation paths.

4.7   Construction of the Analysis Model

On the basis of the IM a second step of the transformation builds a TPN dependability model, by generating a subnet for each model element of the IM [5].

Table 2. Elements of the TPN model

Element	Description
Place	<name> <initial tokens>
Transition	<name> <random variable> <memory policy> <guard> <priority>
Input arc	<from place> <to transition> <weight>
Output arc	<from transition> <to place> <weight>
Subnet	Nested TPN sub-model

A TPN model is composed of a set of elements as listed in Table 2. Places, transitions and subnets all have a name, which is local to the subnet where they are defined. Transitions are described by a random variable (specifying the distribution of the delay necessary to perform the associated activity) and a memory policy field (a rule for the sampling of the successive random delays from the distribution). A transition has a guard, that is a Boolean function of the net marking, and a priority used to solve the conflict. The weights on input and output arcs may be dependent from the marking of the net. Subnets are a convenient modeling notation to encapsulate portion of the whole net, thus allowing for a modular and hierarchical definition of the model.

Notice that the class of TPNs defined here is quite general. If the TPN model contains only instantaneous and exponential transitions, then it is a GSPN that can be easily translated into the specific notation of the automated tools able to solve it [8,10]. If deterministic transitions are included as well, then the model is a DSPN, which under certain conditions can be analytically solved with specific tools like UltraSAN, and TimeNET. If other kinds of distributions of the transition firing times are included, then simulation can be used to solve the TPN model.

We take advantage from the modularity of the TPN models defined above, to build the whole model as a collection of subnets, linked by input and output arcs over interface places. For each node of the hypergraph, one or two subnets are generated, depending from node type. The basic subnets represent the internal state of each element appearing in the IM, and model the failure and repair processes.

Fault Activation Subnets. The fault activation subnets (called basic subnets hereafter) include a set of places and transitions that are also interfaces towards other subnets of the model. Places called H and F model the healthy and failed state of the component represented by the IM node (Fig. 5). Fault activation subnets of stateful elements also include place E to represent the erroneous state of the component. For a stateless node, transition `fault` models the occurrence of a fault and the consequent failure of the node. For a stateful node, the occurrence of a fault generates first a corrupted internal state (error), modeled by the introduction of a token in E. After a latency period, modeled by transition `latency`, this error brings to the failure.

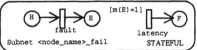

Fig. 5. Fault activation subnets for stateless and stateful nodes

For each FTS and SYS node, a basic failure subnet containing only two interface places, namely H and F, is generated in the TPN model. Indeed, FTS and SYS nodes represent composite elements, and their internal evolution is modeled through the subnets of their composing elements.

Propagation Subnets. By examining the U hyperarcs of the IM, the transformation generates a set of propagation subnets, which link the basic subnets. For instance, suppose node A is linked by a U hyperarc to node B in the IM. In this case, we want to model the fact that a failure occurred in the server B may propagate to the client A, corrupting its internal state. The propagation subnet B->A shown in Fig. 6 models this phenomenon (immediate transitions are depicted by thin bars).

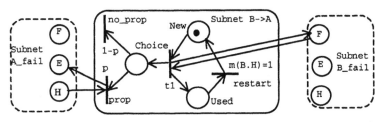

Fig. 6. Error propagation from node B to node A

The propagation subnet becomes enabled only after element B has failed. At that time, a token is put into place B.F, and the propagation subnet is activated. The subnet moves with probability p the token being in place A.H to place A.E. This models the introduction of an error in element A. A single token circulates among the two places New and Used, to allow the propagation subnet to be activated only once for each failure of B (t1 cannot fire until a token is moved from place Used to New).

Consider now a type C hyperarc, linking a FTS node P with its composing nodes. The fault-tree associated with the arc expresses the logic with which the failures of the composing elements propagate towards the failure of P. Also, the dual of the fault-tree (obtained by exchanging each AND gate with an OR gate and vice versa) represents the way the composed element P gets repaired when the composing element are recovered. Thus, the fault-tree is translated into a failure propagation subnet, and its dual counterpart is translated into a "repair propagation" subnet. These two subnets are linked to the basic subnets of all the elements connected by the C hyperarc. Note that the Boolean conditions of the fault trees can be represented in Petri nets either by enabling conditions of transitions or by explicit subnets corresponding to AND or OR gates [5].

Repair Subnets. The repair subnet of a node is activated by the failure occurred in the fault activation subnet of the same node. For instance, Fig. 7 shows the repair subnets for stateless and stateful hardware nodes. The two transitions `implicit` and `explicit` represent the two different kinds of repair which are needed as a consequence of a transient and permanent hardware fault, respectively. If the node is stateless then the final effect of the repair is the insertion of a token in place H. If it is stateful then the repair also removes a token from place E, modeling the error recovery activity.

Notice that all the parameters needed to define the subnets are found in the IM in the obvious fields.

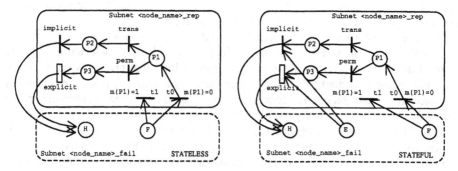

Fig. 7. Repair subnets of hardware nodes

Subnets for Mapping from Architecture to Service Level. C hyperarcs linking SYS nodes are handled in the same way like C hyperarcs linking FTS nodes. When a SYS node does not have an associated fault tree, then we implicitly associate to it a simple fault tree representing the OR relation of all the composing elements.

The markings of places H and F for the SYS node at the top level of the IM define a partition between proper and improper service: whenever a token reaches place F, the service (the object of the dependability evaluation) is considered as failed. Accordingly, the solution of the dependability model should provide the average number of tokens in H to get asymptotic availability figures and the time of the first occurrence of a token in F to get reliability figures.

5   Refinement of the Dependability Model

We identified and elaborated the following options to perform refinement in the structural dependability model as the UML model becomes more detailed:

- Mapping the behavioral diagrams describing redundancy management directly to TPN subnets.
- Constructing subnets on the basis of the refined modeling of usage and fault activation in the used resources.

These options will be described in the following sections.

5.1   Refined Modeling of Redundancy Management

The behavioral diagrams describing redundancy and resource management are natural candidates to be used during refinement since they describe the core logic of the dependability model. In Sect. 4, fault trees were constructed on the basis of the statechart diagram of the redundancy manager in a class based redundancy scheme. The fault tree representing logic conditions (as a static snapshot) can be integrated with the fault activation and repair subnets by using the Petri net places E, F and H representing the state of the components. However, in this way sophisticated repair/recovery scenarios and temporal dependencies could not be taken into account.

In the refinement step, also the dynamics of replica management (sequence of failure events and repair actions) can be considered. Statecharts of selected objects are mapped directly to Petri nets by a model transformation that preserves the dynamic semantics of the statechart [15]. This way the designer is allowed to use the full power of statecharts (state hierarchy, concurrency etc.) to describe application-dependent replication and recovery strategies. It has to be emphasized that only the statecharts of the objects responsible for replica management and recovery are considered in this refinement step. They are interfaced with the other parts of the system by events describing failure occurrences (error reports), and actions initiating repairs. Accordingly, instead of using the places corresponding to the *states* of the components (as in the case of fault trees), the integration of the resulting subnets requires additional TPN places representing the *changes* in the system as follows:

- Input places of the refined subnets represent events. By default, the basic subnet responsible for fault activation puts a token into the place representing the corresponding failure event when it occurs (i.e. state changes from H to F). In a further refinement step, more precise error detection and coverage can also be modeled (similarly by statecharts).
- Output places of the refined subnets represent actions. The subnet belonging to the statechart puts a token into a place representing a repair action when it is generated. By default, this action triggers a TPN transition corresponding to the explicit repair in the component (i.e. target of the action) affected by the repair. Again, based on this interface the repair actions can be refined in subsequent steps.

This approach was introduced first in [16] and adapted to the fault tolerance infrastructure defined by FT-CORBA [23] in [21]. In this adaptation, first a high-level dependability model is constructed that allows the analysis of the fault tolerance strategies and properties directly supported by the standard infrastructure. In the refinement step, the detailed behavioral model, i.e. the UML statechart of the Replication Manager is transformed to a TPN. This subnet forms the core of the dependability model by replacing the original, generic subnet. In this way the analysis of application-dependent, specific replication strategies and recovery policies can be supported.

5.2   Rationale of the Refined Fault Modeling

The modeling and analysis methodology described in Sect. 4 is able to deliver a first, system-level estimate of the dependability attributes based on aggregate measures, like fault occurrence and error propagation rates. However, as error propagation depends both on the attributes of the corresponding components and on the *workload distribu-*

tion in the system, a more refined model in the later phases of the design process should reflect these factors separately.

Frequently, a timeliness and/or performance analysis is performed on the system prior to dependability evaluation, especially if the system has to satisfy severe temporal constraints. We sketch here a dependability modeling style which can reuse the models constructed for performance analysis.

The main scope of the refined methodology is the modeling of the effects of permanent and transient operational faults in resources, dominantly implemented in hardware, and the propagation of errors via hardware, software components, and messages, respectively. A crucial problem results from structure altering faults and error propagation effects not included in a functional model of the system. For instance, two functionally independent threads sharing a resource may interact through a parasitic coupling if a fault affects this resource. (The theoretical background would even allow for modeling faults in the very computer core, like the CPU-memory setup. However, such a fine granular modeling is practically infeasible due to the complexity of the model.) Fortunately, each critical application has some well-defined damage confinement regions designed to limit the propagation of errors within them. Accordingly, an appropriate modeling style assures a proper handling of structure altering faults. The main rule is to describe explicitly all the resource sharing within of a damage confinement region. Direct computational faults are restricted in our model to transient faults local to components, and redundancy-based solutions are modeled explicitly.

5.3   The General Resource Model (GRM)

OMG did elaborate the General Resource Model (GRM [25]), providing a standardized notation to describe resource types, their static or dynamic interaction with the system, together with their management. The services required from and delivered by the resources are characterized by means of QoS parameters defined according to the actual analysis objective. GRM is a (sub)profile defined for transformation based analysis. The standard profile offers several notations to describe schedulability, performance, and time. GRM can be extended for several analysis objectives, including dependability assessment.

For the sake of completeness, we shortly summarize the main concepts of GRM (Fig. 8).

In case of *static resource usage modeling* the dynamics of the client-server interaction is neglected, and only a comparison of the *QoS values* required by the *client* and offered by the *resource instance* is performed. A typical system level static quantitative QoS analysis task is a worst case assessment of the sufficiency of the total capacity offered by the resources matched against the total of the requests.

Dynamic usage modeling explicitly describes the order and timing of the client-resource interaction steps. A *resource instance* may offer multiple different kinds of *services*. Each kind of a service use is represented by a *scenario*, a temporally ordered series of *action* executions, as *steps* using specific service(s) offered by a resource. *QoS values* are assigned to the service invocations (*required QoS value*), and to the resource service instances (*offered QoS*).

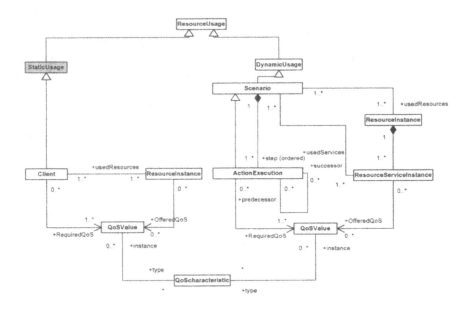

Fig. 8. The OMG General Resource Model

Resources can be classified according to the *protection kind* used either as *unprotected* or *protected*. The latter offers *services* to be used simultaneously only by a single client under an *access control policy* administered by a *resource broker*. A *resource manager* supervises the creation and administration of (typically software) resources according to a *resource control policy*. GRM introduces further technical classifications on resources, like by *purpose* (processor, communication resource, or device), or by activeness (whether they require a trigger or not).

5.4   Modeling of Fault Occurrences

A GRM-based model, as a starting point describes the logic of interactions between the application and the underlying platform. The initial structure of this model is frequently the byproduct of the previous performance analysis. However, dependability analysis necessitates the simultaneous tracing of the information flow in the fault-free and in a faulty case (or all candidate faulty cases) of the system in order to estimate the probabilities of the observable difference in their behavior.

This way the interaction model has to be extended in order to cover all the anticipated faulty cases. This is done by *qualitative fault modeling*. This uninterpreted type of modeling uses a small set of *qualitative values* from an enumerated type, like *{good, faulty, illegal}* to construct an abstract model reflecting the state of the resources and the potential propagation of errors through the system via invocations and messages. The value of *illegal* serves here to model the fault effects resulting in a violation of functional constraints. For instance, a data may not conform to a type related restriction due to a memory fault forcing it out of the legal range or catastrophic distortions of the control flow may cause a crash. The designer can select the set of qualitative values arbitrarily, according to the aim of the analysis. For instance values of *early* and *late* can extend the domain of qualitative values for timeliness analysis in the potentially faulty case.

Stateful components in the system, like resources can take their actual state from this domain of qualitative values. They change the state upon internal fault activation, repair and error propagation.

- Temporal and permanent operational faults in the resources originate in external effects occurring independently from the processes internal to the system. The appearance of the selected fault or fault mode (in case if a resource can be affected by different kinds of faults) at the fault site is triggered by a separate *fault activation process* independently of the internal functioning of the system (Fig. 9). The fault activation process has a direct access to the resources in order to activate the selected fault(s) by forcing a transition of the state of the component to *faulty*. Frequently, fault activation is restricted, for instance by a single fault assumption. All these restrictions can be included into the fault activation process.

- *External repair actions* can be included into the model as independent processes, as well. Built-in *automated recovery actions* can be modeled as special service invocations forcing the state of the resource to *good*.

Rates can be associated to steps of fault activation and repair processes as QoS values. Their rule is identical to that in the corresponding TPN subnets described in Sect. 4. The changes of fault states in resources are reflected in the activation of different scenarios for service invocations.

5.5   Modeling of Propagation

The *propagation of faulty* and *illegal* values in the scenarios of dynamic usage models (i.e. in message sequence charts or statecharts) represents error propagation during an interaction between a component and resource.

Usage scenarios have to be extended by including fault states as branch conditions if the interaction potentially exposes different behaviors on *good* and *faulty* data or resource states. Usually this extension transforms the scenarios to non-deterministic ones, for instance to express probabilistic error manifestation. The arrival of a *faulty* input data to a stateful resource or component may trigger a *good* to *faulty* transition. Similarly, the invocation of a *faulty* component may result in a *faulty* output delivered by the service.

Quantitative measures can be associated to the different scenarios, including the input request arrival frequencies (rates) of the different kinds of data, probabilities assigned to the non-deterministic branches.

Please note, that the main benefit of using this detailed model is that the quantitative dependability model is cleanly decomposed into the workload model (rate of service invocation), activation and repair (separate processes), and error manifestation (interaction scenarios).

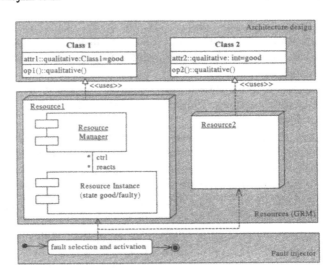

Fig. 9. The fault modeling architecture according to the GRM

The model transformation technology that maps fault activation and usage scenarios to dependability sub-models is the message sequence chart and statechart to TPN transformation introduced in Sect. 5.1 [15].

6   Implementation of the Model Transformation

In HIDE the enriched UML model of the target design was transformed to the mathematical model (TPN for dependability evaluation) by a custom-built model transformation. Later, to avoid the impreciseness of an ad-hoc implementation, the mathematically precise paradigm of graph transformations was selected as the foundation of the definition and implementation of the model transformation. A general framework called VIATRA (Visual Automated model TRAnsformations [11]) was worked out that is also flexible enough to cover the changing UML standard.

In VIATRA, both the UML dialect (standard base UML and its profiles, on one hand restricted by modeling conventions and on the other hand enriched by dependability requirements and local dependability attributes) and the target mathematical notation are specified in the form of UML class diagrams [32] following the concepts of MOF metamodeling [24]. Metamodels are interpreted as type graphs (typed, attributed and directed graphs) and models are valid instances of their type graphs [33]. The transformation steps are specified by graph transformation rules in the form of a 3-tuple (LHS, N, RHS) where LHS is the left-hand side graph, RHS is the right-hand side graph and N is an optional negative application condition. The application of the rule rewrites the initial model by replacing the pattern defined by LHS with the pattern of the RHS. Fig. 10 shows, for example, how an UML object of a class stereotyped as "stateful hardware" becomes an IM node of type SFE_HW with the same name (the source and target objects are linked together by a reference node in the figure). The operational semantics of the transformation (i.e. the sequence of rules to be applied) is given by a control flow graph. As both LHS and RHS can be specified visually (in the form of UML class diagrams), we have an expressive and easy-to-understand notation for the transformation designer.

In the case of dependability modeling, VIATRA is applied to the UML dialect described in Sect. 3 in order to generate first the IM model according to the metamodel given in Fig. 1 then (in a second step) the TPN model itself. The generic TPN description is then tailored to the input language of the selected tool by a minor post-processing step. The first step of the model transformation from the point of view of the transformation designer is depicted in Fig. 11.

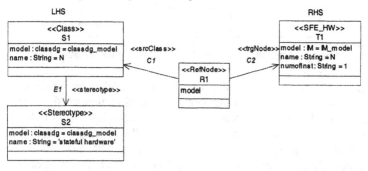

Fig. 10. Definition of a simple transformation rule

The modeler does not have to deal with these internal representations, since the executable program generated from the rules will perform the transformation automatically [32]. The general technological concept of VIATRA is the use of the XMI standard (for arbitrary MOF-based metamodel). Accordingly, the UML CASE tool is interfaced with the transformator by utilizing its XMI export facility. The output of the transformation is again in XMI format, thus the final syntax tailoring steps can be performed by XSLT or dedicated programs.

The first step of our model transformation (from UML structural diagrams to the IM) was defined by only slightly more than 50 rules (e.g. the processing of class diagrams required 28 rules). The subsequent step of constructing the various modules of the TPN can be performed either by similar graph transformation rules or by a Java program [28].

VIATRA is used to construct the fault trees from the statechart diagrams of the redundancy managers as well. Moreover, the generic transformation from UML statecharts to TPN was also developed in this framework.

7 Assessment of the Approach

The input of the dependability analysis is the set of UML structural diagrams. These diagrams were enriched to allow the designer to identify redundancy structures and provide the parameters needed for the definition of the dependability model. The extensions adhere to standard UML and to the OMG GRM profile. The restrictions imposed on the designer concern only the modeling of redundancy structures. The class based redundancy approach correlates with the usual architecture of distributed fault tolerant object-oriented systems (e.g. Fault Tolerant CORBA [23]).

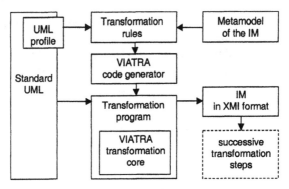

Fig. 11. Application of VIATRA in the first transformation step

The semantic correctness of the dependability model relies on the abstraction represented by the IM. In the IM, each element is assigned an internal fault activation and repair process, while relations specify the way for the propagation of failure and repair events. These local effects are represented in the TPN by separate subnets that can be checked formally (contrary to the above UML diagrams, TPN has formal semantics).

The number of model elements in the transformation is in the same order of magnitude as the number of model elements in the UML design. This statement derives from the projection defined when the IM is constructed, since the TPN subnets belonging to IM elements have a fixed number of model elements. A hand-made model could save on the number of modeling elements at the expenses of the modularity.

8   Conclusion

In this paper we described a transformation from structural UML diagrams to TPN models for the quantitative evaluation of availability and reliability. Our transformation is an attempt to build first a quite abstract system-level dependability model with tractable dimensions that can be subsequently enriched and refined by substituting coarse representation of some elements with a more detailed one.

We identified two points in the model where the refined sub-models can be acquired: both the behavioral diagrams describing redundancy and the resource usage (based on the GRM) are candidates of model transformations that result in refined sub-models to be included in the dependability model.

Besides the structural dependability modeling of the production cell benchmark [6], we successfully applied the model refinement approach in the case of FT-CORBA architectures [21].

In addition, further work is ongoing to refine the methodologies described here and to collect evidence on the feasibility and usefulness of the approach. This work is performed in the frame of the PRIDE project, supported by the Italian Space Agency, where the transformation described in this paper is being implemented as a part of the 'HRT UML Nice' toolset specifically tailored for the design and validation of real-time dependable systems.

References

1. Ajmone Marsan, M., and G. Chiola: On Petri nets with deterministic and exponentially distributed firing times. Lecture Notes in Computer Science, Vol. 226, pp. 132-145, 1987.
2. Ajmone Marsan, M., G. Balbo, and G. Conte: A Class of Generalized Stochastic Petri Nets for the Performance Analysis of Multiprocessor Systems. ACM TOCS, pp. 93-122, 1984.
3. Allmaier, S., and S. Dalibor: PANDA - Petri net analysis and design assistant. In Proc. Performance TOOLS'97, Saint Malo, France, 1997.
4. Betous-Almeida, C., and K. Kanoun: Dependability Evaluation - From Functional to Structural Modeling. In Proc. SAFECOMP 2001, pp. 239-249, Springer Verlag, 2001.
5. Bondavalli, A., I. Majzik, and I. Mura: From structural UML diagrams to Timed Petri Nets. European ESPRIT Project 27439 HIDE, Del. 2, Sect. 4, http://www.inf.mit.bme.hu/, 1998.
6. Bondavalli, A., I. Majzik, and I. Mura: Automatic Dependability Analysis for Supporting Design Decisions in UML. Proc. Fourth IEEE Int. Symposium on High-Assurance Systems Engineering (HASE'99), November 17-19, 1999, Washington DC, 1999, pp. 64-71.
7. Bondavalli, A., M. Dal Cin, D. Latella, I. Majzik, A. Pataricza, and G. Savoia: Dependability Analysis in the Early Phases of UML Based System Design. International Journal of Computer Systems - Science & Engineering, Vol. 16 (5), Sep 2001, pp. 265-275.
8. Chiola, G.: GreatSPN 1.5 software architecture. In Proc. Fifth International Conference on Modelling Techniques and Tools for Computer Performance Evaluation, Torino, Italy, 1991, pp. 117-132.
9. Choi, H., V. G. Kulkarni, and K. S. Trivedi: Markov regenerative stochastic Petri nets. Performance Evaluation, Vol. 20, pp. 337-357, 1994.
10. Ciardo, G., J. Muppala, and K. S. Trivedi: SPNP: stochastic Petri net package. In Proc. International Conference on Petri Nets and Performance Models, Kyoto, Japan, 1989.
11. Csertán, Gy., G. Huszerl, I. Majzik, Zs. Pap, A. Pataricza, and D. Varró: VIATRA - Visual Automated Transformations for Formal Verification and Validation of UML Models. In Proc. 17th Int. Conference on Automated Software Engineering (ASE 2002), Edinburgh, Scotland, 23-27 September 2002, IEEE CS Press, 2002.
12. Frolund, S., and J. Koistinen: Quality of Service Specificaton in Distributed Object Systems Design. In Proc. of the 5th USENIX Conf. on Object-Oriented Technology and Systems (COOTS), May 3-7, San Diego, California, USA, 1999, pp. 69-89.
13. Ganesh, J. P. , and J.B. Dugan: Automatic Synthesis of Dynamic Fault Trees from UML System Models. Proc. of the IEEE Int. Symp. on Software Reliability Engineering, 2002
14. Goseva-Popstojanova, K., and K.S. Trivedi: Architecture Based Software Reliability. In Proc. of the Int. Conf on Appplied Stochastic System Modeling (ASSM 2000), Kyoto, Japan, March 2000.
15. Huszerl, G., and I. Majzik, A. Pataricza, K. Kosmidis, and M. Dal Cin: Quantitative Analysis of UML Statechart Models of Dependable Systems. The Computer Journal, Vol 45(3), May 2002, pp. 260-277
16. Huszerl, G., and I. Majzik: Modelling and Analysis of Redundancy Management in Distributed Object-Oriented Systems by Using UML Statecharts. In: Proc. of the 27th Euromicro Conference, pp. 200-207., Warsaw, Poland, 4-6. September 2001.
17. Huszerl, G., and K. Kosmidis: Object Oriented Notation for Modelling Quantitative Aspects. In Proc. Workshop of the International Conference on Architecture of Computing Systems (ARCS 2002), Karlsruhe, Germany, 2002, VDE Verlag Berlin, pp. 91-100.
18. Issarny, V., C. Kloukinas, and A. Zarras: Systematic Aid for Developing Middleware Architectures. In Communications of the ACM, Issue on Adaptive Middleware, Vol. 45(6), pp. 53-58, June 2002.
19. Laprie, J.-C. (editor): Dependability: Basic Concepts and Terminology. Series Dependable Computing and Fault Tolerant Systems, volume 5, Springer Verlag, 1992

20. Laprie, J.-C. and K. Kanoun: Software Reliability and System Reliability. In M.R. Lyu (editor), Handbook of Software Reliability Engineering, pp 27-69, McGraw Hill, New York, 1995
21. Majzik, I., and G. Huszerl: Towards Dependability Modeling of FT-CORBA Architectures. In A. Bondavalli, P. Thevenod-Fosse (eds.): Dependable Computing EDCC4. Proc. 4th European Dependable Computing Conference, Toulouse, France, 23-25 October 2002, LNCS 2485, Springer Verlag, Berlin Heidelberg, pp. 121-139, 2002.
22. Nelli, M., A. Bondavalli, and L. Simoncini: Dependability Modelling and Analysis of Complex Control Systems: An Application to Railway Interlocking. In Proc. 2nd European Dependable Computing Conference (EDCC-2), pp. 93-110, Springer Verlag, 1996.
23. Object Management Group: Fault Tolerant CORBA. CORBA 2.6, Chapter 25, formal/01-12-63, OMG Technical Committee, http://www.omg.org/, 2001.
24. Object Management Group: Meta Object Facility Version 1.3, http://www.omg.org/, September 1999.
25. Object Management Group: UML Profile for Schedulability, Performance, and Time. Final adopted specification. http://www.omg.org/, 2001.
26. Object Management Group: Unified Modeling Language. Specification v1.4, http://www.uml.org/, 2000.
27. Pataricza, A.: From the General Resource Model to a General Fault Modeling Paradigm? Workshop on Crititcal Systems Development with UML at UML 2002, Dresden, Germany.
28. Poli, S.: Dal Linguaggio di Specifica UML ai modelli a rete di Petri stocastiche: generazione per la valutazione di Dependability. Master thesis (in Italian), University of Pisa, 2000.
29. Rabah, M., and K. Kanoun: Dependability Evaluation of a Distributed Shared Memory Multiprocessor System. In Proc. 3rd European Dependable Computing Conference (EDCC-3), pp. 42-59, Springer Verlag, 1999.
30. Sanders, W. H., W. D. Obal II, M. A. Qureshi, and F. K. Widjanarko: The UltraSAN modeling environment. Performance Evaluation, Vol. 21, pp. 1995.
31. SURF-2 User guide. LAAS-CNRS, 1994.
32. Varró, D., and A. Pataricza: Metamodeling Mathematics: A Precise and Visual Framework for Describing Semantic Domains of UML Models. In Proc. UML 2002, International Conference on UML, Dresden, Germany, pp. 18-33, LNCS-2460, Springer Verlag, 2002.
33. Varró, D., G. Varró, and A. Pataricza: Designing the Automatic Transformation of Visual Languages. Science of Computer Programming, 44(2002):205-227, 2002.
34. Walter, M., C. Trinitis, and W. Karl: OpenSESAME: An Intuitive Dependability Modeling Environment Supporting Inter-Component Dependencies. In Proc. of the 2001 Pacific Rim Int. Symposium on Dependable Computing, pp. 76-84, IEEE Computer Society, 2001.
35. Xu, J., B. Randell, C.M.F. Rubira-Calsavara, and R.J. Stroud: Toward an Object-Oriented Approach to Software Fault Tolerance. In D.K. Pradhan and D.R. Avresky (eds.): Fault-Tolerant Parallel and Distributed Systems. IEEE CS Press, pp. 226-233, 1994.

Specification–Level Integration of Simulation and Dependability Analysis

Swapna S. Gokhale[1], Joseph R. Horgan[2], and Kishor S. Trivedi[3]

[1] Dept. of Computer Science and Engineering
University of Connecticut, Storrs, CT 06269
ssg@engr.uconn.edu
[2] Applied Research, Telcordia Technologies
445 South Street, Morristown, NJ 07960
jrh@research.telcordia.com
[3] Dept. of Electrical and Computer Engineering
Center for Advanced Computing and Communication
Duke University, Durham, NC 27708
kst@ee.duke.edu

Abstract. Software architectural choices have a profound influence on the quality attributes supported by a system. Architecture analysis can be used to evaluate the influence of design decisions on important quality attributes such as maintainability, performance and dependability. As software architecture gains appreciation as a critical design level for software systems, techniques and tools to support testing, understanding, debugging and maintaining these architectures are expected to become readily available. In addition to providing the desired support, data collected from these tools also provides a rich source of information from the point of view of performance and dependability analysis of the architecture. This paper presents a performance and dependability analysis methodology which illustrates the use of such data. The methodology thus seeks a three way integration of distinct and important areas, namely, formal specification, specification simulation/testing and performance and dependability analysis. We illustrate the key steps in the methodology with the help of a case study.

1 Introduction

Software architecture is receiving increasing appreciation as a critical design level for software systems, as they continue to grow in size and complexity. The software architecture of a system defines its high level structure, exposing its gross organization as a collection of interacting components [5]. Software architecture represents the design decisions that are made in the early phases of a system and these decisions are usually difficult to change or reverse. These architectural choices have a profound influence on the non functional attributes that can be supported by a system. Software architecture analysis can be used to assess the degree to which a given software architecture supports important quality attributes such as maintainability, reliability, reusability and performance.

R. de Lemos et al. (Eds.): Architecting Dependable Systems, LNCS 2677, pp. 245–266, 2003.

Architectural description languages (ADLs) are formal languages that can be used to represent the architecture of a software system. They focus on the high level structure of the overall system rather than the implementation details of any specific source module. ADLs are intended to play an important role in the development of software by composing source modules rather than by composing individual statements written in conventional programming languages. A number of architectural description languages have been proposed recently, such as Rapide [11], UniCon [15], and WRIGHT [1]. As software architecture design gains prominence, the development of techniques and tools to support understanding, testing, debugging, reengineering, and maintaining software architectures will become an important issue. Li et al. propose a tool for understanding, testing, debugging and profiling software architectural specifications in SDL [9]. Zhao et al. propose a technique for architecture understanding based on program dependence graphs for ACME [21]. ACME provides an architecture description interchange language which permits a subset of ADL tools to share architectural information that is jointly understood, while tolerating the presence of information that falls outside their common vocabulary [4].

Software architectures specified in ADLs such as SDL and LOTOS, and other modeling languages such as UML can also be used for performance and dependability analysis, by constructing quantitative models from these specifications. Wohlin et al. develop a performance analysis methodology for specifications written in SDL [20]. Marsan et al. present an extension of LOTOS, which enables a mapping from the extended specifications to performance models [12]. Steppler develops a tool for the simulation and emulation of formal specifications in SDL, with an eye towards analyzing these specifications for the non functional attribute of performance [16]. Heck et al. describe a hierarchical performance evaluation approach for formally specified protocols in SDL [7]. Bondavalli et. al. present a dependability analysis procedure based on UML designs [2]. Wang et al. discuss a performance and dependability analysis methodology for specifications in Estelle [19]. Argus-I is a quality focussed environment which assists specification based analysis and testing at both the component and architecture levels. Argus-I is based on specifying software architecture augmented by statecharts. Argus-I provides support for numerous analysis techniques from type checking to model checking and simulation. Argus-I also supports preliminary performance analysis by determining how often each architectural entity is invoked during simulations [18].

The different approaches described in the literature focus on various analysis types such as model checking, checking for interface mismatches, and structural and behavioral analysis. A very basic performance analysis may be facilitated, which essentially provides a count of the different types of architectural entities executed during simulation. Model–based performance analysis, which involves translation of the architectural specification into a quantitative performance model is not supported. Model–based performance analysis can not only enable the performance prediction of the present architectural specification, but it can also facilitate the exploration of architectural alternatives. In addition, by superimposing failure and repair information, model–based performance analysis can also enable dependability analysis at the specification level. Even in the approaches where model–based performance analysis is supported, the major drawback is the lack of adequate information to parameterize the quantitative models constructed from software specifications. As the techniques for software architecture testing and simulation become more mature and tools become readily available, the data generated during simulation and testing can provide a rich source of information for subsequent model parameterization. A similar approach has been demonstrated at the source code level, where execution trace data collected from extensive testing of the application was used to extract and parameterize the architectural model of the system [6]. Our present paper outlines an approach which seeks a three way integration, namely, formal specification, specification simulation/testing, and performance and dependability analysis. The glue between specification, performance and dependability analysis and simulation and testing is provided by the measurements obtained during simulation and testing. These measurements are used to parameterize the quantitative model of the system. Our methodology is facilitated by Telcordia Software Visualization and Analysis Tool Suite (TSVAT), developed at Telcordia Technologies for architectural specifications in SDL [10].

The rest of the paper is organized as follows: Section 2 provides an overview of Specification and Description Language (SDL) and Stochastic Reward Nets (SRNs). Section 3 illustrates the various steps in the performance and dependability analysis methodology with the help of a case study. Section 4 presents conclusions and directions for future research.

2 Background

The methodology centers around systems specified using the Specification and Description Language (SDL) and the quantitative modeling paradigm of Stochastic Reward Nets (SRNs). In this section we present an overview of Specification and Description Language (SDL) and Stochastic Reward Nets (SRNs).

2.1 Specification and Description Language (SDL)

An architecture can be specified using an informal notation (box and arrow diagrams), however, such notations are error–prone and ambiguous. An architecture specified in a formal specification language eliminates the ambiguity and provides a clear basis for analysis. We choose Specification and Description Language as a CEFSM (Communicating Extended Finite State Machine) specification language to specify software architecture. We use formal specification as a means to specify software architecture. The choice of SDL as an architecture description language is motivated due to the following reasons: (i) SDL is an International Telecommunication Union (ITU) standard [24]. Many telecommunications system software specifications are rendered in SDL, (ii) SDL is a formal language with a well–defined semantics. Several commercial off–the–shelf tools can be used to investigate architectural models formalized in SDL, (iii) SDL meets the requirements for an executable architectural specification language [11]. SDL allows dynamic creation and termination of process instances and their corresponding communication paths during execution. Hence it is capable of modeling the architectures of dynamic systems in which the number of components and connectors may vary during system execution, and (iv) SDL can present all four views of software architecture [8]. These four views include the logical view which describes the design's object model, the process view which describes the design's concurrency and synchronization aspects, the physical view which describes the mapping of the software onto hardware and presents the distributed aspects of the design, and the development view which describes the software's static organization in the development environment. For example, SDL uses delay and non delay channels to indicate the relative physical locations of components as described in the physical view of the design.

An SDL specification can be viewed as CEFSM (Communicating Extended Finite State Machine) model. A CEFSM model is often defined as a tuple: $CEFSM = (EFSM, Channel)$, including a set of EFSMs and a set of channels. Each EFSM is defined as a FSM with the addition of variables to its states. An EFSM is a quintuple $(S, S_0, I, 0, T)$ where S is a set of states, S_0 is the set of initial states, I is the set of input events and enabling conditions, 0 is the set of action tasks and output events, and the T maps an input set and the old state to tasks and/or outputs and a set of new states. Each state in an EFSM is defined by a set of variables, including state names. The transition T of an EFSM is then given by: $[< u_0, u_1, \ldots, u_n > +input^*, task^*; output^* + < u_0', u_1', \ldots, u_n' >]$, where u_0 and u_0' are the names of the states, $< u_i, \ldots, u_n >$ and $< u_1', \ldots, u_n' >$ are the values of the extended variables, n is the number of variables, "+" means coexistence, and "[,]" denotes a sequenced pair. Each channel consists of three elements, a source component, a destination component, and a signal list, which is the list of signals that can be sent through the channel.

2.2   Stochastic Reward Nets (SRNs)

Stochastic reward nets (SRNs) are a generalization of generalized stochastic Petri nets (SPNs), which in turn are a generalization of stochastic Petri nets (SPNs). We first describe SPNs, then GSPNs, and then SRNs.

Stochastic Petri Nets (SPNs). A Petri net (PN) is a bipartite directed graph with two disjoint set of nodes called places and transitions [17]. Directed arcs in the graph connect places to transitions (called input arcs) and transitions to places (called output arcs). Places may contain an integer number of entities called tokens. The input places of a transition are the set of places which connect to that transition through input arcs. Similarly, output places of a transition are those places to which output arcs are drawn from that transition. In a graphical representation of a PN, places are represented by circles, transitions are represented by bars and the tokens are represented by dots or integers in the circles (places).

The state or condition of the PN is associated with the presence or absence of tokens in various places in the net. A marked PN is obtained by associating tokens with places. The marking of a PN is the distribution of tokens in the places of the PN. A marking is represented by a vector $M = (\#(P_1),\#(P_2),\#(P_3), \ldots, \#(P_n))$, where $\#(P_i)$ is the number of tokens in place i and n is the number of places in the net. The condition of the net may enable some transitions to fire. A transition is considered enabled to fire in the current marking if each of its input places contains the number of tokens assigned to the input arc (called the arc multiplicity). The firing of a transition is an atomic action in which the designated number of tokens are removed from each input place of that transition and one or more tokens (as specified by the output arc multiplicity) are added to each output place of that transition, possibly resulting in a new marking of the PN. If exponentially distributed firing times correspond with the transitions, the result is a stochastic PN.

Generalized Stochastic Petri Nets (GSPNs). Generalized stochastic Petri nets (GSPNs) allow transitions to have zero firing times in addition to exponential firing times [17]. The former are called immediate transitions and the latter are called timed transitions. Other extensions to SPNs in the development of GSPNs include the inhibitor arc. An inhibitor arc is an arc from a place to a transition that inhibits the firing of the transition when a token is present in the input place.

In any marking of the PN, a number of transitions may be simultaneously enabled. The tie between the simultaneously enabled transitions can be broken by specifying probabilities, or by a race. Priorities are non negative integers that permit a partial ordering of transitions. Whenever a transition with priority D is enabled, all transitions with priority less than D are inhibited from firing. If probabilities are assigned to transitions, they are interpreted as weights of each transition. With some probability, any of the enabled transitions may be the first to fire; any enabled transition with positive probability may fire next. Immediate transitions which can be simultaneously enabled must have either priorities or probabilities assigned to avoid ambiguity in the net. For timed transitions, the decision as to which transition fires next can be decided by a race; the transition with the highest firing rate is most likely to fire next.

Stochastic Reward Nets (SRNs). Stochastic Reward Nets (SRNs) are a superset of GSPNs [17]. SRNs substantially increase the modeling power of GSPNs by adding guard functions, marking dependent arc multiplicities, general transition probabilities and reward rates at the net level.

A guard function is a Boolean function associated with a transition. Whenever the transition satisfies all the input and inhibitor conditions in a marking

M, the guard is evaluated. The transition is considered enabled only if the guard function evaluates to true.

Marking dependent arc multiplicities allows either the number of tokens required for the transitions to be enabled (the number of tokens removed from the input place), or the number of tokens placed in an output place to be a function of the current marking of the PN. Such arcs are called variable cardinality arcs.

Measures. SRNs provide the same capability as Markov reward models [14]. A Markov reward model is a Markov chain with reward rates (real numbers) assigned to each state. A state of an SRN is actually a marking (labeled $(\#(P_1),\ \#(P_2),\ \ldots,\ \#(P_n))$, if there are n places in the net. The set of all possible markings that can be reached in the net can be subdivided into two categories: tangible markings and vanishing markings. For each tangible marking, a reward rate is assigned based on the overall measure of interest. These measures may include reliability, safety and performance measures.

Several measures can be obtained using Markov reward models. These include the expected reward rate both in the steady state and at a given time, the expected accumulated reward until absorption or a given time, and the distribution of the accumulated reward until absorption or until a given time [17].

3   A Case Study

In this section we present the steps involved in the performance and dependability analysis process with the help of a case study.

3.1   System Specification in SDL

The first step in the methodology is the system specification in SDL. We use a PBX system as an example system in our case study. The block level SDL specification of a PBX system is shown in Figure 1. The system consists of two distributed blocks. The block *CallHandler* controls the call processing functions and the block *ResManager* involves inventory control and remote database access. The *CallHandler* block receives three signals over channel *C1*, namely, *offhook, dig and hangUp*. The first signal announces the caller's intent to place a call, the second signal is a digit of a telephone number and the *hangUp* signal is sent either after the call is complete, if there is a change in the caller's intention to pursue the call, due to the unavailability of the resources required to place a call, or due to the unavailability of the callee to accept the call (callee is busy). The *CallHandler* process outputs the signals *dialT, busyT, connt, ringT* and *ring* over the channel *C2*. Communication between the *CallHandler* block and the *ResManager* block occurs over channels *C3* and *C4*. Channel *C3* is used to communicate the request and release messages for resources and channel *C4* is used to send reply messages regarding the availability of the resources to proceed with the call. Channels *C3* and *C4* are delaying channels which indicates that the two blocks can be implemented on different CPUs with a non-negligible delay.

This reflects the reality that the database information can be stored remotely. Figure 2 shows the partial process level specification of the *CallHandler* block. The *Caller* process interacts with the call originator party and the *Callee* process handles the terminator party. The *Caller* process waits for the call originator to pick up the phone and announce the intent to make a phone call. Once a phone is off hook, the *Caller* process checks whether the resources are available to handle the call. If so, it waits for the originator to input the phone number, digit by digit. It determines the type of call (local, long-distance, operator) based on the number input. It also tears down the call once it is finished. The block *Res-Manager* has two processes: *CMgr* (not shown here) and *TMgr* which controls two types of resources. The *Caller* process communicates with the *TMgr* process in order to determine the availability of the resources. The partial process level specification of *TMgr* is shown in Figure 3. The SDL specification of the PBX system consisted of approximately 300 lines of SDL code.

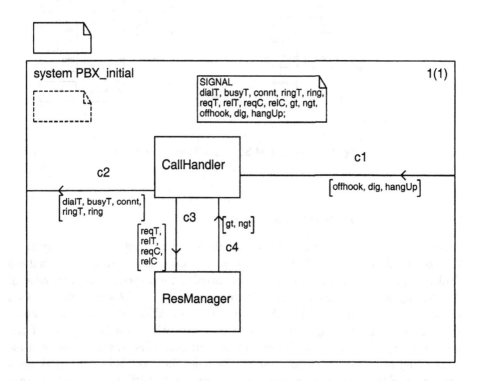

Fig. 1. Block level SDL specification of PBX system

process Caller

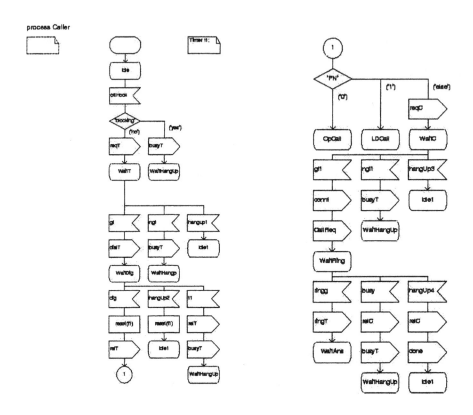

Fig. 2. Process level SDL specification of *Caller*

3.2   Specification Simulation/Testing

The next step in the methodology is to simulate/test the system specified in SDL. We use the SDL version of the Telcordia Software Visualization and Analysis Toolsuite (TSVAT), developed to support architectural specification, debugging and testing for this purpose. TSVAT contains a suite of tools, χSlice, χVue, χProf, χRegress, and χATAC. We primarily use χATAC in our methodology. The technique underlying this toolsuite is the creation of a flow graph of the specification, thus laying out its execution structure. The simulator is then instrumented to collect execution traces. The trace file records how many times a given part of the specification, such as a process, a transition, a decision, a state input, or a data flow, has been exercised in each simulation of the specification, or at the end of the testing process. χATAC reports coverage with respect to the following well-known criteria: function coverage, basic transition coverage, and decision coverage. Function coverage simply checks that each process of the SDL specification has been executed at least once. A basic transition is simply a statement sequence of the specification that is always executed sequentially,

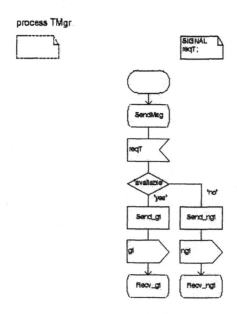

Fig. 3. Process level SDL specification of *TMgr*

including states and decision constructs (no internal branching constructs). Basic transition coverage checks that each basic transition has been executed at least once, which implies that each statement has been executed at least once. Decisions are conditional branches from one basic transition to another. They could be states or decision constructs. Decision coverage checks that each such situation, decision matching or input mapping has been executed, so that all true and false paths have been taken as well as all input alternatives and decision alternatives. χATAC aids in the testing process by prioritizing specification transitions, states and decisions. Some transitions or states dominate others in the same process in that, if the dominating one is covered by a test, then many others must also be covered. The dominating ones are found by analyzing the flow graph of the specification, and indicate a good starting place for designing test cases. If the dominating ones are covered, then the coverage of the specification can be increased significantly with just a few test cases. Each test case in this context is one simulator execution of the specification. We have developed our own specification simulation tool, however χATAC can work cooperatively with the existing commercial tools such as Telelogic SDT [22] and Telelogic ObjectGeode [23].

Figure 4 shows a screen from χATAC. The dark SDL segments indicate the dominating ones, that is, if a test case is designed to cover these then the coverage of the specification can be increased significantly. The SDL specification of the *Caller* was tested using 18 test cases. The test cases ensured that all the blocks and decisions in the SDL specification were executed at least once, providing 100% block and decision coverage.

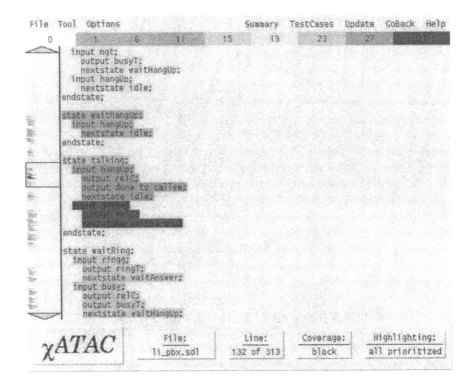

Fig. 4. A snapshot of SDL specification in ATAC

The execution traces collected during the testing of the specification can then be used to extract branching probabilities of the various decisions in the specification, as described in Section 3.4. It is important to note that the methodology described here provides a way to determine the branching probabilities using a set of simulations. The representativeness of these branching probabilities will depend on how representative the simulations are of the actual usage of the system. If the operational profile [13] is available, then the simulation process can be guided by the operational profile. In that case, the branching probabilities obtained would be reflect what would be observed during the actual usage of the system.

3.3   Translation from a SDL Specification to a SRN Model

The SDL representation of the architecture of the system is then translated to a stochastic reward net (SRN) model for performance analysis. The translation is performed according to the following rules:

1. A state in the SDL representation is mapped to a place in the SRN.
2. A task in the SDL specification is represented as a place and a transition. The place represents the initiation/beginning of the task, and the transition models the time required for the execution of the task.
3. A decision is modeled as a place which represents the beginning of the execution of the decision, a transition which represents the time required to execute the decision, and an intermediate place which represents the completion of the decision execution. ¿From the intermediate place, there are as many immediate transitions as the possible outcomes of the decision.
4. The behavior of the timer *T1* is captured as follows: *Pinit_1* represents the initial state of the timer. Immediate transition *t_11* is fired when there is a token in the place *WaitT*, depositing a token in the place *Pstart_1*. The enabling condition for the transition *t_11* is listed in Table 1. This corresponds to the task of setting the timer *T1*. Deterministic transition *t1* represents the duration of the timer. Immediate transition *t_12* is used to reset the timer, should the event(s) the timer is set for occur, before the timer expires. In this case, the system is waiting for a user to input the digit, or for an *onhook* signal from the caller. The enabling condition for the transition *t_12* is listed in Table 1. If the time duration represented by the deterministic transition elapses, transition *t_1* fires, depositing a token in the place *Pdone_1*. This corresponds to the firing of the timer. A token in the place *Pdone_1*, simultaneously enables two immediate transitions *WaitDigFlush* and *pdone_1_tr*. The former transition flushes the token from the place *WaitDig*, and the latter achieves the dual tasks of resetting the timer and the initiation of the tasks following the firing of the timer. The transition *WaitDigFlush* was set to have a higher priority than the transition *pdone_1_tr*. As a result, when a token is deposited in the place *Pdone_1*, the transition *WaitDigFlush* fires and flushes the token out of the place *WaitDig*. The enabling condition for the transition *WaitDigFlush* is also shown in Table 1.
5. Outputs are not represented explicitly using any SRN construct.
6. Inputs are represented by transitions.

The set of rules described above to transform an SDL representation to SRN are heuristic. A part of the transformation can be automated, for example, translation of states and tasks in the SDL specification to places and transitions respectively in the SRN model can be possibly automated. In order for the process to be completely automated, more experience with a variety of SDL specifications needs to be gathered.

The SRN model for the *Caller* process specified in SDL is depicted in Figure 5. The enabling functions for the model are listed in Table 1. The SRN representation of the *TMgr* process is shown in Figure 6.

3.4   SRN Model Parameterization

The next step in the process is to parameterize the SRN model. The parameters of the SRN model can be broadly classified into five categories, depending on the sources of information used for the parameterization:

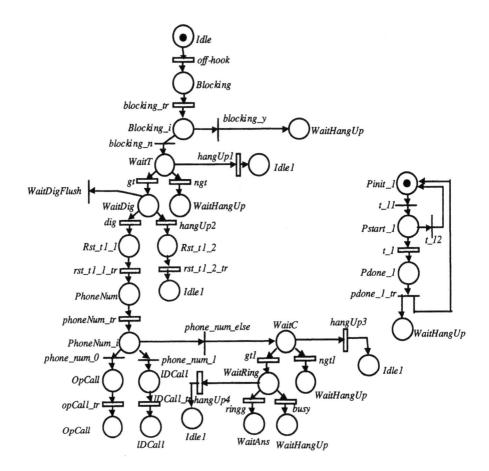

Fig. 5. SRN model of the process *Caller*

Table 1. Enabling functions for transitions in Figure 5

Transition	Enabling function
t_11	(#(WaitDig) = 1)
t_12	(#(Rst_t1_1)=1 V (Rst_t1_2)=1)
WaitDigFlush	(#(Pdone_1)=1)

Execution Time Parameters. These parameters are associated with the execution of the tasks and decisions in the SDL specification. These parameters are dependent heavily on the implementation details. SDL specifications can also be used to generate code in a semi–automatic fashion, and the measurements obtained from the execution of this partial code can also be used to obtain the distributions and values of these parameters. The execution time parameters will also depend on the hardware characteristics. We assume that the hardware

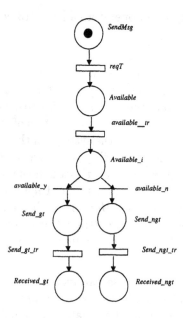

Fig. 6. SRN model of the process *TMgr*

characteristics are homogeneous. In the present analysis, these parameters follow an exponential distribution with mean 1.0 time unit.

User Inputs. These parameters model the inputs resulting from the actions of the user. These inputs are expected by the system at various stages of execution. In this system, they include the *offhook* signal, all the *hangUp* signals, as well as the digits input by the user. The distributions and the actual values of these parameters can be derived from historical data, or can be based on the knowledge of the experts who are intimately familiar with the system and its field usage. In the event that the system is novel and not much information is available about the system, these parameters can be guesstimated.

Branching Probabilities. These reflect the probabilities of occurrence of the various outcomes of a decision. These values can also be derived from historical data, or can be based on expert knowledge. The trace data collected during the simulation/testing of the SDL specification can be used to determine these branching probabilities. The SDL version of Telcordia Software Visualization and Analysis Toolsuite (TSVAT) facilitates the collection of such trace data. In the SDL specifications for the *Caller*, the occurrence probabilities of the type of call, namely, operator call, long distance call, and normal call need to be determined. Out of the 19 test cases used, 13 execute the transition *phonenum_tr*. Long distance call and operator calls each occur once out of the 13 test cases, whereas, 11 test cases simulate a normal call. Hence, the probability of a long distance call is 1/13, the probability of an operator call is 1/13, while the probability of a normal call is 11/13.

Inputs from Other Components/Processes. Most real life software systems are inherently distributed, and hence require interactions between the various components of the system. Since the SRN model is constructed from process level specification, it is natural for some of the parameters of the model to draw from the execution of the other processes in the system. In the PBX system, the inputs *gt* and *ngt* which indicate the availability and unavailability of the resources respectively are received by the process *Caller* upon the completion of the *TMgr* process. The firing rates of the transitions *gt* and *ngt* can be obtained from the solution of the SRN model of the *TMgr*. Also, the hardware communication delays among processes will add places/transitions to the SRN model. In the present paper, we assume that these communication delays are negligible.

Failure/Repair Parameters. These parameters model the failure/repair behavior of the processes and/or each task within a process and are necessary to compute various measures such as the reliability, availability and safety of an application. This information can be obtained by consulting with experts who are familiar with the application or can be guesstimated.

3.5   Reachability Graph Generation

The next step in the analysis methodology is the generation of the reachability graph. Each distinct marking of the PN constitutes a separate state of the PN. A marking is reachable from another marking if there exists a sequence of transition firings which occur from the original marking that results in the new marking. The reachability graph of a PN is the set of markings that are reachable from the other markings. The markings of a GSPN are classified into two types: tangible and vanishing. A marking is tangible if the only transitions enabled (if any are enabled) are timed transitions. A marking is vanishing if one or more immediate transitions are enabled in the marking.

The reachability graph shown in Figure 7 includes only the tangible markings. The markings shaded in grey indicate the absorbing markings, that is the system is destined to stay in these markings forever upon reaching there. In the initial state, the system has a token each in places *Idle* and *Pinit_1*. Upon firing of the transition *offhook*, the next state includes a token in the places *Blocking* and *Pinit_1*. After the firing of several transitions and intermediate transient markings, the system terminates in one of the four absorbing states. The absorbing state with tokens in the places *WaitHangUp* and *Pinit_1* is reached when the resources required to place a call are unavailable, when the callee is busy, or when the timer *T1* fires while waiting for a user to input the digits. The absorbing state with a token in the place *Pinit_1* is reached when the call being placed is either a long distance call or an operator assisted call (processing of these calls is not shown here for the sake of simplicity). The absorbing state with tokens in places *Idle_1* and *Pinit_1* is reached when the user hangs up while waiting for a resource availability check, or while providing the digits of the telephone number to be dialed. The final absorbing state, with tokens in the place *Pinit_1* and *WaitAns*, indicate successful completion of the call, with the user waiting for the callee to answer the phone. The reachability graph is generated using the tool SPNP (Stochastic Petri Net Package) [3], which is also used in the subsequent section for performance and dependability analysis.

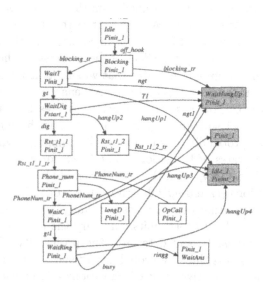

Fig. 7. Reachability graph generated from the *Caller* model

3.6   Performance and Dependability Analysis

In this section, we illustrate how our integrated specification, testing and analysis methodology can be used for performance and dependability analysis. The examples presented in this section are for the purposes of illustration, and the analysis is by no means complete. A detailed description of how SRN models and in particular SPNP can be used to obtain various performance measures of interest can be found in [17].

The performance measure of paramount importance from the caller's point of view is the probability of successful call completion. Call completion is indicated by the arrival of a token in the place *WaitAns* in Figure 5. The call completion probability is influenced by several factors, namely, the probability that the resources are available to complete the call, the value of the timer *T1*, the users tendency to hang up during the process of placing a call and lastly the probability that the called party or the callee is free to accept the call. Of these, the first two are system dependent parameters, while the latter two are environmental parameters which are not under the direct control of the system. We demonstrate how the system dependent parameters influence the probability of successful call completion using the SRN model.

Initially we study the impact of resource availability on the probability of successful call completion. The input transitions *gt* and *gt1* indicate the resource availability, while the transitions *ngt* and *ngt1* indicate resource unavailability. The values of these transitions are obtained from the solution of the SRN model representing the *TMgr* specification. We will address the issue of how these values can be obtained by solving the SRN shown in Figure 6 in the sequel. For the time being, we attempt to study the effect of these values on the successful call completion probability. Figure 8 indicates that when a token is present in place *WaitT*, three timed transitions are simultaneously enabled: *hangup1*, *gt* and *ngt*. The decision as to which of these three transitions fires next is thus decided by a race, the transition with maximum firing rate has the highest chance of being fired next. The probability of successful call completion will be dependent on the relative firing rates of transitions *gt* and *ngt*, for a given firing rate of transition *hangUp1*. Similarly, when there is a token in place *WaitC*, the relative firing rates of transitions *gt1* and *ngt1* determine the probability of successful call completion, for a given firing rate of transition *hangUp3*. Thus, we hold firing rate of transitions *gt* and *gt1* at 9.0 units, and vary the ratio of the firing rates of *gt* and *ngt* (*gt1* and *ngt1*), and determine the probability of successful call completion. Figure 8 shows that the probability of successful call completion is almost unaffected as the relative rates of transitions *gt* and *ngt* (*gt1* and *ngt1*) changes from 10000 to 100. However, some drop in the probability is observed when the relative rate is 10, followed by a significant drop in the case when the rate of resource availability is the same as the rate of resource unavailability. The firing rates of the transitions *hangUp1* and *hangUp3* are held at a value which is 0.01% of the firing rate of transition *gt*, implying that the user hanging up is very unlikely compared to the probability of having an available resource.

The rate of transitions *gt* and *gt1* is a function of the probability that the resource is actually available as well as the firing rates of the transitions *reqT*, *available_tr*, and *send_gt_tr* shown in the Figure 8. Similarly, the rate of transitions *ngt* and *ngt1* is a function of the probability that the resource is unavailable as well as the rates of the transitions *reqT*, *available_tr*, and *send_ngt_tr*. It is important to note that the transitions *reqT* and *available_tr* are common to both *gt* and *ngt*. The transition *reqT* incorporates the communication delay incurred while sending the resource request from the caller to the *TMgr*. The transition *send_gt_tr* signifies the processing as well as the communication delay incurred if the resource is available, while the transition *send_ngt_tr* signifies the processing as well as the communication delay incurred if the resource is unavailable. It is entirely conceivable that the delay in case of the former is longer than the delay in case of the latter, since some additional processing might be required if the resource is available (such as obtaining the resource id and other details regard-

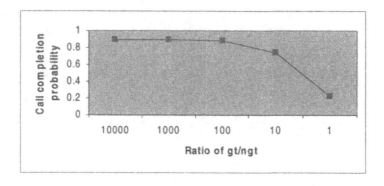

Fig. 8. Effect of resource availability on call completion probability

ing the resource and then forwarding these details to the *Caller* process), when compared to the case when the resource is unavailable. The rate of transitions *gt* and *gt1* is the inverse of the mean time until absorption in state *Received_gt*, while the rate of transitions *ngt* and *ngt1* is the inverse of the mean time until absorption in state *Received_ngt*. In the previous example, in order to study the influence of the relative firing rates of *gt* and *ngt* (*gt1* and *ngt1*) on the call completion probability, we held the rate of transitions *gt* and *gt1* at 9.0 units. Let us assume that the call completion probability is acceptable when the ratio of the firing rates of *gt* and *ngt* is 10.0. As a result, the transition rate of *ngt* and *ngt1* is 0.9, and thus the mean time until absorption in state *Received_ngt* is 1.111 units. If we assume that the tasks corresponding to the availability and unavailability of resources, as represented by transitions *send_gt_tr* and *send_ngt_tr* respectively have the same mean time, then to achieve the relative rates among the transitions *gt* and *ngt*, resources availability should exceed approximately 91%. The probability of resource being available controls only the relative firing rates of transitions *gt* and *ngt*. The actual firing rate of the transition *gt* is controlled by the transitions *send_gt_tr*, *reqT* and *available_tr*. We now study the effect of the firing rates of the above three transitions on the firing rate of *gt*. For the sake of simplicity, we assume that the transitions *send_gt_tr*, *reqT*, *available_tr* and *send_ngt_tr* have the same firing rate. This assumption is being made for the sake of illustration, and the analysis itself is not limited by this assumption. Figure 9 shows the effect of the firing rate of transitions *available_tr*, *send_gt_tr* and *send_ngt_tr* on the firing rate of transition *gt* (and *gt1*). It can be seen that the firing rate of the transitions in the *TMgr* process should be at least 3.4 units, to allow the firing rate of the transition *gt* to be at an acceptable level of 0.11 units.

Next we study the influence of the timer duration on the probability of successful call completion. The timer is set when the *Caller* process is waiting for a user to input the digit. The timer is thus expected to achieve two goals, provide the user with sufficient time to supply the digit, and reset the system if the

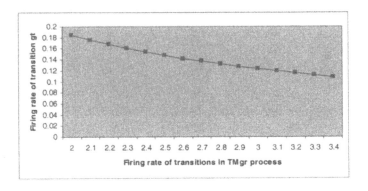

Fig. 9. Effect of firing rate of transitions in $TMgr$ on transition gt

input is not received in a reasonable duration. If the duration of the timer is too small (firing rate too high), then the user will not have enough time to supply the digit, resulting in repeated resets and very low probability of call completion. On the other hand, if the timer duration is too high, then the resources consumed by the *Caller* process while waiting for the user will be unavailable for subsequent callers. As a result, an optimal value for the timer needs to be determined. Figure 10 shows that the probability of successful call completion remains around 85% while the timer rate is less than 0.1 units (timer duration greater than 10 units). As the timer rate increases beyond 1 unit (timer duration less than 1 unit), the probability of call completion drops dramatically.

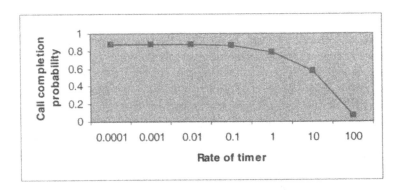

Fig. 10. Influence of the timer on call completion probability

The SRN model produced by a transformation of the SDL specification can also be used for the analysis of dependability attributes such as reliability, availability and safety. In order to conduct reliability analysis, information regarding the failure behavior will be needed. Such failure information can be available at the process level or at the level of each task within a process. Similarly, information regarding the repair behavior at the process level or at the task level will be necessary for meaningful availability analysis. Safety analysis will require the ability to categorize the failures into safe and unsafe. Various examples of the use of SRNs for reliability, availability and safety analysis exist in the literature [3].

We illustrate the use of SRN model for dependability analysis with the help of an example. Figure 11 shows the SRN model of the process *TMgr* augmented with the failure behavior of each task in the process. The probability of immediate transitions *available_y* and *available_n* is set to 0.9 and 0.1 respectively. These transitions reflect the availability and the unavailability of the resources respectively. These branching probabilities were computed from trace data. The failure rate of the transitions *Fail_Available*, *Fail_Send_gt* and *Fail_Send_ngt* are set to 0.001. The SRN model is then solved to compute various performance and dependability measures using SPNP. The probability of resource availability or success is computed to be 0.82, whereas the probability of resource unavailability is computed to be 0.09, and the probability of failure is computed to be 0.09. The mean time to absorption (MTTA) is computed to be 1001.99.

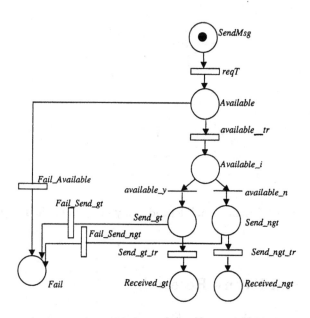

Fig. 11. SRN model of process *TMgr* with task failures

To summarize, the following steps are involved in the three way integration of specification, simulation/testing and performance/dependability analysis:

1. Specification of the system in SDL.
2. Simulation/testing of the specification and collection of execution traces.

3. Transformation of SDL specification to a Stochastic Reward Net (SRN) model.
4. Parameterization of the SRN, partly using the execution trace data collected in Step(2), and partly from external sources.
5. Reachability graph generation
6. Performance and dependability analysis.

Figure 12 shows the steps in the performance and dependability analysis methodology. Notice that Step(2) and Step(3), namely, simulation/testing of the specification and transformation of the specification into a SRN model can be performed in parallel.

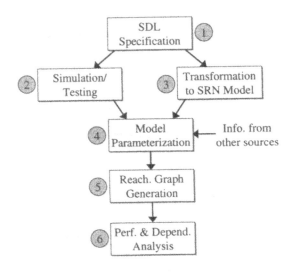

Fig. 12. Steps in the performance and dependability analysis methodology

4   Conclusions and Future Research

In this paper we present a methodology which integrates three distinct areas in architecture design: specification, simulation and testing and performance and dependability analysis. As architecture design and analysis gain prominence in system building process, the development of tools to support various activities in a systematic manner appears to be inevitable. Such tools not only help in automating and streamlining the design and testing process, but also provide a rich source of information to conduct performance and dependability analysis. We demonstrated the various steps involved in this methodology with the help of an example. Our future research includes extending the methodology to analyze other non functional attributes such as flexibility. Demonstrating the applicability of this methodology to a real–world system is also the topic of future research.

References

1. R. Allen. *"A formal approach to software architecture"*. PhD thesis, Dept. of Computer Science, Carnegie Mellon University, Pittsburgh, NC, 1997.
2. A. Bondavalli, I. Mura, and I. Majzik. "Automated dependability analysis of UML designs". In *Proc. of Second IEEE International Symposium on Object-Oriented Real-Time Distributed Computing*, 1998.
3. G. Ciardo, J. Muppala, and K.S. Trivedi. "SPNP: Stochastic Petri Net Package". In *Proceedings of the International Workshop on Petri Nets and Performance Models*, pages 142–150, Los Alamitos, CA, December 1989. IEEE Computer Society Press.
4. D. Garlan, R.T. Monroe, and D. Wile. "ACME: An architecture description interchange language". In *Proc. of CASCON 97*, pages 169–183, Toronto, Canada, November 1997.
5. D. Garlan and M. Shaw. *Advances in Software Engineering and Knowledge Engineering, Volume 1, edited by V. Ambriola and G. Torotora*, chapter An Introduction to Software Architecture. World Scientific Publishing Company, New Jersey, 1993.
6. S. Gokhale, W.E. Wong, K.S. Trivedi, and J.R. Horgan. "An analytic approach to architecture-based software reliability prediction". In *Proc. of Intl. Performance and Dependability Symposium (IPDS 98)*, pages 13–22, Durham, NC, September 1998.
7. E. Heck and D. Hogrefe. "Hierarchical performance evaluation based on formally specified communication protocols". *IEEE Trans. on Computers*, 40(4):500–513, April 1991.
8. P.B. Krutchen. "The 4+1 view model of architecture". *IEEE Software*, pages 42–50, November 1995.
9. J.J. Li and J.R. Horgan. "A toolsuite for testing software architectural specification". *Software Quality Journal*, 8(4), June 2000.
10. J.J. Li and J.R. Horgan. "Simulation-trace-based software component performance prediction". In *Proc. of 33rd Annual Simulation Symposium*, April 2000.
11. D. Luckham, L.A. Augustin, J. Kenney, J. Veera, D. Bryan, and W. Mann. "Specification and analysis of system architecture using Rapide". *IEEE Tran. on Software Engineering*, 21(4):336–355, April 1995.
12. M.A. Marsan, A. Bianco, L. Ciminera, R. Sisto, and A. Valenzano. "A LOTOS extension for the performance analysis of distributed systems". *IEEE/ACM Transactions on Networking*, 2(2):151–165, April 1994.
13. J.D. Musa. "Operational profiles in software-reliability engineering". *IEEE Software*, 10(2):14–32, March 1993.
14. A. Reibman, R. Smith, and K.S. Trivedi. "Markov and Markov Reward Model Transient Analysis: An Overview of Numerical Approaches". *European Journal of Operational Research*, 40:257–267, 1989.
15. M. Shaw, R. DeLine, D.V. Klein, T.L. Ross, D.M. Young, and G.Zelesnik. "Abstractions for software architecture and tools to support them". *IEEE Trans. on Software Engineering*, 21(4):314–335, April 1995.

16. M. Steppler and B. Walke. "Performance analysis of communication systems formally specified in SDL". In *Proc. of Workshop on Software and Performance*, Santa Fe, NM, 1998.

17. L.A. Tomek and K.S. Trivedi. *Software Fault Tolerance, Edited by M. R. Lyu*, chapter Analyses Using Stochastic Reward Nets, pages 139–165. John Wiley and Sons Ltd., New York, 1995.

18. M.E.R. Vieira, M.S. Dias, and D.J. Richardson. "Analyzing software architectures with Argus-i". In *Proc. of the Intl. Conference on Software Engineering*, pages 758–761, 2000.

19. C.Y. Wang and K.S. Trivedi. "Integration of specification for modeling and specification for system design". In *Proc. of Fourteenth Intl. Conference on Applications and Theory of Petri Nets*, pages 24–31, 1993.

20. C. Wohlin and D. Rapp. "Performance analysis in the early design of software". In *Proc. of 7th International Conference on Software Engineering for Telecommunication Switching Systems*, pages 114–121, Bournemouth, England, 1993.

21. J. Zhao. *New Technologies on Computer Software, M. Li, Editor*, chapter "Using Dependence Analysis to Support Software Architecture Understanding", pages 135–142. International Academic Publishers, September 1997.

22. http://www.telelogic.com.

23. http://www.telelogic.com/products/additional/objectgeode.

24. International Telegraph and Telephone Consultative Committee. *"SDL User Guideliness"*, Blue Book, IXth Plenary Assembly, pages 14–25, International Telecommunication Union, November 1989.

Using Architectural Properties to Model and Measure Graceful Degradation

Charles Shelton and Philip Koopman

Electrical and Computer Engineering Department
Carnegie Mellon University
Pittsburgh, PA 15213, USA
{cshelton,koopman}@cmu.edu

Abstract. System-wide graceful degradation may be a viable approach to improving dependability in computer systems. In order to evaluate and improve system-wide graceful degradation we present a system model that will explicitly define graceful degradation as a system property, and measure how well a system gracefully degrades in the presence of multiple combinations of component failures. The system's software architecture plays a major role in this model, because the interface and component specifications embody the architecture's abstraction principle. We use the architecture to group components into subsystems that enable reasoning about overall system utility. We apply this model to an extensive example of a distributed embedded control system architecture to specify the relative utility of all valid system configurations. We then simulate working system configurations and compare their ability to provide functionality to the utility measures predicted by our model.

1 Introduction

Dependability is a term that covers many system properties such as reliability, availability, safety, maintainability, and security [1]. System dependability is especially important for embedded computer control systems, which pervade everyday life and can have severe consequences for failure. These systems increasingly implement a significant portion of their functionality in software, making software dependability a major issue.

Graceful degradation may be a viable approach to achieving better software dependability. If a software system can gracefully degrade automatically when faults are detected, then individual software component failures will not cause complete system failure. Rather, component failures will remove the functionality derived from that component, while still preserving the operation of the rest of the system. Specifying and achieving system-wide graceful degradation is a difficult research problem. Current approaches require specifying every system failure mode ahead of time, and designing a specific response for each such mode. This is impractical for a complex software system, especially a fine grained distributed embedded system with tens or hundreds of software and hardware components.

R. de Lemos et al. (Eds.): Architecting Dependable Systems, LNCS 2677, pp. 267–289, 2003.

Intuitively, the term graceful degradation means that a system tolerates failures by reducing functionality or performance, rather than shutting down completely. An ideal gracefully degrading system is partitioned so that failures in non-critical subsystems do not affect critical subsystems, is structured so that individual component failures have a limited impact on system functionality, and is built with just enough redundancy so that likely failures can be tolerated without loss of critical functionality.

In order to evaluate and improve system-wide graceful degradation, we present a system model that enables scalable specification and analysis of graceful degradation. We base the model on using the system's interface definitions and component connections to group the system's components into subsystems. We hypothesize that the software architecture, responsible for the overall organization of and connections among components, can facilitate the system's ability to implicitly provide graceful degradation, without designing a specific response to every possible failure mode at design time. We define a failure mode to be a set of system components failing concurrently. By using the model to measure how gracefully a system degrades, we predict that we can identify what architectural properties facilitate and impede system-wide graceful degradation.

We demonstrate the usefulness of our model by applying it to a representative distributed embedded system and showing how we can achieve scalable analysis of graceful degradation. Our example system is a gracefully degrading elevator control system that was designed by an elevator engineer and implemented in a discrete event simulator (an earlier version of this system was presented in [2]). We use the simulator to perform fault injection experiments by failing nodes during the system's operation to observe how well the system gracefully degrades, and compare the results to the predictions of our model.

The rest of the paper is organized as follows. Section 2 identifies the problem of specifying graceful degradation and how our model is scalable. Section 3 provides a description of the key features of our model. Section 4 details our elevator control system architecture in terms of the defined components and interfaces. Section 5 shows how we applied our system model for graceful degradation to the elevator architecture to specify the system utility function. Section 6 describes a preliminary fault injection experiment we performed to validate the model. Section 7 describes previous related work. Finally, section 8 ends with conclusions and future work.

2 Specifying Graceful Degradation

For graceful degradation to be possible, it must be possible to define the system's state as "working" with other than complete functionality. In many systems, a substantial portion of the system is built to optimize properties such as performance, availability, and usability. We must be able to define the minimum functionality required for primary missions, and treat optimized functionality as a desirable, but optional, enhancement. For example, much of a car's engine control software is devoted to emission control and fuel efficiency, but loss of emission sensors should not strand a car at the side of the road.

Specifying and designing system-wide graceful degradation is not trivial. Graceful degradation mechanisms must handle not only individual component failures, but also combinations of component failures. Current graceful degradation techniques emphasize adding component redundancy to preserve perfect operation when failures occur, or designing several redundant backup systems that must be tested and certified separately to provide a subset of system functionality with reduced hardware resources. These techniques have a high cost in both additional hardware resources and complexity of system design, and might not use system resources efficiently.

We define graceful degradation in terms of system utility: a measure of the system's ability to provide its specified functional and non-functional capabilities. A system that has all of its components functioning properly has maximum utility. A system degrades gracefully if individual component failures reduce system utility proportionally to the severity of aggregate failures. Utility is not all or nothing; the system provides a set of features, and ideally the loss of one feature should not hinder the system's ability to provide the remaining features. It should be possible to lose a significant number of components before system utility falls to zero.

We focus our analysis on distributed embedded computer systems. Distributed embedded systems are usually resource constrained, and thus cannot afford much hardware redundancy. However, they have high dependability requirements (due to the fact that they must react to and control their physical environment), and have become increasingly software-intensive. These systems typically consist of multiple compute nodes connected via a potentially redundant real-time fault tolerant network. Each compute node may be connected to several sensors and actuators, and may host multiple software components. Software components provide functionality by reading sensor values, communicating with each other via the network, and producing actuator command values to provide their specified behavior.

This work is a part of the RoSES (Robust Self-Configuring Embedded Systems) project and builds on the idea of a configuration space that forms a product family architecture [3]. Each point in the space represents a different configuration of hardware and software components that provides a certain utility. Removal or addition of a component to a system configuration moves the system to another point in the configuration space with a different level of utility. For each possible hardware configuration, there are several software configurations that provide positive system utility. Our model focuses on specifying the relative utility of all possible software component configurations for a fixed hardware configuration. For a system with N software components, the complexity of specifying a complete system utility function is normally $O(2^N)$. Our model exploits the system's decomposition into subsystems to reduce this complexity to $O(2^k)$, where k is the number of components within a single subsystem. When we have a complete utility function for all possible software configurations, we can use techniques described in [4] to analyze the utility of system hardware configurations to determine the best allocation of software components to hardware nodes.

3   System Model

System *utility* is a key concept in our model for comparing system configurations. Utility is a measure of how much benefit can be gained from using a system. Overall system utility may be a combination of functionality, performance, and dependability properties. If we specify the relative utility values of each of the 2^N possible configurations of N software components, sensors, and actuators, then we can determine how well a system gracefully degrades based on the utility differences among different software configurations.

Our model enables complete definition of the system utility function without having to evaluate the relative utility of all 2^N possible configurations. Our software data flow model enables scalable system utility analysis by partitioning the system into subsystems and identifying the dependencies among software components. Our system utility model is based on the system's software configurations, and is primarily concerned with how system functionality changes when software components fail.

The fault model for our system uses the traditional fail-fast, fail-silent assumption on a component basis, which is best practice for this class of system. We assume that components can either be in one of two states: working or failed. Working means that the component has enough resources to output its specified system variables. Failed means the component cannot produce its specified outputs. Individual components are designed to shut down when they detect an unrecoverable error, which enables the rest of the system to quickly detect the component's failure, and prevents an error from propagating through the rest of the system. All faults in our model thus manifest as the loss of outputs from failed components. Software components either provide their outputs to the system or do not. Hardware component failures cause loss of all software components hosted on that processing element. Network or communication failures can be modeled as a loss of communication between distributed software components.

Section 3.1 describes our system data flow graph, section 3.2 details how we perform our utility analysis, and section 3.3 identifies some of the key assumptions of our model.

3.1   Data Flow Graph and Feature Subset Definitions

We consider a system as a set of software, sensor, and actuator components. We construct our system model as a directed data flow graph in which the vertices represent system components (sensors, actuators, and software components), and the edges represent the communication among components via their input and output interfaces. We use these interfaces to define a set of *system variables* that represent an abstraction of all component interaction. These variables can represent any communication structure in the software implementation. Actuators receive input variables from the system and output them to the environment, while sensors input variables from the environment to the system. Our data flow graph can be derived directly from the system's software architecture, which specifies the system's components and interfaces, as well as component organization and dependencies.

We then partition the data flow graph into subgraphs that represent logical subsystems that we term *feature subsets*. These feature subsets form the basis for how we decompose the system utility analysis. A feature subset is a set of components (software components, sensors, actuators, and possibly other feature subsets) that work together to provide a set of output variables or operate a system actuator. Feature subsets may or may not be disjoint and can share components across different subsets. Feature subsets also capture the hierarchical decomposition of the software system, as "higher level" feature subsets contain "lower level" feature subsets as components, which further encapsulate other software, sensor, and actuator components.

The feature subset data flow graphs can also represent dependency relationships among components. Each component might not require all of its inputs to provide partial functionality. For example, in an elevator the door controllers can use the inputs from the passenger request buttons to more efficiently open and close the doors based on passenger input, but this is an enhancement to normal door operation that simply waits a specified period before opening and closing the doors. If the door controllers no longer received these button inputs, they could still function correctly.

We annotate our feature subset graph edges with a set of dependency relationships among components. These relationships are determined by each component's dependence on its input variables, which might be strong, weak, or optional. If a component is dependent on one of its inputs, it will have a dependency relationship with all components that output that system variable. A component *strongly* depends on one of its inputs (and thus the components that produce it) if the loss of that input results in the loss of the component's ability to provide its outputs. A component *weakly* depends on one of its inputs if the input is required for at least one configuration, but not required for at least one other configuration. If an input is *optional* to the component, then it may provide enhancements to the component's functionality, but is not critical to the basic operation of the component.

3.2   Utility Model

Our utility model exploits the system decomposition captured in the software data flow view to reduce the complexity of specifying a system utility function for all possible software configurations. Rather than manually rank the relative utility of all 2^N possible software configurations of N components, we restrict utility evaluations to the component configurations within individual feature subsets. We specify each individual component's utility value to be 1 if it is present in a configuration (and providing its outputs), and 0 when the component is failed and therefore not in the configuration.

We also make a distinction between *valid* and *invalid* system configurations. A valid configuration provides some positive system utility, and an invalid configuration provides zero utility. For graceful degradation we are interested in the utility differences among valid system configurations, as the system is still considered "working" until its utility is zero. In general, there are many "trivially" invalid system configurations. A system configuration that strongly depends upon a component that is failed provides zero utility regardless of what other components are present. For example, any system configuration in which the elevator's drive motor has failed cannot provide its basic system functionality and is invalid, so examining the rest of the system's component configuration is unnecessary. However, there is still a set of multiple valid configurations that must be ranked for system utility, and we use our subsystem definitions to specify the utility of these system configurations.

If we restrict our analysis to individual feature subset component configurations, we only need to rank the relative utility values of all valid configurations within each feature subset. For feature subsets with a maximum of $k << N$ components, this is a much more feasible task. We only need to manually rank at most the utilities of 2^k possible configurations for each feature subset Additionally, we can significantly reduce the number of configurations we must consider by using component dependencies to determine the valid and invalid configurations of each feature subset.

We can then determine overall system utility by examining the system configurations of the "top level" feature subsets that provide outputs to system actuators. All other feature subsets utility evaluations are encapsulated within these subsystems that provide external system functionality. We can completely specify the system utility function without manually specifying the relative utility values of all 2^N possible system component configurations, but rather specifying the utilities of 2^k feature subset configurations for each feature subset in the system.

We can use this model to develop a space of systems with varying degrees of graceful degradation. At one end of the spectrum, we have extremely "brittle" systems that are not capable of any graceful degradation at all. In these systems, any one component failure will result in a complete system failure. In our model, this would be a system where every component is a member of at least one required feature subset, and each feature subset strongly depends on all of its components. Therefore, every component must be functioning to have positive system utility.

Similarly, any modular redundant system can be represented as a collection of several feature subsets, where each feature subset contains multiple copies of a component plus a voter. The valid configurations that provide positive utility for each feature subset are those that contain the voter plus one or more component copies. This redundant system can tolerate multiple failures across many feature subsets, but cannot tolerate the failure of any one voter or all the component copies in any one feature subset.

At the other end of the spectrum, an ideal gracefully degrading system is one where any combination of component failures will still leave a system with positive utility. In our model, this system would be one where none of its feature subsets would be labeled as required for basic functionality, and every component would be completely optional to each feature subset in which it was a member. The system would continue to have positive utility until every component failed.

3.3   Assumptions of Our Model

Our model is never any worse than having to consider 2^N system configurations of N components, and in typical cases will be a significant improvement. We have made several assumptions with regard to how these software systems are designed. First, we assume that the parameters of the utility function for each feature subset configuration are independent of the configuration of any other feature subset in the system. We only define different utility functions for different feature subset configurations, in which a configuration specifies whether a component is present and working (providing positive utility) or absent and failed (providing zero utility).

When a feature subset is treated as a component in a higher-level feature subset, that component can potentially have different utility values based on its current configuration, rather than just 1 for working and 0 for failed as with individual software components, sensors, and actuators. This could potentially mean that in order to define the higher-level feature subset's utility function, we would have to define a different utility function for every possible utility value for every feature subset contained as a component in the higher-level feature subset. However, this is only necessary if the encapsulated feature subsets are strongly coupled within higher level feature subsets. Because system architects generally attempt to decouple subsystems, we assume that encapsulated feature subsets are not strongly coupled. If some subsystems are strongly coupled, one could apply multi-attribute utility theory [5] to deal with the added system complexity within the model.

We also assume that the system is "well-designed" such that combinations of components do not interact negatively with respect to feature subset or system utility. In other words, when a component has zero utility, it contributes zero utility to the system or feature subset, but when a component has some positive utility, it contributes *at least* zero or positive utility to the system or feature subset, and never has an interaction with the rest of the system that results in an overall loss of utility. Thus, working components can enhance but never reduce system utility. We assume that if we observe a situation in which a component contributes negative utility to the system, we can intentionally deactivate that component so that it contributes zero utility instead.

Our utility model only deals with software system configurations, and we do not directly account for hardware redundancy as a system utility attribute. However, in general hardware redundancy mechanisms will not affect system functionality, but rather hardware system reliability or availability. To analyze tradeoffs between system functionality and dependability, we could again apply multi-attribute utility theory to judge the relative value of the software configuration's utility and the hardware configuration's reliability and availability to the system's overall utility. This analysis may include factors such as system resource costs and hardware and software failure rates.

4   Example System: A Distributed Elevator Control System

To illustrate how we can apply our system model to a real system, we use a design of a relatively complex distributed elevator control system. This system was designed by an elevator engineer (the second author) and has been implemented in a discrete event simulator written in Java. This elevator system has been used as the course project in the distributed embedded systems class at Carnegie Mellon University for several semesters. Since we have a complete architectural specification as well as an implementation, we can directly observe how properties of the system architecture affect the system's ability to gracefully degrade by performing fault injection experiments in the simulation.

Our view of the elevator system is a set of sensors, actuators and software components that are allocated to the various hardware nodes in the distributed system. The nodes are connected by a real-time fault tolerant broadcast network. All network messages can be received by any node in the system. Since all communication among components is via this broadcast network, all component communication interfaces map to a set of network message types.

Our elevator system architecture is highly distributed and decentralized, and is based on the message interfaces that system components use to communicate. System inputs come from "smart" sensors that have a processing node embedded in the sensing device. These sensors convert their raw sensor values to messages that are broadcast on the network. The software control system, implemented as a set of distributed software components, receives these messages and produces output messages that provide commands to the actuators to provide the system's functionality.

The elevator consists of a single car in a hoistway with access to a set number of floors f. The car has two independent left and right doors and door motors, a drive that can accelerate the car to two speeds (fast and slow) in the hoistway, an emergency stop brake for safety, and various buttons and lights for determining passenger requests, and providing feedback to the passengers. Since the sensors and actuators map directly to the message interfaces among components, we list all the possible interface message types along with their senders and receivers below to define the components and interfaces of the system architecture. In the following notation, the values within the "[]" brackets represent the standard replication of an array of sensors or actuators, and the values within the "()" parentheses represent the values the sensor or actuator can output. For example, the Hall call message type maps to an array of sensors for the up and down buttons on each floor outside the elevator that is f (the number of floors the elevator services) by d (the direction of the button; Up or Down) wide, and each button sensor can either have a value v of True (pressed) or False (not pressed). Unless otherwise noted, "f" represents the number of floors the elevator services, "d" represents a variable that indicates a direction of either Up or Down, "j" is a variable that is a value of either Left or Right (for the left and right elevator doors), and "v" denotes a value that can be either True or False.

The sensor message types available in the system include:
- **AtFloor[f](v):** Output of AtFloor sensors that sense when the car is near a floor.
- **CarCall[f](v):** Output of car call button sensors located in the car.
- **CarLevelPosition(x):** Output of car position sensor that tracks where the car is in the hoistway. x = {distance value from bottom of hoistway}
- **DoorClosed[j](v):** Output of door closed sensors that will be True when the door is fully closed.
- **DoorOpen[j](v):** Output of door open sensors that will be True when the door is fully open.
- **DoorReversal[j](v):** Output of door reversal sensors that will be True when door senses an obstruction in the doorway.

- **HallCall[f,d](v):** Output of hall call button sensors that are located in hallway outside the elevator on each floor. Note that there are a total of 2f - 2 rather than 2f hall call buttons since the top floor only has a down button and the bottom floor only has an up button.
- **HoistwayLimit[d](v):** Output of safety limit sensors in the hoistway that will be True when the car has overrun either the top or bottom hoistway limits.
- **DriveSpeed(s,d):** Output of the main drive speed sensor. s = {speed value}, d = {Up, Down, Stop}

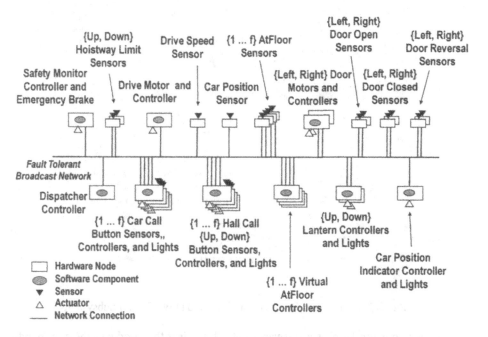

Fig. 1. Hardware View of the Elevator-Control System

The actuator command messages available in the system are:

- **DesiredFloor(f, d):** Command from the elevator dispatcher algorithm indicating the next floor destination. d = {Up, Down, Stop} (This is not an actuator input, but rather an internal variable in the control system sent from the dispatcher to the drive controller)
- **DoorMotor[j](m):** Door motor commands for each door. m = {Open, Close, Stop}
- **Drive(s, d):** Commands for 2-speed main elevator drive. s = {Fast, Slow, Stop}, d = {Up, Down, Stop}
- **CarLantern[d](v):** Commands to control the car lantern lights; Up/Down lights on the car doorframe used by passengers to determine the elevator's current traveling direction.
- **CarLight[f](v):** Commands to control the car call button lights inside the car call buttons to indicate when a floor has been selected.
- **CarPositionIndicator(f):** Commands for position indicator light in the car that tells users what floor the car is approaching.

- **HallLight[f,d](v):** Commands for hall call button lights inside the hall call buttons to indicate when passengers want the elevator on a certain floor.
- **EmergencyBrake(v):** Emergency stop brake that should be activated whenever the system state becomes unsafe and the elevator must be shut down to prevent a catastrophic failure.

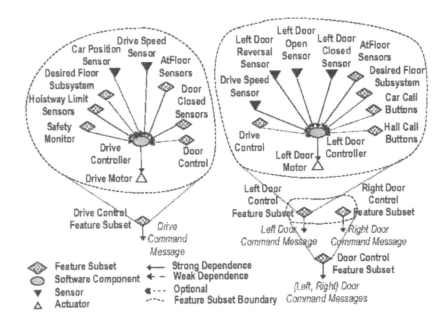

Fig. 2. Feature Subset Graphs of the Door and Drive Control Subsystems

For each actuator, there is a software controller object that produces the commands for that actuator. The drive controller commands the drive actuator to move the elevator based on the DesiredFloor input it receives from the dispatcher software object. The left and right door controllers operate their respective door motors. The safety monitor software monitors the elevator system sensors to ensure safe operation and activate the emergency brake when necessary. The various software objects for the buttons and lights determine when to activate the lights to indicate appropriate feedback to the passengers. Additionally, since the AtFloor sensors are a critical resource for the elevator system, we have redundant "virtual" AtFloor software components that can synthesize AtFloor messages based on data from the car position and elevator drive speed sensors. If some of the physical AtFloor sensors fail, these software sensors can be used as backups. The elevator control system consists of 8 + 4f sensors, 5 + 3f actuators, and 6 + 4f software components, for a total of 19 + 11f components in the system. Figure 1 illustrates how these system components are allocated to hardware nodes in the elevator's distributed control system.

In our experiments, we simulated an elevator with seven floors, meaning that there were a total of 96 components in the system. To specify how well the system gracefully degrades with respect to all possible combinations of component failures, the traditional approach would require a manual ranking of the utility of all $2^{96} = 7.92$ $* 10^{28}$ possible system configurations. Our model exploits the information available from the system architecture to overcome this exponential difficulty.

5   Specifying the Elevator Control System

We can use the component and interface specifications of the elevator control system to apply our system model for graceful degradation. We will not reproduce the entire system data flow graph here, but rather show the subgraphs for each feature subset we identified and how we performed our analysis using these subsystem definitions.

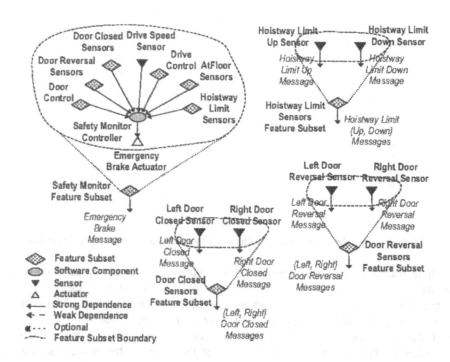

Fig. 3. Feature Subset Graphs of the Safety Monitor Subsystem

5.1   Elevator Feature Subsets

In the elevator system, there are several functional subsystems that map to feature subsets. The primary control systems in the elevator operate the drive and the door motors. Their feature subsets are defined by the inputs and outputs of the drive controller, and left and right door controller software objects. Figure 2 displays these feature subsets and the dependency relationships among their components. In the diagrams we annotated the output variables of each feature subset. The left and right door control feature subsets are nearly identical with the exception of which door sensors and actuators they contain, so only the left door control feature subset is shown in detail.

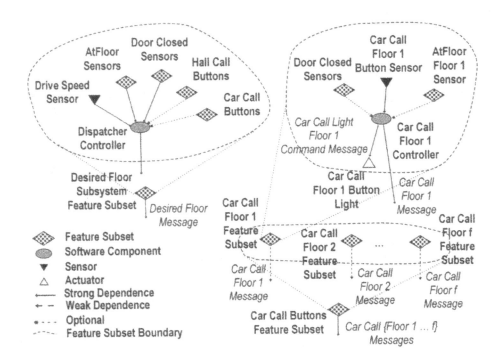

Fig. 4. Feature Subset Graphs for the Desired Floor and Car Call Button Subsystems

These feature subsets are responsible for controlling the drive and door actuators, but they also output their command variables over the network to the rest of the system. This allows subsystems to loosely coordinate their operation without being strongly coupled and dependent on each other. For example, the Door Controllers must receive inputs from the Drive Speed sensor in order to safely operate the door only when the elevator is not moving. However, the Door Controller can also use the command output from the Drive Control feature subset to anticipate when the elevator will stop based on the command sent from the Drive Control feature subset, thus allowing more efficient door operation via sending the door open command slightly before the elevator is level with the destination floor. The Drive Control feature subset encapsulates all of its components, so that it is represented as a single component that outputs the Drive command system variable in the Left and Right Door Control feature subsets. Likewise the Door Control feature subset encapsulates all of the components in the Left and Right Door Control feature subsets.

These feature subsets also contain several identical components, such as the Drive Speed and AtFloor sensors. These components do not represent multiple copies of the same component in the software data flow view, but rather that these feature subsets overlap and share some of their components. The feature subset graphs show dependencies among components, but not whether individual components are replicated for multiple subsystems. There may be multiple redundant sensors installed in the system, but the information about how components are allocated to hardware would be visible in the hardware architecture and is orthogonal to the software data flow view of our system model.

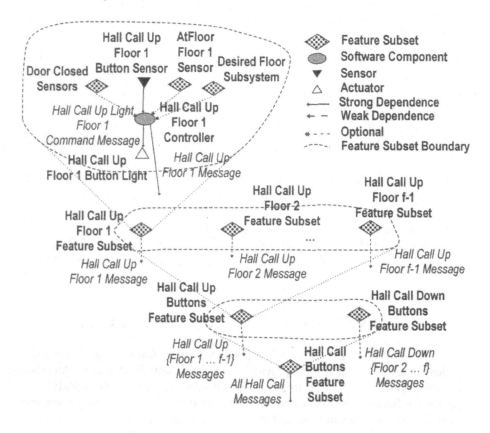

Fig. 5. Elevator Hall Call Button Feature Subsets

We defined several other feature subsets for our elevator system in addition to the Door Control and Drive Control feature subsets. The Safety Monitor software component and its inputs and outputs defines the Safety Monitor feature subset. The Safety Monitor feature subset is responsible for detecting when the elevator system state becomes unsafe, such as the doors opening while the elevator is moving, the doors failing to reverse direction if they bump into a passenger while closing, or the elevator crashing into the top or bottom of the hoistway. In any unsafe situation, the Safety Monitor must trigger the Emergency Brake actuator that shuts down the elevator system to prevent a catastrophic failure. Figure 3 shows the Safety Monitor feature subset along with some of the sensors from which it receives inputs. The Safety Monitor must receive inputs from both the Door and Drive Control feature subsets to ensure that their commands are consistent with the elevator's actual operation determined from the drive speed and door sensors.

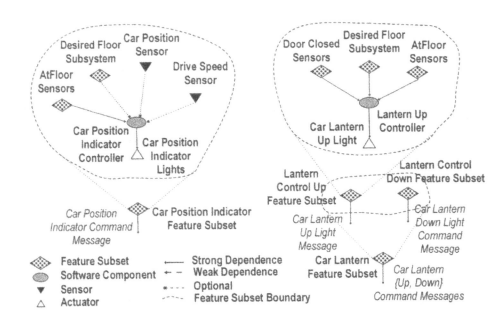

Fig. 6. Car Position Indicator and car Lantern Feature Subsets

The Door Control, Drive Control, and Safety Monitor feature subsets represent the critical elevator subsystems that provide an elevator's basic functionality. An efficient elevator should also respond to passenger requests to move people quickly to their destination floors. The Drive Controller listens to the DesiredFloor system variable to determine its next destination, and this variable is the output of the Desired Floor feature subset. The Desired Floor feature subset contains the Dispatcher software component that implements the algorithm for determining the next floor at which the elevator should stop. The Dispatcher receives inputs from the Car Call and Hall Call buttons to determine passenger intent and compute the elevator's next destination. The Car Call and Hall Call buttons in turn form their own feature subsets that provide the button sensor messages to the rest of the system, but also control the button lights to provide appropriate passenger feedback. Figures 4 and 5 show the feature subset definitions for the Desired Floor, Car Call and Hall Call feature subsets. The feature subsets for the Car Call and Hall Call buttons are similarly defined for each floor since each Car Call and Hall Call software controller have similar input and output interfaces. Each Car Call and Hall Call controller outputs the value of its respective sensor on the network for the rest of the system, but only sends the command messages for its button light to its actuator.

In order to encourage people to move quickly in the elevator, the Car Lantern and Car Position Indicator lights provide feedback to let the passengers know the elevator's current traveling direction, and the elevator's next floor destination. Figure

6 displays the feature subsets for the Car Position Indicator and up and down Car Lantern light subsystems. These features are not essential for the elevator's basic operation, but provide information to the passengers to help them use the elevator more efficiently.

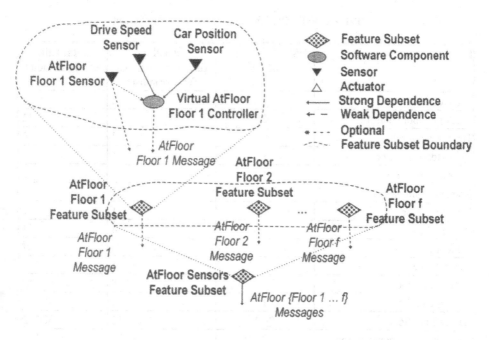

Fig. 7. AtFloor Subsystem Feature Subset Graph

One essential subsystem that is required by all of the other major elevator subsystems is the AtFloor Sensors feature subset. Nearly every feature subset strongly depends on AtFloor sensor information to provide functionality. For example, the Drive Control and Door Control feature subsets need the AtFloor sensor information to correctly operate the drive and door motors. Since this is such a critical feature in the elevator system, our elevator design also has redundant software components. The Virtual AtFloor software components can synthesize AtFloor sensor messages from the Car Position and Drive Speed sensors when the physical AtFloor sensors fail. Thus they are included in the AtFloor sensor feature subset graphs. Figure 7 shows the AtFloor feature subset description for the elevator system in our model.

5.2   Utility Analysis

The elevator system has a total of $19 + 11f$ system components, meaning there are $2^{19 + 11f}$ possible system configurations. The system can provide basic functionality if the minimum components necessary to operate the drive motor, door motors, and maintain safety are present. Thus these 17 components (Drive Controller software, drive speed sensor, drive motor, Left and Right Door Controller components, left and right door motors, all door sensors, Safety Monitor software, hoistway limit sensors, emergency brake actuator) are fixed and must be present in every valid configuration. All other components (such as the button lights and sensors and passenger feedback lights) can be considered optional and present in any configuration. There are $1 + 9f$ optional components that can have 2^{1+9f} possible configurations.

Table 1. Valid Configuration in each Fetaure Subset

Feature subset	# Similar feature subsets	# Valid configurations per feature subset	Total valid configurations
Drive control	1	8	8
Left/right door control	2	16	32
Top door control	1	3	3
Door closed sensors	1	1	1
Door reversal sensors	1	1	1
Hoistway limit sensors	1	1	
Safety monitor	1	1	1
Desired floor	1	4	4
AtFloor per floor	f	9	9f
Top AtFloor	1	f	f
Car call per floor	f	8	8f
Top car call	1	f	f
Hall call per floor	2f-2	16	32f-32
Top hall call up/down buttons	2	f-1	2f-2
Top hall call buttons	1	3	3
Lantern control up/down	2	1	2
Top car lantern	1	3	3
Car position indicator	1	8	8
Total:	16+4f		33+53f

Enough components to provide working AtFloor feature subsets for each floor must be present as well. Therefore, on each floor there must be a working AtFloor sensor or a working VirtualAtFloor component with a working Car Position sensor. If the Car Position sensor breaks, then all AtFloor sensors must work. Since all the AtFloor sensors must work in this situation, they are fixed and have one configuration. However, the VirtualAtFloor components can either work or not work since their failure will not affect the availability of the AtFloor system variables, making 2^f valid combinations for the various VirtualAtFloor components. If the Car Position sensor works, then one or both AtFloor sensor and VirtualAtFloor component must work for each floor, so the only invalid combinations are when both have failed for at least one floor. This means there are 3 valid combinations per floor, making 3^f valid combinations out of the possible 2^{2f}. Thus there are $2^f + 3^f$ valid combinations of components in the AtFloor feature subset.

The total number of possible valid system component configurations after eliminating all configurations that will always have utility zero is $(2^f + 3^f)(2^{1+9f})$. For our elevator with seven floors this is approximately $4.27 * 10^{22}$ configurations that still must be manually ranked. This is a significant reduction from the $7.92 * 10^{28}$ total possible system configurations, but still intractable for specifying system-wide graceful degradation. However, we can exploit the structure of the system design captured in the feature subset definitions to reduce the number of configurations we must rank to completely specify the system utility function.

We have defined $16 + 4f$ distinct feature subsets in the elevator system. If f is small, the largest feature subsets are the left and right door control feature subsets, with 11 components each. Thus we must rank a maximum of $2^{11} = 2048$ configurations in any one feature subset.

Since we can determine the valid and invalid configurations in each feature subset by examining the component dependencies, we can significantly reduce the number of configurations we must consider in each feature subset. For example, in the left and right door control feature subsets, 7 of the 11 components are required for the feature subset to provide utility, meaning we only need to consider the 16 possible configurations of the 4 optional components. If f is large, the number of configurations in feature subsets that contain f components (AtFloor, Car Call, and Hall Call Up/Down) will dominate. However, these feature subsets contain components that are largely orthogonal since each component's functionality is restricted to a different floor. Therefore we can simplify the utility specification of these feature subsets to a linear combination of the utility values of their components, requiring only that we specify f weights for each component utility in the feature subset. Table 1 summarizes the number of valid configurations that must be assigned utility values in each feature subset for a total of $33 + 53f$ feature subset configurations that must be considered across the entire elevator system. For our seven floor elevator, this totals 404 valid feature subset component configurations for the entire system.

We can then determine overall system utility by composing the system configurations of the "top level" feature subsets that provide system functionality. In the elevator system, these feature subsets are the Drive Control, Door Control, Safety Monitor, Car Call, Hall, Call, Car Lantern, and Car Position Indicator feature subsets. All other feature subsets are encapsulated within these seven subsystems that provide external system functionality. Since the Drive Control, Door Control, and Safety Monitor feature subsets must be present to provide minimum elevator functionality, that leaves only $2^4 = 16$ possible configurations of the other four feature subsets in the system. Once we specify the relative utilities of these 16 configurations in addition to the 404 total feature subset configurations, we can completely specify the system utility function. We have greatly reduced the number of configurations we must evaluate from $4.27 * 10^{22}$ system component configurations to 420 feature subset configurations to assess the system's ability to gracefully degrade.

6 Experimental Validation

If our model accurately predicts the relative utility of all system configurations, we can assess how well the system gracefully degrades by observing how system utility changes when the system configuration changes as components fail. To validate our model, we performed some preliminary fault injection experiments on a simulated elevator implementation. A discrete event simulator simulates a real time network with message delay that delivers broadcast periodic messages between system components. Each software component, sensor, and actuator is a software object that implements its message input and output interface to provide functionality. Sensor and actuator objects interact with the passenger objects that represent people using the elevator. Each simulation experiment specifies a passenger profile that indicates how many passengers attempt to use the system, when they first arrive to use the elevator, what floor they start at, and their intended destination. We can specify which elevator system configuration to simulate by setting which components are failed at the start of the simulation.

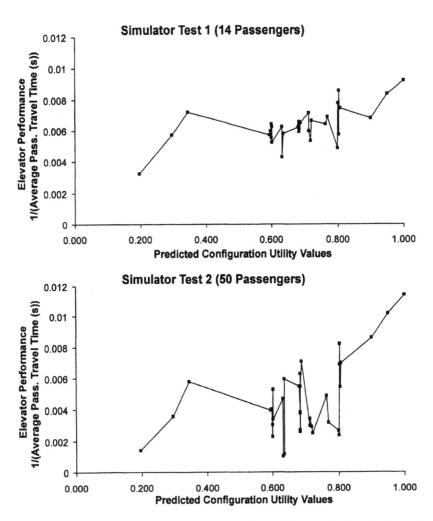

Fig. 8. Utility vs. Average Performance for Selected Elevator System Configurations

In general, system utility should be a measure of how well the system fulfills its requirements, and could incorporate many system properties such as performance, functionality, and dependability. An elevator system's primary function is to efficiently transport people to their destinations, minimizing how long passengers must wait for and ride in the elevator. Therefore, in our simulation experiments, we use the elevator's average performance per passenger as a proxy for measuring system utility. We track how long it takes for each passenger to reach their destination, from the time they first arrive to use the elevator to the time they step off the elevator at their intended floor.

We selected a small subset of the possible valid elevator system configurations, and ran two passenger profiles on each system configuration. The configurations we selected for evaluation included the configuration in which only the minimum required components for basic operation were present, as well as the configuration in which all of the components were working. We also picked several configurations in which different subsets of Car Call and Hall Call buttons were failed so that the elevator could not receive all passenger requests. One encouraging result of our experiment is that every valid configuration we tested eventually delivered all passengers to their destination regardless of which set of system components were failed.

We measured the average performance of each system configuration and compared it to its system utility as predicted by our model. If our model accurately predicted system utility, we should see configurations that have higher utility measures achieve better average performance. Figure 8 graphs the utility of the tested system configurations versus the elevator performance per passenger. The system configurations on the horizontal axis are ordered by utility, so the performance measures should be monotonically increasing. The graphs show a general trend of increasing performance, but it is not monotonically increasing.

However, elevator performance can be largely affected by how frequently passengers arrive and how the dispatcher deals with a loss of button inputs. Our dispatcher algorithm would periodically send the elevator to visit floors for which it was not receiving button information in order to ensure that all passengers eventually get delivered to their destination. Thus, sometimes elevator performance would suffer to ensure that no passengers were stranded. The fact that none of the system configurations tested suffered a complete system failure and delivered all passengers indicates that the system can gracefully degrade in the presence of multiple component failures.

This experiment was limited because we were only able to test a small number of configurations on two passenger profiles. We plan to extend this experimental validation with a wider range of different passenger profiles, as well as test many more different system configurations. We also plan to run these experiments with variants of the elevator architecture that are designed with different degrees of graceful degradation mechanisms.

7   Related Work

Previous work on formally defining graceful degradation for computer systems was presented in [6]. That work proposed constructing a lattice of system constraints that identifies what tasks the system can accomplish based on which constraints it can satisfy. A system that works perfectly satisfies all constraints, and a system that encounters failures might satisfy a looser set of constraints and still provide functionality, but is degraded with respect to some system properties. The difficulty with this model is that in order to specify the relaxation lattice, it is necessary to specify not only every system constraint, but also how constraints are relaxed in the presence of failures. It further requires determining how constraints interact and developing a recovery scheme for every possible combination of failures in order to move between points in the lattice. Because all combinations of component failures must be considered, specifying and achieving graceful degradation is exponentially complex with the number of system components. Our model for specifying graceful degradation overcomes this difficulty by encapsulating utility evaluations within individual subsystem configurations rather than evaluating the system as a whole in a single step. Other work on graceful degradation has focused on developing formal definitions [7, 8], but has not addressed how to apply these definitions to real system specifications, nor how to overcome the problem of exponential complexity for specifying failure modes and recovery mechanisms.

Current industry practice for dealing with faults and failures in embedded systems focuses on the traditional approaches of fault tolerance and fault containment [9]. Software subsystems are physically separated into different hardware modules. Additionally, system resources, such as sensors and actuators, that may be commonly used are replicated for each subsystem. That approach provides assurance that faults will not propagate between subsystems since they are physically partitioned, and fault tolerance is achieved by replicating resources and subsystems. Typically, failures are dealt with by having separate backup subsystems available rather than shedding functionality when resources are lost. This approach is a restricted form of graceful degradation, in that it tolerates the loss of a finite set of components before suffering a complete system failure. However, this methodology is costly because of its high level of redundancy.

A promising approach to achieving system dependability is NASA's Mission Data System (MDS) architecture [10, 11]. This system architecture is being designed for unmanned autonomous space flight systems that must complete missions with limited human oversight. Their architecture focuses on designing software systems that have specific goals based on well defined state variables. The software is decomposed based on the subgoals it must complete to satisfy its primary goal. The software is not constrained to a particular sequence of behavior, but rather must determine the best course of action based on its goals. The potential difficulties with this approach include the effort required to decompose goals into subgoals, and conflict resolution among subgoals at run time. Our framework differs from MDS in that we specifically focus on behavior-based subsystems and the coordination among them through system communication interfaces.

Survivability and performability are related to our concept of graceful degradation. Survivability is a property of dependability that has been proposed to define explicitly how systems degrade functionality in the presence of failures [12]. Performability is a unified measure of both performance and reliability that tracks how system performance degrades in the presence of faults [13]. Our work differs from survivability in that we are interested in building implicit graceful degradation into systems without specifying all failure scenarios and recovery modes *a priori*. Also, we focus on distributed embedded systems rather than on large-scale critical infrastructure information systems. Performability relates system performance and reliability, but our concept of graceful degradation addresses how system functionality can change to cope with component failures. Military systems have long used similar notions to provide graceful degradation (for example, in shipboard combat systems), but had scalability limits and were typically limited to a dozen or so specifically engineered configurations.

8   Conclusions

Our system model provides a scalable approach to determining how well a system gracefully degrades.   Since individual component failures simply transform the system from one configuration to another, we can evaluate how well the system gracefully degrades by observing the utility differences among valid system configurations. By exploiting the fact that systems are decomposed into subsystems of components, we can reduce the complexity of determining the utility function for all possible system configurations from $O(2^N)$ to $O(2^k)$, where N is the total number of software components, sensors, and actuators in the system, and k is the maximum number of components in any one subsystem. Data dependency relationships among components enable efficient elimination of invalid configurations from our analysis. In the elevator system, we used our system model to generate a complete system utility function for all $4.27 * 10^{22}$ valid system configurations by only examining 420 subsystem configurations.

Our model consists of a software data flow graph for determining dependency relationships among software components, sensors, and actuators, and a utility model that provides a framework for comparing the relative utility of system configurations. Since feature subset definitions are based on component input and output interfaces, they can be automatically generated from the software architecture specification. We allow multiple feature subsets that require the same input system variable from another component to share that component. Feature subsets are in general not disjoint, and a component or feature subset encapsulated in one high-level feature subset may belong to several other feature subsets. This allows us to decouple subsystem utility analyses within our model, even if the system itself does not completely encapsulate its subsystems into a strict hierarchy.

For graceful degradation in the elevator system we designed the software components to have a default behavior based on their required inputs, and to treat optional inputs as "advice" to improve functionality when those inputs are available. For example, the Door Control and Drive Control components can listen to each other's command output variables in addition to the Drive Speed and Door Closed sensors to synchronize their behavior (open the doors more quickly after the car stops), but only the sensor values are necessary for correct behavior. Likewise, the Drive Control component has a default behavior that stops the elevator at every floor, but if the Desired Floor system variable is available from the output of the Dispatcher component, then it can use that value to skip floors that do not have any pending requests. Also, the Door Control component normally opens the door for a specified dwell time, but can respond to button presses to reopen the doors if a passenger arrives.

We did not explicitly design failure recovery scenarios for every possible combination of component failures in the system, but rather built the individual software components to be robust to a loss of system inputs. The individual components were designed to ignore optional input variables when they were not available and follow a default behavior. This is a fundamentally different approach to system-wide graceful degradation than specifying all possible failure combinations to be handled ahead of time. Properties of the software architecture such as the component interfaces and the identification and partitioning of critical system functionality from the rest of the system seem to be key to achieving system-wide graceful degradation. The model we developed illustrates how well a system can gracefully degrade by using the software architecture's component connections to decompose the system.

In preliminary experiments on a simulated implementation of the elevator control system architecture we designed, we found that the system was resistant to multiple combinations of component failures, as predicted by the model. We validated the utility estimates we generated with our model by measuring the elevator performance of a set of system configurations that had various combinations of component failures. Since general system utility encompasses both functionality and dependability requirements, the performance of these configurations did not exactly match what our model predicted. However, every system configuration tested delivered all passengers to their destinations in both simulation tests, satisfying the minimum elevator system requirements despite a loss of system functionality. Future work will include running a more comprehensive set of simulation tests for this elevator system, as well as comparing the graceful degradation ability of different elevator architectural designs, and identifying how we can specify the parameters of our system model to more accurately measure system utility attributes and thus more closely represent the actual functionality and performance of system configurations.

Acknowledgments

This work was supported in part by the General Motors Collaborative Research Laboratory at Carnegie Mellon University, the High Dependability Computing Program from NASA Ames cooperative agreement NCC-2-1298, and Lucent Technologies.

References

1. Laprie, J.-C., "Dependability of Computer Systems: Concepts, Limits, Improvements", *Proceedings of the Sixth International Symposium on Software Reliability Engineering*, Toulouse, France, Oct. 1995, pp. 2-11.
2. Shelton, C., Koopman, P., "Using Architectural Properties to Model and Measure System-Wide Graceful Degradation," *Workshop on Architecting Dependable Systems sponsored by the International Conference on Software Engineering (ICSE2002)*, May 2002, Orlando, FL.
3. Nace, W., Koopman, P., "A Product Family Approach to Graceful Degradation," *Distributed and Parallel Embedded Systems (DIPES)*, October 2000.
4. Nace, W., "Graceful Degradation via System-wide Customization for Distributed Embedded Systems," Ph.D. dissertation, Dept. of Electrical And Computer Engineering, Carnegie Mellon University, May 2002.
5. Keeney, R.L., Raiffa, H., Decisions with Multiple Objectives: Preference and Value Tradeoffs, John Wiley & Sons, New York, 1976.
6. Herlihy, M. P., Wing, J. M., "Specifying Graceful Degradation," *IEEE Transactions on Parallel and Distributed Systems*, vol.2, no.1, pp. 93-104, 1991.
7. Jayanti, P., Chandra, T.D., Toueg, S., "The Cost of Graceful Degradation for Omission Failures," Information Processing Letters, vol. 71, no. 3-4, pp.167-172, 1999.
8. Weber, D.G., "Formal Specification of Fault-Tolerance and its Relation to Computer Security," *Proceedings of Fifth International Workshop on Software Specification and Design*, Pittsburgh, PA, USA, May 19-20, 1989.
9. Rushby, J., "Partitioning in Avionics Architectures: Requirements, Mechanisms, and Assurance," NASA Contractor Report CR-1999-209347, June 1999.
10. Dvorak, D., Rasmussen, R, Reeves, G., Sacks, A., "Software Architecture Themes in JPL's Mission Data System," *2000 IEEE Aerospace Conference*, March 2000, Big Sky, MT.
11. Rasmussen, R., "Goal-Based Fault Tolerance for Space Systems using the Mission Data System," *2001 IEEE Aerospace Conference*, March 2001, Big Sky, MT.
12. Knight, J.C., Sullivan, K.J., "On the Definition of Survivability," University of Virginia, Department of Computer Science, Technical Report CS-TR-33-00, 2000.
13. Meyer, J.F., "On Evaluating the Performability of Degradable Computing Systems," *The Eighth Annual International Conference on Fault-Tolerant Computing (FTCS-8)*, Toulouse, France, June 21-23 1978.

Industrial Experience

Dependability Experience in Philips

Frank van der Linden

Philips Medical Systems, Veenpluis 4-6, 5684 PC Best, NL
Frank.van.der.linden@philips.com

Abstract This paper gives an overview of dependability issues of the 12 years in several business units of Philips. Main experiences stem from the development of systems in the telecommunications, consumer electronics and medical imaging domain. Several ways of dealing with these dependability issues and the best practices encountered are reported. The main focus is on architectural concepts and patterns that help to solve dependability issues in systems. Both the solution and the problem sides of dependability are explained by means of examples.

Introduction

Around 1990 PKI (Philips Kommunikations Industrie, Nürnberg) was involved in the development of a telecommunications switch tss (Telecommunication Switching System), which was aimed at a niche market. The *tss Building Block* method was used at PKI between 1985 and 1994 for the development of telecommunication software. Results of this method were published at several places, see [3,4,6]. The main characteristics of such telephony switching systems are:
- embedded control;
- satisfaction of real-time constraints;
- hardware failures shall cause no or only low downtimes;
- it must be easy to implement software configuration changes due to expansion of the functionality, errors, or changing hardware.

Besides the requirements from the customers and the conformance to external standards a number of additional goals are important for the architectural design. Components, then called *Building Blocks* by PKI, are the most important structures in all phases of the development of the tss system. These components are self-describing. In particular, they describe their resource usage themselves.

The tss architecture determines a framework. In order to derive a specific family member several plug-ins are added to the framework. Of course, the framework may be adapted and/or added during the lifetime of the family. This will usually have consequences for specific plug-ins. Parts of the framework are only available for subsets of the product family. In 1995 PKI was sold to Lucent, who kept maintenance versions of the system for several years, but did not continue the commercial use of the tss system family.

R. de Lemos et al. (Eds.): Architecting Dependable Systems, LNCS 2677, pp. 293–307, 2003.
© Springer-Verlag Berlin Heidelberg 2003

In 1995 Philips joined the European co-operation project, ESPRIT 20.477, ARES [1]. In that project Philips' involvement was related to the consumer electronics division. One of Philips' aims was to introduce product family architectures in the consumer domain, and through this way transfer of the knowledge of PKI, and that from external ARES partners. Since consumer electronic equipment have only small resources, specific attention was taken to resource usage, mainly processor time and memory consumption. Of course availability is an important issue as well for these systems. The project resulted in the introduction of a component-based family architecture for the consumer electronics domain.

In 1999 the Philips joined a consortium of several European companies to start a series of ITEA projects: ESAPS (1999-2001) [5,6], CAFÉ (2001-2003) [5] and FAMILIES (2003-2005). The main topic of these projects is to improve the system family development practices of the involved companies. The main department of Philips involved in these projects is the Philips Medical Systems department.

Philips Medical Systems makes medical imaging systems. These systems are used to make pictures of (interior) parts of human bodies for medical (diagnostic) purposes. These systems are subject to many dependability issues. There are legal rules guarding the safety and security of these systems, moreover availability is often an important requirement. Because of the very large sizes of medical images resource consumption is also an issue for these systems.

Within this paper we give an overview of some best practice encountered during 12 years within Philips. It starts with the introduction of dependability for component-based families. The following section deals with an important way of solving dependability issues in these families, the introduction of aspects. Next comes the process design, which is an important issue when dealing with several dependability issues. In particular, we show that the right process design may support graceful degradation. Next we go into an example aspect, recovery, which supports dependability issues like availability and reliability. For specific dependability techniques we give examples in resource management, hardware management, graceful degradation and testing.

Product Families

All developments discussed above were based upon component-based family architectures. A *software product family* is an evolving collection of systems with a lot of commonality built upon the same technology (including the architecture). Reuse of the commonality throughout the family is managed through architectural measures, for instance by only allowing reuse of complete components. A lot of components are common to all products in the family. They form a framework. Variants are built by adding specific components (plug-ins) to the framework. Since the family evolves over time, the structure is less static than presented here. Common components will change and evolve as well. New, common and specific, components will be added.

In dealing with dependability issues, the use of a component-based family has advantages and drawbacks. An advantage is the fact that the issues can be solved once for the complete family. Moreover, when there are already several working systems in the family, the trust in the solution may increase. A drawback is that it may be harder to find a solution in a situation where the surrounding system is variable. Testing or validating the approach may be harder, since not all situations can be tested beforehand. Because of evolution some dependability issues may have to be introduced in an existing family. It may be difficult to smoothly integrate a solution at a later stage.

Specific dependability issues, which are important for families, are maintainability and adaptability. Only architectures that have these qualities will be able to support an evolving family.

Aspects

In order to keep intellectual control over the system functionality, the tss Building Block method introduced *design aspects* as a third dimension for development, this in addition to the more common structure and processing dimensions [7]; see also the next section. Design can be carried out independently for every dimension. Decomposition into aspects provides a functional decomposition of the system. Many aspects are related to technical solutions towards dependability issues. The 'actual' or operational functionality of an embedded system is usually only a small part of the total functionality. The following aspects are distinguished in the tss system:

- Operational
- Configuration
- Error handling
- Debugging
- Operator interface
- Data replication
- Diagnostics
- Overload control
- Recovery
- Test handling
- Performance observations

In addition to redundant hardware several software aspects improve reliability; see Fig 1 for the distinct contributions of aspects to the reliability of the system.

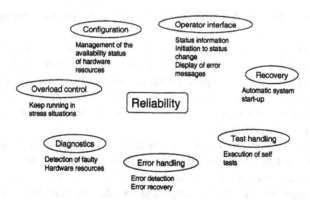

Fig. 1. Aspects of tss contributing to reliability

Aspects are distributed over the complete system. In general each component contains functionality of some or all aspects. The complete functionality of an aspect is a view of the total system functionality. The functionality corresponding to the aspect is distributed over all components, each one contributing its own small part to it. For each aspect a separate design is made. This leads to standard solutions for aspect implementation, or even to automate code generation. In a product family the use of aspects has the advantage that the aspect apply to each configuration, since it comes together with the set of components used in the configuration.

The list of aspects is a tool for the architects to check the functional completeness of the components identified to configure a system. It leads to considering for each component separately:

- which initialisation actions are required by a component,
- which faults can a component have, how can it be influenced by other faults in the system,
- how can the component be configured,
- what is the required reliability,
- which resources may it use,
- etc.

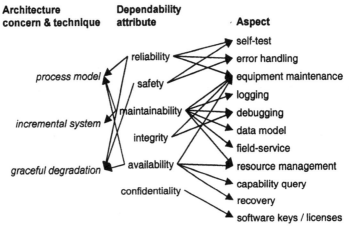

Fig. 2. Relationship between dependability to aspects (r) and to other architecture concerns (l)

Fig. 2 shows the relationship between dependability attributes and aspects we encountered in the medical systems considered. In addition a relationship is shown with other architecture concerns and techniques, which are not treated as aspects. For each of the identified aspects a separate design is made, and often the aspect is addressed by all components. We do not explain all aspects mentioned here. Several of them will be explained in the forthcoming sections.

An architectural pattern for aspects that is often observed within product families is that of an infrastructure component framework. This pattern is present within all families studied. Generic functionality to support the aspect is available in the framework, and separated from the distributed component specific functionality. Components that have to deal with the aspect have to register themselves to the framework. Often this applies to many, or even to all, components. This allows ease of adaptation of the generic parts of the aspects. In contrast, the specific part is distributed across the system, and has to be adapted locally on a per component basis.

An example of the pattern is the component framework that deals with all field-service related functions, such as hardware calibrations, or the setting of configuration parameters; see Fig. 3. A infrastructure framework is present that provides connections between the field service engineers and the software components to be serviced. The framework does not need to know beforehand which are these components. Instead during initialisation, each component needing field-service register their field service functions to the field-service component framework. Typically a component identification, e.g. a string containing a logical component name and version identification, is provided during registration. This helps the service engineer to navigate through the software. The framework keeps a run-time list components that can be serviced. The functionality of the framework provides access to the internal states of the components, through the registered field service functions. A similar framework takes care of other aspects, and for run-time restart, which is a part of process management. During initialisation, each component having a process registers it to the restart framework, so that the component framework can restart the process when needed.

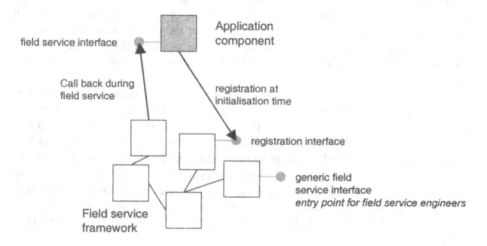

Fig. 3. Field service framework, example

Within the tss system automatic code generation was present for many aspects with standard solutions. This means that for those aspects the component specific code was generated through a proprietary tool. For instance in the field service example above, the registration code and a large part of the code related to the field service interface can be generated automatically. Only simple information is necessary, like component name and version number, the variables that may be accessed and links that may be followed during field service. An initial investigation was performed whether aspect-oriented programming [2] could take up the automatic code generation. This may lead to automatic code generation for many identified aspects. However, we have not yet experiences enough with the use of aspect-oriented programming for our systems to use it for automatic generation of code. Moreover, in a component-based architecture automatic code generation may add new classes to a component, aspect-oriented techniques like weaving code in classes may be less important.

Within the consumer electronics business, the resource restrictions were too severe to apply the infrastructure framework with run-time registration unaltered. However, the principle still was available during development. Configuration was performed before compilation. It was followed by automatic code generation support to perform registration just before compilation time. Extensive use is made of the generation of macros, which transform indirect calls related to the use of an infrastructure framework into direct calls during compilation. Less storage space is needed for access lists; less code is needed for indirect calls. This leads to a (crucial) reduction of the code image (ROM) and memory (RAM) consumption sizes.

Process Model

One very important observation in all encountered product families is the independence of structural and behavioural design. The designer is free to carry out the process design without consequences for the structural design. These build two orthogonal dimensions; e.g. a component may implement zero, one or more process types. In addition not all procedures in a component run under the same process. Since all data is local to components, the synchronisation of data access is done locally, in each component. The process model chosen influences the maintainability, reliability and availability.

In addition to processes also the underlying hardware (processors) is important. The performance of the system is directly dependent on the underlying hardware. For instance the number of processors and their speed. However, it may be expected that the underlying hardware is evolving. Therefore, also the software has to be modelled in such a way that it is able to adapt to new hardware. For instance by determining enough separate threads of execution eases the distribution of processing over more than one processor. By having for each piece of peripheral hardware a management software component, addressing it at a logical level above the driver level, adaptations of the peripheral hardware will be accompanied by only a local software component replacement.

Process management follows the infrastructure framework pattern as described for the aspects, above. The Process Management generic component administers all processes of the system. Each process is defined locally in some component, and registered by the Process Management, together with important data such as priority, dispatch time or dynamic stack size. The Process Management starts and handles the processes according to the obtained data.

Reasons for the non-naive assignment of components to processes is that parallelism has to be carefully designed within a large system. For example a tss system consists of 100 – 200 Components, which are driven by essentially 4 process types (the complete list contains between 30 and 40 process types). These 4 process types determine the main dynamic behaviour of the system. One of these process types is instantiated between 1500 and 4000 times, but instances of process types make the system not really more complicated to understand.

Consider the addition of some component to the system. No recompilation, relinking or reloading of the Process Management is necessary. Instead, those Components, which need a separate process, subscribe it at the Process Management. After adding the component, the system will have an adapted list of processes. Alternatively, if the underlying hardware changes, the Process Management component has to be adapted. However, the components defining the processes do not have to be adapted.

The tss Process Management supports a distinction between process types and process instances. Process design is guided by the following principles:

- autonomous external behaviour is represented by a process internally, e.g. each operator session and each call has its own process instance;
- each communication channel arriving at a hardware unit is handled by one process instance;
- tasks, which have different priorities are represented by process types for each priority;
- sets of tasks, which require fixed amounts of time and should not be delayed because of processor contention are implemented on different real or virtual processors.

These principles lead to few process types and relatively large numbers of process instances. The process support was designed to deal with this situation. Since the tss had its own operating system, process management supported the own process design and configuration. Programming of process synchronisation is limited while the dynamic behaviour profits from the number of independent working process instances. Because each process instance acts on its own data space within the components, the design of the process types can be carried out as if working in a single instance environment.

Moreover, the behavioural system design of a tss system is guided by the principle that processing intensive operations is as much as possible done by peripheral processors. The central processor is reserved for system co-ordination tasks. This separation of functionality in co-ordination tasks, which are visible on the system level and local tasks is vital for performance reasons, because a central processor is a bottleneck in such a system.

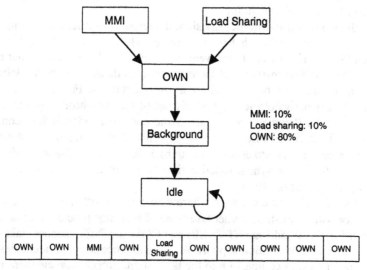

Fig. 4. Virtual processor scheme of tss

In order to support graceful degradation, the tss scheduler works with *virtual processors*; see Fig. 4. Each process is assigned a *category* and within this category it is assigned a priority. For tss these categories are OWN for call processing, MMI for man-machine interface, Load Sharing, Background, and idle. A specific part of the processing time is guaranteed for processes of different categories. This is obtained by a simple round robin scheduling of the categories; see the bottom row of Fig. 4. If a category does not need all of its time, the remaining time is given to another category, in a predefined order, determined by the arrows at the top part of Fig. 4. In a multi-processor system a similar mapping of the categories may be used, keeping a guaranteed processor share.

Because processes in different categories have their own guaranteed part of the processing time, they do not compete with each other for the processor, i.e. a category can be seen as a virtual processor. In particular, the number of call processes that may be active is not dependent on the load of other categories of processes. Specific processes enabling load sharing have their own category, which means that they still get enough processor time, even in overload situations. Moreover operator interaction (MMI) always needs to have a processing budget in overload situations. The degradation of the exchange in overload situations will be controlled via this scheme. In situations when load sharing is less important a large part of the overload processing time may be assigned to call processing, or other necessary tasks.

The use of the virtual processor scheme is facilitated by the fact that the tss system has its own proprietary operating system, where process scheduling could be designed according to their own needs. Until now it is not easy to design a virtual processing scheme on commercially available operating systems. The main problem here is that the tss scheme requires two levels of scheduling. At the top level a fixed round robin scheduling of the categories, with a fixed schema of moving unneeded processor time to other categories. At the second level, within each category, there is an ordinary priority driven process-scheduling scheme. Commercially available systems only provide the second level scheduling.

Within the consumer electronics division, the resource restrictions enforce that the number of processes and threads has to be limited. However a similar approach to tss was used, although no process types were introduced. Each component that needs an activity defines itself its own *virtual threads*, and uses its own internally defined synchronisation mechanisms between different virtual threads. For data exchange between threads it is obligatory to use one of a set of safe synchronisation mechanisms within components. Parameter driven automatic code generation before compilation merges the defined virtual threads into fewer actual threads, taking the defined synchronisation mechanisms into account, resulting in less synchronisation code, because within a single thread the synchronisation times are known. This results in a reduced number of processes at run-time.

Within the Medical System division, hardware costs are often not an issue. A separate processor with a real-time kernel takes care of real-time processing. For non-real-time processing the Windows (NT & XP) and COM (or .NET) support takes care of the process and synchronisation support. A separate process design identifies a small number of processes, in comparison to the tss system. Process management is less of an issue, and most components are within a single process, as the COM support facilitates.

Recovery

After software delivery, after the repairing of system faults and after updates or recon-figurations, the system has to be initialised. During initialisation the data in the system has to be recovered to reflect the state of the system before it was shut off. Moreover in certain error states the system itself may start recovery, in order to return to a con-sistent state. In order to fulfil availability requirements, the recovery has to be fast, and only those parts that are really needed have to be recovered.

Within the professional business the recovery is recognised as a separate aspect, supporting an independent design. It enables a single approach towards recovery, and the component specific recovery actions may be determined locally. The recovery aspect mainly influences the availability of the system. One part of recovery is the initialisation of the system. The recovery aspect eases complexity management and maintainability through separating initialisation from the remainder of the functional-ity. Elements, which are only necessary during initialisation, should not reduce the performance at run-time. When the system has to fulfil performance requirements it is important to execute during initialisation those actions that yield good performance at run-time.

A clear separation between initialisation and run-time eases the understanding of a system. System initialisation can be designed with less complexity than the run-time behaviour. For instance, time restrictions are less severe during initialisation. There-fore, a simpler process structure, e.g. uni-processing, may be chosen at initialisation time. Such a simple process structure eases the implementation of the actions to be done during initialisation.

The distribution of resources can often be done at initialisation time. Run-time processes are freed from the initialisation of resources. During initialisation global system constants get their values and (semi-) stable software structures are mapped upon the available hardware. Fixed links between different parts of the data structures are set up. Binding for later call-back is executed. These are all means to speed up navigating at run-time. If such issues have to be decided at run-time the system would get a more interpretative behaviour. This would add considerable complexity to the run-time. Moreover, maintainability, reliability and availability would be reduced. In the consumer electronics business a lot of such initialisation actions are moved to-wards pre-compilation code generation. This reduces the run-time resource consump-tion. Examples of this are already given in the preceding sections.

Already in the tss system each component has a run-time descriptor available which is the only entrance point for function calling from outside. At a fixed position within the descriptor of the component there is a recovery interface consisting of a fixed set of (about 20) recovery procedures, called *recovery chains*. Each chain per-forms a part of the initialisation. Recovery proceeds by executing each chain for each component available, in an undefined component order. The chains are chosen in such a way that dependencies on other components use only data that are initialised in an earlier chain. This way the actions for the different components of a given chain may be executed in any order. This is a desirable property because the connections be-tween the components are not yet known at initialisation time. The recovery is fin-ished when application processes are started. At that moment the system finds through the configuration aspect that the peripheral hardware is not in operation, although the have power and are available for their activity. The configuration aspect set each piece of peripheral hardware into operation, and monitors its availability during run-time.

There are different levels of recovery. Each level determines a sub-sequence of the recovery chains to be executed. The levels differentiate between a simple 'restart' to a full 'initial load'. Some recovery levels are initiated by the system itself by the error management aspect; the precise level is chosen depending of the severity of the error. Other recovery levels are initiated by operator interaction and are not prompted by faults. For the medical systems domain, COM delivers recovery support. No explicit recovery chains are defined.

It is common practice in the telecommunication world to classify the data into the following three classes; each with their own recovery characteristics

- *Hard data*. These are data that are fixed during the normal operation of the system and are not modifiable at run-time. This is present at the start of recovery, and does not have to be recovered.
- *Soft data*. These are data that have to be kept stable in the system for long periods and have to be consistent even after system failures. Typically the operator sets these data through transactions. For instance these data deals with configuration issues. During recovery after system crashes these data is restored through roll-back to the last consistent state.
- *Dynamic data*. These are data that may change often during run-time and do not have to be restored after system failures. Examples are stacks and temporary variables. These data are lost and will be built up after recovery. So they do not have to be restored during recovery.

Within consumer electronics the systems have to have a high level of availability, and recovery is often not acceptable. In fact, the system should not crash at all. However after power on the system has to be recovered. The consumer expects a fast start-up after power on, meaning that the number of recovery actions at start-up is very limited. With respect to the data classification above this means that the amount of soft data should be limited. Instead, the majority of the data is hard or dynamic. In order to achieve the high level of availability the control and process synchronisation of the system is treated as a specific aspect that needs separate design. Again the design uses an infrastructure framework. Resource constraints may result in binding a large part of the variability at compile time. This is supported by a fixed connection of the component activities to the process control at compile time as well.

Logical Resources

Many embedded systems have severe restrictions to resource consumption. Therefore explicit resource management is often needed. In many cases we encountered the *logical resources* pattern; see Fig. 5. Logical resources abstract away from actual resources, and are a way to provide application processing with more ideal resources than the actual resources. The introduction of logical resources addresses availability and maintainability. Logical resources can roughly be divided into two classes. The first one consists of abstraction from hardware objects and builds the basis on which the application processing is performed. It allows hardware configuration changes without changing the applications on top. The second class has to do with non-hardware-related logical objects, the software structures that are treated as resources by application processing. For example, with the telecommunications infrastructure systems the logical-resource-management deals with data for signalling, logical lines, and facility data (call forwarding, follow me, ...).

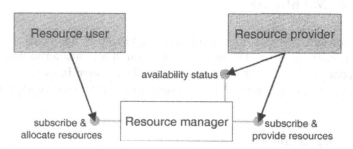

Fig. 5. Logical resource management

Logical resource management deals with logical resources and maps them to physical resources. The pattern provides a specific resource manager for each kind of logical resource. Customer applications needing logical resources allocate them at the resource manager; see Fig. 5 left hand side. Components managing physical resources supply these to the resource manager; see Fig. 5 right hand side. The resource manager is responsible for performing the right actions towards customer applications in case a physical resource becomes unavailable. This may result in the removal of the resource from the customer, or assigning another one to it. An important case where removal and addition of logical resources occurs is the run-time adaptation of hardware. The removal of the hardware makes its resources unavailable for application processing. The addition and subsequent recovery of the new hardware makes the resources available again. In cases of more software related logical resources, the resource manager performs a translation of other logical, hardware related, resources towards the kind of resource they provide. This may make them a customer of another resource manager.

The resource manager acts like a software bus, reducing the mutual knowledge of resource suppliers and customers to that of an abstract resource. The resource manager transmits messages about the availability of the resources. The standardisation of the resource managers as a design pattern provides an abstract interface for the communication between resource supplier and customer components. This enables automatic code generation for there resource managers. Moreover the complete set up is such that it is avoided to provide a global system configuration files. As a consequence it avoids a complicated handling of the system flexibility.

Within the Medical imaging systems an additional *capability query* aspect is added to logical resources. Several peripheral devices have different capabilities, e.g. each kind of equipment has a set of distinct basic movements, through which several kinds of movements are possible, but others are not possible with the equipment. Certain complex movements may be built using the basic movements. Different complex movements are seen as different logical resources that may, or may not be provided by the system. The capability query aspect collects information about which kinds of basic movements are possible. Resource management translates these to a collection of logical resources dealing with the complex movements that may be provided to the end-user.

Equipment Maintenance

Within professional systems, the configuration aspect keeps and holds the complete system in a consistent state. The central control unit has to guarantee this. This unit holds the configuration and the state of the complete system in the form of data. It controls connected components, which in turn may control other components. The main tasks are:

- recovery
- software image distribution/management
- control data distribution/management
- fault management
- hierarchical control

The configuration aspect deals with the conceptual scheme of the system. It uses a consistent database containing a model of the system. It performs logical actions at the database concerning the usability of e.g. hardware and the (logical) resources. Several pieces of peripheral hardware may be unusable due to hardware faults. There are special components keeping track of the maintenance condition of the hardware, whether or not the hardware is operational or serviceable. In particular, this holds for the operational condition of the main processor itself.

The equipment maintenance aspect addresses maintainability. An important point in the equipment maintenance is the structure of the control software in the controlling equipment. Changes within a component low down in the control hierarchy have consequences for the control software of components higher up in the control hierarchy. When equipment is added or removed, the corresponding control software must be adapted to the new situation, e.g. by just adding or removing components.

The chosen solution is to mirror the hardware structure in the software. All of the non-central hardware is mirrored into software, providing virtually error-free hardware for applications. This means that applications do not need to care about maintenance aspects of the hardware they are involving. Thereby it uses the logical resource scheme, discussed above. Each relevant part of the hardware has its own software counterpart in the form of a component. Furthermore, several resource managers are available interconnecting these components, and providing logical resources towards the applications.

Control software components have the same interconnection structure as their controlled hardware counterparts. One or more components represent each hardware module type. Each level of hardware modules in the control hierarchy is represented by a generic control component. There are specific control components for each hardware module type.

Within the Medical Imaging equipment the capability query aspect is also related to the Equipment maintenance. A querying mechanism is used to find the set of basic movements that may be done with the present equipment.

Graceful Degradation

Graceful degradation is supported by a number of aspects, all contributing to it. In this section we provide for example how the aspects in the tss system deal with graceful degradation.

For dealing with graceful degradation in overload situations the overload aspect is in control. The virtual processor scheme provides enough processing time, even in the overload situation. Typical overload actions are to stop accepting new calls. During overload time operators should have acceptable response times to enable configuration changes to reduce the overload situation

In case of hardware errors, other aspects establish graceful degradation. The aspect of tests handling detects internal or external hardware faults. Each processor, both peripheral and central, may have processes running, which tests the processor itself. Test handling deals with the initiation of these test processes and the checking of the results. Each component maintaining a piece of hardware should have such test processes. This way the component itself can initiate tests and check the hardware it is responsible for. When an error is detected in a piece of peripheral hardware, the error handling aspect takes over. It may use diagnostic software to locate and determine the severity of the error.

The aspect of error handling re-establishes the configuration after hardware failures. Each exception is of a fixed format containing a text for a report and a recovery level. If the component itself cannot deal with the fault, a program exception statement is called. The exception may lead to partial or complete recovery of the system.

When an error occurs in a peripheral card, the corresponding maintenance component first tries to determine the nature of the error (hard, transient, or soft). In the case of a hard error, the peripheral card is taken out of operation. Because parts of the peripheral hardware can be taken out of operation during run-time, the system may continue to work with reduced capacity. The maintenance component itself takes care of blocking the access to the erroneous piece of hardware. Therefore the remainder of the system can continue without disturbance. When the piece of hardware is replaced the maintenance personnel can put the replaced hardware into operation again by an operator interface action without having to disturb the remainder of the system, which is still operational. Transient errors are dealt with by the maintenance component itself, without interaction of the operator interface. In this case only the peripheral card will be recovered.

Within the Medical imaging systems the capability query aspect deals with finding the basic movements of the hardware present. In case of hardware failures part of the exiting movements may be blocked. This results in a smaller set of movements that may be supported. The equipment still works, but with less functionality for moving.

Incremental Building and Testing

Another approach to address maintainability is the introduction of strict incremental building and testing. In order to facilitate this, the components are organised in many (>20) layers. Often this is a derived structure, which is a refined version of the layered splitting of the system into subsystems. Each component is contained in exactly one layer. The layering ensures that all components that import a given component C reside in strictly higher layers than C itself. This way the components in higher layers depend only on the components in lower layers and not vice versa. Note that components in the same layer do not call each other. The layered structure makes it possible to build, compile, load and test the system from the bottom up.

This must not be confused with the 'built a little, test a little' principle which quite popular nowadays (code added, built and tested on a daily basis). This principle does not define beforehand what has to be built and tested in which order. The layered structure predefines an incremental structure upon which building and testing takes place.

During the architectural design phase, the responsibilities (functionality and interfaces) of the components are determined. During the component implementation phase, the functionality is implemented independent of the implementation of other components. In fact there may be a considerable time between the implementation of the different components. Special techniques, which are best suited for the application area, may be used to design and implement certain components. Components may be tested on a platform consisting of other components comprising the lower layers in the architecture. When the executable images of the different components are still identifiable within the final system, the executable image of a component is easily removed and/or replaced by another version.

Components are first tested on a platform consisting of other components comprising the lower-layers in the architecture. The system is thus tested in an incremental way, where more functionality is added in each step. The lower part has already achieved some stability. In a practical development situation this has been proven to be a major advantage in reducing system test time. Components may be added to test the next delta of functionality. To isolate faults, components may be removed before additional tests are executed. No new production (compilation and linking) is necessary. This ensures that no new faults are incorporated in such a production process. When the executable images of the different components are still identifiable within the target system the localisation of faults will be eased.

Components are compiled and linked independently. This is necessary to achieve the parts-list approach to software. If a component has passed all tests successfully and is running stable in one system, it is regarded as a reusable component for other members of the product family too. Only in the case that new failures are detected in new family members a component may need to be reconsidered.

Besides the functional black box test and the stress test, the system integration test does white box testing. It is performed to provide the system group with a feed back about the actual implementation and to support the localisation of errors in the test. The feed back for the system team provides the basis for global optimisation and evolutionary improvement of the architecture.

Conclusions

For several years dependability issues have been addressed within Philips. Best practices in dependability deal with the recognition of separate aspects during design. The determination of aspects helps to focus on specific solutions, to address dependability. There is no straightforward one to one dependency between aspects and dependability issues, however a relationship is available. Moreover dependability will be attained only if other architectural measures are treated, which cannot easily be identified as aspects. In this paper we identified at least the issues of the process model, graceful degradation and the incremental system.

This document shows how the architectural concerns and the determination of the aspects help to solve specific dependability issues for Philips' products. We have approached the relationship from different angles. We have shown how an architectural concern, process model, will influence the dependability properties. We have treated dependability from the aspect view: recovery, resource management, and equipment maintenance. Finally we have chosen to look from different architectural techniques used, graceful degradation, and incremental systems and their relationship to dependability and aspects.

Acknowledgements

This work has been performed in the Eureka Σ! 2023 Programme, ITEA project ip00004, CAFÉ. Main inputs and feedback came from my former colleagues, Jürgen Müller, André Postma, and Jan Gerben Wijnstra from Philips Research, René Krikhaar from Philips Medical Systems and Lothar Baumbauer from Lucent.

References

1. Mehdi Jazayeri, Alexander Ran, Frank van der Linden (eds.), *Software Architecture for Product Families*, Addison Wesley, 2000.
2. Gregor Kiczales, John Lamping, Anurag Mendhekar, Chris Maeda, Cristina Lopes, Jean-Marc Loingtier, John Irwing: *Aspect-Oriented Programming*, Proceedings ECOOP, 1997.
3. Frank van der Linden and Jürgen K. Müller: *Creating Architectures with Building Blocks*, IEEE Software, Nov. 1995.
4. Frank van der Linden, Jürgen K. Müller: *Composing Product Families from Reusable Components*, Bonnie Melhart, Jerzy Rozenblit (eds.) Proceedings 1995 International Symposium and Workshop on Systems Engineering of Computer Based Systems, IEEE, pp. 35–40 (1995).
5. Frank van der Linden, *Software Product Families in Europe: The Esaps & Café Projects*, IEEE Software, pp. 41–49, July/August 2002.
6. Frank van der Linden, *Engineering Software Architectures, Processes and Platforms for System Families – ESAPS Overview*, Gary Chastek (ed.), Proceedings SPLC2, Springer LNCS 2379, pp. 383–397, 2002.
7. Jürgen K. Müller, *Aspect Design with the Building Block Method*, Proceedings of the First Working IFIP Conference on Software Architecture, February 1999.

Author Index

Lecture Notes in Computer Science

For information about Vols. 1–2698
please contact your bookseller or Springer-Verlag